DATE DUE

1976
The Supreme Court Review

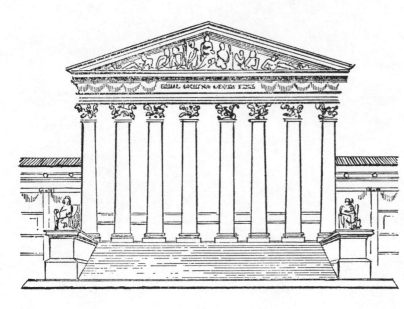

1976
The

"Judges as persons, or courts as institutions, are entitled to
no greater immunity from criticism than other persons
or institutions . . . [J]udges must be kept mindful of their limitations and
of their ultimate public responsibility by a vigorous
stream of criticism expressed with candor however blunt."
—*Felix Frankfurter*

". . . while it is proper that people should find fault when
their judges fail, it is only reasonable that they should recognize the
difficulties. . . . Let them be severely brought to book,
when they go wrong, but by those who will take the trouble
to understand them."
—*Learned Hand*

THE LAW SCHOOL

THE UNIVERSITY OF CHICAGO

Supreme Court Review

EDITED BY

PHILIP B. KURLAND

 THE UNIVERSITY OF CHICAGO PRESS

CHICAGO AND LONDON

INTERNATIONAL STANDARD BOOK NUMBER: 0-226-46428-8
LIBRARY OF CONGRESS CATALOG CARD NUMBER: 60–14353

THE UNIVERSITY OF CHICAGO PRESS, CHICAGO 60637
THE UNIVERSITY OF CHICAGO PRESS, LTD., LONDON

83 82 81 80 79   6 5 4 3 2

FOR
ANN AND JOHN

Give me the world if Thou wilt,
but grant me an asylum
for my affections.
—Tulka

CONTENTS

DANIEL D. POLSBY

BUCKLEY v. VALEO: THE SPECIAL NATURE OF POLITICAL SPEECH

I. Introduction

President Richard Nixon epitomized for his contemporaries both the possibilities and the realities of American democracy as has no President since George Washington. Just as Washington symbolized our republic's most hopeful age, Nixon was "the one" for an age of heartbreak. From now on, the tenability of various political arrangements and institutions will be referred, again and again, to the promise and performance of Richard Nixon. The Federal Election Campaign Act amendments of 1974,[1] signed into law only two months after Nixon resigned, are in a sense a major legacy of his administration. Just as the growing malaise and restlessness of the electorate through the Vietnam period made sweeping reform of federal elections possible, Watergate and its extraordinary transpirations made it necessary.

Daniel D. Polsby is Assistant Professor of Law, Northwestern University.

The author gratefully acknowledges the help of Professor Glen O. Robinson, who shared in the formulation of everything herein although he should not be held accountable for any of it.

[1] Pub. L. No. 93–443, 88 Stat. 1263 (1974). The relevant provisions are set out in the Appendix to the Court's opinion in Buckley v. Valeo, 424 U.S. 1, 144–235 (1976).

The Federal Election Campaign Act was further amended in 1976 to meet the constitutional objections raised by the Supreme Court in *Buckley v. Valeo.* The statute will be discussed herein as amended in 1974, the form in which it was presented in *Buckley.*

By common agreement, the FECA amendments are the most ambitious and thoroughgoing reforms of the election process ever enacted by Congress.[2] They have about them a tinge of the heroic, for they challenge a number of conventional assumptions concerning the nature of constitutional liberty and, more broadly, the proper relation between the individual and the state in a self-governing polity. The amendments impose a number of limitations on how much money candidates for federal office may spend on their campaigns and how much money private individuals may contribute to, or even independently spend on behalf of, those campaigns. They provide for federal subsidy to presidential campaigns, for detailed reporting and record-keeping of income and outgo by candidates and political committees, and for a Federal Election Commission with an expansive authority to enforce the election laws. Numerous constitutional issues are raised by these provisions—equal protection questions,[3] separation of powers questions, and a profusion of First Amendment questions. Most important, however, are the propositions in the last category.

The statute suggests a species of First Amendment issues that has come to be associated with the honored name of the late Professor Alexander Meiklejohn—questions that probe the interrelationship between free speech and the government of a democratic state. *Buckley v. Valeo*,[4] the massive litigation in which the FECA amendments were subjected to constitutional review, decides for the first time some old unanswered questions about these relationships. The divergent responses of the United States Court of Appeals for the District of Columbia Circuit and the Supreme Court to the interplay between the amendments' negative provisions, which impose contribution and expenditure limitations on candidates for federal office and their contributors, and the positive provisions, establishing public subsidy for presidential campaigns,[5] render some of the prop-

---

[2] 424 U.S. at 7.

[3] Some of these are mentioned in Fleishman, *The 1974 Federal Election Campaign Act Amendments: The Shortcomings of Good Intentions*, 1975 DUKE L. J. 851, 883–99. See also SCHWARZ, PUBLIC FINANCING OF ELECTIONS: A CONSTITUTIONAL DIVISION OF THE WEALTH 25, 62 (1975).

[4] 424 U.S. 1 (1976); 519 F.2d 821 (D.C. Cir. 1975).

[5] For simplicity's sake I confine discussion to presidential campaigns. Public financing is provided only for these; contribution and expenditure limitations, as well as reporting requirements, are applicable to all elections to federal office.

erties of constitutional free speech clearer than they have been heretofore.

Before getting on with the discussion, I shall describe the FECA amendments briefly, in order to give an idea of the kind of regime they establish. The amendments are divided into four principal sections. The first of these amends the criminal code to impose (1) limitations on how much money candidates for federal office may spend in search both of a party's nomination and for election;[6] (2) ceilings on amounts that may be contributed to a particular candidate's campaign by individuals, as well as an overall ceiling on an individual's donations;[7] and (3) limits on independent expenditures of money in behalf of or against a "clearly identified candidate" by individuals not formally connected with a candidate's campaign organization.[8] The provisions that establish a Presidential Election Campaign Fund[9] are meant (1) to subsidize a part of the cost of campaigns for a major party's presidential nomination according to a matching fund formula that rewards a candidate for demonstrating a broad base of political support;[10] (2) to pay the cost of party

---

[6] The contribution and expenditure ceilings as they stood in the 1974 amendments were codified in Title 18 of the United States Code. All candidates for federal office were subjected to these, from presidential aspirants to candidates for delegate to Congress from Guam. The limits differed, of course; candidates for a major party's nomination for president were limited to $10 million overall expenditures before the conventions; nominees were allowed $20 million thereafter until the general election. Candidates for election to the House of Representatives were limited to $70,000 in the primary or general election; candidates for senator to $100,000 in primary, and $150,000 in general elections. A useful synopsis of the amendments' key provisions is provided by the Court of Appeals, 519 F.2d at 844–50.

[7] "Persons" and "committees" are required to observe limits on what may be contributed to a candidate's campaign. A person may contribute up to $1,000 to a candidate for each primary and general election, up to an annual limit of $25,000. Section 608(b) (2) "political committees" must observe a $5,000 ceiling with respect to each candidate, but are not subject to any overall limitations. In order to qualify as a "political committee" and be thus freed of the overall ceiling, the organization must support five or more candidates, have at least fifty contributors, and have been registered with the Federal Election Commission for at least six months.

[8] § 608(e), 424 U.S. at 193.

[9] The fund is financed solely by taxpayers' checkoffs. Consenting taxpayers so indicate on their tax returns and one dollar of tax liability will be transferred from general revenues into the fund.

[10] A candidate cannot tap into the fund until he raises at least $5,000, in at least twenty different states, in contributions of $250 or less. Candidates who meet these eligibility requirements are entitled to matching grants, a public dollar for every private dollar raised, but excluding all privately collected amounts of over $250 in any single contribution.

conventions;[11] and (3) to pay $20 million to the candidates of major parties, and less to those of minor parties, in order to finance the general election campaign.[12] Third are detailed reporting and record-keeping provisions which require campaign organizations and political committees to maintain careful account of their income, and their expenditures and political purposes, and to keep these matters currently on file with the Federal Election Commission.[13] The fourth part of the amendments establishes this Commission to receive such records as are required to be kept, to enforce the election laws, to make rules further to facilitate their policies, and generally to police the election process with a broad and flexible administrative jurisdiction.[14]

To say no more of them, then, the 1974 amendments make running for federal office a regulated industry, with all the familiar trappings—reports to file, forms to fill out, regulations to observe, and a regulatory commission to live with. But they also reflect a more or less coherent theory of constitutional free speech.

---

[11] Major and minor parties are not treated identically by the fund. Major parties receive $2 million to pay for their nominating conventions but must promise, in order to receive the Election Fund grant, not to supplement it with any private money. A minor party—one whose candidate received less than 25 percent but more than 5 percent of the vote at the last presidential election—takes the same pledge not to seek private funding but gets a lesser amount, proportioned to the relationship between its percentage of the major parties' vote. In addition to major and minor parties, the FECA amendments make special provisions for "new" parties defined as those which did not receive as much as 5 percent of the vote. A "new" party and its candidates would not get public money unless and until, following the general election, its candidate for president received as much as 5 percent of the vote. At that point, a "new" party would receive payment on the same basis that a "minor" party would have—assuming, of course that something remains in the fund after the election is held.

[12] Major party candidates are entitled to $20 million from the fund, and minor party candidates to a lesser amount, proportioned to their performance in the immediate past presidential election. Here again, candidates are ineligible to receive public financing unless they agree not to use private contributions to finance their campaign unless (and to the extent that) the fund is insufficient to meet the full $20 million ceiling.

[13] 2 U.S.C. §§ 432–34.

[14] 2 U.S.C. § 437. To illustrate the breadth of the Commission's contemplated activity, 2 U.S.C. § 437(g)(a)(B)(5) provides: "If the Commission determines, after investigation, that there is reason to believe that any person has engaged, or is about to engage in any acts or practices which constitute or will constitute a violation of this Act, it may endeavor to correct such violation by informal methods of conference, conciliation, and persuasion."

II. Individual Interests and Collective Interests in Free Speech

The FECA amendments are systematically directed at maximizing one sort of speech interest that is a practical corollary of democratic government. This idea has been referred to as the Meiklejohn interpretation of the First Amendment.[15] On the road to this goal, the amendments displace a more familiar but harder to characterize free speech interest, an individual interest, a "natural right," that does not explicitly depend for legitimacy or sanction on an instrumental relationship to some larger social purpose. The basic problem is this: in a situation where the speech opportunities of a group in the aggregate, or of the average member of a group, could be maximized, enhanced, or even made initially possible only by abridging the speech of an individual, what (if anything) does the First Amendment command to be done? Dozens of cases test the individual interest in speech against some countervailing individual or social value; these are the great occasions for "absolutists" to trade oratorical flourishes with "balancers," "categorizers," and the other sects of the lawyers' church of epistemology. But before the *Buckley* case, the Supreme Court had had only glancing encounters with the sort of individual versus collective conflict that the amendments present.

The complexity of this conflict should not be underestimated. It is a mistake to conceive of this confrontation as pitting the individual (one actor) against the state (another and distinct actor). Because they live in a society, individuals have an interest in the proper government of the state; moreover, the state—at least the one established by our Constitution—has an important concern with the idiosyncratic interests of individuals. One balances when and what one can. But there are limits to balancing, both as a technique for accommodation and as a metaphor. The individual and collective interests in speech do not necessarily collide. For example, in *Barr v. Matteo*[16] and *New York Times Co. v. Sullivan*,[17] they run in the

---

[15] Brennan, *The Supreme Court and the Meiklejohn Interpretation of the First Amendment,* 79 Harv. L. Rev. 1 (1965).

[16] 360 U.S. 564 (1959).

[17] 376 U.S. 254 (1964).

same direction. But these interests may collide; and the FECA amendments effect such a collision.

The purpose of the amendments was to promote political equality by furthering equality of speech opportunities in order to protect the political process from undue influence by the wealthy. One form of Congress's attack on inequality of speech was to make communications over and above a certain dollar amount a crime. A single example, borrowed from the opinion of Judge Edward A. Tamm, dissenting in the Court of Appeals,[18] should, for the moment, suffice to illustrate the sweep of the prohibition. Under the FECA amendments, a person who, independently and on his own initiative, placed a full-page advertisement in the *Washington Post* urging the defeat of an incumbent president—an act that would entail exceeding the $1,000 independent expenditure limitation imposed by § 608(e) of the amendments—could be fined and sent to prison. Even granting the seriousness of the problem, solutions so rigorous give off a whiff of brimstone. One feels that orderly political speech during election campaigns should be out of Congress's reach to ban, if any speech is. In *Mills v. Alabama*,[19] the Supreme Court said that "no test of reasonableness can save a state law from invalidation as violative of the First Amendment when that law makes it a crime for a newspaper editor to do no more than urge people to vote one way or another in a publicly held election." But Professor Joel Fleishman has pointed to the peculiarly paradoxical character of political speech. At the same time that the public interest in "robust, wide-open debate" is greatest, so also is the public need to prevent abuses.[20]

The individual interest in free speech is a familiar (if rather untidy) part of our law. Although certain kinds of collective interests have always been recognized as qualifications of some sort on the individual interest in public expression, the evolutionary thrust of constitutional free speech has generally been in the direction of finding larger and more certain zones of immunity for individual choice to stand its ground against countervailing social purposes. This raveling of the individual interest can be seen from many signs —among them the growth of the "over-breadth,"[21] "void-for-vague-

---

[18] 519 F. 2d at 916.   [19] 384 U.S. 214, 220 (1966).

[20] Fleishman, note 3 *supra*, at 863.

[21] Aptheker v. Secretary of State, 378 U.S. 500 (1964); NAACP v. Button, 371 U.S. 415 (1963).

ness,"[22] and "less drastic means"[23] tests for constitutional regulations of speech; the lapidary restatement of the "clear and present danger" doctrine by *Brandenburg v. Ohio;*[24] the requirement that in defamation cases involving public figures, "actual malice" be proved with "convincing clarity";[25] and even from the extra immunity that otherwise-illegal "speech" may get when its locus is a private home.[26]

The collective interest in free speech is a less familiar, but certainly not an unheard-of, concept in our law. It received its classic exposition by Alexander Meiklejohn, who saw the ethical justification for free speech as an outgrowth of the human condition. Human beings are both free and yet social by nature; they require social institutions to make it possible for them to live together with one another, institutions which do not affront the underlying substance of their individual freedom. The one institution that is compatible with these opposite impulses toward control and freedom is self-government, a state of affairs that is characterized by the consent of the governed and is contrasted with "alien government." Alien government "is easy to understand," says Meiklejohn. "A ruler, by some excess of strength or guile or both, without the consent of his subjects, forces them into obedience."[27]

Self-government, however, is anything but simple: "in such a society, the governors and the governed are not two distinct groups of persons. There is only one group—the self-governing people."[28] The subjective element that characterizes the relationship between a free person and his government Meiklejohn calls "consent," by which is meant, not that a person is assumed to agree with everything his government does, but rather that he shall have had an opportunity to

---

[22] Baggett v. Bullitt, 377 U.S. 360 (1964); Cramp v. Board of Public Instruction, 368 U.S. 278 (1961).

[23] United States v. Robel, 389 U.S. 258 (1967); Shelton v. Tucker, 364 U.S. 479 (1969). See Note, *Less Drastic Means and the First Amendment*, 78 YALE L.J. 464 (1969).

[24] 395 U.S. 444 (1969).

[25] Garrison v. Louisiana, 379 U.S. 64 (1964); New York Times Co. v. Sullivan, 376 U.S. 254 (1964).

[26] Stanley v. Georgia, 394 U.S. 557 (1969).

[27] *Free Speech and Its Relation to Self Government* 5–6 (1948) (hereinafter "*Free Speech*"). Meiklejohn does not discuss the possibility that the people might consent to a despotic form of government, a possibility that cannot be dismissed either on *a priori* logical, or on historical, grounds.

[28] *Id.* at 6.

participate in the process of government. "[N]o man is called upon
to obey a law unless he himself, equally with his fellows, has shared
in making it."[29]

What makes the distinction between free societies and despotic
societies important is the power of government. All government is
inherently dangerous, because "being stronger than any one of us,
than any group of us, [it] can take control over all of us."[30] How,
then, is the power of government to be controlled? "A government
of free men can properly be controlled only by itself. Who else
could be trusted by us to hold our political institutions in check?"[31]
The special importance of free speech, then, is that it is the mechanism whereby individual citizens exercise influence over the government. And the idea of self-government is the basic, atomic principle
of our society:[32]

> To that fundamental enactment all other provisions of the Con-
> stitution, all statutes, all administrative decrees, are subsid-
> iary and dependent. All other purposes, whether individual or
> social, can find their legitimate scope and meaning only as they
> conform to the one basic purpose that the citizens of this nation
> shall make and shall obey their own laws, shall be at once their
> own subjects and their own masters.

This focus intensifies the functions of free speech by clarifying
its purpose. The First Amendment "is not the guardian of unregu-
lated talkativeness. It does not require that, on every occasion, every
citizen shall take part in public debate. . . . What is essential is not
that everyone shall speak, but that everything worth saying shall
be said."[33] As Meiklejohn goes on to explain, regulations of speech
that are aimed at making the most of limited discussion time are in-
offensive. The vice to be avoided is treating speakers unequally because of the substance of their ideas:[34]

> [T]hough citizens may, on other grounds, be barred from
> speaking, they m·y not be barred because their views are
> thought to be false or dangerous. . . . No speaker may be de-
> clared "out of order" because we disagree with what he intends
> to say. And the reason for this equality of status in the field of
> ideas lies deep in the very foundations of the self-governing

---

[29] *Id.* at 10–11.   [31] *Id.* at 12.   [33] *Id.* at 25.

[30] *Id.* at 11–12.   [32] *Id.* at 15.   [34] *Id.* at 26–27.

process. When men govern themselves, it is they—and no one else—who must pass judgment upon unwisdom and unfairness and danger . . . . The principle of the freedom of speech springs from the necessities of the program of self-government. It is not a Law of Nature or of Reason in the abstract. It is a deduction from the basic American agreement that public issues shall be decided by universal suffrage.

When Meiklejohn says it is for the people themselves to determine how far free speech may (and must) go, he leaves it somewhat ambiguous precisely how this determination is to be made.[35] I read Meiklejohn as embracing the view that individuals do not personally decide, *ad libitum*, the propriety of their speech in particular cases. Rather, as an incident of the social contract, each individual must defer to the decisions of our democratic institutions. "Under the Constitution, we are agreed together that we will be, by corporate action, self-governed."[36] In short, the individual interest in speech is subordinate to the idea of self-government, "the source both of our freedoms and of our . . . obligations to one another and to the common cause in which we all share."[37]

In recent years the Supreme Court has found fragmentary reference to Meiklejohn's thought helpful in explaining the peculiar status of free speech, from *Barr v. Matteo*,[38] which, as Professor Harry Kalven wrote, "almost literally incorporated Alexander Meiklejohn's thesis that in a democracy the citizen as ruler is our most important public official,"[39] to *Garrison v. Louisiana*,[40] which based its result, in part, on the proposition that "speech concerning public affairs is more than self-expression; it is the essence of self-government." But these were not cases that squarely pitted the individual interest in free speech against the collective interest. Only a handful of cases do this.

The most important of these cases is *Red Lion Broadcasting Co.*

---

[35] Professor Kenneth Karst has criticized Meiklejohn on this point: "The state lacks 'moderators' who can be trusted to know when 'everything worth saying' has been said, and the legislature lacks the capacity to write laws that will tell a moderator when to make such a ruling." *Equality as a Central Principle in the First Amendment*, 43 U. CHI. L. REV. 20, 40 (1975).

[36] *Free Speech* 105.   [37] *Ibid.*   [38] 360 U.S. 564 (1959).

[39] Kalven, *The New York Times Case: A Note on "The Central Meaning of the First Amendment,"* 1964 SUPREME COURT REVIEW 191, 209.

[40] 379 U.S. 64, 74–75 (1964).

v. FCC,[41] which concerns the Federal Communications Commission's fairness doctrine, one branch of which obliges a broadcast licensee to offer reply time to a person whose character is impugned during an on-the-air discussion of a controversial matter of public importance. In *Red Lion*, the FCC had found the broadcaster's conduct out of compliance with the fairness doctrine, but the licensee stood on its constitutional rights and argued that its freedom of speech was being abridged.

The Supreme Court was unimpressed. "Where there are substantially more individuals who want to broadcast than there are frequencies to allocate, it is idle to posit an unabridgeable First Amendment right to broadcast,"[42] wrote Mr. Justice White for a unanimous Court. "A license permits broadcasting, but the licensee has no constitutional right to be the one who holds the license or to monopolize a radio frequency to the exclusion of his fellow citizens."[43] "This is not to say that the First Amendment is irrelevant to public broadcasting,"[44] Mr. Justice White emphasized. It is to say that the peculiarities of the broadcast medium transform the applicable considerations:[45]

> Because of the scarcity of radio frequencies, the Government is permitted to put restraints on licensees in favor of others whose views should be expressed on this unique medium. But the people as a whole retain their interest in free speech by radio and their collective right to have the medium function consistently with the ends and purposes of the First Amendment. It is the right of the viewers and listeners, not the right of the broadcasters, which is paramount.

The "collective right" of free speech derives from Meiklejohn, whose formulation startlingly parallels the Court's: "[T]he point of ultimate interest is not the words of the speakers, but the minds of the hearers."[46] This instrumental interpretation of free speech interest is novel, and to the extent that "collective rights" and "individual rights" are inherently in tension, it is also heterodoxical. But it is not unconsidered or inadvertent. Mr. Justice White pounds the point home: "It is the purpose of the First Amendment to preserve

---

[41] 395 U.S. 367 (1969).

[42] *Id.* at 388.

[43] *Id.* at 389.

[44] *Ibid.*

[45] 395 U.S. at 390.

[46] *Free Speech* 25.

an uninhibited marketplace of ideas in which truth will ultimately prevail, rather than to countenance monopolization of that market, whether it be by the Government itself or a private licensee."[47] And again: "It is the right of the public to receive suitable access to social, political, esthetic, moral, and other ideas and experiences which is crucial here. That right may not constitutionally be abridged either by Congress or by the FCC."[48]

Red Lion is still the clearest elaboration of the "collective right" of free speech that the Court has yet articulated, and one is tempted to wonder whether it is not a sport. In *Columbia Broadcasting System, Inc. v. Democratic National Committee*,[49] the Court had a ready-made opportunity to explain this new First Amendment principle in another FCC matter, one concerning a radio station's Commission-approved policy of refusing to accept paid announcements on controversial subjects from members of the public. Business Executives' Move for Vietnam Peace, an antiwar lobbying group, attempted to get a radio station in Washington, D.C., to run a number of spot announcements to the effect that American armed forces ought to be withdrawn from Vietnam and other overseas installations. The Court of Appeals for the District of Columbia Circuit, reversing the Commission's endorsement of the licensee's judgment, absolutely sizzled with ardor for this "new effort by members of the public to assert *their* First Amendment interests in the operations of radio and television,"[50] the constitutional right, in other words, of the public to access to the air. The Supreme Court reversed, but on grounds that do not clearly suggest a position, one way or another, on the collective right interpretation of the First Amendment. The Court conceded that it is the public's First Amendment rights, rather than those of the licensee, which are paramount. On the one hand, the Court took the cautious view that Congress should be the one to decide how the public's speech opportunities are to be maximized. Congress had, the Court noted, considered the possibility of guaranteeing members of the general public a right of access to the air by imposing common carrier status on licensees but had rejected that approach, preferring to make broadcasters "public trustees" under the supervision of the Federal Communications Commission. This scheme, in place and functioning for two generations, should not be

---

[47] 395 U.S. at 390.   [48] *Ibid.*   [49] 412 U.S. 95 (1973).
[50] Business Executives' Move for Vietnam Peace v. FCC, 450 F.2d 642, 649 (1971).

displaced "simply because one segment of the broadcast constituency casts its claims under the umbrella of the First Amendment."[51] Nothing in this sort of approach adumbrates any constitutional novelties. On the other hand, the Court's opinion is liberally sprinkled with citations to *Red Lion* as precedent for its holding. The Court even quotes Meiklejohn that the point of First Amendment reference is the mind of the listener rather than the speech of the speaker; "what is essential is not that everyone shall speak, but that everything worth saying shall be said."[52] And indeed, the Court's ambivalence on the nature of the free speech guarantee is heightened by Mr. Justice Stewart's concurring opinion, which takes a most unequivocal view of the issue:[53]

> [T]he Court of Appeals held, and the dissenters today agree, that the First Amendment *requires* the Government to impose controls upon private broadcasters—in order to preserve First Amendment "values." The appellate court accomplished this strange convolution by the simple device of holding that private broadcasters *are* Government. This is a step along a path that could eventually lead to the proposition that private *newspapers* "are" Government. Freedom of the press would then be gone. In its place we would have such governmental controls upon the press as a majority of this Court at any particular moment might consider First Amendment "values" to require. It is a frightening specter.

The frightening specter to which Mr. Justice Stewart alludes is evidently not the finding of "state action" by the Court of Appeals. That finding was only the portfolio for a much more basic notion: that free speech, instead of being a guarantee of some sort which individuals enjoy as against the rest of society, becomes just the opposite—a guarantee that the Congress will attempt to maximize free speech over the entire society, even if it means silencing certain individuals and groups in order to do it.

Another recent case bears on or approaches the collective interest in free speech without squarely presenting the conflict of this right with any individual interest. *Miami Herald Publishing Co. v. Tornillo*[54] holds unconstitutional a state law giving political candidates a right to demand reply space from newspapers which had

---

[51] 412 U.S. at 103.

[52] *Id*. at 122.

[53] *Id*. at 133.

[54] 418 U.S. 241 (1974).

attacked them. The Court reviewed the various arguments for a constitutional right of access, including the sinister implications of an increasingly monopolistic newspaper industry, and neither denied them nor discounted their importance, but instead demurred:[55]

> However much validity may be found in these arguments, at each point the implementation of a remedy such as an enforceable right of access necessarily calls for some mechanism, either governmental or consensual. If it is governmental coercion, this at once brings about a confrontation with the express provisions of the First Amendment and the judicial gloss on that Amendment developed over the years.

Tornillo, however, is not squarely in point, because it is much less obvious in the print media than in the broadcast media that one person's speech excludes another's.[56] Accordingly, the question for the Court was whether the state law would bring about an excessive entanglement of government in constitutionally protected liberties, rather than the extent to which the collective interest in free speech may be a qualification on the individual interest.

In *Buckley v. Valeo*, however, the individual-collective antinomy of free speech was squarely presented and had to be resolved. The

---

[55] *Id.* at 254.

[56] This distinction between print and broadcast media of communications is conventional, and I rely on it as such with little confidence that it could withstand a scrupulous analysis. Newspapers are not free to print limitless columns; if there develop unusual departures from economically necessary ratios of commercial to noncommercial space, newspapers lose money and die.

The traditional justification for special regulation of broadcast speech is by Justice Frankfurter in National Broadcasting Co. v. United States, 319 U.S. 190, 226 (1943): "Freedom of utterance is abridged to many who wish to use the limited facilities of radio. Unlike other modes of expression, radio inherently is not available to all. That is its unique characteristic, and that is why, unlike other modes of expression, it is subject to governmental regulation." Some critics have pointed out, however, that the spectrum is not "inherently" limited at all, any more than any other finite resource. The "limitation" is simply the outcome of trading off the costs of building more sophisticated transmission and reception gear, on the one hand, against the conservation of a "free" but limited resource, on the other. This balancing process, it must be stressed, when it occurred, gave no account of the long-run costs to society of striking the balance in such a way that government supervision of the contents of broadcasts would be necessary forever after. See generally, LEVIN, THE INVISIBLE RESOURCE (1971). See also Robinson, *The FCC and the First Amendment: Observations on Forty Years of Radio and Television Regulation*, 52 MINN. L. REV. 67, 88 (1967). Dr. Charles Jackson of the FCC states flatly that "Spectrum scarcity . . . is a phantom." *Technology for Spectrum Markets* 17 (1976) (doctoral dissertation, on file at Barker Engineering Library, Massachusetts Institute of Technology, Cambridge, Mass.).

Supreme Court's opinion has more than its share of dark places and contradictions. But in the end it managed to pick its way through the FECA amendments with a minimum of strain and, at times, considerable ingenuity. The end result it reached was to decide, squarely and *ex cathedra*, that the individual right of free speech may be too big for any simple utilitarian calculus of social choice and collective decision-making to embrace.

III. THE COURTS' OPINIONS

The Court of Appeals received the amendments' mass of strictures and obligations without a single note of skepticism. On the contrary, it wrote as though the reforms were all but constitutionally required.[57] The amendments were, it said, intended by Congress "as a comprehensive approach to a set of conditions and abuses that have spread over the years to infect the nation's federal election campaigns."[58] "Infect"? "Affect" would have been a more neutral word, but the language of dispassion was reserved for other days and narrower occasions. Quoting Justice Frankfurter, the court continued: "Speaking broadly, what is involved here is the integrity of our electoral process, and, not less, the responsibility of the individual citizen for the successful functioning of that process. The case thus raises issues not less than basic to a democratic society."[59] The court invoked the shades of Lincoln and Theodore Roosevelt to witness the importance of election reform and the country's historic commitment to it,[60] against the backdrop of legislative findings, largely agreed to by plaintiffs, which establish the case for reform.

The Court of Appeals began its argument with a very important premise, that election reform cannot realistically be made to work on a piecemeal basis. For seventy years Congress has been trying to enact disclosure requirements and campaign expenditure ceilings in order to preserve the electoral process from undue influence by the rich.[61] But "[t]he achievements of the statutes were overmatched by

---

[57] It rejected only one part of the amendments, an obscure reporting provision, codified at 2 U.S.C. § 437a, which required lobbying organizations supporting or opposing candidates to file reports with the Commission. 519 F.2d at 843.

[58] *Id.* at 835.

[59] *Ibid.*, quoting United States v. United Auto Workers, 352 U.S. 567, 570 (1957).

[60] 519 F.2d at 835–36.

[61] The history of federal corrupt election practices legislation is set out in a usefully brief form in Appendix C of the court's opinion, *id.* at 904.

what proved to be wholesale circumvention," especially because of
the "proliferation of political committees that purported to be independent and outside the knowledge and control of the candidates."[62]
It is not the fundamental unworkability of reforms in this area that
undid the earlier efforts, stressed the court: "[W]e have arrived at
the comprehensiveness of the present Acts through the failure of
piecemeal regulation to preserve the integrity of federal elections."[63]
The underlying factor pointing toward reform is the increasing
scarcity of money to run election campaigns. "An estimated $400
million was spent in 1972 for nomination and election campaigns—
almost a 300% increase since 1952, in a period when the consumer
price index rose 57.6%."[64] It quotes Congress's finding:[65]

> The unchecked rise in campaign expenditures coupled with the
> absence of limitations on contributions and expenditures, has in-
> creased the dependence of candidates on special interest groups
> and large contributors. Under the present law the impression
> persists that a candidate can buy an election by simply spending
> large sums in a campaign.

And as money grows scarcer, reliance on larger contributors has
grown more intense: "[O]ne percent of the people accounted for
90 percent of the dollars contributed to federal candidates, political
parties and committees. Just 2–3 percent, the wealthiest people in
the country, are responsible for about 95 percent of the financing
for Congressional elections."[66] And reliance on rich people for campaign money produces undesirable effects in the body politic:[67]

> Large contributions are intended to, and do, gain access to the
> elected official after the campaign for consideration of the con-
> tributor's particular concerns. Senator Mathias not only de-
> scribes this but also the corollary, that the feeling that big
> contributors gain special treatment produces a reaction that the
> average American has no significant role in the political process.

If this finding is accepted—and Congress did accept it[68]—then
certain assumptions concerning the democracy of our government

---

[62] *Id.* at 837.   [63] *Id.* at 907.   [64] *Id.* at 837.

[65] *Ibid.* quoting H. R. Rep. No. 93–1239, 93d Cong., 2d Sess. 3 (1974).

[66] 519 F.2d at 837.   [67] *Id.* at 838.

[68] S. Rep. No. 93–689, 93d Cong., 2d Sess. 4–5; Findings I, ¶¶ 108, 110, 118, and 170–
71 (1974).

must be reexamined. Self-government (argued the court) implies a
relative equality of status between those who speak to the public on
matters of policy; if the wealthy have special access to decision-
makers, the premise of equality is compromised.[69] "It would be
strange indeed if, by extrapolation outward from the basic rights of
individuals, the wealthy few could claim a constitutional guarantee
to a stronger political voice than the unwealthy many because they
are able to give and spend more money, and because the amounts
they give and spend cannot be limited."[70] And to make it clear that
equality of access is being accorded a First Amendment function
and status, the Court pointedly observes that, although parts of the
FECA amendments make it a crime to speak in excess of one's
statutory allotment:[71]

> There is a positive offset . . . [in] that the statute taken as whole
> affirmatively enhances First Amendment values. By reducing
> in good measure disparity due to wealth, the Act tends to
> equalize both the relative ability of all voters to affect electoral
> outcomes, and the opportunity of all interested citizens to be-
> come candidates for elective federal office. This broadens the
> choice of candidates and the opportunity to hear a variety of
> views.

In spite of the formally "strict" standard of judicial scrutiny that
the court accepted as appropriate in reviewing speech-burdening
legislation,[72] once it is clear that "First Amendment values" are constitutionally secondary to the democratic values which the amendments were designed to protect, all that remains is to decide whether
one believes the congressional findings concerning the extent to
which private cupidity has compromised public elections. And who,
reading the newspapers even irregularly between 1972 and 1974,
would be inclined to doubt them? The court approved virtually the
entire package of reforms with a series of more or less conclusory
thrusts: Contribution and expenditure limitations are constitutional
("in the context of past abuses and present needs the statutory con-

---

[69] The Court underlines this point by citation to Harper v. Virginia Board of
Elections, 383 U.S. 663 (1966), and several of its progeny, Lubin v. Panish, 415 U.S.
709 (1974); Bullock v. Carter, 405 U.S. 134 (1972); and Phoenix v. Kolodziejski, 399
U.S. 204 (1970), all of which rely, in varying degrees, on the proposition that money
should not be a criterion for the exercise of fundamental rights such as voting or
standing for election.

[70] 519 F.2d at 841.   [71] Ibid.   [72] Id. at 843.

tribution limit . . . serves a compelling governmental interest"),[73] even those which would limit the speech of a private individual relative to a "clearly identified candidate" ("a necessary and constitutional means of closing a loophole that would otherwise destroy the effectiveness of other statutory provisions").[74] Similarly, there can be no objection to the extensive public disclosure of contributions (disclosure "has an impact on personal privacy in political association," but this "is outweighed by the compelling state interest in disclosure").[75] Public financing is unobjectionable because "Congress has determined that providing public funding . . . would advance the general welfare of the nation."[76]

The Supreme Court's conclusion on the First Amendment issues in *Buckley* differed so much from that of the Court of Appeals that one might suppose their perceptions of the underlying facts or law would be entirely different. Except on one point, however, the two courts' view of the case differed hardly at all. Neither court doubted Congress's broad remedial authority over federal elections. Neither blinked the facts developed in the legislative history of the case. But the two courts appear to diverge on one crucial point—what guarantee the First Amendment offers to an individual as against the rest of society. The Court of Appeals, in the end, joins Meiklejohn in hanging the right of free speech from the ceiling joists of democracy. The Supreme Court rejected that doctrinal view decisively.

Two preliminary remarks may be offered about the Supreme Court's opinion. First, it is a political decision, in the sense that, unlike the opinion of the Court of Appeals, the Supreme Court's opinion does not seem to rest on a single, coherent view of free speech. Second, it is an anti-heroic document, in which the Court backs off grandeur or exuberance of expression at every opportunity, preferring to affect its driest persona, studious to find a middle way between the extremes of the FECA amendments and no election reform at all.

The Court notes that the amendments' contribution and expenditure limitations "operate in an area of the most fundamental First Amendment activities"[77] and goes on to add that "political associa-

---

[73] *Id*. at 851–52.

[74] *Id*. at 853.

[75] *Id*. at 867.

[76] *Id*. at 879.

[77] 424 U.S. at 14.

tion as well as political expression" is protected.[78] But expression and association are not the same thing. The latter interest is subject to greater regulatory encroachment than the former, as will be apparent from the Court's analysis:[79]

> A restriction on the amount of money a person or group can spend on political communication during a campaign necessarily reduces the quantity of expression by restricting the number of issues discussed, the depth of their exploration, and the size of the audience reached. This is because virtually every means of communicating ideas in today's mass society requires the expenditure of money. . . .
> The expenditure limitations contained in the Act represent substantial rather than merely theoretical restraints on the quantity and diversity of political speech. . . .

Thus, by establishing the rather tight equation between the expenditure of money and constitutionally protected speech, the Court prepares the way for holding that expenditure limitations violate the First Amendment. And refusing to allow the proposition that "campaign speech" and "spending money" were constitutionally separable, the Court also rejects the proposition that the regulation of expenditures might be tolerable if their effect on free speech were only incidental. "[T]his Court has never suggested that the dependence of a communication on the expenditure of money operates itself to introduce a nonspeech element or to reduce the exacting scrutiny required by the First Amendment."[80] The Court likewise disallowed limitations both on a candidate's use of his own private fortune in pursuit of election to office and on the right of a person unconnected with a campaign organization to spend unlimited amounts of money to advance or retard the cause of a particular candidate, rejecting the Court of Appeals' suggestions that this was merely "a loophole-closing provision."[81] In addition to registering a certain skepticism that this sort of provision could truly be effective against one determined to exercise undue influence on a candidate, the Court indicated that, in its view, independent expenditures have not been shown to be a danger. If they are coordi-

---

[78] *Id.* at 15. This dichotomy between speech and association later becomes important to the Court's analysis as the underlying idea behind treating contributions and expenditures as constitutionally separable.

[79] *Id.* at 19.   [80] *Id.* at 16.   [81] 519 F.2d at 853.

nated with the candidate in whose behalf they are made, they will be treated as contributions and subjected to limitation; if not coordinated, there is little danger of there being a *quid pro quo* from the candidate.[82]

The Court's argument here avoids rather than grapples with the basic issue. The suggestion is that a ban on independent expenditures on behalf of a candidate fails for want of an adequate government interest, because candidates will not really be grateful for money independently spent to promote their candidacies. This seems a dubious conclusion. The more basic question is whether Congress can ban gratitude-producing behavior simply because it may result in certain persons having more influence than their aliquot share of the electoral total would theoretically give them. For a Meiklejohnian, the question is not difficult. People are "entitled" to so much influence as is compatible with the proper functioning of democratic self-government. Conventional First Amendment theory does not address itself to how much political influence an individual is "entitled" to exercise. While Congress might provide that this or that particular means of procuring a politician's gratitude will be prohibited—hence, for example, the prohibition of bribery—it is not at all clear that equality of influence is compatible with the promise of free speech.

That the Court was ready to declare an immanent incompatibility between free speech and equality of influence becomes clear in its discussion of limitations on candidates' spending their own money in pursuit of election. Candidates do not give up any free speech rights by qualifying to run for office, argues the Court. Indeed, there is special reason not to hinder candidates' communications with the public, "so that the electorate may intelligently evaluate the candidates' personal qualities and their positions on vital public issues before choosing among them on election day."[83] Furthermore, added the Court, the public interest advanced by this restriction is solely that of "equalizing the relative financial resources of candidates competing for elective office."[84] The Court goes on to document the weakness of this interest in rather an odd way. First it notes that personal wealth may actually work against a candidate's fund-raising efforts because potential contributors may not believe that a rich candidate really needs their help. "Second, and more

---

[82] 424 U.S. 44–45.　　　　　[83] *Id.* at 53.　　　　　[84] *Id.* at 54.

fundamentally, the First Amendment simply cannot tolerate §608(a)'s restriction upon the freedom of a candidate to speak without legislative limit on behalf of his own candidacy."[85]

The first of these reasons seem a throwaway. Suppose wealth is sometimes a handicap, is Congress barred from legislating on the premise that it usually is not? But the second reason is pregnant with implications for what sort of guarantee against collective limitation the First Amendment represents. The Court simply refuses to accept the equalization premise—no matter how well-documented—against the assertion that this is just the sort of speech the Constitution was meant to protect. The Court elaborates: "There is nothing invidious, improper, or unhealthy in permitting such funds to be spent to carry the candidate's message to the electorate. . . . In the free society ordained by our Constitution it is not the government but the people—individually as citizens and candidates and collectively as associations and political committees—who must retain control over the quantity and range of debate on public issues in a political campaign."[86]

This is the most basic proposition placed at issue in *Buckley v. Valeo*. The First Amendment secures rights to be exercised by each citizen in *propria persona* and not *in communi*. Governmental abridgments that are aimed at enlarging the collective interest by suppressing individual expression, even in the presence of massive documentation that the two interests are in hopeless conflict, are unconstitutional.[87]

This does not mean that the individual interest in free speech can never be asked to compromise with other and conflicting values. The concept of First Amendment absolutism does not address itself to the tension between individual free speech concerns and those of the sort that Meiklejohn espoused. Indeed, Meiklejohn himself was a most powerful proponent of the First Amendment as an "absolute."[88] The question is not whether individual free speech is an

---

[85] *Ibid.*   [86] *Id.* at 56–57.

[87] *Red Lion*, however, is still intact, as the Court makes clear as it repeats that broadcast speech is "special" in some sense. *Id.* at 49 n.55. No doubt the Court will continue on this line until Dr. Jackson's views, see note 56 *supra*, gain a wider following. When this happens, however, the Court will be faced with an awkward set of choices—either bring the regulation of broadcast speech into line with that pertaining to newspapers, throwing a fifty-year-old regulatory establishment overboard, or find some other justifying rationale to explain broadcasting's special status.

[88] "[T]he provisions of the Bill of Rights are 'universal' statements. In affirmative form they say 'all are'; when negative, they say 'none are.' And such statements are

absolute value, but whether individuals may be prevented from acquiring too much political influence by a too-vigorous exercise of
the individual right to free speech. The Court's disposition of this
question says that at the pinch, where the individual interest in
speech in an obviously protected zone of discussion is seriously interfering with public matters going to the heart of democratic self-
government, the individual interest takes precedence.

The Court's treatment of contribution limits is sharply different
from its treatment of expenditure limits:[89]

> By contrast with a limitation upon expenditures for political
> expression, a limitation upon the amount that any one person
> or group may contribute to a candidate or political committee
> entails only a marginal restriction upon the contributor's ability
> to engage in free communication. A contribution serves as a
> general expression of support for the candidate and his views,
> but does not communicate the underlying basis for the support.
> The quantity of communication by the contributor does not in-
> crease perceptibly with the size of his contribution, since the
> expression rests solely on the undifferentiated, symbolic act of
> contributing. . . . A limitation on the amount of money a person
> may give to a candidate or campaign organization thus involves
> little direct restraint on his political communication, for it
> permits the symbolic expression of support evidenced by a con-
> tribution but does not in any way infringe the contributor's
> freedom to discuss candidates and issues.

In other words, while expenditures are themselves "speech," and
subject to something like absolute protection in the context of an
election campaign, contributions are more nearly like "association."
They do not express ideas but merely communicate a solidarity
between the candidate and contributor. As such, of course, they
are entitled to deference and First Amendment protection. Yet, although association is "closely allied to freedom of speech and a right

---

'not open to exceptions.' As universals, they refer, validly or invalidly, clearly or
unclearly, to every member of the class which their terms designate. If you believe
that 'all are,' it is nonsense to say that 'some are not.' If you believe that 'none are,'
you thereby believe, whether you know it or not, that 'some are' is false. The
'absolute' assertion, like every other intelligible assertion 'means what it says' or,
at least, what it tries to say." Meiklejohn, *The First Amendment Is an Absolute*,
1961 SUPREME COURT REVIEW 245, 248. Compare the similar and opposite views of
Justice Douglas, concurring in *Columbia Broadcasting System*, 412 U.S. at 156.

[89] 424 U.S. at 20–21.

which, like free speech, lies at the foundation of a free society,"[90] it is conceptually distinct from speech and (apparently) entitled to a lesser degree of protection.

There are sound, chiefly historical, grounds for distinguishing between speech and association and giving the latter interest a somewhat lesser deference.[91] But the Court's effort to distinguish contribution and expenditure ceilings does not appear to rest on a historical but on a doctrinal point. The showing that it makes on this basis is not convincing. Granted that freedom of association is merely ancillary to speech, a means of amplifying and effectuating communication but logically secondary to speech itself. The same thing is true of expenditures of money in aid of speech. How, then, are the constitutional differences that the Court sees in contributions and expenditures to be defended?

The Court does little persuading on this score—its argument is no more than what I have reproduced above. It does not acknowledge, except to reject out of hand, the validity of a sort of secondary speech interest in a contributor's possible decision that his communications dollar will be maximized by going into the political war chest of his favorite candidate. Indeed, this secondary speech interest may be of at least two common sorts. First, a judgment that a person's own ideas might gain widest acceptance if a political candidate could be found to espouse them. Second, there could well be imagined a privilege, analogous to that pertaining to the defense of third persons from assaults, for a contributor to aid a candidate—an unpopular one, let us say; or one whose ideas are misunderstood—to make his views more widely known. Why should not either of these be sufficient to establish contributions as an expressive activity at least the equal of expenditures? Professor Ralph Winter has argued: "A limit on the amount an individual may contribute to a political campaign is a limit on the amount of political activity in which he may engage."[92] But what sort of a limit is it? Perhaps it is a not-very-limiting limit, the sort of limit that may be got around by a diligent speaker but which still embodies at least a degree of reform

---

[90] *Id.* at 625, quoting Shelton v. Tucker, 364 U.S. 479, 486 (1970).

[91] See Fellman, *Constitutional Rights of Association*, 1961 Supreme Court Review 74, 76–84.

[92] Winter, *Money, Politics and the First Amendment*, in Campaign Finances 45, 60 (1971). Professor Winter was co-counsel to plaintiffs in *Buckley*, where, of course, he maintained his earlier-stated views.

by requiring that the speaker make the effort to communicate himself instead of simply giving the candidate money. This is apparently
the tack that the Court pursues with rather an ingenious and original
argument.

The Court invites us, in effect, to imagine that, somehow, political
contributions can be distilled and the "true speech" elements of the
contribution removed. The residuum is an expression of solidarity
with the candidate and little more. Since the quality of this expression is little affected by a limitation on amount, a contribution ceiling
constitutes a small and hence a constitutionally innocuous burden.
As for the "true speech" elements—those that pertain to argument,
persuasion, and reasoned debate—with the independent expenditure
limitations deleted from the statute, the would-be contributor is at
liberty to pursue these interests to his heart's content. He can say
what he wants, to whom he wants. His speech interest is interfered
with in only one important way: the contributor loses the liberty to
use a political candidate as a sort of sound truck, to amplify the
power of his own private views by channeling them through the
mouth of a political leader (or someone who wants to be). And
while the speech interest implicit in that liberty is by no means negli-
gible, it is also precisely here, in the fear that politicians may be
bought or simply seem to be bought by their most solvent angels,
that there subsists the greatest danger to democratic government.

Evidence that politicians are regularly bought by malefactors
of great wealth is hard to come by. But there is plainly an enormous
amount of shopping going on. Defendant-appellees documented this
point with painstaking thoroughness.[93] Of dozens of examples, one
must suffice for the present—a letter to Senator Henry Jackson, a
candidate for the 1972 Democratic nomination, from M. T. Mehdi,
representing The Action Committee on American-Arab Relations.
Mehdi wrote:[94]

> The Arab American and American Arabist, viewing you as a
> serious man . . . have decided to offer you the opportunity to
> wage your campaign for nomination as a freer man and with a
> greater possibility to succeed.
>
> More specifically, we are offering you our financial support.
> Presently, there are pledges ranging from $800,000 to $1 mil-
> lion. . . . Furthermore, I am happy to advise you that we are

---

[93] Appellees' brief, pp. 46–65.   [94] *Id.* at 52 n.42.

ready to offer you at least twice as much financial support as the Jewish funds you are seeking and you can realistically expect.

Mehdi later added: "We are looking for one great strong politician to stand on his feet and say 'To hell with Israel.' "[95] Such overtures support Senator Russell Long's statement, relied on in part by the Court of Appeals in sustaining the contribution ceilings, that "when you are talking in terms of large campaign contributions . . . the distinction between a campaign contribution and a bribe is almost a hair's line difference."[96]

Contribution limits may be distinguished from expenditure limits, then, on the practical ground that large political contributions present palpably greater dangers to democratic government than do large political expenditures. At least where the possibility of independent expenditure is preserved, limits on contribution do not impose unacceptable burdens on "true" political speech. But the Court finds[97] a stronger and more elementary ground for distinguishing between contribution and expenditure limitations which is more soundly rooted in First Amendment doctrine. Contribution and expenditure limits focus on quite different legislative purposes. Limiting contributions is meant to keep very wealthy contributors from acquiring too much influence with and regard from elective politicians. Expenditure ceilings are meant to promote political equality among candidates by equalizing the amount of money each may spend in pursuit of election. The former restrictions are not aimed at a speech interest, nor do they necessarily or logically require that political speech will be diminished in quality or in quantity in any political campaign. But expenditure limits are undeniably aimed at speech.[98] The evil which they mean to correct is political inequality (a condition with which inequality of speech opportunities is identi-

---

[95] 4 NATIONAL JOURNAL 68 (1972).

[96] Hearings on S. 3496, Amendment No. 732, S. 2006, S. 2965, and S. 3014, before the Senate Committee on Finance, 89th Cong., 2d Sess. 78 (1966), quoted at 519 F.2d 838.

[97] 424 U.S. at 14–23.

[98] Judge Tamm put this point very persuasively: "The interests in preventing corruption and undue influence are fully effectuated by [disclosure and contribution limits], and what is then accomplished through expenditure ceilings escapes me. If a senatorial candidate can raise $1 from each voter, what evil is exacerbated by allowing that candidate to use all that money for political communication?" 519 F.2d at 917 (dissenting opinion).

fied). The mechanism by which they accomplish this aim is to suppress speech in excess of that which is practically inconsistent with political equality.

Professor John Hart Ely, in trying to make sense of a number of recent "symbolic speech" cases, suggested that the critical question in determining the constitutionality of a given prohibition on some form of conduct that is asserted to have a First Amendment significance is "whether the harm that the state is seeking to avert is one that grows out of the fact that the defendant is communicating, and more particularly out of the way people can be expected to react to his message, or rather would arise even if the defendant's conduct had no communicative significance whatever."[99] This rule clarifies the principle on which the prohibition on destroying draft cards can be sustained.[100] The state's interest is in maintaining an orderly selective service, and while the pursuit of this interest might incidentally burden some forms of symbolic expression (such as burning draft cards, spoiling records, or sitting in at offices), the government interest has little or nothing to do with anyone's interest in free expression. Likewise, a prohibition on too-large contributions to candidates does not inevitably mean that a candidate must have less money to campaign with: it simply means that he will have to pursue new ways of getting money. But the assertedly evil thing about unlimited expenditures "grows out of the fact that the defendant is communicating." It is this manifest congressional purpose, then, which makes contribution ceilings unconstitutional. "In the free society ordained by our Constitution it is not the government but the people . . . who must retain control over the quantity and range of debate on public issues in a political campaign."[101]

---

[99] Ely, *Flag Desecration: A Case Study in the Roles of Categorization and Balancing in First Amendment Analysis*, 88 Harv. L. Rev. 1482, 1497 (1975).

[100] See United States v. O'Brien, 391 U.S. 367 (1968).

[101] 424 U.S. at 57. The Court suggested another, rather lesser reason for validating contribution ceilings, and although it does not spell out the implications of its observation, these are consistent with the theory of the First Amendment as a sort of natural right in and of itself, rather than an instrumental value on the road to some other desideratum: "While contributions may result in political expression if spent by a candidate or an association to present views to the voters, the transformation of contributions into political debate involves speech by someone other than the contributor." *Id.* at 21. This point would obviously be an irrelevancy if the Court were following the Meiklejohn interpretation of the First Amendment. In Meiklejohn's view, the focus is on the polity, and it makes no difference *whose* speech is to be protected—the question is always *what* speech. But the aspect of free speech that attaches importance to the verbal imagination itself and to expression as a natural right and function of human beings, is not, after all, transferable.

The Court's invalidation of limitations on candidates' expenditures of personal money on their election campaign is the most sweeping constitutional holding in the opinion. Elsewhere, even in connection with the independent expenditure limitations, the Court is careful to avoid the language of absolutism. Provisions are unconstitutional, not because the First Amendment absolutely forbids something, but because in the particular circumstance presented the social interest is not great enough to displace the free speech interest. There is no such trimming of sails here. The implication is that of all First Amendment rights, the right to stand for public office using one's own money to communicate with the electorate is the most basic of all, for it guarantees a candidate a right "to speak without legislative limit on behalf of his own candidacy."[102] This seems if not obvious, at least an entirely allowable reading of the First Amendment.

It is also an interpretation with which the Court does not seem entirely comfortable, for it presently returns to it in its discussion of public financing with the cryptic notation that, of course, the "acceptance of public financing entails voluntary acceptance of an expenditure ceiling."[103] In other words, no sooner does the Court resolve a most fundamental First Amendment question in a manner highly favorable to the interest in personal liberty, than it takes it all back again, letting expenditure ceilings in the back door by allowing them as a condition to a candidate's accepting public financing. This is a curious holding indeed, in view of the stature that the Court elsewhere accords the right to be surrendered. Why, if this right is so important, so nearly absolute, can it be cut off by a presidential candidate's acceptance of the one and only large pool of ready cash on which he may lawfully draw? The clash of the holdings is startling. And as the Court does not explicate this issue at all, it is worth a moment's digression.

There are many cases discussing whether the government may accomplish some result by imposition of a condition on the receipt of a public benefit when it cannot accomplish the result directly. The leading and most famous of them is *McAuliffe v. Mayor of New Bedford*,[104] a mandamus, brought by a policeman following his dismissal from the New Bedford force for violating a city police regulation which provided: "No member of the Department shall

---

[102] *Id.* at 54.   [103] *Id.* at 95.   [104] 155 Mass. 216 (1892).

be allowed to solicit money or any aid, on any pretence, for any
political purpose whatever." Justice Holmes's opinion launched a
famous epigram: "The petitioner may have a constitutional right to
talk politics, but he has no constitutional right to be a policeman."[105]

> [T]here is nothing in the Constitution . . . to prevent the city
> from attaching obedience to this rule as a condition to the office
> of policeman, and making it part of the good conduct required.
> . . . There are few employments for hire in which the servant
> does not agree to suspend his constitutional right of free speech,
> as well as of idleness, by the implied terms of his contract. The
> servant cannot complain, as he takes the employment on the
> terms which are offered him.

McAuliffe has been criticized on a number of cogent grounds.[106]
But eighty-four years later, the Supreme Court decided *Buckley* as
Holmes decided *McAuliffe*—a politician may have a constitutional
right to talk politics, but he has no constitutional right to tap the
Election Fund.

There is another doctrine in this part of the law, which takes care
of all the cases that the *McAuliffe* doctrine cannot take care of. The
leading case of this other doctrine is *Frost & Frost Trucking Co. v.
Railroad Commission*,[107] which decided that a state, with undisputed
"power to prohibit the use of the public highways in proper cases,"
could not require a private trucker to become a common carrier as a
condition of using the highways. The Court began with the proposition that the federal Constitution would obviously prohibit a
statutory requirement that a private trucker become a common carrier. If Frost could not be compelled directly to become a common
carrier, could compulsion by condition be allowed? "If so," said
the Court:[108]

---

[105] *Id.* at 220.

[106] See ROBINSON & GELLHORN, THE ADMINISTRATIVE PROCESS 653 (1974): "What
does Holmes mean when he says that no person has a right to a government job?
Does this privilege concept mean that a government employee can be dismissed for
any reason—because he has red hair? Wears a mustache? Is a homosexual? Is a
Methodist, votes or (she) wears miniskirts? . . . What does Holmes mean, in other
words, when he concludes that a government employee surrenders his constitutional right of free speech?" Robinson and Gellhorn never betray Holmes's meaning. A number of these questions are discussed in Van Alstyne, *The Demise of the
Right-Privilege Distinction in Constitutional Law*, 81 HARV. L. REV. 1439 (1968).

[107] 271 U.S. 583 (1926).

[108] *Id.* at 593–94. The Court's opinion was written by Justice Sutherland. Holmes
dissented. *Id.* at 600.

constitutional guaranties, so carefully safeguarded against direct
assault, are open to destruction by the indirect but no less effective process of requiring a surrender, which, though, in form
voluntary, in fact lacks none of the elements of compulsion. . . .
In reality, the carrier is given . . . a choice between the rock and
the whirlpool,—an option to forego a privilege which may be
vital to his livelihood or submit to a requirement which may
constitute an intolerable burden.

   It would be a palpable incongruity to strike down an act of
state legislation which, by words of express divestment, seeks
to strip the citizen of rights guaranteed by the federal Constitution, but to uphold an act by which the same result is accomplished under the guise of a surrender of a right in exchange
for a valuable privilege which the state threatens otherwise to
withhold. It is not necessary to challenge the proposition that,
as a general rule, the state, having power to deny a privilege
altogether, may grant it upon such conditions as it sees fit to
impose. But the power of the state in that respect is not unlimited; and one of the limitations is that it may not impose conditions which require the relinquishment of constitutional
rights. If the state may compel the surrender of one constitutional right as a condition of its favor, it may, in like manner,
compel a surrender of all. It is inconceivable that guaranties
embedded in the Constitution of the United States may thus be
manipulated out of existence.

Both *Frost* and *McAuliffe* are still good law;[109] but this branch of
law has not advanced since then. The nearest thing to synthesis that
exists here is a sort of rule of reason, such as the one laid down by the
Supreme Court in *Slochower v. Board of Higher Education:* "To
state that a person does not have a constitutional right to government
employment [or other valuable things] is only to say that he must
comply with reasonable, lawful, and nondiscriminatory terms laid
down by the proper authorities."[110]

---

[109] Especially *McAuliffe*. In Kelley v. Johnson, 425 U.S. 238, 246 (1976) (text
at n.8), the Court leaves little doubt that it would approve regulations of the same
sort upheld in *McAuliffe*. See also, Bishop v. Wood, 96 S. Ct. 2074 (1976), an even
more recent case which points in the same direction.

[110] 350 U.S. 551, 555 (1956). To illustrate the malleability of this rule of reason, it
should be observed that there is fairly current and respectable authority for each
of the following propositions: (1) Federal government may condition employment
in the career civil service on an employee's agreement to foreswear various political
activities which are conceded to be protected by the First Amendment. United
States Civil Service Commission v. National Association of Letter Carriers, 413
U.S. 548 (1973); United Public Workers v. Mitchell, 330 U.S. 75 (1947). (2) A
state may not remove a schoolteacher for publishing a letter (some of whose de-

Huge differences of opinion exist, however, with respect to what is "reasonable." In every case the continuation of a government benefit of some sort—a job, welfare assistance, unemployment compensation, a right to practice law—is made to turn on the surrender of a constitutional right arising under the First, Fourth, Fifth, or Fourteenth Amendment. No question arises, obviously, if the regulation sought to be imposed does not require the surrender of a constitutional right. It is only where a person is made, in Justice Sutherland's figure, to choose between "the rock and the whirlpool"—to give up a right everyone has, to obtain a benefit not everyone can get —that a question arises. I doubt that these cases can be resolved into a consistent principle. But at least they largely support the notion that no conditioned surrender of a constitutional right is acceptable unless there is some substantial relation between the governmental interest sought to be vindicated and the actual forfeiture of the individual interest that is required to be forgone. If this thread is all the law that can be got out of the unconstitutional condition cases, then it is extremely difficult to see why otherwise illegal expenditure ceilings can be made legal by a candidate's acceptance of public funding.

The governmental interests vindicated by public financing are not logically inconsistent with allowing private contributions to campaigns. These interests are chiefly of two kinds. First, they prevent candidates from becoming unduly dependent on wealthy political underwriters. Second, they equalize candidates' respective abilities

tails are inaccurate) critical of the actions of the school board. Pickering v. Board of Education, 391 U.S. 563 (1968). (3) A state may not base nonrenewal of an untenured professor's year-to-year contract on the fact that the professor made public statements critical of university administrators or regents. Board of Regents v. Roth, 408 U.S. 564 (1972); Perry v. Sindermann, 408 U.S. 593 (1972). (4) A Canal Zone Policeman may be dismissed from office for "inveigh[ing] against his superiors in public with intemperate and defamatory lampoons . . . ." Meehan v. Macy, 392 F.2d 822, 835 (D.C. Cir.), modified on reconsideration, 425 F.2d 469 (D.C. Cir. 1968). (5) A state may not put a policeman to the choice of answering possibly incriminating questions or being removed from office. Garrity v. New Jersey, 385 U.S. 493 (1967). (6) A state may not disbar a lawyer for failure to produce possibly incriminating, subpoenaed documents. Spevack v. Klein, 385 U.S. 511 (1967). (7) A state may not remove a professor from his academic appointment because he invokes the Fifth Amendment before the Internal Security Subcommittee of the Senate. Slochower v. Board of Higher Education, 350 U.S. 551 (1956). (8) Government may not condition receipt of unemployment compensation on a recipient's forgoing religious scruples about working on Saturday. Sherbert v. Verner, 374 U.S. 398 (1963). (9) A state may condition public assistance to families with dependent children on the recipients' forgoing their right to exclude agents of the state from their home. Wyman v. James, 400 U.S. 309 (1971).

to communicate with the electorate. But the first of these purposes does not depend on private contributions being entirely excluded from the election process. It can be substantially satisfied by a public grant large enough to make a candidate, if not indifferent to the generosity of private contributors, at least not subservient to them. Furthermore, in view of the validity of contribution ceilings, the fear of a candidate's being "bought" seems unrealistic at best.

The second of these reasons is, of course, fully consistent with the permissible governmental objective of equalizing candidates' financial ability to compete with one another for election. But, granting the validity of this congressional policy, why is limiting candidates' expenditures more constitutionally palatable as a condition than as an outright ban? The Court must harbor some notion that the equalizing function of public financing would be substantially impaired or overthrown by unlimited expenditures in addition to the public subsidy. It nowhere makes this finding explicit, and I suggest that it is a dubious proposition at best. At some point in a promotional campaign—whether the subject is underarm deodorant or a candidate for president—diminishing returns set in. Eventually, the consumer (or voter) gets as much information as he wants to make up his mind, and it seems improbable that any privately financed flood of jingles, bumper stickers, or interruptions of prime time television will override this decision. Yet the evidence that any sort of private financing, even that which is carefully limited by contribution ceilings, is inimical to the purposes of public financing ought to have been clear and unambiguous to support the Court's result.

One could imagine other public purposes to be served by public financing, for example, assurance that a candidate would have at least a minimally sufficient cache of money with which to conduct his campaign. But this purpose is also consistent with candidates supplementing their public subsidies from nonpublic sources. The foregoing considerations point to the conclusion that the Court made a mistake in allowing expenditure ceilings to ride in on the coattails of public financing. There is no good reason for the Court to allow this restraint, especially when it takes the strong position on expenditure ceilings that it does. The Court's failure even to allude to this issue has the flavor of a tacit agreement among the Justices that expenditures of private money in elections is a bad thing for which there exists no obviously constitutional remedy. Hence, expenditure limits are to be cursed with the tongue but blessed with the hand, an understandable political compromise, not dismissible out-of-hand as bad policy, but unconvincing as law and contrary to the fundamental logic of the bulk of the decision.

IV. ELECTION FINANCE MONOPOLY

Public subsidy is the most direct means of relieving the alleged tendency of presidential candidates to become unduly protective of their large contributors' private interests. It is a means that neither places limits on political speech, as contribution and expenditure ceilings are in practice intended to do, nor intrudes into a sensitive zone of personal privacy, as disclosure provisions do. All of the obvious reasons, therefore, make the public financing of elections the most attractive remedial tool contemplated by the FECA amendments.[111]

There is, nevertheless, a menacing dimension to public financing that escaped the Supreme Court's notice. Even more than the old, wholly private system of funding presidential elections, public financing concentrates in a very few, highly partisan, very interested persons the power to impede, facilitate, or deny various candidates access to the money they need to run for office. Public financing of elections increases the risk that the government of the United States will come to approximate that of many large business corporations where existing management is able to perpetuate its control over company affairs without its controlling any significant share of voting stock. Businessmen accomplish this feat through keeping a monopoly over an indispensable element of conducting corporate affairs—information. Of course, secretiveness comes from competitive necessity; but it also means that the performance of management may be difficult for a shareholder to judge. Politicians could accomplish the same controlling purpose by maintaining a partial monopoly over an indispensable ingredient of political affairs —money.

Appellants argued this concern vehemently, but wrapped the argument in a curious package, asking that it be viewed as essentially an Establishment Clause sort of problem. Involving government in a meta-governmental process like elections is undesirable, they argued, for the same reasons that government-established religions are

---

[111] See Fleishman, Public Financing of Election Campaigns, 52 N. CAR. L. REV. 349 (1973).

undesirable. "[T]he similarities between partisan politics and religion are so great that the same concerns that protect religious liberty should also protect political liberty, and . . . the necessity of
avoiding governmental dominance and entanglement is likewise
comparable as between religion and partisan political activity."[112]
The Supreme Court appears to have thought that the issue had little
merit, for its response to it was terse to the point of abruptness:[113]

> But the analogy is patently inapplicable to our issue here.
> Although "Congress shall make no law . . . abridging the free-
> dom of speech, or of the press," Subtitle H is a congressional
> effort, not to abridge, restrict, or censor speech, but rather
> to use public money to facilitate and enlarge public discussion
> and participation in the electoral process, goals vital to a self-
> governing people. Thus, Subtitle H furthers, not abridges,
> pertinent First Amendment values.

Only in a footnote did the Court acknowledge that it had at least
grasped the appellants' Establishment Clause argument. But with a
single sentence, it dismissed it:[114]

> Appellants voice concern that public funding will lead to
> governmental control of the internal affairs of political parties,
> and thus to a significant loss of political freedom. The concern
> is necessarily wholly speculative and hardly a basis for invali-
> dation of the public financing scheme on its face.

Chief Justice Burger, however, saw things differently:[115]

> But, in my view, the inappropriateness of subsidizing, from
> general revenues, the actual political dialogue of the people—
> the process which begets the Government itself—is as basic to
> our national tradition as the separation of church and state also
> deriving from the First Amendment.

Whether or not the Chief Justice's historical point is correct, at
least the underlying concern with excessive entanglement of government in essentially private and constitutionally sheltered matters
cannot be lightly dismissed. In several recent cases—written by Chief
Justice Burger, by no coincidence—the Court makes the notion of

---

[112] Reply Brief of Appellants, pp. 55–56.   [114] *Id*. at 93 n.126.

[113] 424 U.S. at 92–93.   [115] *Id*. at 248.

excessive entanglement the key concept in relating the Establishment
Clause to the Free Exercise Clause of the First Amendment. In *Walz
v. Tax Commission*,[116] the Chief Justice's opinion for the Court sustaining the First Amendment constitutionality of states exempting
churches from property taxation stressed that allowing the exemption was the lesser of two evils:[117]

> Determining that the legislative purpose of tax exemption is not
> aimed at establishing, sponsoring, or supporting religion does
> not end the inquiry, however. We must also be sure that the
> end result—the effect—is not an excessive government entangle-
> ment with religion. The test is inescapably one of degree.
> Either course, taxation of churches or exemption, occasions
> some degree of involvement with religion. Elimination of ex-
> emption would tend to expand the involvement of government
> by giving rise to tax valuation of church property, tax liens, tax
> foreclosures, and the direct confrontations and conflicts that
> follow in the train of those legal processes.

He expressed similar views in *Lemon v. Kurtzman*,[118] where the
Court rejected two state plans for the reimbursement of parochial
schools for a part of the salaries of teachers of secular subjects. The
Chief Justice wrote that such plans leave states in an impossible
dilemma. Either money is granted with no strings (or state supervision) attached, creating a great risk that the money might be spent
on impermissibly spiritual disciplines, or restrictions must be imposed
on how the money might be spent. To choose the latter would mean
that a "comprehensive, discriminating, and continuing state surveil-
lance will inevitably be required to ensure that these restrictions are
obeyed and the First Amendment otherwise respected. . . . These
prophylactic contacts will involve excessive and enduring entanglement between state and church. . . . It is a relationship pregnant with
dangers of excessive government direction of church schools and
hence of churches."[119]

This idea of excessive entanglement as an implicit inhibition on

---

[116] 397 U.S. 664 (1970).

[117] *Id.* at 674. Professor Morgan has read Burger's opinion to suggest that "subtle
governmental control over the internal affairs of religious institutions . . . is a danger
and an evil independent of any strife which the entanglement might generate."
Morgan, *The Establishment Clause and Sectarian Schools*, 1973 SUPREME COURT
REVIEW 57, 65, n.32.

[118] 403 U.S. 602 (1971).   [119] *Id.* at 619–20.

expression of private conscience has not been limited to religious clause cases. The fear of entanglement is the principal motif in the *Miami Herald* case, where the Court stressed the perishability of free speech and its incompatibility with government-sponsored intervention, which "inescapably dampens the vigor and limits the variety of public debate."[120]

The Chief Justice's dissent to the portions of the Court's opinion sustaining public financing stresses these same themes. Two conceptually distinct objections to public financing can be read into the dissent. First, there is the notion that public financing may provide a springboard for later attempts to impose a whole range of requirements on delegate selections and convention activities. "Does this foreshadow judicial decisions allowing the federal courts to 'monitor' these conventions to assure compliance with court orders or regulations?"[121] This objection is surely not frivolous. One can easily imagine future lawsuits to enjoin the payment of funds to candidates because they are not "bona fide" or some such thing. In addition some courts could conclude that the payment of money to a presidential candidate transforms his actions into "state action" which could be held to trigger various constitutionally based affirmative obligations.[122] But these dangers seem remote. More mundane issues would more likely pose more serious problems concerning the propriety or legality of the Commission's paying out funds to a candidate. Suppose, for example, some question arose over whether an ostensibly independent expenditure relative to a candidate had in fact been collusively arranged by the candidate. Since entitlement to Election Fund money is contingent on accepting expenditure limitations, such a collusive act, in addition to being a crime, might disentitle a candidate to his federal subsidy. Rival candidates or members of the public might well try to enjoin disbursement of subsidies until the truly independent character of some expenditure could be established. This sort of delay could well prove fatal to a

---

[120] 418 U.S. at 257. "A responsible press is an undoubtedly desirable goal, but press responsibility is not mandated by the Constitution and like many other virtues it cannot be legislated." *Id*. at 256.

[121] 424 U.S. at 250.

[122] See Business Executives' Move for Vietnam Peace v. FCC, 450 F.2d 642 (D.C. Cir. 1971), *reversed*, Columbia Broadcasting System Co., Inc. v. Democratic National Commiteee, 412 U.S. 94 (1973); Brown v. O'Brien, 469 F.2d 563 (D.C. Cir. 1972), *vacated*, 409 U.S. 1 (1972).

presidential campaign. It is not too much, one hopes, to rely on the native caution of the judiciary to ensure that injunctions do not issue except in the clearest cases.

This dissent had a second objection, however, of even more concern because it is no longer in the realm of speculation. It suggested that the political branches of government cannot be relied on to administer public financing fairly. Congress and the President both failed to seize this opportunity to show the Chief Justice up. The Supreme Court gave the Congress thirty days from 30 January, the day *Buckley* was decided, in which to reconstitute the Election Commission in legal form, a grace period that was extended once. By 2 March, the *Washington Post* reported "Liberal Hopefuls Running Out of Cash."[123] The story mentioned that "the new Federal Campaign Finance Law, with its limit of $1000 on personal contributions, also makes fast raising of large sums of money very difficult."[124]

On 2 April, the House passed a reconstitution bill, and the *Washington Post's* story on the event noted that "Congress is already 10 days beyond a March 22 deadline set by the Supreme Court," and that "while the FEC is in suspended animation, presidential candidates running in the primaries can't get the federal matching funds they are entitled to, because one of the functions of the FEC is to distribute them."[125] By 15 April, the holdup of reconstitution legislation was serious enough to call for a *Post* editorial:[126]

> The presidential candidates have good reason to sue Congress for non-support. After arguing for weeks over changes in the campaign law, the Senate and House have gone off on a 10-day Easter vacation without quite finishing the bill. This leaves the Federal Election Commission in limbo for a few more weeks—and leaves the candidates unable to collect any matching funds on the eve of the crucial Pennsylvania and Texas primaries. . . . Some argue that the real cause of many campaigns' distress is the $1000 limit on individual contributions, which has—as intended—shut off the large gifts from "fat cats" that were so important in past years' campaigns. The ceiling has certainly changed the nature of the money-raising game; it has also made matching funds doubly important

---

[123] Washington Post, 2 March 1976, A-1, col. 4.

[124] *Id*. at A-4, col. 2.   [126] *Id*. 15 April 1976, A-22, cols. 1–2.

[125] *Id*. 2 April 1976, A-1, col. 1 and A-21, col. 1.

as a timely supplement. By turning off that tap, Congress has disrupted the new system and may have severely undercut some candidates' fortunes at a critical point. The Congressional dallying is all the more inexcusable because there was no good reason for it. The legislation was not bogged down in any substantive dispute; the . . . conferees have essentially settled all their differences and were on the verge of reporting a relatively sound bill when they recessed.

The *Post* ended by asking the President to announce his support of the conference bill in order to "dispel any suspicion that candidate Ford is trying to prolong the confusion, undercut any particular contenders, or otherwise profit from his challengers' distress."[127]

Three days later, David S. Broder, the *Post*'s distinguished political reporter, questioned the wisdom of publicly financed campaigns in the perspective of unfolding current events, from 30 January, the date *Buckley* was decided, to Easter:[128]

If secret, dirty, private money in large cash chunks was at the root of Watergate, as many believed, then the cure was to give presidential candidates an alternate source of supply—good, clean Treasury money, contributed by the taxpayers.

A few people raised some questions about that solution: Suppose, they said, the presidential candidates are made dependent on a system of public finance and then Congress cuts off their funds? What greater power could one give to a set of incumbent politicians than to let them determine the schedule and scale of funds flowing to those seeking the presidency? What safeguard will there be against abuse of that power?

This reporter remembers a conference on campaign finance where exactly those questions were put to the lobbyist for a famous reform group and that gentleman assured the questioner that he was conjuring up hypothetical evils that could never occur. Any interruption in public financing by members of Congress would stir such a public outcry, the reformer said, that the incumbents would be signing their political death warrants.

That assurance, friends, is cold comfort to the presidential candidates who find themselves this week with empty treasuries, because Congress has gone home for the Easter holiday without renewing the legislation that gives the contenders the federal matching funds they counted on to sustain their efforts in the coming crucial weeks.

---

[127] *Ibid.*   [128] *Id.* 18 April 1976, B-7, cols. 7–8.

The campaigns of Republican presidential challenger Ronald Reagan and of all three active Democratic contenders—Jimmy Carter, Henry Jackson and Morris Udall—are hurting. The beneficiaries of Congress' lassitude are President Ford, who has plenty of opportunities for free publicity, and Sen. Hubert Humphrey of Minnesota, who has no current campaign expenses and whose chances of winning the Democratic nomination depend on a stalemate among the active contenders. The less Carter, Jackson, Udall and Reagan can campaign in the next six weeks, the better off Mr. Ford and Humphrey are.

Now, it so happens that the candidates most congressional Republicans would like to see nominated is their old friend Jerry Ford. And the favorite of most congressional Democrats is their old pal Hubert. Anyone who believes that it's coincidence that Congress left the other candidates financially stranded is likely to be someone who is probably still waiting for the Easter Bunny to deliver a brand new canary-yellow convertible. . . . This is exactly the kind of abuse of power of which the reformers were warned. And it is clear proof that if the experiment in public finance is to be continued after this year, the distribution of funds by an accepted formula must be made automatic, and taken totally out of the hands of those incumbent congressional politicians who have proved their unwillingness to divorce their personal concerns from their public responsibilities.

On 1 May, the *Post* carried the front-page headline, "Sen. Jackson Will Suspend Campaigning." According to the *Post*, "A shortage of money 'purely and simply' forced Jackson's decision, one staff lieutenant said. 'Immediate cash flow problems'—an inability to pay cash for television time and other expenses that can't be charged—made it impossible for Jackson to go on."[129] On 11 May, the President signed the reconstitution legislation, and the Election Fund money began flowing again.

It would be simplistic to suggest that the failure of several of the Democrats' better-known personalities to win their party's 1976 presidential nomination could properly be laid on the absence of anticipated Election Fund revenues. There are, after all, losers every election year, and it is seldom possible to assign one or another specific shortcoming to blame for their campaigns' breaking down. Moreover, it must be remembered that winners are generally spared

---

[129] *Id.* 1 May 1976, A-1, cols. 7–8.

the embarrassment of cash crunches. For example, Senator Jackson's financial fortunes in May would undoubtedly have been greatly enhanced if, in March and April, he had had the success that some other recent candidates for president have had in persuading nationally influential interpreters of current events (such as the television networks' news departments or nationally syndicated political journalists) that his mediocre showings in the early primaries were actually smashing moral victories, cleverly disguised.

The fact remains that the financing of presidential nomination campaigns is an important part of getting a nomination, and in 1976 the rules pertaining to financing were changed in the middle of the game. The question must be faced whether it is realistic to look for such upheavals in the future or whether the costs of moving from a private to a public system of election subsidy are already substantially in the past.

These are not easy questions to answer. The FECA amendments appear to make entitlements to federal funds fairly cut-and-dried.[130] But no matter how automatic the disbursements appear on the face of the statute there remains a structural difficulty not easily overcome. The expenditure limitations applicable to candidates for a presidential nomination—$10 million overall and not more in any one state than double the limit applicable to a candidate for a party's nomination for senator—are pegged to the Consumer Price Index,[131] a measure of inflation in the economy that may not fairly reflect increases in the costs of running for president. Indeed, according to above-mentioned figures relied on by the Court of Appeals,[132] over the past twenty-five years, the costs of running for president have inflated roughly five times faster than the Consumer Price Index, a trend which, if it continues in the future, may throw a crippling financial constraint on a candidate's ability to seek nomination. When and if such money problems occur, and are widely perceived to be imposing an arbitrary and untenable restraint on a candidate's ability to get through to the electorate, the statutory limits will have to be changed. Because this eventuality seems quite likely to occur, it is not unfair to say that Congress has reserved for itself, *sub silentio* of course, a continuing presence in presidential campaign

---

[130] 26 U.S.C. §§ 9004, 9006, 424 U.S. at 205–07, 208–09.

[131] 18 U.S.C. § 608(d); 424 U.S. at 192–93.

[132] 519 F.2d at 837.

finance. In light of their performance on their maiden run, no one should entertain high hopes that this role will be performed acceptably.

Furthermore, there remains room under the public financing reforms for the executive branch to do a little tampering of its own. Because the obligations of the Federal Election Fund cannot be met from general revenues, the pot is not necessarily large enough to pay for all the entitlements that accrue under any of the amendments' provisions.[133] Suppose the several candidates' aggregate entitlements exceed the amount of money in the Federal Election Campaign Fund? Section 9006(d) provides if the Secretary of the Treasury "or his delegate determines that the moneys in the fund are not, or may not be, sufficient to satisfy the full entitlements of the eligible candidates of all political parties, he shall withhold from such payment such amount as he determines to be necessary to assure that the eligible candidates of each political party will receive their pro rata share of their full entitlement."

A significant residual power remains in the hands of the political branches of the government to manipulate the outcomes of campaigns for nomination or election by holding up public subsidy money on which candidates' ability to communicate with the electorate is founded. The power of incumbent politicians to affect the election process in undemocratic ways is, indeed, greater than ever, an ironic and bewildering upshot for these Watergate-inspired reforms.

Given the likelihood that Congress will eventually have to revisit the existing scheme of public financing, it is not entirely academic to reflect on the similarities between the entirely private system of election finance which the FECA amendments aimed to displace and the mostly public system which they establish. In either case, the occasion for abuse seems to be the shortness of money with which to run political campaigns. In a wholly private system, this scarcity of money gives politicians great incentives to stay on excellent terms with rich contributors. Following the FECA amendments, however, with contribution limitations left standing, it becomes impossible for a candidate to tap one or a very few under-

---

[133] Nor is it practical, as Professor Fleishman points out, to allow entitlements to be satisfied out of general revenues: "Given the innate tendency of subsidization to encourage and facilitate candidates, the Treasury could be bankrupted." Note 111 *supra*, at 388.

writers for seed money or for help over rough spots. As a result, Congress is in a position of much greater power over presidential candidates than can safely be allowed. One wonders whether there might not be an approach which combines public and private financing of elections in such a way that neither sector would have the excessive power over candidates that a monopoly position over the disbursement of money implies.

The most conspicuous hedge against congressional dominance of election finance is rich contributors, on whom politicians have traditionally relied when it was necessary to raise large sums of money without delay. But to make use of the rich for this purpose, contribution ceilings—surely among the most democratically justifiable of the FECA reforms—would have to be abolished. Before that step is even considered, and the *status quo ante* is restored with all of its demonstrated potential for abuse, other means of counterbalancing Congress's power ought to be explored.

One acceptable way of supplementing public subsidy of election campaigns might be to elaborate on existing provisions of the Internal Revenue Code which allow a tax credit of one-half of contributions up to twenty-five dollars to candidates for public office.[134] Suppose a full tax credit—or even a double or triple credit—were allowed on smaller contributions, say of two, five, or ten dollars. It seems plausible to suppose that if such provisions were available, they would be used by a very large portion of the tax-paying public. If they were, three distinct benefits would be realized. First, candidates' reliance on wealthy contributors would be diminished even further than it is now. If contributions of $1,000 made up only a negligible fraction of a candidate's total campaign revenues, then no one who had contributed the maximum to a campaign could look for, nor would sensible people expect him to receive, any special favors from candidates once they were elected. Second, the existence of large amounts of private money in politics removes the extraordinary leverage that the political branches of the government now have over political campaigns. If public subsidy is merely helpful, but not absolutely indispensable to the orderly progress of candidates' primary and general election efforts, Congress and the executive are both deprived of their only significant incentive to tamper with the disbursement of monies to various campaigns. A repeat

---

[134] 26 U.S.C. § 41.

of Congress's performance in the 1976 primary elections would be much less likely to occur in the first place, and much less likely to affect the eventual outcome of the process even if it did. Finally, supplementing public subsidy with private money could assure that election campaigns were adequately financed. Most students of the subject believe American elections to be seriously underfinanced.[135] And under the FECA reforms, the expenditures limitation of $20 million for each major party will represent a drastic reduction from spending levels typical of recent campaigns.[136] Given the complexity of a good citizen's choice for president—in contrast, for example, to his consumer's choice among beers, breath fresheners, and denture adhesives—it does not seem extravagant to demand that candidates for high office do more, rather than less, communicating with and explaining to the public of what they think about public matters, and, by direction or indirection, what sort of people they are.

All of the foregoing presupposes, of course, that expenditure ceilings would be deleted from the reforms. The Court was remiss in its failure to do this itself as a matter of constitutional law, for all of the reasons that its own opinion persuasively urges: expenditure limits make no significant contribution to remedying the abuses which stimulated the FECA amendments while seriously impeding, to no discernible worthwhile purpose, a number of important, speech-related interests. But the Court's failure to follow its own logic on expenditure limits should not hinder Congress, which should consider this matter again and amend the amendments to assure that no one person or coherent group of persons, interested in the outcome of elections, could effectively stifle or even seem capable of stifling a candidate's efforts to seek office, by playing tricks—bureaucratic or parliamentary—with the underlying financing of election campaigns.

V. Conclusion

Buckley v. Valeo is not a gaudy landmark, but it is a landmark, for it makes the clearest acknowledgment that has yet been given by the courts of the multivalency of the First Amendment. Free speech interests of the highest and most hallowed sort were on

---

[135] See ALEXANDER, MONEY IN POLITICS (1972); ALEXANDER, FINANCING THE 1968 ELECTION (1971); Fleishman, note 3 *supra*, at 878, and authorities therein cited at n.174.

[136] Appellees' brief, p. 67.

the line—an individual interest in unlimited speech on political topics, and a collective interest in keeping the poison of selfish interest out of the wellspring of democracy. There has never been a more treacherous case for balancing interests and harmonizing values, but the Supreme Court negotiated the tangle of the FECA amendments, leaving significant parts of the reforms undisturbed but announcing that there is an irreducible core of individual liberty of free expression which cannot be made to yield to the emergencies that sometimes overtake the democratic process.

By upholding public financing of elections against constitutional attack, the Court opened the way for what is probably the most practically valuable idea to be embodied in the FECA amendments. By making a grubstake available to candidates who want to be elected president, public financing will encourage candidates who may not have ties to wealth but who are well qualified to run for office. It will tend to reduce wealth-related influence on candidates and consequently on elective politicians, and it can help to assure that campaigns for public office are adequately funded. Indeed, public financing is such a good idea that one hopes Congress will not be long in extending it to Senate and House campaigns as well. It is natural to assume that incumbents will not be eager to guarantee themselves at least minimally funded opponents in their reelection campaigns. But if public subsidy of presidential elections is a good idea, so is it also (and for the same reasons) a good idea for all federal elections.

Public financing of elections also carries serious dangers of excessive entanglement of existing government in the process of choosing new elective officials and the undue domination of the process by people with a personal stake in an election's outcome. These dangers could be substantially removed if Congress would delete the spending limitations that are attached to acceptance of public financing and would create incentives to low and middle income taxpayers to contribute money to political campaigns.

The most important aspect of *Buckley v. Valeo* is what it did not do—specifically, the Supreme Court's refusal to follow the lead of the Court of Appeals and announce a radical new departure in the meaning of constitutional free speech. Although the revelations that accompanied Watergate undoubtedly pose hazards to the idea of self-government fully as great as the Court of Appeals apparently assumed, speech is not "free" in any very important sense if it is protected only when and to the extent that such protection is consistent with a congressionally defined notion of political equality. Yet, given that this is the issue on which the two courts divided, it is disturbing to reflect on the differences in background of the judges on the two courts. The Court of Appeals is unusually well endowed with members whose careers had given them first-hand experience in political campaigns. By contrast, the Justices of the Supreme Court do not, by and large, appear to have comparable political credentials, although none is an innocent in the political thicket.

If we set any store by what Mr. Justice White in his dissenting opinion called "the word of those who know,"[137] the strong consensus is that, considering the state of American politics, very substantial sacrifices of the individual speech interest are warranted, indeed are necessary for the preservation of democratic values in government. The Court of Appeals capped its opinion with a disturbing metaphor—that of the dog in Aesop's fable who, lunging for the illusive bone reflected in the water, loses the real one that he had in his mouth. That real bone is the speech interest that is compatible with what Meiklejohn called "the common cause in which we all share."[138] The bone in the water, the idea of free speech as an individual liberty—something that belongs to a person by inherent right regardless of what Congress may desire—may have, as the Court of Appeals suggests, a tincture of unreality. But the other bone is all too familiar. It is, at present, lodged in the throat of almost everyone in the world. Almost every country in the world, including those behind the iron curtain, can display a constitution that guarantees freedom of expression to the people—to the extent, of course, that the people's representatives may deem proper. With *Buckley v. Valeo* in hand, we can boast that our Constitution protects something far scarcer in history than that sort of freedom. And with the knowledge of the caliber of people who sometimes get their hands on our government, it is well that this is so.

---

[137] 424 U.S. at 261. As an architect of the John F. Kennedy presidential election campaign, Mr. Justice White may be among "those who know."

[138] *Free Speech* 105.

RICHARD SCHIRO

COMMERCIAL SPEECH: THE DEMISE OF A CHIMERA

The Supreme Court's rejection of an absolutist interpretation of the First Amendment has produced intriguing debates as the Court has sought perimeters and standards for exceptions to the Amendment. The clear and present danger doctrine and its variants such as the "fighting words" doctrine, libel, and obscenity are the first three exceptions. From its enigmatic inception in a seemingly offhand sentence in *Valentine v. Chrestensen*,[1] until its demise in *Virginia State Board of Pharmacy v. Virginia Citizens Consumer Council*,[2] the commercial speech exception could be viewed as the fourth.[3] Unlike the other three, however, commercial speech was generally thought to occupy a middle ground, that is, to be "less protected" rather than "unprotected."

In the years following *Valentine* the commercial speech exception's use by the Court was so infrequent that it has a history but

Richard Schiro is Assistant Professor of Law, Wharton School, University of Pennsylvania.

[1] 316 U.S. 52 (1942).

[2] 425 U.S. 748 (1976).

[3] One commentator has differentiated commercial speech from the categories of unprotected speech on the ground that the latter "are supposedly harmful in and of themselves. Commercial speech is not damaging per se to state interests." Redish, *The First Amendment in the Marketplace: Commercial Speech and the Values of Free Expression*, 39 GEO. WASH. L. REV. 429, 431 (1971). In this article commercial speech will be referred to interchangeably as a doctrine or an exception.

barely any development.[4] Nevertheless, commercial speech[5] has remained a persistent factor in constitutional discussion.[6]

In recent years the commercial speech doctrine has been increasingly criticized by the Court.[7] In *Bigelow v. Virginia*[8] the Court devalued significantly the doctrine's constitutional currency by explicitly overturning the assumption "that advertising, as such, was entitled to no First Amendment protection."[9] Perhaps, however, because the advertising of an abortion referral service was out of the ordinary, the Court seemed unwilling fully to reformulate the constitutional status of commercial speech. Less than a year after *Bigelow*, in the *Pharmacy* case, the Court expressly abolished the doctrine by "concluding that commercial speech, like other varieties, is protected."[10]

---

[4] See DeVore & Nelson, *Commercial Speech and Paid Access to the Press*, 26 HASTINGS L.J. 745 (1975); Resnik, *Freedom of Speech and Commercial Solicitation*, 30 CALIF. L. REV. 655 (1942); Note, *Discrimination in Classified Advertising—Pittsburgh Press Company v. Pittsburgh Commission on Human Relations*, 38 ALBANY L. REV. 847 (1974); Note, *The Commercial Speech Doctrine: The First Amendment at a Discount*, 41 BROOKLYN L.J. 60 (1974); Note, *Commercial Speech —An End in Sight to Chrestensen?* 23 DE PAUL L. REV. 1258 (1974); Note, *Freedom of Expression in a Commercial Context*, 78 HARV. L. REV. 1191 (1965); Note, *Regulation of Commercial Speech: Commercial Access to the Newspapers*, 35 MD. L. REV. 115 (1975); Note, *The First Amendment and Advertising: The Effect of the "Commercial Activity" Doctrine on Media Regulation*, 51 N.C. L. REV. 581 (1973); Note, *Commercial Speech Is Not Protected by the First Amendment*, 48 TUL. L. REV. 426 (1974); Note, *The First Amendment and Commercial Advertising: Bigelow v. Commonwealth*, 60 VA. L. REV. 154 (1974).

[5] Commercial speech has been defined as "communication concerned solely with promoting the sale of commercial services or products, which services or products are themselves not speech traditionally protected by the first amendment. [Commercial speech is] traditional commercial advertising of products and services the public purchases and uses regularly." Redish, note 3 *supra*, at 432.

[6] "Whenever some new regulation of mass communications is contemplated, *Valentine v. Chrestensen*-type considerations are usually present." GILLMOR & BARRON, MASS COMMUNICATION LAW 166 (2d ed. 1974).

[7] Pittsburgh Press Co. v. Pittsburgh Commission on Human Relations, 413 U.S. 376, 388; *id.* at 393 (Burger, C.J., dissenting); *id.* at 398 (Douglas, J., dissenting); *id.* at 401 (Stewart, J., dissenting, supported by Blackmun, J., in a separate opinion) (1973); Lehman v. City of Shaker Heights, 418 U.S. 298, 314–15 n.6 (1974) (Brennan, J., dissenting, joined by Justices Stewart, Marshall, and Powell). For Justice Douglas's oft-quoted criticisms of the doctrine, see note 18 *infra*.

[8] 421 U.S. 809 (1975).

[9] *Id.* at 825.

[10] 425 U.S. at 770 (1976).

I. History of the Doctrine

A. VALENTINE: THE SEMINAL CASE

The commercial speech exception was first expressly stated in 1942 in *Valentine v. Chrestensen*, where the Court upheld Chrestensen's conviction for violating an ordinance banning distribution in the streets or other public places of any "commercial and business advertising matter."[11] He had distributed handbills promoting paid visits by the public to his former Navy submarine on one side, and on the reverse protesting an official New York City action affecting his business. Chrestensen argued that the ordinance violated his First Amendment rights of freedom of speech and press. After noting its unequivocal interest in protecting freedom of communication in the streets from being unduly burdened by governmental regulations, the Court held "that the Constitution imposes no such restraint on government as respects purely commercial advertising."[12]

In this single sentence the Court first announced the existence of a commercial speech exception. The opinion left unresolved three central questions. First, what kind of test determined commercial speech —motive, content, method of distribution, or some combination of these? The *Valentine* opinion vaguely offered a "primary purpose" or motive test. The Court implied that Chrestensen's motive in distributing the handbill was commercial. In fact, the handbill's first version, which, Chrestensen was advised, violated the ordinance, spoke only of the submarine visits. The noncommercial content in the second handbill was "the protest against official conduct [affixed] to the advertising circular with the intent, and for the purpose, of evading the prohibition of the ordinance."[13] Second, was

---

[11] The ordinance at issue in *Valentine* stated: "*Handbills, cards and circulars.*— No person shall throw, cast or distribute, or cause or permit to be thrown, cast or distributed, any handbill, circular, card, booklet, placard or other advertising matter whatsoever in or upon any street or public place, or in a front yard or court yard, or on any stoop, or in the vestibule or any hall of any building, or in a letterbox therein; provided that nothing herein contained shall be deemed to prohibit or otherwise regulate the delivery of any such matter by the United States postal service, or prohibit the distribution of sample copies of newspapers regularly sold by the copy or by annual subscription. This section is not intended to prevent the lawful distribution of anything other than commercial and business advertising matter." 316 U.S. at 53 n.1.

[12] *Id.* at 54.   [13] *Id.* at 55.

commercial speech to be wholly unprotected and, therefore, prohibitable, or was it to be merely less protected and, therefore, more regulable?[14] Third, and most basic, what was the justification for removing commercial speech from full First Amendment protection?[15] Again, only indirectly did *Valentine* provide an explanation here. Immediately following its statement that "the exercise of the freedom of communicating information and disseminating opinion" may not be unduly burdened by government regulation, the Court stated that "no such restraint" exists "as respects purely commercial advertising."[16] From this juxtaposition the inference can be drawn that, in the Court's eyes, "commercial advertising" did not convey "information and opinion"; or, to the extent it did so, it only warranted some lesser degree of First Amendment protection than was accorded speech more fully communicating information and disseminating opinion.[17]

---

[14] Even those forms of speech accorded full First Amendment protection are susceptible to some regulation. "[A]ll schools of thought [on the scope of the First Amendment] . . . are in substantial agreement . . . that government has some power to regulate the 'how' and 'where' of the exercise of the freedom [of speech]; . . ." Brennan, *The Supreme Court and the Meiklejohn Interpretation of the First Amendment*, 79 HARV. L. REV. 1, 5 (1965).

[15] The idea of varying degrees of First Amendment protection for various kinds of speech has been much discussed. "The guarantee given by the First Amendment is not, then, assured to all speaking. It is assured only to speech which bears, directly or indirectly, upon issues with which voters have to deal—only, therefore, to the consideration of matters of public interest. Private speech, or private interest in speech, on the other hand, has no claim whatever to the protection of the First Amendment. If men are engaged, as we so commonly are, in argument, or inquiry, or advocacy, or incitement which is directed toward our private interests, private privileges, private possessions, we are, of course, entitled to 'due process' protection of those activities. But the First Amendment has no concern over such protection. . . . [W]e draw sharply and clearly the line which separates the public welfare of the community from the private goods of any individual citizen or group of citizens." Meiklejohn, *Free Speech and Its Relation to Self-Government*, in POLITICAL FREEDOM 79–80 (1948). While Meiklejohn is perhaps the leading exponent of this tier system of speech, similar formulations have been discussed by others: ANASTAPLO, THE CONSTITUTIONALIST 113–29 (1971); Kalven, *The New York Times Case: A Note on "The Central Meaning of the First Amendment*," 1964 SUPREME COURT REVIEW 191, 217. For a similar approach to commercial speech, see Emerson, *Toward a General Theory of the First Amendment*, 72 YALE L.J. 877, 948–49 n.93 (1963).

[16] 316 U.S. at 54.

[17] As to a rationale for lesser First Amendment status for commercial speech, one commentator offered three: (1) "[S]ince both manufacture and sale of certain products may be prohibited, regulation of lesser incidents of the commercial process must also be permitted"; (2) advertising is really economic activity rather than a form of speech; (3) utilizing Meiklejohn's theory, some speech is preferred because

Perhaps because of these deficiencies in the *Valentine* opinion the commercial speech doctrine was viewed as constitutionally unsound and deemed unworthy of further attention by the Court. For example, Justice Douglas's oft-quoted opinion of 1959 was that, "The ruling was casual, almost offhand. And it has not survived reflection."[18] Nevertheless, the doctrine remained alive another seventeen years.

B. THE HANDBILLING/CANVASSING CASES

One of the earliest handbilling cases can be viewed as providing the roots for, and an interesting counterpoint to, the holding in *Valentine*. Three of the four cases consolidated in *Schneider v. State*[19] involved ordinances that banned handbilling on any issue—not solely "advertising matter" as in *Valentine*—in streets, parks, and other public places.[20] The Court found the anti-littering rationale of these ordinances unpersuasive. "[T]he purpose to keep the streets clean and of good appearance is insufficient to justify an ordinance which prohibits a person rightfully on a public street from handing literature to one willing to receive it."[21]

---

it furthers First Amendment purposes, while other speech is less preferred because it does not. Note, note 4 *supra*, 48 TUL. L. REV. at 429–31.

Interestingly, Chrestensen's defense was based on his claim to First Amendment protection for the "protest" side of his circular, not the commercial advertising side. "The respondent contends that, in truth, he was engaged in the dissemination of matter proper for public information, none the less so because there was inextricably attached to the medium of such dissemination commercial advertising matter." 316 U.S. at 55. In effect, Chrestensen, the first "victim" of the doctrine, failed to argue the key constitutional point in his defense.

[18] Cammarano v. United States, 358 U.S. 498, 514 (1959) (Douglas, J., concurring). Justice Douglas's "reflection" stemmed, no doubt, from the fact that in at least one post-*Valentine* case he affirmed the commercial speech exception by observing for the Court that, "The right to use the press for expressing one's views is not to be measured by the protection afforded commercial handbills." Murdock v. Pennsylvania, 319 U.S. 105, 111 (1943). His opinion in *Cammarano*, sixteen years later, argued against a distinction between commercial and noncommercial speech: "The profit motive should make no difference, for that is an element inherent in the very conception of a press under our system of free enterprise." 358 U.S. at 514. See also, Dun & Bradstreet, Inc. v. Grove, 404 U.S. 898, 904–05 (1971) (Douglas, J., dissenting from denial of certiorari).

[19] 308 U.S. 147 (1939).

[20] The three handbills at issue in *Schneider* dealt with a variety of public topics: announcing a meeting to discuss the war in Spain, a labor dispute, and the administration of state unemployment insurance.

[21] 308 U.S. at 162. In contrast, the ordinance upheld in *Valentine* had the intent of preventing "an undesirable invasion of, or interference with, the full and free

The Town of Irvington ordinance at issue in the fourth case consolidated in *Schneider* banned house-to-house canvassing for any reason without first obtaining a permit from the police.[22] The petitioner was a Jehovah's Witness who distributed religious booklets house to house and sought small contributions. In holding the ordinance unconstitutional on First Amendment grounds, the Court said:[23]

> While it affects others, the Irvington ordinance . . . affects all those, who, like the petitioner, desire to impart information and opinion to citizens at their homes. If it covers the petitioner's activities it equally applies to one who wishes to present his views on political, social or economic questions. The ordinance is not limited to those who canvass for private profit; nor is it merely the common type of ordinance requiring some form of registration or license of hawkers, or peddlers. It is not a general ordinance to prohibit trespassing. It bans unlicensed communication of any views or the advocacy of any cause from door to door, and permits canvassing only subject to the power of a police officer to determine, as a censor, what literature may be distributed from house to house and who may distribute it.

The Irvington ordinance sought to regulate a method of distribution (canvassing), but the Court ignored that issue and spoke only in terms of protecting the canvasser's purpose of imparting "information and opinion." In addition, the Court rejected any distinction based on the canvassing's content: "If it covers the petitioner's activities it equally applies to one who wishes to present his views on political, social or economic questions."[24]

---

use of the highways by the people in fulfillment of the public use to which streets are dedicated." 316 U.S. at 54–55. The Second Circuit, however, had maintained that the ordinance had an anti-littering rationale. 122 F.2d at 513.

[22] 308 U.S. at 157.

[23] *Id*. at 163.

[24] *Ibid*. In Lovell v. Griffin, 303 U.S. 444, 451 (1938), decided the year before *Schneider*, the Court struck down as unconstitutional on its face an ordinance which banned handbilling anywhere of " 'literature' in the widest sense" without first obtaining a permit from the city manager. The petitioner violated the ordinance by distributing religious pamphlets without a permit; no money was involved in the distribution. Since the *Schneider* opinion used *Lovell* as a precedent in both the three non-Jehovah's Witnesses handbilling cases and the one Jehovah's Witnesses canvassing case, it appears from *Lovell* and *Schneider* together that the Court struck down ordinances which infringed upon a person's First Amendment in-

In its last paragraph, the *Schneider* opinion prophetically isolated commercial activity from the protection established earlier in the opinion for imparting "information and opinion."[25] Said the Court, "We are not to be taken as holding that commercial soliciting and canvassing may not be subjected to such regulation as the ordinance requires."[26] Although the *Valentine* opinion contained no citations or references to precedent, arguably this language in *Schneider* was the source for the Court's finding Chrestensen's handbill different from the handbills in *Schneider*.[27] For, as noted earlier, *Valentine* contrasted the two-sided handbill at issue there with speech containing information and opinion. Even without a specific citation, *Valentine* can be viewed as a continuation of *Schneider*'s motive test—affording protection only where there was a primary purpose of disseminating information and opinion—and thus as giving substance to the commercial speech exception foreshadowed in *Schneider*.[28]

In *Jamison v. Texas*,[29] decided shortly after *Valentine*, the Court

---

terests (motive) and did not draw distinctions as to the speech's content (religious or political) or method of distribution (handbilling or canvassing, with or without a permit required). *Cf.* Talley v. California, 362 U.S. 60 (1960). Of course, the ordinances at issue in these two cases were so intolerably broad that such distinctions, aimed at defining the commercial speech doctrine, would have been pointless.

[25] Recognition that the First Amendment safeguards the communication of "information and opinion" continued in Cantwell v. Connecticut, 310 U.S. 296, 310 (1940).

[26] 308 U.S. at 165. Earlier in the opinion the Court implied that the ordinance might have been valid if "limited to those who canvass for private profit." *Id.* at 163.

[27] Language in *Schneider* can also be read as precedent for the result in another leading commercial speech case, Breard v. Alexandria, 341 U.S. 622, 640 (1951). The Court's statement in *Breard* that the city council has "the duty of protecting its citizens against the practices deemed subversive of privacy and of quiet" is similar to language in *Schneider* recognizing a municipality's right to legislate against certain distribution tactics including trespassing. 308 U.S. at 161, 164. The Court used similar "time, place, and manner" language in Cantwell v. Connecticut, 310 U.S. 296, 307 (1940), indicating its willingness to approve legislation drawn narrowly enough to reflect a "judgment that the playing of a phonograph on the streets should in the interest of comfort or privacy be limited or prevented."

[28] That *Valentine* stated a motive or primary purpose test is well acknowledged. Resnik, note 4 *supra*, at 657. Note, *Developments in the Law-Deceptive Advertising*, 80 HARV. L. REV. 1005, 1028 (1967).
  "But a motive test raises unmanageable problems of definition. Moreover, whose motive should be determinative—the author's, publisher's or distributors'? A more fundamental defect of a motive distinction is that it is irrelevant to the reasons why social, religious, or political expression is protected." Note, note 4 *supra*, 78 HARV. L. REV. at 1203.

[29] 318 U.S. 413 (1943).

refined its view of commercial activity by again rejecting distinctions of content or method of distribution and continuing to focus on motive. The city acknowledged that the handbills were distributed to further the Jehovah's Witnesses' religious activity, but argued that the handbills in fact had a commercial purpose because they "contained an invitation to contribute to the support of that activity by purchasing books related to the work of the group."[30] Referring to "almost precisely the same" conduct in *Schneider*, the Court held that this handbill was protected because its primary purpose was distribution of "information and opinion" of a religious nature. The fact that the handbill had what could be termed commercial content did not make it commercial speech.

Shortly after *Jamison*, two cases decided on the same day, *Murdock v. Pennsylvania*[31] and *Martin v. Struthers*,[32] further defined the commercial speech doctrine in the context of handbilling and canvassing. The Court in *Murdock* used *Schneider* and *Jamison* to strike down "an ordinance which as construed and applied requires religious colporteurs to pay a license tax as a condition to the pursuit of their activities."[33] As with *Jamison*'s handbilling, the Court held that *Murdock*'s door-to-door soliciting was a "religious venture" protected by the First Amendment, not a commercial endeavor. Although it foresaw problems in drawing lines between religious and purely commercial activity,[34] the Court asserted that, "the mere fact that the religious literature is 'sold' by itinerant[35] preachers rather than 'donated' does not transform evangelism into a commercial enterprise."[36]

---

[30] *Id.* at 416.

[31] 319 U.S. 105 (1943).

[32] 319 U.S. 141 (1943).

[33] 319 U.S. at 110.

[34] *Ibid.*

[35] When an ordinance similar to that in *Murdock* was applied to a Jehovah's Witnesses preacher who worked full-time canvassing door to door in only one community, the Court struck that down as well. "We referred to the itinerant nature of the activity in the *Murdock* case merely in emphasis of the prohibitive character of the license tax as so applied. Its unconstitutionality was not dependent on that circumstance." Follett v. McCormick, 321 U.S. 573, 577 (1944).

[36] 319 U.S. at 111. The rationale of *Murdock* was used the same day in Jones v. Opelika, 319 U.S. 103 (1943) (*Jones #2*), to overrule Jones v. Opelika, 316 U.S. 584 (1942) (*Jones #1*). *Jones #2* relied on *Murdock* to strike down an occupational license tax as an unconstitutional restraint on religious freedom. Just one year earlier in *Jones #1* the Court found that: "When proponents of religious or social theories use the ordinary commercial methods of sales of articles to raise propaganda funds, it is a natural and proper exercise of the power of the State to charge reasonable fees for the privilege of canvassing . . . . It is prohibition and unjustifiable abridgment which are interdicted, not taxation." 316 U.S. at 597. The prompt re-

Murdock carried one step further *Jamison*'s exclusion of seemingly commercial activity from the commercial speech doctrine:
Jamison had merely "advertised" by handbill the sale of religious
literature to support religious activities, whereas Murdock actually
"sold" such literature door to door for the same purpose. Both efforts
were found by the Court to be noncommercial activity protected
by the First Amendment.

The facts in *Martin v. Struthers* differed from those in *Murdock*
only in that (a) the door-to-door canvassing was not to distribute
religious literature and solicit book sales but to distribute leaflets
advertising a Jehovah's Witnesses meeting, and (b) the ordinance
at issue did not impose a license tax but forbade summoning residents
to their doors to receive "handbills, circulars or other advertisements."[37] The Court easily found this canvassing protected by its
First Amendment motive and, therefore, not within the commercial
speech exception.[38] *Struthers* was the first Jehovah's Witnesses case
where the societal interest supporting the restrictions on canvassing
was distinctive enough and strong enough to compete with the First
Amendment's interest in protecting that activity. That societal interest was homeowner's privacy.[39] In no prior case did the municipality have a more compelling rationale for upholding "reasonable
police and health regulations of time and manner of distribution."[40]
The facts in this case could well have justified the Court's using a
method-of-distribution test to reach an unprotected speech result,
rather than a motive test to reach the opposite result.

The Court took note of the privacy rationale for the ordinance:
"The City, which is an industrial community most of whose residents are engaged in the iron and steel industry, has vigorously

---

versal of this position only one year later may be explained by a change in Court
personnel. The majority opinion in *Jones #1* was written by Justice Reed, joined
by Justices Roberts, Frankfurter, Byrnes, and Jackson. The dissenters were Justices Stone, Black, Douglas, and Murphy. In *Jones #2* and *Murdock* Rutledge replaced Byrnes and shifted the balance of the Court. The *Jones #2* opinion was
one paragraph, *per curiam*, and the dissents there were filed as part of *Murdock*.

[37] 319 U.S. at 142.   [38] *Id.* at 146–47.

[39] Prior to *Martin v. Struthers* the possibility of using a privacy rationale for restrictions on canvassing was noted approvingly in *Schneider* and *Cantwell*. See note
27 *supra.* The Court also commented on this possibility in *Murdock*: "[T]he present ordinance is not narrowly drawn to safeguard the people of the community in
their homes against the evils of solicitations." 319 U.S. at 116.

[40] 319 U.S. at 147.

argued that its inhabitants frequently work on swing shifts, working nights and sleeping days so that casual bell pushers might seriously interfere with the hours of sleep although they call at high noon."[41] The Court found this privacy interest outweighed by the First Amendment's interest in protecting door-to-door canvassing. In reaching this conclusion the Court balanced privacy (and the possibilities of burglary as well) against a broad statement of the First Amendment purposes to be fulfilled by protecting from regulation the door-to-door distribution of religious leaflets:[42]

> While door to door distributers of literature may be either a nuisance or a blind for criminal activities, they may also be useful members of society engaged in the dissemination of ideas in accordance with the best tradition of free discussion. The widespread use of this method of communication by many groups espousing various causes attests its major importance.

In sum, the Court said, "Door to door distribution of circulars is essential to the poorly financed causes of little people."[43]

In *Martin v. Struthers* the Court again ignored any distinctions based on manner of distribution or content (merging religion with labor and politics just as in *Schneider*), and instead spoke of the First Amendment motive, reflected in the content, for "the dissemination of ideas in accordance with the best tradition of free discussion."[44]

C. A SECOND SEMINAL EFFORT: BREARD V. ALEXANDRIA

The line of cases involving handbilling/canvassing by Jehovah's Witnesses ended at this point,[45] but a significant, rather enigmatic, commercial speech case, *Breard v. Alexandria*,[46] was decided just a few years later. At issue was a city ordinance that prohibited door-to-door solicitation without the prior consent of the homeowner.

---

[41] *Id*. at 144.   [42] *Id*. at 145.

[43] *Id*. at 146. The irony, of course, is that the Court's examples could hardly be considered "the poorly financed causes of little people." Justice Jackson's dissent questions whether that phrase is descriptive of Jehovah's Witnesses. 319 U.S. at 166.

[44] 319 U.S. at 145.

[45] Follett v. McCormick, 321 U.S. 573 (1944), another Jehovah's Witnesses case, followed *Martin v. Struthers* by a few months, but it merely refined a rather narrow point. See note 35 *supra*.

[46] 341 U.S. 622 (1951).

Breard appealed his conviction on three grounds, only one of which is pertinent here.[47] His novel contention was that the ordinance, as applied to his door-to-door selling of magazine subscriptions, was an abridgment of freedom of the press.[48]

Justice Reed, a dissenter in *Murdock* and *Struthers*, wrote the Court's opinion upholding the constitutionality of the ordinance, finding that a homeowner's right to privacy outweighed whatever First Amendment rights this distributor (and, by implication, the publishers utilizing him) had to solicit magazine subscriptions by this method.[49] With some effort the Court found that *Struthers* "is not necessarily inconsistent with the conclusion reached in this case."[50] The difference was that "the free distribution of dodgers 'advertising a religious meeting,' "[51] which was at issue in *Struthers*, contained "no element of the commercial," and "the opinion was narrowly limited to the precise fact of the free distribution of an invitation to religious services."[52] In contrast, Breard's activity was the "solicit[ation of] subscriptions for nationally known magazines."[53] In response to Breard's contention that "the mere fact that money is made out of the distribution does not bar the publications from First Amendment protection,"[54] the Court explained: "We agree that the fact that periodicals are sold does not put them beyond the protection of the First Amendment. The selling, however, brings into the transaction a commercial feature."[55]

---

[47] The two other grounds argued by *Breard* were that the ordinance violated (1) the Due Process Clause by unreasonably burdening his right to engage in a lawful private business; and (2) the Commerce Clause. *Id.* at 629–41.

[48] "Finally we come to a point not heretofore urged in this Court as a ground for the invalidation of a Green River ordinance. This is that such an ordinance is an abridgment of freedom of speech and the press. Only the press or oral advocates of ideas could urge this point. It was not open to the solicitors for gadgets or brushes." *Id.* at 641.

[49] 341 U.S. at 644. In *Struthers*, where the ordinance was struck down as violative of the First Amendment, the Court observed: "The ordinance does not control anything but the distribution of literature, and in that respect it substitutes the judgment of the community for the judgment of the individual householder." 319 U.S. at 143–44. In contrast, the Court in *Breard* stated: "To the city council falls the duty of protecting its citizens against the practices deemed subversive of privacy and of quiet." 341 U.S. at 640.

[50] *Id.* at 643. Justice Black, author of the majority opinion in *Martin v. Struthers*, dissented. "Since this decision cannot be reconciled with the *Jones, Murdock* and *Martin v. Struthers* cases, it seems to me that good judicial practice calls for their forthright overruling." *Id.* at 649–50.

[51] *Id.* at 642.   [53] *Id.* at 624.   [55] *Id.* at 642.

[52] *Id.* at 643.   [54] *Id.* at 641–42.

The Court in *Breard* appears to have used two different tests to resolve two different issues. As noted earlier, in upholding the contested ordinance the Court applied a method-of-distribution test, balancing homeowners' privacy against the merits of door-to-door canvassing. But in attempting to reconcile *Breard* with its predecessor, *Struthers*, the Court utilized a motive analysis. Certainly the distinction between *Breard* and *Struthers* cannot be method of distribution, for the house-to-house canvassing was identical in each. Nor can the distinction be content: the political, economic, and social discussions in some of Breard's magazines would seem to be as entitled to First Amendment protection as the religious literature distributed in *Struthers*.[56]

If the test, then, is motive, the question is how the Court determined a commercial motive in Breard's activity and a fully protected First Amendment motive in *Struthers*. The Court spoke of Breard's "selling" and seemed to assume that this one word, standing alone, conveyed the distinction that the Court perceived between the two cases. If Breard's "selling" indicated that he had a different motive than Martin, who distributed his literature free, with the result that Breard's activity was regulated as less protected commercial speech but Martin's was not, then how does this "selling" distinguish *Breard* from *Murdock* (a case not discussed in the *Breard* opinion)? In both *Breard* and *Murdock* the canvassers went house to house receiving money in exchange for literature which, if considered solely on the basis of content in either case, was entitled to full First Amendment protection.[57]

There are three possible bases for reconciliation of *Breard* with *Murdock* and *Struthers*. On the basis of a motive test, a possible reconciliation of these cases is that Breard's sale of magazine subscriptions on behalf of his profit-seeking employer was found by the Court to be primarily a commercial activity, and therefore less protected, albeit not completely unprotected, by the First Amendment than the less commercial sale of religious literature by the nonprofit Jehovah's Witnesses in *Murdock* or the distribution of leaflets advertising a religious meeting in *Struthers*. In other words, the fact of

---

[56] "[A] distinction based purely upon content fails to explain *Breard*, since at least some of the magazines sold contained substantial social or political advocacy." Note, note 4 *supra*, 78 HARV. L. REV. at 1203.

[57] See discussion of *Murdock* in text *supra*, at notes 31–36.

"selling" in *Breard* is really the motive or primary purpose test,[58] with the distinction being the presence or absence of a profit motive.[59] The difficulty with such vague motive differentiations is that they offer no identifiable guidelines for future cases.

A second reconciliation of these cases is possible by applying a method-of-distribution test.[60] The *Breard* opinion not only specifically noted that magazine subscriptions may be obtained by methods other than canvassing,[61] but actually balanced these alternatives against the right of privacy framed in the ordinance: "This makes the constitutionality of Alexandria's ordinance turn upon a balancing of the conveniences between some householders' desire for privacy and the publisher's right to distribute publications in the precise way that those soliciting for him think brings the best results."[62]

In applying this test, the Court in *Breard* did not examine the constitutionality of a particular method of distribution per se. The cases are no more consistent on that basis than on an analysis of content or motive.[63] Nor did the Court balance a particular method of distribution against some competing interest such as homeowners' privacy. Rather, the Court seemed to apply the test by balancing a societal interest such as privacy against the ability of the distributor, determined by his economic strength, to pursue some alternative method-of-distribution. This is more accurately termed the "alternative methods of distribution" test. Viewed in this way, the distinction between *Breard* and *Murdock/Struthers* may be in the Court's

---

[58] See Note, note 4 *supra*, 51 N.C.L. Rev. at 585.

[59] See Note, note 4 *supra*, 78 Harv. L. Rev. at 1203.

[60] The Court later observed in *Bigelow* that, contrary to the accepted interpretation, *Valentine* had a method-of-distribution, rather than a motive, rationale. 421 U.S. at 819.

[61] 341 U.S. at 644.

[62] *Ibid*. Note that the Court here made no distinction between the distributor and the publisher.

[63] Both *Schneider*, 308 U.S. at 164, and *Struthers*, 319 U.S. at 145, exalted the historic importance of door-to-door dissemination of First Amendment protected speech. But when Breard engaged in precisely that activity, he was restrained. At least one leading commentator disapproves of constitutional protection for door-to-door solicitation regardless of motive or content. Zechariah Chafee was approvingly quoted by the Court in *Breard* for his condemnation of house-to-house canvassing by " 'peddlers of ideas and salesmen of salvation in odd brands . . . as much as the regular run of commercial canvassers.' " 341 U.S. at 639 n.27, quoting Chafee, Free Speech in the United States 407 (1941).

view that the economic strength of this distributor and his pub-lishers[64] was sufficient that their use of door-to-door canvassing was not crucial to the dissemination of their ideas.[65] Hence the result that homeowners' privacy outweighed Breard's canvassing but did not outweigh the identical activity by the Jehovah's Witnesses.[66]

If alternative methods of distribution are the telling factor, the Court erred, first, by not considering the economic strength of the Jehovah's Witnesses Church,[67] and second, by not weighing seri-ously the impact a widely adopted ban on door-to-door solicitation undeniably would have on the magazine industry.[68] Finally, the vital question is whether the *Breard* result meant that the activities of struggling newspapers and journals which sell door-to-door would be found more like those of the publishers in *Breard* or those of itinerant preachers.

Yet even if the word distinctions were less murky, the cases up to and including *Breard* would not have formulated a viable com-mercial speech doctrine.[69] If, as the Court said in *Breard*, *Struthers*

---

[64] 341 U.S. at 644.

[65] "National magazines are generally able to advertise and secure distribution by means that do not interfere with the protection of privacy, safety, and aesthetic standards. The proponents of political or religious points of view frequently cannot afford or obtain extensive advertising, while they may be able to secure the free services of their own members." Note, note 4 *supra*, 78 HARV. L. REV. at 1203.

[66] *Struthers* identified canvassing as "essential to the poorly financed causes of little people." 319 U.S. at 146.

[67] 319 U.S. at 166 (Jackson, J., dissenting).

[68] The Court was aware in *Breard* that 50–60 percent of all magazine subscrip-tions were secured by door-to-door solicitation, but evidently did not consider this to be critically important. 341 U.S. at 635 n.18.

[69] *Struthers* is distinguishable from *Breard*, said the Court, because *Struthers* in-volved "free" distribution whereas *Breard* involved "selling." But then how is *Breard* distinguishable from *Murdock*, which involved selling? The difference is that Murdock sold religious literature, whereas Breard sold commercial magazines. But that difference is constitutionally unsound because the content of Breard's magazines should be as much preferred by the First Amendment as was Murdock's religious activity. The distinction, then, is that the Court found Murdock's pri-mary purpose to be religious activity, as contrasted to Breard's profit-seeking mo-tive. But that distinction is also infirm because many profit-seeking activities are fully protected by the First Amendment, *e.g.*, newspapers, Grosjean v. American Press Co., 297 U.S. 233 (1936), books, Smith v. California, 361 U.S. 147 (1959); *but cf.* Ginzburg v. United States, 383 U.S. 463 (1966), and movies, Joseph Burstyn, Inc. v. Wilson, 343 U.S. 495 (1952). The distinction, then, could be that Breard was a distributor and, therefore, unprotected, but that the magazine companies as publishers would have been protected had they acted independently. That dis-tinction, however, is also problematical, for in an early handbilling case the Court observed: "The ordinance cannot be saved because it relates to distribution and

is to be read as "narrowly limited to the precise fact of the free distribution of an invitation to religious services," despite the clear language in *Struthers* encompassing that literature within "the dissemination of ideas . . . by many groups espousing various causes,"[70] and if *Breard's* language about "selling" created no discernible inconsistency with *Murdock*, then the Court simply defined commercial speech in terms of what it was not. And sales by a religious denomination in furtherance of its religious efforts were not commercial speech.[71]

The apparently irreconcilable conflict between these cases can be resolved if *Murdock/Struthers*, as well as the other Jehovah's Witnesses cases involving handbilling and canvassing, are deemed unique because of their religious element. If these religion cases are viewed as a sequence separate and distinct from the commercial speech doctrine, then the oft-noted contradictions in these early handbilling/ canvassing cases disappear. Public, direct proselyting by the Jehovah's Witnesses meant that the issue of their religious freedom was framed within the Free Speech Clause rather than the Freedom of Religion Clause of the First Amendment. The Court was unwilling to create a precedent of restraint in these cases, which were brought to it structured in a free speech context, because such a precedent might then be used, not to restrain analogous instances of nonreligious speech infringing upon other societal interests, but to restrain religious freedom of other sects.[72]

Aside from these religion cases, there were only two commercial speech cases related to this point, *Valentine* and *Breard*. *Valentine* really stated no rationale for its commercial speech doctrine. If, as the Court observed more than thirty years later, it was a method-of-

---

not to publication. 'Liberty of circulating is as essential to that freedom as liberty of publishing; indeed, without the circulation, the publication would be of little value.' " Lovell v. Griffin, 303 U.S. 444, 452 (1938).

[70] 319 U.S. at 145.

[71] The Court never faced a difficult line-drawing problem within the Jehovah's Witnesses cases themselves. Church-sponsored door-to-door selling of subscriptions to non-religious magazines would, no doubt, have fallen outside the commercial speech exception as easily as did similar selling of religious literature. But what about newspaper advertisements for vacancies in a church-owned and operated, profit-seeking and profit-making, home for the elderly?

[72] See Jones v. Opelika, 316 U.S. 584, 621 (Murphy, J., dissenting). This is not to say, however, that these religion cases do not have precedential value in free press cases. See, *e.g.*, Pittsburgh Press Co. v. Pittsburgh Commission on Human Relations, 413 U.S. 376, 383 (1973).

distribution case, by a balancing of Chrestensen's speech distributed by handbilling in the streets against the competing societal interest of minimizing interference with the free use of those streets the Court could have produced the same result without the necessity of first reducing the status of Chrestensen's speech by terming it commercial. As for *Breard*, the Court used only the motive test to distinguish it from the religion cases. *Breard's* result was produced by balancing the societal interest in homeowners' privacy against the distributor's and publishers' interest in realizing their First Amendment rights (and a profit) by this particular method of distribution. As with *Valentine*, the same result could have been achieved as easily without reducing the First Amendment status of the speech by terming it commercial.[73]

In sum, in the religion cases the Court was unwilling to restrict the Jehovah's Witnesses' proselytizing activity, regardless of its tactics, because such a precedent might be applied to restrict religion in other circumstances rather than to restrict similar nonreligious activity. That leaves only two cases, *Valentine* and *Breard*, each distinguishable on its facts so that neither one separately nor both together can be seen as establishing a commercial speech doctrine. Yet, the doctrine was invoked for twenty-five years after *Breard*.

II. The Doctrine's Impact on Other First Amendment Exceptions

A. NEWSPAPERS AS COMMERCIAL PUBLICATIONS

The libel exception to the First Amendment protections contains a noteworthy commercial speech element in its landmark case, *New York Times Co. v. Sullivan*.[74] The doctrine posed a threshold bar-

---

[73] In 1970 the Court upheld the constitutionality of a federal statute (Title III of the Postal Revenue and Federal Salary Act of 1967, 39 U.S.C. § 4009, 1964 ed., Supp. IV), under which a householder may require that a mailer remove his name from its mailing list and stop all future mailings to his home. Neither *Breard* nor *Valentine* was cited as authority, perhaps because the opinion did not distinguish commercial from noncommercial speech. Rather, the result was produced by the householder's right to privacy outweighing the mailer's First Amendment right to communicate ideas. Rowan v. U.S. Post Office Department, 397 U.S. 728 (1970).

[74] 376 U.S. 254 (1964). In light of the fact that the New York Times appellation is equally applicable to the later *Pentagon Papers Case*, New York Times v. United States, 403 U.S. 713 (1971), the textual reference to the case hereinafter will use *Sullivan* as its designation.

rier for the Court to hurdle in order to reach the historic libel result in *Sullivan*. One of the plaintiff's arguments was that "the constitutional guarantees of freedom of speech and of the press are inapplicable here, at least so far as the Times is concerned, because the allegedly libelous statements were published as part of a paid, 'commercial' advertisement."[75] The four clergymen who, as signatories to the advertisement at issue, were the Times's co-defendants were not joined in this part of the argument.[76] And in that lies at least part of the Court's confusion about the commercial speech component here.

The Court's exact language in distinguishing *Valentine* is worth noting:[77]

> The publication here was not a "commercial" advertisement in the sense in which the word was used in *Chrestensen*. It communicated information, expressed opinion, recited grievances, protested claimed abuses, and sought financial support on behalf of a movement whose existence and objectives are matters of the highest public interest and concern. . . . *That the Times was paid for publishing the advertisement is as immaterial in this connection as is the fact that newspapers and books are sold.* . . . Any other conclusion would discourage newspapers from carrying "editorial advertisements" of this type, and so might shut off an important outlet for the promulgation of information and ideas by persons who do not themselves have access to publishing facilities—who wish to exercise their freedom of speech even though they are not members of the press. . . . The effect would be to shackle the First Amendment in its attempt to secure "the widest possible dissemination of information from diverse and antagonistic sources."

Much subsequent confusion regarding commercial speech could have been avoided if the Court, rather than distinguishing the *Valentine* rule and thereby further legitimizing it, had chosen *Sullivan* as the occasion to minimize if not eliminate the commercial speech exception. Instead, the Court simply disposed of the plaintiff's argu-

---

[75] 376 U.S. at 265.

[76] On the purely libel elements of the case, it has been noted that, "The Court never reached the question whether these defendants [the clergymen] were sufficiently connected with the publication to be treated as publishers." Kalven, note 15 *supra*, at 194 n.13.

[77] 376 U.S. at 266. (Emphasis added.)

ment on this point as a threshold question.[78] The need to do so, given the result of the case, was obvious: If the plaintiff had successfully argued that the commercial speech exception lowered the defendant's (the Times's) First Amendment protective barrier and had then hopped over that barrier, the Court could hardly have used this case, as it did, to create a new, higher protective barrier for the media for alleged libel of public officials.

The method by which the Court circumvented *Valentine* did little to sort out the persistent confusion surrounding content, motive, and method of distribution as analytic tools for determining commercial speech. The finding that this advertisement was not commercial speech by the Times certainly was vital to an expansive use of First Amendment protection, but the reasoning to reach that result was indirect and somewhat faulty.

In regard to the Times the Court's analysis of its position vis-à-vis the commercial speech doctrine had to be in terms of motive, since the Times had no voice in the advertisement's content, and since method of distribution was never at issue in the case. But a motive analysis of the Times's participation would surely have produced a finding of commercial speech, for the Times's key role was the commercial decision whether to accept this advertisement for publication.[79] To avoid this commercial speech result, the Court drew an incorrect analogy between the Times's role here and that of a bookseller. This analogy successfully shifted the analysis away from the necessary starting point of the newspaper's motive and eventually to the advertisement's content,[80] and thereby provided the Times's extrication from the snares of the commercial speech doctrine.

---

[78] The secondary importance of the issue within the rather revolutionary result of the *Sullivan* case is illustrated by its being accorded but a brief footnote in Kalven's immediate post-*Sullivan* commentary. See Kalven, note 15 *supra*, at 194 n.12. Still, the doctrine was sufficiently acknowledged at the time that the Court could not simply ignore the plaintiff's commercial speech contention.

[79] As the Court subsequently indicated in *Pittsburgh Press*, 413 U.S. at 387, the "editorial judgment" whether to accept an advertisement is not sufficient by itself to provide First Amendment protection to a newspaper in all circumstances. But that a newspaper has the right under the First Amendment to accept or reject advertisements in its sole discretion is well established. See Associates & Aldrich Company, Inc. v. Times Mirror Company, 440 F.2d 133, 135 (9th Cir. 1971); Chicago Joint Bd., Amalgamated Clothing Workers v. Chicago Tribune Co., 435 F.2d 470, 478 (7th Cir. 1970).

[80] This shift is the basis for comments that "the primary purpose test was effectively overruled by the court's decision in *New York Times v. Sullivan*." Redish, note 3 *supra*, at 457.

The bookseller analogy was not apt because the transaction raised in the plaintiff's commercial speech argument was not the sale of a newspaper to a reader/consumer, but rather the sale of advertising space in the newspaper. The motive in such a sale could only have been commercial, for if this particular advertisement—the content of which "communicated information, expressed opinion, recited grievances"—had not been placed by the individual defendants, either the same space would have been sold to another advertiser (commercial or otherwise), or, if no purchaser for that space appeared, the newspaper that day would simply have been that much smaller. The newspaper's motive in selling this advertising space was not to communicate information or disseminate opinion; the motive was to make a profit. Only subsequently did the Times engage in the First Amendment protected activity of selling for a profit the clergymen's speech via the advertisement to the public.

A bookseller, in contrast, sells only to a reader/consumer. In addition to its commercial motive, such a sale has the effect, and perhaps the motive as well, of communicating information and disseminating opinion and is thus deemed protected activity under the First Amendment.[81] Only at the point of actually selling its newspapers to the public was the Times's role similar to the bookseller's. In the transaction with the clergymen for advertising space, the Times's role was analogous to book publishing, not to retail book selling. And then the analogy is precise and valid only if the book publisher inserts advertising copy as pages in the book. Such insertions dilute the First Amendment clarity of that publisher's motive, at least as to the sale of advertising space on the insert pages as distinct from publication and distribution of the book itself.

The plaintiff's commercial speech argument logically must have been directed to this first transaction for advertising space, for only at that point was the motive of the Times independently determinable.[82] The Court itself framed the issue in terms of the Times's being "paid for publishing the advertisement," not in terms of its being paid for retail sale of newspapers. At the point of this second transaction—selling newspapers to reader/consumers—the Times's

---

[81] E.g., Smith v. California, 361 U.S. 147, 150 (1959).

[82] In fact, the plaintiff's commercial speech argument was not this finely drawn, although it did point in the right direction. "And the Times itself . . . submitted [the ad] to the advertising Acceptability Department . . . . The Times charged the regular commercial advertising rate of almost five thousand dollars, . . ." Brief for Appellee at p. 31.

profit-seeking motive was protected by well-established First Amendment precedents which have found it irrelevant whether "dissemination takes place under commercial auspices."[83] In view of these precedents plaintiff Sullivan surely realized the futility of directing his commercial speech argument at the latter sale.[84]

Once the Court achieved this shift in focus from the unprotected commercial transaction raised by the plaintiff's commercial speech argument to a subsequent protected transaction, it had only to imbue that second transaction with a protected First Amendment quality in order to overcome the plaintiff's contention. That quality was not automatic, notwithstanding the First Amendment precedents which protect dissemination of information and opinion under commercial auspices, because the element of the newspaper's sale to the reader-consumer at issue was an advertisement, not an editorial or news story generated by the Times itself.[85] Protection was obtained by

---

[83] *Smith*, 361 U.S. at 150 (1959). See also *Grosjean*, 297 U.S. 233, 249 (1936); *Burstyn*, 343 U.S. at 501. "If a newspaper's profit motive were determinative, all aspects of its operations—from the selection of news stories to the choice of editorial position—would be subject to regulation if it could be established that they were conducted with a view toward increased sales. Such a basis for regulation clearly would be incompatible with the First Amendment." *Pittsburgh Press*, 413 U.S. at 385.

[84] Arguably any newspaper's sale of advertising space should be fully protected by the First Amendment because the profits from such selling are essential to fulfillment of the newspaper's news and editorial functions. But see United States v. Hunter, 459 F.2d 205, 213 (4th Cir. 1972), rejecting that argument and holding constitutional as applied to newspaper classified ads that provision of the 1968 Civil Rights Act prohibiting discriminatory notices for the sale or rental of dwellings. The argument is that a newspaper's activities cannot be dissected; they all further its First Amendment purposes. What result for a conglomerate corporation involved in several industries, one of which is newspaper publishing? Are corporate activities unrelated to the newspaper's First Amendment function eligible for First Amendment protection? What if those unrelated activities subsidize the newspaper? Would it matter how the subsidy was transmitted—for example, a fully documented, interest-bearing loan as compared to an overhead allocation by the accountant? Finally, aside from this question whether the newspaper's First Amendment status can shield unrelated corporate activity, what about the converse: can this corporate activity become so intertwined with the newspaper's operations that the paper's First Amendment status is nullified, if not totally, then perhaps as to certain articles? See S.E.C. v. Texas Gulf Sulphur Company, 446 F.2d 1301, 1306 (2d Cir. 1971), citing the commercial speech doctrine in support of a ruling that a corporate press release, like a corporate registration statement or prospectus, lacks full First Amendment protection.

[85] In *Pittsburgh Press* the Court drew a distinction between restrictions there authorized for classified ads and "any restriction whatever, whether of content or layout, on stories or commentary originated by Pittsburgh Press, its columnists, or its contributors." 413 U.S. at 391.

terming this an "editorial advertisement" with a purpose, unlike the *Valentine* advertisement, of communicating preferred speech—information, opinion, grievances, etc. Of course, the clergymen's unimpeachable motive of debating one of the great issues of the day and simultaneously obtaining "financial support on behalf of a movement whose existence and objectives are matters of the highest public interest and concern"[86] made it that much easier to adjudge this content to be "editorial." Thus, sandwiching the opinion's exculpatory sentence for the Times—that it was immaterial that the Times was paid for this advertisement—is broad, clear language first about the highly preferred First Amendment content of the advertisement, and then about the highly preferred First Amendment motive of the clergymen in placing the editorial advertisement.

In sum, the commercial speech argument could not be asserted by the plaintiff in regard to the clergymen because their advertisement's preferred content, as well as their motive in disseminating that content, made their entire effort highly protected speech. But, as to the Times, the plaintiff's commercial speech argument was applicable and telling. The Court was compelled, therefore, to abandon *Valentine*'s motive test, which had produced an unprotected result in *Breard* and would have done the same in *Sullivan*. For even though the clergymen's motive was protected, the Times's participation in furthering that motive by selling advertising space could not be. But, by shifting the analysis to content the Court could protect this "editorial advertisement" both as uttered by the clergymen and as "distributed" by the Times. With both the advertiser and the publisher thus protected, the Court could then link their First Amendment roles: publication of such an advertisement must be encouraged because it is "an important outlet for the promulgation of information and ideas by persons who do not themselves have access to publishing facilities—who wish to exercise their freedom of speech even though they are not members of the press."[87]

If the commercial speech issue was only a minor, unavoidable hurdle before reaching the result in *Sullivan*, it was at the core of the Court's analysis in *Pittsburgh Press Co. v. Pittsburgh Commission on*

---

[86] 376 U.S. at 266. These fund-raising efforts were apparently as entitled to protection as similar efforts on behalf of religion which the Court protected in *Jamison* and *Murdock*. See discussion in text *supra*, at notes 29–36.

[87] 376 U.S. at 266.

Human Relations.[88] The defendant, Pittsburgh Press, was found by the Commission to have violated an ordinance which prohibited discriminatory hiring on the basis of sex. Its violation consisted of aiding employer discrimination by carrying "help-wanted" advertisements in sex-designated columns even when the advertised jobs did not have valid occupational qualifications based on sex. The Press contended that its "exercise of editorial judgment" at two points—(1) whether to accept the advertisement in the first place, and (2) once accepted, where to place it in the newspaper—brought its role in the dissemination of these classified ads within the protection of the First Amendment.[89] The Court rejected this argument, and held that the Commission's order banning sex-designated column headings did not violate the First Amendment.

Just as the Court in *Sullivan* linked motive to content from one transaction to another in order to avoid the commercial speech doctrine with its consequences of less First Amendment protection, so the Court in *Pittsburgh Press* performed the same process, but in reverse, in order to retain the publisher's activity within the perimeters of that doctrine and thereby find it unprotected by the First Amendment. The Court first found the classified employment advertisements to be "classic examples of commercial speech."[90] It then performed its catenating process in opposite directions simultaneously.[91]

In *Sullivan* the preferred First Amendment content of the advertisement was used to elevate the publisher's commercial motive and thus achieve a protected speech result. In *Pittsburgh Press* the Court found to the contrary. The discriminatory commercial content of the classified ads vitiated whatever First Amendment status the editorial decisions may have had. And, just as the clergymen's high motive in *Sullivan* helped define a preferred status for the advertisement's content, so, to the contrary in *Pittsburgh Press*, the advertiser's suspect motive further tarnished the already questioned status of the content:[92]

> Under some circumstances, at least, a newspaper's editorial judgments in connection with an advertisement take on the character of the advertisement and, in those cases, the scope

---

[88] 413 U.S. 376 (1973).   [89] *Id.* at 386.   [90] *Id.* at 385.

[91] In fact, the Court actually stated the question before it in the alternative. *Id.* at 386.

[92] *Id.* at 386, 387–88.

of the newspaper's First Amendment protection may be affected by the content of the advertisement. . . .

By implication at least, an advertiser whose want ad appears in the "Jobs—Male Interest" column is likely to discriminate against women in his hiring decisions. Nothing in a sex-designated column heading sufficiently dissociates the designation from the want ads placed beneath it to make the placement severable for First Amendment purposes from the want ads themselves. The combination, which conveys essentially the same message as an overtly discriminatory want ad, is in practical effect an integrated commercial statement.

Apparently the Court did not consider this line of reasoning forceful enough to produce the holding, for it also found the converse: that the editorial judgments affected the want ads. The Pittsburgh Commission on Human Relations in its Decision and Order had found "that the advertisements were placed in the respective columns according to the advertiser's wishes, either volunteered by the advertiser or offered in response to inquiry by Pittsburgh Press."[93] Since the Press always deferred to the advertiser's wishes, the Court reinterpreted what the Press asserted was an individualized judgment on the placement of each advertisement to be a more generalized "judgment whether or not to allow the advertiser to select the column."[94] Then, focusing on this conduct by the Press (as distinct from the advertiser's role), the Court concluded that it did not merit First Amendment protection because it actually aided the discrimination. "The advertisements, *as embroidered by their placement*, signaled that the advertisers were likely to show an illegal sex preference in their hiring decisions."[95]

This second sequence, using the editorial judgment's discriminatory character (even though essentially a product of the advertiser's instructions) to deprive the want ads of First Amendment protection, seems even more grounded than the first sequence in the illegal nature of the advertisements rather than their commercialism.[96] The Court stated:[97]

---

[93] *Id*. at 379–80.   [94] *Id*. at 386.

[95] *Id*. at 389. (Emphasis added.)

[96] The Court later confirmed in *Bigelow* that the classified ads' illegality was significant in reaching the result in *Pittsburgh Press*, 421 U.S. at 821. Illegality was similarly important to the result in Ginzburg v. United States, 383 U.S. 463 (1966), discussed in text *infra*, at notes 105–19.

[97] 413 U.S. at 389. This balancing process is an established analytic technique for deciphering a governmental regulation in light of the First Amendment. "A dis-

Any First Amendment interest which might be served by advertising an ordinary commercial proposal and which might arguably outweigh the governmental interest supporting the regulation is altogether absent when the commercial activity itself is illegal and the restriction on advertising is incidental to a valid limitation on economic activity.

In sum, the *Pittsburgh Press* opinion lessened the First Amendment status of the classified ads by terming them commercial speech. Then, in conjunction with the advertiser's apparently discriminatory and assuredly commercial motive, it linked this commercial content-motive to the publisher's editorial judgments, thereby reducing the latter's First Amendment status. As a result, the state's interest in these regulations, which encompassed the Press's conduct in order to achieve the elimination of sex-discrimination in hiring, outweighed the First Amendment's interest in this lower status, and illegal, form of speech.

Yet neither *Sullivan* nor *Pittsburgh Press* is a resounding affirmation of the commercial speech doctrine. The Court in *Sullivan* leapfrogged the doctrine with a minimum of effort and attention, saving its analysis for the crucial libel issue. And, despite the doctrine's centrality to the *Pittsburgh Press* result, the Court used that opinion as an occasion to imply the doctrine's demise. Mr. Justice Powell, writing the opinion for the majority of five, observed that, were it not for the Press's activity being illegal[98] as well as commercial, there might be sufficient merit in its contention that "the exchange of information is as important in the commercial realm as in any other" to warrant abrogating "the distinction between commercial and other speech."[99]

B. OBSCENITY

Obscenity is another First Amendment exception which has a commercial speech thread of some significance. The import of commercialism attendant on the sale of allegedly obscene material was

---

tinction must be drawn between cases in which legal sanctions are imposed for the specific purpose of restricting speech and those in which the control of speech is a by-product of government action that is otherwise permissible." Kalven, note 15, *supra*, at 216.

[98] For a discussion of the ramifications of this illegality component, see DeVore & Nelson, note 4 *supra*, at 761–64.

[99] 413 U.S. at 388.

first explicitly noted in *A Book Named "John Cleland's Memoirs of a Woman of Pleasure" v. Attorney General of Massachusetts.*[100] The plurality opinion found that the book was not "utterly without redeeming social value" and, therefore, that it was not obscene under one part of the tripartite obscenity test established in *Roth v. United States.*[101] The opinion then went on to discuss merchandising methods as an additional consideration for applying the third part of the *Roth* test:[102]

> On the premise . . . that *Memoirs* has the requisite prurient appeal [the first criterion] and is patently offensive [the second criterion], but has only a minimum of social value [the third criterion], the circumstances of production, sale, and publicity are relevant in determining whether or not the publication or distribution of the book is constitutionally protected. Evidence that the book was commercially exploited for the sake of prurient appeal, to the exclusion of all other values, might justify the conclusion that the book was utterly without redeeming social importance.

This idea that the purveyor's conduct should be added to the obscenity calculation was first mentioned in Chief Justice Warren's concurring opinion in *Roth.*[103] As elaborated by the plurality opinion in *Memoirs,*[104] the idea seemed to become a variant of the commercial speech doctrine, speaking in terms of evaluating a method of distribution, and then using that evaluation to judge the work's social importance.

In *Ginzburg v. United States,*[105] decided the same day as *Memoirs,*

---

[100] 383 U.S. 413 (1966).   [101] 354 U.S. 476 (1957).

[102] 383 U.S. at 420. The plurality opinion was written by Mr. Justice Brennan, joined by Chief Justice Warren and Justice Fortas. They were joined in the six-to-three vote by Justices Black, Douglas, and Stewart.

[103] "It is not the book that is on trial; it is a person. The conduct of the defendant is the central issue, not the obscenity of a book or picture. The nature of the materials is, of course, relevant as an attribute of the defendant's conduct, but the materials are thus placed in a context from which they draw color and character. A wholly different result might be reached in a different setting." 354 U.S. at 495 (Warren, C.J., concurring).

[104] Of the three Justices joining the plurality opinion, only Justice Douglas wrote a separate concurring opinion. In it he dissented from this idea that a court might infer an evaluation of a work's social value from the manner of its distribution. 383 U.S. at 427. Justices Black and Stewart concurred for reasons expressed in their respective dissents in Ginzburg v. United States, 383 U.S. 463, 476, 497·(1966).

[105] 383 U.S. 463 (1966).

a majority of the Court used this approach to reach an obscenity finding.[106] In a much fuller exposition than *Memoirs*, the Court expanded this commercialism idea by mixing it as an evaluative ingredient with each of the three conjunctive parts of the *Roth* obscenity test, not solely with the social value part as in *Memoirs*.[107] The *Ginzburg* opinion began by acknowledging that in the cases decided since *Roth* the Court had "regarded the materials as sufficient in themselves for the determination of the [obscenity] question."[108] But now, given the fact that "the prosecution charged the offense in the context of the circumstances of production, sale, and publicity"[109] and stipulated that the materials were not obscene,[110] the Court was willing to include "consideration of the setting in which the publications were presented as an aid to determining the question of obscenity."[111]

The Court linked the particular form of commercialism ("pandering") in Ginzburg's method of distribution to the materials' content in order to judge the materials obscene. The question is, however, whether the commercial element in the pandering was sufficient by itself to produce the *Ginzburg* result.[112] The opinion cited *Sullivan* in support of the proposition that a profit motive in the sale of the publications was entitled to "no weight."[113] Content was likewise eliminated as a factor because the Court assumed, along with the prosecutor, that the materials "cannot themselves be adjudged obscene in the abstract."[114] That left Ginzburg's method of distribution based on appeal to prurient interests, and here the Court saw the commercial speech doctrine as a supportive analogy rather than as an integral element of the pandering itself. "Material sold solely to produce sexual arousal, like commercial advertising, does not escape

---

[106] The *Ginzburg* five-man majority was comprised of the *Memoirs* plurality plus Justices White and Clark, both of whom dissented in *Memoirs*.

[107] 383 U.S. at 470.   [109] *Ibid.*   [111] *Id.* at 465–66.

[108] *Id.* at 465.   [110] *Id.* at n.4.

[112] One commentator, at least for purposes of shaping his own thesis, thinks so. "The usefulness of *Ginzburg* lies in its recognition of the doctrine that when commercial purposes dominate the matrix of expression seeking first amendment protection, first amendment directives must be restructured." Barron, *Access to the Press—A New First Amendment Right*, 80 HARV. L. REV. 1641, 1663 (1967). Barron's thesis was rejected by the Court in Miami Herald v. Tornillo, 418 U.S. 241 (1974).

[113] 383 U.S. at 474. But see *id.* at 497 (Harlan, J., dissenting).

[114] 383 U.S. at 474.

regulation because it has been dressed up as speech, or in other contexts might be recognized as speech."[115] Just as its commercial motivation altered the First Amendment status of Chrestensen's handbill, so the commercial appeal to prurient interests altered Ginzburg's
materials.[116] And, as a final step, the conclusion to be drawn from
this method of distribution was that "the transactions here were
sales of illicit merchandise, not sales of constitutionally protected
matter."[117]

What the Court did in *Ginzburg*, then, was use the inherent illicit-
ness of the defendant's distribution-by-appeal-to-prurient-interests
to infer obscenity in the materials' content.[118] For the commercial
speech doctrine, the point is not that it became a central element in
obscenity theory, although this pandering analysis has remained
valid since *Ginzburg*.[119] Nor does it matter whether commercial
speech actually inhered in pandering, or instead served as an analogous instance of regulable speech. The net effect of the commercial
speech doctrine's use remained the same. The Court used the same
reasoning process with regard to obscenity as it did with classified
advertising (*Pittsburgh Press*) and libel (*Sullivan*). Generally stated,
the process was to link the commercial speech element of the case
either to purer, more preferred speech elements in order to reach a
protected speech result (*Sullivan*) or to other less preferred speech
elements (*Pittsburgh Press* and *Ginzburg*) to reach an unprotected
result. Utilization or avoidance of the commercial speech doctrine
was a factor in each case, but the doctrine by itself was insufficient
to produce the result.

C. CLEAR AND PRESENT DANGER

The clear and present danger exception of the First Amendment
also has a commercial speech thread. The doctrine's impact here

---

[115] *Id*. at n.17.

[116] "The *Ginzburg* theory that an overriding commercial purpose may alter first
amendment imperatives vis-à-vis legislative power to regulate a particular area is
not new doctrine. Valentine v. Chrestensen . . . ." Barron, note 112 *supra*, at 1662
n.52.

[117] 383 U.S. at 474–75.

[118] *Cf.* Sonderling Broadcasting Corp., WGLD-FM, 41 F.C.C.2d 777 (1973),
aff'd sub nom., Illinois Citizens Comm. for Broadcasting v. FCC, 515 F.2d 397, 404
(D.C. Cir. 1975).

[119] See Hamling v. United States, 418 U.S. 87, 130 (1974).

was on the political advertising cases[120] where the forum for the speech was usually either a public transit vehicle or a campus newspaper. Prior to *Lehman v. City of Shaker Heights*[121] a cluster of cases in the 1960s raised the issue of First Amendment protection for political advertising. In one of the first litigated cases, *Wirta v. Alameda–Contra Costa Transit District*,[122] the plaintiff, intending to pay the established rates, sought to place in the defendant's public transit buses antiwar posters which quoted a former President of the United States and urged writing letters to the then President. The California Supreme Court utilized the commercial speech doctrine in overturning the bus company's refusal to carry this political advertising:[123]

> Not only does the district's policy prefer certain classes of protected ideas over others but it goes even further and affords total freedom of the forum to mercantile messages while banning the vast majority of opinions and beliefs extant which enjoy First Amendment protection because of their noncommercialism. . . .
>
> A long line of decisions has established the rule that commercial messages do not come within the orbit of the First Amendment and may be regulated or prohibited by the Government in the same manner as other business affairs. . . . In the case at bar, the policy of the district reverses these acceptable priorities and perversely gives preference to commercial advertising over nonmercantile messages.

Subsequent cases relied on *Wirta* to reach the same protected speech–open forum result on similar facts.[124] As a group these cases

---

[120] The commercial speech exception did not arise in the well-known line of cases which formulated the clear and present danger doctrine, beginning with Schenck v. United States, 249 U.S. 47 (1919), and continuing through Brandenburg v. Ohio, 395 U.S. 444 (1969).

[121] 418 U.S. 298 (1974).

[122] 64 Cal. Rptr. 430 (1967). *Wirta* prompted at least three case notes: Note, *Municipal Transit District's Refusal to Accept Anti-War Advertisement while Permitting Commercial and Election-Related Advertising Violates First Amendment*, 82 HARV. L. REV. 1379 (1969); Note, *Transit District May Not Constitutionally Restrict Paid Advertising so as to Exclude Opinions and Beliefs within the Ambit of First Amendment Protection*, 43 NOTRE DAME LAWYER 781 (1968); Note, *Public Transit Advertising*, 10 WM. & MARY L. REV. 244 (1968).

[123] 64 Cal. Rptr. at 434. For a comment on commercial television's similar reversal of First Amendment priorities, see C.B.S. v. Democratic Nat'l Comm., 412 U.S. 94, 201 (1973) (Brennan, J., dissenting).

[124] Kissinger v. New York City Transit Authority, 274 F. Supp. 438 (S.D. N.Y.

illustrate near-universal[125] recognition of the reduced First Amendment status of commercial speech and the usefulness of that lower
status as counterpoint to achieve protection for controversial, highly
valued speech in the form of political advertising.

This pattern of using the commercial speech doctrine as a constitutional foil in political advertising cases ended in *Lehman v. City of
Shaker Heights*.[126] Prior to *Lehman* the rule seemed to be that once
a public forum—campus newspaper, public transit ad, or whatever—

1967), was decided after the California Court of Appeals decision but before the
California Supreme Court decision in *Wirta*. In *Kissinger* the court ruled that antiwar advertisements proffered by a radical student group, with the intention to pay
for them, must be accepted by the transit authority absent proof of a clear and
present danger to occur from accepting them. *Id*. at 442. In order to distinguish the
California Court of Appeals decision in favor of the transit district in *Wirta*, the
court noted that the New York C.T.A. had accepted other political posters prior
to rejecting plaintiffs' posters, whereas the transit district's rejection of the posters
in *Wirta* was in accord with an established regulation for accepting political advertising only at election time. *Id*. at 443 n.6. When the California Supreme Court
reversed the intermediate appellate court in *Wirta*, it referred to *Kissinger*'s clear
and present danger language. 64 Cal. Rptr. at 438.

Political advertising cases after *Kissinger* and *Wirta* produced similar results:
Hillside Community Church, Inc. v. City of Tacoma, 76 Wash.2d 63 (1969)
(advertisements less provocative than those in *Kissinger* must be posted by
defendant after having already signed a contract to do so); Zucker v. Panitz, 299 F.
Supp. 102 (S.D. N.Y. 1969) (students' antiwar advertisement intended for the
school paper found to be as much school related as student news stories and edi-
torials on the war); Lee v. Bd. of Regents of State Colleges, 306 F. Supp. 1097 (W.D.
Wis. 1969) (campus newspaper is an important First Amendment vehicle and,
therefore, must accept political as well as commercial advertisements); Radical
Lawyers Caucus v. Pool, 324 F. Supp. 268 (W.D. Tex. 1970) (advertisement for
radical lawyers' meeting must be published in state bar association publication which
accepted other political comment); Ross v. Goshi, 351 F. Supp. 949 (D. Hawaii
1972) (political billboards may not be totally banned while commercial signs are
allowed).

[125] In Business Executives' Move for Vietnam Peace v. FCC, 450 F.2d 642 (D.C.
Cir. 1971), *rev'd sub nom*. C.B.S. v. Democratic Nat'l Committee, 412 U.S. 94 (1973),
the issue was "the permissibility of discrimination, within a given block of advertising time, against 'controversial' speech and in favor of commercial and 'noncontroversial' speech." 450 F.2d at 659. The Court of Appeals for the District of Columbia joined the "unbroken line of authority" in the *Wirta* line of cases to find
"that once a forum, subject to First Amendment constraints, has been opened up
for commercial and 'noncontroversial' advertising, a ban on 'controversial' editorial
advertising is unconstitutional unless clearly justified by a 'clear and present
danger.'" *Ibid*. In reaching that result the Court of Appeals recognized commercial speech's "less fully protected" status under the First Amendment. *Id*. at 658 n.38.
When the Supreme Court reversed, it distinguished the *Wirta* line of cases used
by the Court of Appeals: "In none of those cases did the forum sought for expression have an affirmative and independent statutory obligation to provide full
and fair coverage of public issues, such as Congress has imposed on all broadcast
licensees." 412 U.S. at 129–30.

[126] 418 U.S. 298 (1974).

—was opened to commercial speech, it could not be closed to non-commercial, political advertising.[127] In contrast, the Court in *Lehman* allowed commercial advertising to continue, but foreclosed access for political advertising by finding no public forum and thus nullifying any speech issue. In an unsatisfying opinion the Court failed to reconcile the *Lehman* result with the unanimously contrary results of the prior cases, none of which had reached the Supreme Court. The close, perhaps indistinguishable, similarity between the facts in *Lehman* and in the earlier political advertising cases may explain why the *Lehman* opinion failed to discuss those decisions. Instead they were merely acknowledged by listing without discussion in a footnote.[128]

In *Lehman* the plaintiff "sought to promote his candidacy [for the state legislature] by purchasing car card space on the Shaker Heights Rapid Transit System."[129] The transit system, following a long-established policy of the city council against any political or public issue advertising on the buses, rejected his advertisement. The Ohio courts refused declaratory or injunctive relief, finding that neither commercial nor political advertising on rapid transit vehicles was protected by the First Amendment.[130] In affirming by a five-to-four vote,[131] the Supreme Court glossed over the First Amendment interests involved.[132] By analogizing the city's operation of a transit system to a private commercial venture, the Court found advertising space in a bus to be simply an element of that venture rather than a forum capable of raising the speech issue. Thus the decision to exclude political advertising from that space was similar to other business decisions such as the cost of a fare or the location of bus stops. The Court found the reasons for this exclusionary decision—to avoid (*a*) jeopardizing revenue from long-term commercial advertising, (*b*) subjecting passengers to political propaganda,[133] (*c*) showing

---

[127] See generally Kalven, *The Concept of the Public Forum: Cox v. Louisiana,* 1965 SUPREME COURT REVIEW 1.

[128] 418 U.S. at 301 n.5.   [129] *Id.* at 299.

[130] 34 Ohio St.2d 143 (1973).

[131] Mr. Justice Blackmun's opinion for a plurality of the Court was joined by Chief Justice Burger and Justices White and Rehnquist. Justice Douglas concurred separately. Mr. Justice Brennan's dissent was joined by Justices Stewart, Marshall, and Powell.

[132] Lehman's equal protection argument was briefly disposed of on grounds similar to those applied to his First Amendment argument. 418 U.S. at 303–04.

[133] See Public Utilities Comm'n v. Pollak, 343 U.S. 451, 467–69 (1952) (Douglas, J., dissenting).

any favoritism among candidates, and (d) "sticky administrative problems . . . in parceling out limited space"—to be "reasonable legislative objectives advanced by the city in a proprietary capacity."[134] In light of these objectives, said the Court, "[T]he managerial decision to limit car card space to innocuous and less controversial commercial and service oriented advertising does not rise to the dignity of a First Amendment violation."[135]

By refusing to find a public forum and thus not reaching the First Amendment issue, the Court may have reduced commercial speech to its nadir in terms of First Amendment protection. In its very failure to note and discuss the implications and impact of this "commercial venture" analysis on the commercial speech doctrine, the *Lehman* plurality undermined whatever First Amendment protection, if any, commercial speech hitherto possessed. Mr. Justice Blackmun, author of the plurality opinion in *Lehman*, implied in his opinion for the Court in *Bigelow v. Virginia*[136] that the *Lehman* result was reached by a balancing process.[137] In fact, the Court performed no balancing of the First Amendment's interest in *Lehman*'s political advertising against the city's interests in its regulation. It simply found the city's legislative objectives reasonable, and failed to identify the First Amendment interests at stake, namely, exclusion of preferred political speech (albeit in the form of advertising) and inclusion of less preferred commercial speech at a public forum. In effect, commercial speech was not recognized as a form of speech at all in *Lehman*. It was permitted on the bus strictly as an element of a commercial venture rather than on the basis of its First Amendment status. If commercial speech had a First Amendment stature, then surely it should have at least triggered the finding of a public forum and a subsequent balancing of interests.[138] After *Lehman* it could be

---

[134] 418 U.S. at 304.

[135] *Ibid.* Justice Douglas was the fifth vote for the majority in this five-to-four decision. His concurrence on the ground of preserving passengers' privacy proceeded from the same premise as the plurality opinion, that a public transit vehicle is not a forum for speech. *Id.* at 305.

[136] 421 U.S. 809 (1975).

[137] "Advertising, like all public expression, may be subject to reasonable regulation that serves a legitimate public interest. See *Pittsburgh Press* . . . ; *Lehman.* . . . [A] court may not escape the task of assessing the First Amendment interest at stake and weighing it against the public interest allegedly served by the regulation." *Id.* at 826. For a discussion of the analytic shortcomings in the *Lehman* decision, see Note, *The Public Forum in Nontraditional Areas*, 51 WASH. L. REV. 142 (1975).

[138] In the dissent's view, shared by as many members of the Court as the plurality

argued that commercial speech did not even warrant limited First Amendment status.

In contrast to reducing commercial speech to its constitutional nadir, *Lehman* can also be interpreted as elevating such speech in preference to political speech expressed in the form of advertising. At least *Lehman*'s result may do that, even if the plurality opinion's language and intent do not. Mr. Justice Brennan's dissent, using language very similar to that in *Wirta*, noted this anomaly. "To hold otherwise, and thus sanction the city's preference for bland commercialism and noncontroversial public service messages over 'uninhibited, robust, and wide-open' debate on public issues, would reverse the traditional priorities of the First Amendment."[139] Given the omission of any commercial speech discussion in the plurality opinion, however, it is unlikely that such a result was intended.

The marginal but useful role played by the commercial speech doctrine in protecting more preferred political advertising was comprehensible prior to *Lehman*. The results were in accord with well-established First Amendment priorities.[140] *Lehman* conflicted with both the prior reasoning and the prior results. Of the city's four regulatory rationales, only preserving passengers' privacy had precedent,[141] and, in fact, this is the rationale for which *Lehman* is fre-

---

view, "A forum for communication was voluntarily established when the city installed the physical facilities for the advertisements." 418 U.S. at 314. And, whatever may be the status of commercial speech vis-à-vis speech on political and social issues, "it is 'speech' nonetheless," with sufficient stature so that once "such messages have been accepted and displayed, the existence of a forum for communication cannot be gainsaid." *Id.* at 314–15.

[139] *Id.* at 315. In Spence v. Washington, 418 U.S. 405 (1974), decided the same day as *Lehman*, Mr. Justice Rehnquist, in dissent, indicated he found this same implication in the *Lehman* result. In *Spence* the Court found unconstitutional, as applied to a college student who hung the United States flag upside down with a peace symbol taped to each side from his apartment window in protest, a Washington statute which prohibited improper use of the flag. Mr. Justice Rehnquist noted that the Court had upheld "a virtually identical statute" in Halter v. Nebraska, 205 U.S. 34 (1907). 418 U.S. at 418. The Court distinguished *Halter* on the ground that it was decided almost twenty years before the Court applied the First Amendment to the states, and also apparently because *Halter* involved commercial activity (placing a flag representation on beer bottles) unlike that at issue in *Spence*. Id. at 413 n.7. Mr. Justice Rehnquist commented on this second distinction of *Halter*: "The Court may possibly be suggesting that political expression deserves greater protection than other forms of expression, but that suggestion would seem quite inconsistent with the position taken in *Lehman* v. *Shaker Heights* . . . by nearly all Members of the majority in the instant case." *Id.* at 419–20.

[140] See Note, note 28 *supra*, 80 HARV. L. REV. at 1035.

[141] Packer Corp. v. Utah, 285 U.S. 105 (1932). See generally Haiman, *Speech*

quently cited.[142] But if the plurality opinion was grounded in privacy, how could it ignore the equal protection issue, since the decision's result allowed commercial advertising, which has as great an impact on passengers as political advertising,[143] to continue but excluded political advertising?

At least so far as the commercial speech doctrine is concerned, *Lehman* can be viewed as an aberration. Although a subsequent political advertising case cited *Lehman* as direct authority,[144] the doctrine's demise only two years later indicates that, given its membership, the *Lehman* plurality was intent on upholding what it perceived as reasonable government regulation notwithstanding the First Amendment issue at stake. One year later in *Bigelow*, with a weaker governmental regulatory interest and a more potent First Amendment issue, Mr. Justice Blackmun and Chief Justice Burger joined the *Lehman* dissenters. Justices White and Rehnquist dissented. And one year after *Bigelow*,[145] Mr. Justice White also joined the First Amendment side of the balance, leaving only Mr. Justice Rehnquist in dissent. Although Mr. Justice Blackmun cited *Lehman* in his opinions for the Court in *Bigelow* and *Pharmacy*, he never alluded to *Lehman* as an aberration.

The *Lehman* result is an unfortunate First Amendment precedent, although its future impact may be minimal in light of the opinion's narrowness and lack of a majority. In terms of.commercial speech, precisely because the plurality opinion ignored the First Amendment issues, *Lehman* did little to inhibit the doctrine's impending demise.

---

v. Privacy: Is There a Right Not to Be Spoken To? 67 Nw. U. L. Rev. 153 (1972).

[142] Bigelow v. Virginia, 421 U.S. 809, 828 (1975); Erznoznik v. City of Jacksonville, 422 U.S. 205, 209 (1975); Southeastern Promotions, Ltd. v. Conrad, 420 U.S. 546, 556 (1975); Chicago Area Military Project v. City of Chicago, 508 F.2d 921, 926 (7th Cir. 1975). For a critique of the privacy rationale's use in *Lehman*, see Note, *Public Forum—Captive Audience—Transit Advertising on Municipally Owned Transit System*, 13 Duquesne L. Rev. 1003, 1008–12 (1975).

[143] "There is certainly no evidence in the record of this case indicating that political advertisements, as a class, are so disturbing when displayed that they are more likely than commercial or public service advertisements to impair the rapid transit system's primary function of transportation." 418 U.S. at 319 (Brennan, J., dissenting).

[144] Buck v. Impeach Nixon Committee, 419 U.S. 891 (1974).

[145] Virginia State Bd. of Pharmacy v. Virginia Citizens Consumer Council, 425 U.S. 748 (1976).

III. The Doctrine's Demise

A. THE ABORTION ADVERTISEMENT

Repeated expressions of dissatisfaction with the commercial speech doctrine in recent years were not resolved by the doctrine's application in *Bigelow v. Virginia*.[146] *Bigelow* was one more in the line which failed to confront the commercial speech question and resolve it on its own merits or lack thereof. The opinion followed the reasoning in *Sullivan*, with the result that this allegedly commercial advertisement was transformed into an editorial advertisement on one of the crucial issues of the day. And that issue well explains the decision. For whatever may have been in the Court's mind on the commercial speech doctrine at the time *Bigelow* was decided, the fact that the contested advertisement was for an abortion referral agency made this the least likely of cases for resolving the doctrine's future. The abortion decisions, *Roe v. Wade*[147] and *Doe v. Bolton*,[148] were not universally well received.[149] That fact, far more than the tattered condition of the commercial speech doctrine, must have been foremost in the Court's mind. Despite the disclaimer that *Bigelow* was a First Amendment not an abortion case,[150] the decision is best viewed as an attempt to buttress, or at least avoid undermining, the abortion decisions. After tending to this primary task, it may well be that the Court sought secondarily in *Bigelow* to forecast the commercial speech doctrine's demise, perhaps even anticipating that the likely instrument for that occasion, namely, *Virginia State Board of Pharmacy v. Virginia Citizens Consumer Council*, was already on its way to the Court.[151]

When a weekly newspaper distributed mainly at the University

---

[146] 421 U.S. 809 (1975).

[147] 410 U.S. 113 (1973).

[148] 410 U.S. 179 (1973).

[149] See, *e.g.*, Epstein, *Substantive Due Process by Any Other Name: The Abortion Cases*, 1973 SUPREME COURT REVIEW 159.

[150] 421 U.S. at 815 n.5. In contrast, in remanding the same case to the Virginia Supreme Court three years earlier, the Court suggested a reconsideration of the *Bigelow* result in light of the Court's abortion decisions. 413 U.S. 909 (1973).

[151] The grant of certiorari in *Pharmacy*, 420 U.S. 971 (1975), preceded the *Bigelow* decision by three months.

of Virginia published an advertisement[152] for abortion services in New York City, its editor, Jeffrey C. Bigelow, was charged with violating a Virginia statute which forbade encouraging abortions "by the sale or circulation of any publication or in any other manner."[153] The Virginia courts rejected the defendant's claim that the statute was unconstitutional, found him guilty, and levied a fine.[154] The United States Supreme Court decided the abortion cases while Bigelow's appeal was pending before it. Thereafter, it vacated the state court judgment in *Bigelow* and remanded for reconsideration in light of those decisions.[155] The Virginia Supreme Court reaffirmed the conviction, finding *Roe* and *Doe* inapplicable because "[n]either mentioned the subject of abortion advertising."[156] On a second appeal, the United States Supreme Court held the Virginia statute, in its form as used to prosecute Bigelow,[157] an unconstitutional infringement of Bigelow's First Amendment rights, and reversed.[158]

---

[152] The advertisement's text read:

"UNWANTED PREGNANCY
LET US HELP YOU
Abortions are now legal in New York.
There are no residency requirements.
FOR IMMEDIATE PLACEMENT IN ACCREDITED
HOSPITALS AND CLINICS AT LOW COST
Contact
WOMEN'S PAVILION
515 Madison Avenue
New York, N. Y. 10022
or call any time
(212) 371-6670 or (212) 371-6650
AVAILABLE 7 DAYS A WEEK
STRICTLY CONFIDENTIAL. We will make
all arrangements for you and help you
with information and counseling."
421 U.S. at 812.

[153] The statute at the time of Bigelow's prosecution read: "If any person, by publication, lecture, advertisement, or by the sale or circulation of any publication, or in any other manner, encourage or prompt the procuring of abortion or miscarriage, he shall be guilty of a misdemeanor." Va. Code Ann. § 18.1–63 (1960).

[154] 213 Va. 191 (1972).

[155] 413 U.S. 909 (1973).

[156] 214 Va. 341 (1973).

[157] Shortly after its use to prosecute Bigelow, the Virginia statute was amended to restrict its "application, with respect to advertising, to an abortion illegal in Virginia and to be performed there . . . . [T]here is no dispute here that the amended statute would *not* reach appellant's advertisement." 412 U.S. at 813 n.3.

[158] Mr. Justice Blackmun was author of the Court's opinion. Mr. Justice Rehnquist,

On the First Amendment issue[159] the Court's first effort was to correct the Virginia Supreme Court's "central assumption . . . that the First Amendment guarantees of speech and press are inapplicable to paid commercial advertisements."[160] Citing a string of commercial speech related cases, including *Pittsburgh Press, Sullivan, Ginzburg,* and *Murdock,* the opinion noted that just because an advertisement "had commercial aspects" or "involved sales," or because the advertiser's or publisher's motive "may have involved financial gain" does "not negate all First Amendment guarantees" for the advertisement.[161] This language at the outset seemed to indicate that the commercial speech doctrine's end might be at hand.

The opinion then narrowed *Valentine* without overruling it:[162]

> But the [*Valentine*] holding is distinctly a limited one: the ordinance was upheld as a reasonable regulation of the manner in which commercial advertising could be distributed. The fact that it had the effect of banning a particular handbill does not mean that [*Valentine*] is authority for the proposition that all statutes regulating commercial advertising are immune from constitutional challenge. The case obviously does not support any sweeping proposition that advertising is unprotected *per se.*

It is curious that the Court read *Valentine*'s rationale as grounded on the method of distribution, since that case generally is viewed as having adopted a primary purpose (motive) rationale.[163] One explanation for this reading is that the Court wanted to isolate and narrow *Valentine,* weakening its precedential value for *Bigelow*: if the *Valentine* result of restricting commercial speech were viewed as having a motive rationale, then that case would have been difficult to distinguish in reaching a protected speech result for the *Bigelow* advertisement, which surely had a commercial motive. But with the motive test thus eliminated by reinterpreting *Valentine,* and since

---

joined by Mr. Justice White, wrote a dissenting opinion. Mr. Justice Blackmun also wrote the Court's opinion in *Pharmacy,* with Mr. Justice Rehnquist alone dissenting.

[159] The Court first resolved in Bigelow's favor the question of his "standing to challenge a statute on First Amendment grounds as facially overboard," but then found that issue moot because of the statute's amendment in 1972. 421 U.S. at 815–18.

[160] *Id.* at 818.   [161] *Ibid.*

[162] 421 U.S. at 819–20. The *Pharmacy* opinion later interpreted this language in *Bigelow* to mean that *Valentine*'s "continued validity was questioned." 425 U.S. at 760.

[163] See text *supra,* at note 28.

method of distribution was not at issue, the Court could apply a content analysis to the *Bigelow* advertisement.

The Court had a choice of two paths to reach a protected speech result for the abortion advertisement. The advertisement could be termed pure commercial speech similar to that in *Pittsburgh Press*, and then be accorded sufficient First Amendment protection as commercial speech to outweigh whatever state interest the Virginia statute might have represented. That choice would have capitalized on the implication in *Pittsburgh Press* that legal instances of commercial speech might well outweigh certain state interests.[164] As noted earlier, however, the fact that the advertisement concerned abortion made *Bigelow* an ill-advised choice for resolving the commercial speech doctrine. So the Court chose another path. It found that the abortion advertisement contained information of public interest on one of the crucial issues of the day, as in *Sullivan*. It then accorded that editorial advertisement First Amendment protection as a form of preferred speech, thereby outweighing the state's interest in its regulation.

In treading this path the Court had to follow *Sullivan* and to distinguish *Pittsburgh Press*. The latter presented some difficulty because its classified want ads, which closely resembled the abortion advertisement, had been termed "classic examples of commercial speech" by analogy to *Valentine* and in distinction from *Sullivan*.[165] The best that could now be gleaned from *Pittsburgh Press* was the "principle that commercial advertising enjoys a degree of First Amendment protection."[166] Then, in order to neutralize the precedential impact of those classified ads, which had not received First Amendment protection in accordance with this principle, the Court emphasized that this was due to their illegality. Since illegality "was particularly stressed," said the Court, the inference can be drawn that "the advertisements would have received some degree of First Amendment protection if the commercial proposal had been legal."[167] Aside from illegality, other distinctions between the want ads and the abortion referral advertisement were fine ones.[168] But,

---

[164] 413 U.S. at 389.   [165] *Id.* at 385.   [166] 421 U.S. at 821.

[167] *Ibid.* See text *supra*, at notes 95–98, for a discussion of the interplay between illegality and the commercial speech doctrine in producing the *Pittsburgh Press* result.

[168] Mr. Justice Rehnquist in his *Bigelow* dissent was "unable to perceive any relationship between the instant advertisement and that for example in issue in . . . *Sullivan*," and was likewise unable "to distinguish this commercial proposition from that held to be purely commercial in *Pittsburgh Press*." 421 U.S. at 832.

since the Court intended to make such distinctions by finding information of public interest in the abortion advertisement, its task was more easily accomplished if the few preferred speech phrases in that advertisement stood in sharp contrast to the illegality of the classified ads.

The brief discussion of *Sullivan* simply demonstrated the concept that paid advertisements can be found to communicate information and disseminate opinion, and thereby merit full constitutional protection.[169] This set the stage for using *Sullivan's* content analysis in order to reach a protected speech result for the abortion advertisement. With the groundwork established, the opinion began the process of elevating this advertisement to preferred status by noting "important differences" between the abortion advertisement and the *Valentine* and *Pittsburgh Press* advertisements. "The advertisement published in [Bigelow's] newspaper did more than simply propose a commercial transaction. It contained factual material of clear 'public interest.' "[170] Disagreeing with dissenting Justices Rhenquist and White, who deemed the abortion advertisement "a classic commercial proposition directed toward the exchange of services rather than the exchange of ideas,"[171] the majority hung its First Amendment hat on the advertisement's editorial-like "exercise of the freedom of communicating information and disseminating opinion."[172] This was found first in the advertisement's statement that abortions were legal in New York without residency requirements.[173] From this copy, which comprised two lines in a sixteen-line advertisement, the Court stretched the advertisement's First Amendment scope. If "viewed in its entirety," the advertisement's message was "of potential interest and value to a diverse audience—not only to readers possibly in need of the services offered, but also to those with a general curiosity about, or genuine interest in, the subject matter or the law of another State and its development, and to readers seeking reform in Virginia."[174] Then, it was but one more step to find that "the activity advertised pertained to constitutional interests," and

---

[169] *Id.* at 820–21.   [171] *Id.* at 831.   [173] *Ibid.*

[170] *Id.* at 822.   [172] *Id.* at 822.

[174] *Ibid.* In his dissent Mr. Justice Rehnquist accurately presaged the basis for eventual abolition of the commercial speech doctrine: "If the Court's decision does, indeed, turn upon its conclusion that the advertisement here in question was protected by the First and Fourteenth Amendments, the subject of the advertisement ought to make no difference." *Id.* at 831.

therefore, that Bigelow's "First Amendment interests coincided with the constitutional interests of the general public."[175]

This finding, that the information–public interest content of the abortion advertisement was preferred speech warranting more First Amendment protection than that accorded commercial speech, was considerably more tenuous in *Bigelow* than it had been when utilized by the Court in *Sullivan*. Far more of the advertisement's copy in *Sullivan* could be termed information and opinion than the scant two sentences in the *Bigelow* advertisement. In fact, while the *Sullivan* advertisement had both information and opinion, with the latter being the more important ingredient in terms of traditionally preferred First Amendment speech, the *Bigelow* advertisement contained only information. Moreover, the Court in *Sullivan* valued the content itself and never had to strain to view the advertisement "in its entirety." Finally, the clergymen-advertisers in *Sullivan* had a preferred First Amendment motive in seeking to raise funds for their civil rights cause. This made it easier for the Court to find that the advertisement itself was preferred speech. In contrast, the motive of the advertiser in *Bigelow* was simply to further the entrepreneurial efforts of the abortion referral agency; the fact that abortion was a major public issue was irrelevant.

Despite these shortcomings, the analogy of the *Bigelow* advertisement to the *Sullivan* advertisement was potent enough to produce a protected speech result. Two major factors are noteworthy. The analogy was apt because both cases are premised on the right-to-know element of the First Amendment. The statement in *Sullivan* that the advertisement's information, grievances, etc. "are matters of the highest public interest and concern" is an implicit enunciation of the public's right to know, its right to have that interest fulfilled and that concern satisfied. In *Bigelow* the reference was more direct. In the Court's view, Virginia by this statute was trying, "under the guise of exercising internal police powers, [to] bar a citizen of another State from disseminating information about an activity that is legal in that State."[176] So, to the extent that the *Bigelow* opinion's process of elevating the advertisement's content to preferred speech was questionable because of the content's near-total commercialism, the result may be legitimate because of its primary grounding in the right to know. Of course, this common thread of a right-to-know

---

[175] *Id*. at 822.   [176] *Id*. at 824–25.

concept in *Sullivan* and *Bigelow* may only be discernible under the strong light of hindsight: that concept's use by the Court in the *Pharmacy* decision to eliminate the commercial speech doctrine.[177] Still, if the concept was central to the doctrine's eventual demise, logically it may appear in earlier cases which led to that end.

Unlike *Sullivan*, the Court in *Bigelow* did not have to shift the focus of the First Amendment discussion from the commercial sale of advertising space to the protected sale of newspapers to reader-consumers. Granted that Bigelow, like the Times, had sold space to an advertiser. But the statute under which Bigelow was prosecuted prohibited encouraging abortions by, among other things, "the sale or circulation of any publication." That language itself focused on the protected sale to reader–consumers. So, once the advertisement was assessed as preferred speech, the Court could rely on the well-established line of cases protecting the sale of First Amendment speech for commercial motives.[178]

Near the end of the opinion the Court indicated exactly how telling was the fact that the defendant was a publisher, not an advertiser:[179]

> The strength of appellant's interest was augmented by the fact that the statute was applied against him as publisher and editor of a newspaper, not against the advertiser or a referral agency or a practitioner. The prosecution thus incurred more serious First Amendment overtones.

Those overtones included the possibility of Virginia's exercising similar censorial power "over a wide variety of national publications or interstate newspapers."[180] If other states did likewise, that would undermine the intent and purpose of the First Amendment.[181]

With the advertisement thus elevated to preferred First Amendment status, and with the right to know neatly interwoven as a sup-

---

[177] 425 U.S. at 763–65.

[178] The Court's reasoning was not this explicit, but that line of cases was cited by the Court at the outset of its discussion on the First Amendment issue. 421 U.S. at 818.

[179] *Id.* at 828.   [180] *Ibid.*

[181] *Id.* at 829. This language tempts an interpretation that, if the commercial speech doctrine had been applied more against advertisers and less against publishers, it might have survived. The *Pharmacy* decision, and the defendants there, belie such a view.

portive factor, the Court was unwilling to interpret the result very expansively. Its answer to the question how much constitutional protection should be accorded advertising was evasively couched in the negative, stating only that it was incorrect for the Virginia courts to assume "that advertising, as such, was entitled to no First Amendment protection."[182] It also said that, even if related to commercial activity, "[a]dvertising is not thereby stripped of all First Amendment protection."[183] In terms of constitutional status, neither of these statements accorded commercial speech any more protection than was implicit in the doctrine from its beginning, or that it received from the *Pittsburgh Press* dictum.

The Court's language was evasive in two ways. First, as noted earlier, the *Bigelow* opinion sought to protect only this "abortion advertisement," not all commercial advertising. Once this was achieved by elevating the advertisement to a preferred speech level, the Court could not then elaborate protective standards for ordinary commercial advertising. Second, the Court did not have to discuss "the extent to which constitutional protection is afforded commercial advertising under all circumstances and in the face of all kinds of regulation"[184] because Virginia's interest in this regulation was found to be minimal. No extensive balancing discussion was required. The advertised activities were part of another state's internal affairs over which Virginia had no supervisory power, and the advertised services would be delivered outside Virginia, in a place where they were legal.[185] In that light, said the Court, again interweaving the right-to-know concept, Virginia was "asserting an interest in regulating what Virginians may *hear* or *read* . . . [and] in shielding its citizens from information about activities outside Virginia's borders, activities that Virginia's police powers do not reach."[186] Such an interest "was entitled to little, if any, weight under the circumstances."[187]

---

[182] *Id*. at 825.   [183] *Id*. at 826.   [184] *Ibid*.

[185] *Id*. at 827. Subsequent to publication of the advertisement at issue in *Bigelow*, New York enacted a statute forbidding operation of abortion referral services for a profit. New York Laws 1971, ch. 725, effective July 1, 1971, now codified as Art. 45, § 4501.1. The statute was held constitutional in S.P.S. Consultants, Inc. v. Lefkowitz, 333 F. Supp. 1373 (S.D. N.Y. 1971). Even though the services advertised in *Bigelow* subsequently became illegal, the Court found that irrelevant in banning Virginia's effort to forbid its citizens "from using in New York the then legal services of a local New York agency." 425 U.S. at 827.

[186] *Id*. at 827–28.   [187] *Id*. at 828.

With such a deliberately narrow result, reached by reasoning away from the commercial speech doctrine, by fashioning some new, intermediate level of protected speech, and without having to assess a significant state interest, the opinion quite naturally left unresolved major questions as to the post-*Bigelow* status of commercial speech. *Bigelow* did, in fact, expand the protection accorded commercial speech. Whereas *Sullivan* had required that the advertisement contain information and opinion in order to merit the full First Amendment protection, *Bigelow* only required information of public interest. But the opinion provided no guidance as to the elements of public interest–information advertising.

How would a post-*Bigelow* advertisement fare under the commercial speech doctrine if it pertained to an issue less controversial than abortion but contained more information than did the *Bigelow* advertisement? For example, would an advertisement for insect spray dispensed from an aerosol can be elevated from pure commercial speech if, in addition to its sales message, it contained a discussion of the aerosol-created environmental problem and indicated why that product's dispenser would not have an adverse environmental impact?[188] Or, even if the insect spray advertisement contained the same amount of information as did the abortion advertisement, would the aerosol environmental issue be deemed of public interest equal to the abortion advertisement so that a court would be justified in viewing the product advertisement "in its entirety" in order to reach a protected speech result?[189] Did the *Bigelow* result mean that informative but uninteresting advertising about everyday products would be unprotected?

In fact, the public interest level for this abortion advertisement might prove nonreplicative. More narrowly, much of this advertisement's public interest may have stemmed from the illegality of abortions at the time of its publication, rather than from interest in the abortion issue per se. Since this advertisement was speech on a highly controversial, formerly illegal, activity, and since it was the abortion discussion, even in a commercial context, which the Court might have wanted to protect now that abortions were legal, the

---

[188] See Fairness Report, 48 F.C.C.2d 1, 22–28 (1974); Public Interest Research Group v. FCC, 522 F.2d 1060 (1st Cir. 1975).

[189] *FTC Says Corporate Image Ads Exempted from Regulation by First Amendment,* 712 Antitrust & Trade Reg. Report A-3 (1975).

likelihood was remote that many future advertisements would be contested in similar circumstances.

Bigelow was equally uninformative on how to assess the state's regulatory interest to be balanced against the First Amendment's interest in public interest–information advertising. In fact, the Court explicitly refused to decide "the precise extent to which the First Amendment permits regulation of advertising that is related to activities the State may legitimately regulate or even prohibit."[190] The Court was not prepared to select the appropriate tests here. Whether the First Amendment interest would be balanced against the state's interest using the reasonableness standard usually applied to economic regulation, or the compelling state interest standard applied to regulation of speech,[191] remained unanswered.[192]

In sum, from one perspective *Bigelow* can be viewed as expanding the class of fully protected advertising to include advertisements which lack opinion but still contain public interest–information content. Some observers[193] and courts[194] interpreted *Bigelow* as virtually eliminating the commercial speech doctrine. Yet from another, more telling, perspective, *Bigelow* reinforced the reduced First Amendment status of commercial speech. By its unwillingness to view this advertisement as pure commercial speech and then balance it against a weak, almost nonexistent state interest in order to reach a protected speech result, the *Bigelow* opinion, in effect, declared that commercial speech has no First Amendment status. If it did, that status should have been able to outweigh Virginia's interest.

----

[190] 421 U.S. at 825. A footnote at this point in the opinion distinguished those cases in which the Court upheld state regulation of advertising related to certain professions as having been decided on the basis of the Due Process Clause. *Ibid.* n.10.

[191] *Compare* Williamson v. Lee Optical Co., 348 U.S. 483 (1955), *with* United States v. O'Brien, 391 U.S. 367, 376–77 (1968).

[192] The Court's statement on this question was enigmatic, at best. "To the extent that commercial activity is subject to regulation, the relationship of speech to that activity may be one factor, among others, to be considered in weighing the First Amendment interest against the governmental interest alleged." 421 U.S. at 826. The Court's reference at this point to "reasonable regulation" was probably not intended to establish a standard for the balancing test. But see, Note, *Prohibition of Abortion Referral Service Advertising Held Unconstitutional*, 61 CORNELL L. REV. 640, 650 (1976).

[193] *Freedom to Advertise*, ED. & PUB., 5 July 1975, at p. 6.

[194] Anderson, Clayton & Co. v. Washington State Dep't of Agriculture, 402 F. Supp. 1253, 1256–57 (W.D. Wash. 1975).

An explanation which neutralizes this negative effect is that this advertisement's uniquely controversial subject matter required that it be protected as preferred rather than commercial speech. The timing of its publication was quite coincidental in the battle over legalizing abortion. The Court had to accord it full protection under well-established First Amendment precedents for preferred speech, rather than plow new ground for a dubious doctrine, in order to blunt the attacks upon the abortion decisions. In that light, and again with the benefit of hindsight, much of the language in *Bigelow* was a prelude to the *Pharmacy* decision's abolition of the commercial speech doctrine.

B. DRUG PRICE ADVERTISING

The *Bigelow* opinion's deliberate ambiguities on the status and future application of the commercial speech doctrine were resolved by the Court's decision less than a year later in *Virginia State Board of Pharmacy v. Virginia Citizens Consumer Council.*[195] In the retrospective light of the *Pharmacy* decision, *Bigelow*, which protected public interest–information advertising, appears as a transition between the content test (information and opinion) adopted in *Sullivan* and the expansion of that test in *Pharmacy* to include mundane informational advertising, devoid even of *Bigelow's* public interest element. The Meiklejohn rationale, adopted by the Court in *Sullivan*, also produced the *Pharmacy* result. In *Sullivan* the Court decided that discussion about public officials, even to the point of making hitherto libelous statements, must be protected by the First Amendment in the interest of furthering public speech. In *Pharmacy* the First Amendment's reach was extended to informational advertising likewise in order to "enlighten public decisionmaking in a democracy."[196]

Plaintiff, Virginia Citizens Consumer Council,[197] claimed that a Virginia statute which declared a pharmacist guilty of unprofes-

---

[195] 425 U.S. 748 (1976). Mr. Justice Blackmun wrote the Court's opinion for the seven-to-one vote. Chief Justice Burger and Mr. Justice Stewart joined the Court's opinion, but also filed separate concurring opinions. Mr. Justice Rehnquist dissented. Mr. Justice Stevens did not participate.

[196] *Id*. at 765.

[197] Additional plaintiffs were the Virginia State AFL-CIO and "an individual Virginia resident who suffers from diseases that require her to take prescription drugs on a daily basis." *Id*. at 753 & n.10.

sional conduct for advertising prescription drug prices[198] violated its members' First Amendment right to know.[199] This consumers'-right-to-know approach was necessitated by a lower court decision several years earlier in *Patterson Drug Company v. Kingery*,[200] where a similar statute was attacked on the ground, among others, that it violated the freedom of speech of the plaintiff discount drug retailer. The court there rejected that argument, and the decision was not appealed.[201] The lower court in *Pharmacy* easily distinguished its consumer plaintiffs from the "sellers of drugs" who were plaintiffs in *Kingery*.[202]

The Supreme Court had no difficulty in securing VCCC's standing under the right-to-know component of the First Amendment:[203]

> Freedom of speech presupposes a willing speaker. But where a speaker exists, as is the case here,[204] the protection afforded is to the communication, to its source and to its recipients both. This is clear from the decided cases. . . . If there is a right to advertise, there is a reciprocal right to receive the advertising, and it may be asserted by these appellees.

Since the right to know is reciprocal to a right to advertise, the ad-

---

[198] The Virginia statute provided: "Any pharmacist shall be considered guilty of unprofessional conduct who . . . (3) publishes, advertises or promotes, directly or indirectly, in any manner whatsoever, any amount, price, fee, premium, discount, rebate or credit terms for professional services or for drugs containing narcotics or for any drugs which may be dispensed only by prescription." Section 54-524.35 Va. Code Ann. (1974).

[199] Plaintiffs' complaint also attacked the statute on Fourteenth Amendment due process grounds, 425 U.S. at 749, but the Court's opinion referred to that Clause only for First Amendment purposes. *Ibid.*, n. 1.

[200] 305 F. Supp. 821 (W.D. Va. 1969).

[201] The court in *Kingery* did enjoin the enforcement of the statute to the extent that it was used to regulate prescription drug prices by prohibiting discounts. But it did so only because the statute, by not actually fixing the prices, was "so vague and uncertain that an offending pharmacist is denied due process of law." *Id.* at 827.

[202] 373 F. Supp. 683, 686 (E.D. Va. 1974).

[203] 425 U.S. at 756-57. The lower court rendered such a sympathetic but particular description of these plaintiffs—elderly, physically infirm, poor, dependent on medicines for their well-being—in establishing their right to prescription drug prices, that it may have narrowed the applicability of its decision. 373 F. Supp. at 684. The Supreme Court reiterated this description at one point, but its holding was carefully phrased to apply broadly to the commercial speech doctrine. 425 U.S. at 763-64.

[204] The Court's footnote at this point noted the parties' stipulation that absent the statutory prohibition " 'some pharmacies in Virginia would advertise, publish and promote price information regarding prescription drugs.' " *Id.* at 756 n.14.

vertisers rebuffed in *Kingery* were now vindicated. Had a "speaker" rather than a "listener/viewer" brought the commercial speech doctrine before the Court at this juncture, the result would have been identical.[205] Presumably, however, this right to know would not yield prescription drug price information if such advertising were a lower order of speech meriting reduced First Amendment protection when confronted with a state regulatory interest. The heart of the *Pharmacy* opinion was devoted to excising the commercial speech doctrine from First Amendment theory.

Mr. Justice Blackmun's opening review of the doctrine's creation and use was brief. *Valentine* was barely stated, having been previously narrowed in *Bigelow*. *Breard* was noted as "perhaps" a source of "further support" for the doctrine.[206] The opinion then acknowledged the doctrine's inherent disabilities in citing cases such as *Sullivan*, which circumvented commercial speech, and *Pittsburgh Press*, where the doctrine by itself was not enough to produce an unprotected speech result.[207]

This review of the doctrine ended with the *Bigelow* case. The opinion may have overstated the *Bigelow* result by saying that there "the notion of unprotected 'commercial speech' all but passed from

---

[205] In the period between the Supreme Court's decisions in *Bigelow* and *Pharmacy*, restrictions on advertising were repeatedly attacked. See. *e.g.*, Terminal-Hudson Electronics, Inc. v. Dep't of Consumer Affairs, 407 F. Supp. 1075 (C.D. Calif. 1976) (three-judge court), *vacated sub nom.* Bd. of Optometry, State of California v. California Citizens Action Group, 426 U.S. 916 (1976), with direction for lower court to reconsider in light of *Pharmacy;* Brown v. Stackler, 404 F. Supp. 1405 (N.D. Ill. 1975) (individuals have standing to contest state statute prohibiting the publication and advertisement of prices for prescription eyeglasses). Also, just prior to the *Bigelow* decision, the Federal Trade Commission proposed trade regulation rules intended "to allow disclosure of accurate prescription drug price information by retail sellers to prospective purchasers and to eliminate restraints, burdens or controls imposed by non-federal law and by private, state and local governmental action on such disclosure by any means of communication, including but not limited to advertising." 40 FED. REG. 24031, 24032 (1975). Following the *Pharmacy* decision, the FTC postponed indefinitely staff reports on this proposed rule. 41 FED. REG. 27391 (1976). The American Civil Liberties Union passed a resolution to protect speech by business enterprises when they "use advertising media to propagate their views on policy issues." CIVIL LIBERTIES, Jan. 1976, at p.1. The ACLU's position corresponded to the Court's in *Bigelow*, but stopped considerably short of the Court's eventual position protecting commercial speech in *Pharmacy*.

[206] 425 U.S. at 758.

[207] *Id.* at 758–59. *Accord*, Terry v. California State Bd. of Pharmacy, 395 F. Supp. 94, 100 (N.D. Cal. 1975). *Pharmacy* completed the revision of *Pittsburgh Press* begun in *Bigelow;* the case's result was now based solely on the classified ads' illegality, without regard to commercial speech considerations expressed in the opinion.

the scene."[208] Mr. Justice Blackmun accurately fingered "the subject matter of the advertisement in Bigelow" as the reason for that decision's having kept alive "[s]ome fragment of hope for the continuing validity of a 'commercial speech' exception."[209] He also noted that the *Bigelow* result was achieved by finding "public interest" in what appeared to be a purely commercial advertisement.[210] Finally, and most significantly, the *Pharmacy* opinion at this point picked up *Bigelow*'s reference to Meiklejohn's theory of "public speech." That earlier opinion had presciently observed, "The relationship of speech to the marketplace of products or of services does not make it valueless in the marketplace of ideas."[211] This is the seminal language for according commercial speech full constitutional status by incorporating it as an element of the democratic polity's "public speech."

Recognizing that *Bigelow* had really reached a preferred speech result, the Court was now prepared to face squarely "the question whether there is a First Amendment exception for 'commercial speech.' "[212]

> Our pharmacist does not wish to editorialize on any subject, cultural, philosophical, or political. He does not wish to report any particularly newsworthy fact, or to make generalized observations even about commercial matters. The "idea" he wishes to communicate is simply this: "I will sell you the X prescription drug at the Y price." Our question, then, is whether this communication is wholly outside the protection of the First Amendment.

With the doctrine's history neutralized and *Bigelow*'s precedential value appropriately positioned, the issue was now joined.

The Court began its delineation of the First Amendment's interest in protecting commercial speech by eliminating, on the basis of a string of precedents, profit motive as a consideration in determining First Amendment status. If there was to be a distinguishing factor for assessing commercial speech, it had to be content,[213] and then only purely commercial content, not the editorial advertisements or factual advertisements of public interest which earlier cases had protected. Unlike *Bigelow*, where the Court had strained to move away

---

[208] 425 U.S. at 759.

[209] *Id*. at 760.

[210] *Ibid*.

[211] *Ibid*. Quoting from 421 U.S. at 825–26.

[212] 425 U.S. at 761.

[213] *Ibid*.

from the advertisement's commercialism and attain the high ground of preferred speech, now the focus remained on pure commercial speech.

If the First Amendment were fully to protect such speech, said the Court, it would be responding to several interests. The advertiser's solely economic interest qualified for such protection, based on ample precedent in labor dispute cases.[214] (Presumably the economic interest of the advertisement's publisher would also be included.) The equally economic interest of the consumer, tinged with exigencies of age, poverty, and illness which beset these plaintiffs, was likewise worthy of full protection.[215]

The primary beneficiary of full First Amendment protection for commercial speech, however, would be society. As it had earlier, the Court made sure that the focus was on purely commercial advertising. It acknowledged that individual advertisements of the type protected in *Bigelow* are of public interest, and that some element of public interest could presumably be added to even the most routine advertisement.[216] But such an addition need not be artificially made simply to gain constitutional protection. In broad, clean strokes the Court encompassed purely commercial advertising within the Meiklejohn concept of full First Amendment protection for the polity's preferred public speech, and thereby ended the commercial speech doctrine:[217]

---

[214] Mr. Justice Rehnquist's view, as stated in his *Bigelow* dissent, was vindicated. See note 174 *supra*. See Young v. American Mini Theatres, Inc., 96 S. Ct. 2440, 2451 (1976).

[215] 425 U.S. at 763–64.

[216] *Id*. at 764. The Court observed, in a subtle reinforcement of its position that advertising is really vital "public speech," that the consumer's interest in this commercial information might well be "keener by far, than his interest in the day's most urgent political debate." *Id*. at 764. "It is, after all, such consumer goods that people work and earn a livelihood in order to acquire." Fuentes v. Shevin, 407 U.S. 67, 89 (1972).

[217] 425 U.S. at 765. In his separate concurring opinion Mr. Justice Stewart explicitly rejected an interpretation of *Pharmacy* which would accord commercial speech First Amendment status equal to "ideological communication." Since his opinion was written to rebut an interpretation of *Pharmacy* which might preclude government regulations directed at false and deceptive advertising, and since Mr. Justice Stewart concluded his discussion of the differences between "ideological expression" and "commercial price and product advertising" by noting that the truth of the latter can be empirically tested, it may be that Mr. Justice Stewart only intended to emphasize the constitutionality of regulating commercial speech in order to ensure its truthfulness. In this he agrees with the majority. *Id*. at 771–73. In a footnote, however, he observed: "The information about price and

Moreover, there is another consideration that suggests no line between publicly "interesting" or "important" commercial advertising and the opposite kind could ever be drawn. Advertising, however tasteless and excessive it sometimes may seem, is nonetheless dissemination of information as to who is producing and selling what product, for what reason, and at what price. So long as we preserve a predominantly free enterprise economy, the allocation of our resources in large measure will be made through numerous private economic decisions. It is a matter of public interest that those decisions, in the aggregate, be intelligent and well informed. To this end, the free flow of commercial information is indispensable. . . . And if it is indispensable to the proper allocation of resources in a free enterprise system, it is also indispensable to the formation of intelligent opinions as to how that system ought to be regulated or altered. Therefore, even if the First Amendment were thought to be primarily an instrument to enlighten public decisionmaking in a democracy, we could not say that the free flow of information does not serve that goal.

The Court must have felt compelled to eliminate the commercial speech doctrine, rather than attempt to define its limits in some way, because of the ever increasing importance of advertising in propelling, molding, and simply informing our highly commercial society. Advertising is now a dominant mode of speech in the United States.[218] Myriad components of our society, not only business, speak

---

product conveyed by commercial advertisements may of course stimulate thought and debate about political questions." *Id*. at 780 n.8. This language seems to reject the majority opinion's position that, for purposes of public speech, advertising information is itself the idea worthy of First Amendment protection, and is not simply a potential catalyst for political thought and debate.

Such a reinterpretation of the Court's opinion in a separate concurring opinion might pass without comment. Mr. Justice Stewart's view was soon cited by the Court, however, to support the idea that the First Amendment will tolerate regulation of "commercial price and product advertising" that it would not tolerate for "ideological communication." Young v. American Mini Theatres, Inc., 96 S. Ct. 2440, 2451 n.32 (1976). The *Young* majority was formed by Chief Justice Burger, and Justices White, Powell, Rehnquist (who dissented in *Pharmacy*), and Stevens (who did not participate in *Pharmacy* and wrote the *Young* opinion). Interestingly, Mr. Justice Stewart dissented in *Young*. If all of this simply means regulating commercial advertising for truth, an obvious impossibility for ideological speech, then the incorporation of commercial speech into Meiklejohn's public speech remains unimpaired.

[218] In 1972 the estimated expenditures for advertising in the United States were $23,300 million. U.S. Bureau of the Census, Dep't of Commerce, Statistical Abstract of the U.S. 790 (96th ed. 1975). (All numbers in this note are stated in millions, and are rounded off to the nearest million.) In that same year the estimated receipts for movie theaters were $13, *id*. at 787; for sale of all books and pamphlets $2,915, *id*. at

it incessantly, everywhere. Those same components hear it, see it, and most importantly, rely on it, even unconsciously. Surely this prompted the Court's growing uneasiness about the commercial speech anomaly. If the dominant mode of speech in our society is not to merit full constitutional protection, the rationale for such an incongruity must be profound and clearly enunciated. The commercial speech doctrine was neither; it became increasingly illogical and was eventually overwhelmed by the marketplace.

Having defined the First Amendment's interest in protecting prescription drug price advertising by elevating commercial speech to fully protected status under that Amendment, the Court then assessed the state's interest in regulating that speech. The Board of Pharmacy listed expert services, crucial to their customers' health, which pharmacists allegedly provide, and argued that absent the state's ban on prescription drug price advertising these services would cease as a result of the instability which aggressive price competition, made possible by advertising, would precipitate in the profession.[219] The Court's response was brief and direct. At the outset of the opinion, while accepting the parties' stipulation that pharmacy is a profession,[220] the Court had noted that about 95 percent of all prescriptions are filled with dosages prepared by the manufacturer rather than by pharmacists' compounding.[221] Based on that, and the fact that regulations other than this advertising ban maintained pharmacists' professional standards, the Court observed that "this case concerns the retail sale by the pharmacist more than it does his professional standards."[222] Not only was this statute of no benefit to the state's "strong interest" in maintaining pharmacists' professional standards, it also insulated the pharmacist from price competition and allowed "a substantial, and perhaps even excessive, profit in

---

526; for newspapers, net after subtracting advertising revenues, $2,308, *id*. at 522; for periodicals, net after subtracting advertising revenues, $1,504, *ibid;* for television and radio sales, $8,176, *id*. at 775;—for a total of $14,916. The difference between these expenditures and those for advertising is $8,384. What these figures demonstrate is how much advertisers spent in order to communicate with the public, compared to how much the public spent to receive communications of all forms.

[219] 425 U.S. at 767–68.   [220] *Id*. at 750 n.3.   [221] *Id*. at 752.

[222] *Id*. at 768. Here, as in *Bigelow*, 421 U.S. at 825 n.10, the Court distinguished well-known cases, such as Head v. New Mexico Bd., 374 U.S. 424 (1963), in which similar advertising bans, advanced on similar justifications, had been sustained. Those decisions were grounded in the Fourteenth Amendment, whereas this case, like *Bigelow*, was advanced on a First Amendment theory, 425 U.S. at 769.

addition to providing an inferior service."[223] The antidote prescribed by the Court was to assume "that people will perceive their own best interests if only they are well enough informed, and that the best means to that end is to open the channels of communication rather than to close them."[224] The right to know operates in the economic marketplace as well as the marketplace of ideas.

This line of reasoning by the Court provides varied future applications for *Pharmacy*. Linking the First Amendment right to know with an advertising ban's anticompetitive impact on prices creates a catch-22 situation which restrictive trade practices will find difficult to avoid. If individuals or corporations combine to restrain competition in interstate commerce, they are subject to private and governmental actions under the Sherman Act. The *Pharmacy* decision is noteworthy because it indicates the Court's willingness to find, not simply that an advertising ban is a restraint on competition sufficient to violate the Sherman Act, but also that a causal connection exists between such an advertising ban and an anticompetitive effect on prices.

One way in which anticompetitive practitioners might seek to avoid the Sherman Act is to implement such practices pursuant to a directive from a state legislature. Under the rule of *Parker v. Brown*,[225] such a program would then be an act of the sovereign for governmental purposes rather than in restraint of trade.[226] For example, after *Goldfarb v. Virginia State Bar*,[227] which held attorneys subject to the Sherman Act, a state bar association might seek to have its state legislature require that association by law to adopt and enforce a minimum fee schedule. That legislative enactment would constitute the state action required for a private citizen to apply the First Amendment right to know against the restrictive practice, as was done in *Pharmacy*.

Although not all restrictive practices will be remediable simply by exposure under the right to know, the *Pharmacy* decision will be applicable to more than just prices. The Court wanted to inform the

---

[223] *Ibid.* For a detailed analysis of a similar advertising ban, which supports the Court's conclusions, see Benham & Benham, *Regulating through the Professions: A Perspective on Information Control*, 18 J. LAW & ECON. 421 (1975).

[224] 425 U.S. at 770.   [225] 317 U.S. 341 (1943).

[226] *Id.* at 352; but see Cantor v. Detroit Edison Co., 96 S. Ct. 3110 (1976).

[227] 421 U.S. 773 (1975).

public about "the entirely lawful terms that competing pharmacists are offering."[228] Price may be the principal competitive term for pharmacists, but for other products or services other information may be just as, if not more, beneficial to the consumer.[229]

Finally, since the right to know in *Pharmacy* was invoked by consumers as a correlative of pharmacists' desire to exercise their First Amendment right and advertise to those consumers, then the reverse should also apply. That is, after *Pharmacy* a retailer's First Amendment rights allow him to advertise prices in violation of an advertising ban in order to fulfill the consumers' right to know by the information set forth in those advertisements.

With the First Amendment's interest in protecting commercial speech firmly established, and the state unable to demonstrate the compelling interest in its regulation required to outweigh that constitutional interest, it remained only for the Court to delimit commercial speech's new freedom.[230] First, ample precedents exist for imposing "time, place, and manner" restrictions on protected speech.[231] Indeed, *Valentine* avoided being overruled in the end by being reread as a method-of-distribution case, and thereby coming within this restriction. A second permissible restriction on commercial speech is illegality, and the citation for this was *Pittsburgh Press*.[232] Again, a once prominent commercial speech case survived by reinterpretation. And, the Court also excluded from this ruling "the special problems of the electronic broadcast media.[233]

The fourth permissible restriction applied to "false" or "deceptive or misleading" commercial speech.[234] One possible interpretation of the *Pharmacy* result would be that commercial speech's new

---

[228] 425 U.S. at 770.

[229] The Court stressed in a footnote that it was expressing no opinion as to whether "the distinctions, historical and functional, between professions, may require consideration of quite different factors." *Id.* at 773 n.25. Chief Justice Burger wrote a separate concurring opinion to emphasize that point. *Id.* at 773–74. The professions are generally thought to be unique because they render services, which are not price distinctive, rather than dispense standardized goods. The *Pharmacy* opinion's unequivocal avoidance of any discussion regarding the professions indicates that the import for this case lies in the commercial arena apart from them.

[230] Three of the four restrictions set forth in *Pharmacy* were also noted in *Bigelow*, 421 U.S. at 828. Only "the special problems of the electronic broadcast media," identified as the fourth restriction in *Pharmacy*, were excluded in *Bigelow*, and that for the obvious reason that *Bigelow* involved print.

[231] 425 U.S. at 771.   [233] *Id.* at 773.

[232] *Id.* at 772.   [234] *Id.* at 771.

freedom in the name of the consumers' right to know constitutes a setback for other consumer-oriented efforts to eliminate false and deceptive advertising. In order to preclude such thinking, the Court explained in a lengthy footnote that commercial speech remains "differentiable" from other forms of speech, and that these differences "suggest that a different degree of protection is necessary to insure that the flow of truthful and legitimate commercial information is unimpaired."[235] Perhaps with undue optimism, the Court observed that the truth of most commercial statements is "more easily verifiable." Thus, it may be "less necessary to tolerate inaccurate statements for fear of silencing the speaker," and it may even be permissible to allow certain prior restraints.[236] This, probably more than "time, place, and manner" restrictions, will be the future battleground to test how firmly the Court believes that free flow of commercial information is vital to this democratic society. For, while the opinion's concluding paragraph made clear that Utopia was not at hand for the hucksters and rogue merchants, the vast majority of merchants and their speech are not so easily defined:[237]

> What is at issue is whether a State may completely suppress the dissemination of concededly truthful information about entirely lawful activity, fearful of that information's effect upon its disseminators and its recipients. Reserving other questions, we conclude that the answer to this one is in the negative.

IV. CONCLUSION

The commercial speech doctrine existed for thirty-four years as an exception to the First Amendment's protection. Yet each time the Court upheld or overturned a regulation of commercial speech, it was not by an application of the doctrine alone. Another, more telling element was inevitably present. In *Schneider*, *Murdock*, and the other Jehovah's Witnesses cases, that element was religion; in *Breard*, it was privacy; in *Sullivan*, it was the compelling political and social commentary included in the speech; in *Pittsburgh Press* and *Ginzburg*, illegality was crucial. Much of this weakness in the doctrine's application stemmed from the seminal case, *Valentine v. Chrestensen*, an enigmatic decision susceptible of varied interpretation.

---

[235] *Id.* at 771–72 n.24.   [236] *Id.* at 772 n.24.   [237] *Id.* at 773.

In recent years the Court not only circumvented the doctrine but repeatedly cast doubts on its validity while doing so. In a sequence of decisions it carved ever broader exceptions to the doctrine by extending First Amendment protection to speech which was increasingly commercial. Finally, in the *Pharmacy* decision the Court confronted the essence of commercial speech, devoid of redeeming opinion or public interest content. Pure commercial speech was elevated to fully protected First Amendment status because of its central importance to the life of the democratic polity. The consumers' right to hear such speech and the merchant's right to speak it were firmly established.

Commercial speech is a misnomer for this line of cases and this doctrine. The result in each case stemmed from other rationales. To the extent the phrase "commercial speech" exerted any influence, it should not have, for there never was a doctrine. During those thirty-four years, it was a haunting shadow rather than a reality.

WALTER HELLERSTEIN

MICHELIN TIRE CORP. v. WAGES: ENHANCED STATE POWER TO TAX IMPORTS

In *Michelin Tire Corp. v. Wages*,[1] the Supreme Court abandoned a century of precedent in holding that the Import-Export Clause[2] does not bar a state from imposing a nondiscriminatory ad valorem property tax on imported goods. The provision forbidding the states from laying "any Imposts or Duties on Imports or Exports"[3] was never intended to prohibit such a levy, the Court now tells us, and the case first suggesting that it did, *Low v. Austin*,[4] was "wrongly decided."[5] Over a mild protest of Mr. Justice White,[6] the Court thus obviated any examination of the principal issue the parties had briefed: whether Michelin's tires, while sitting in a warehouse in Gwinnett County, Georgia, had retained their "distinctive charac-

Walter Hellerstein is Assistant Professor of Law, The University of Chicago.

The author wishes to thank Professors Walter J. Blum, Gerhard Casper, Kenneth W. Dam, Jerome R. Hellerstein, Phil C. Neal, and Geoffrey R. Stone for their helpful comments on an earlier draft of this article.

[1] 423 U.S. 276 (1976).   [2] U.S. Const., Art. I, § 10, cl. 2.

[3] *Id.* The complete text of the Clause reads: "No State shall, without the Consent of the Congress, lay any Imposts or Duties on Imports or Exports, except what may be absolutely necessary for executing its inspection Laws: and the net Produce of all Duties and Imposts, laid by any State on Imports or Exports, shall be for the Use of the Treasury of the United States; and all such Laws shall be subject to the Revision and Controul of the Congress."

[4] 13 Wall. 29 (1872).   [5] 423 U.S. at 301.   [6] *Id.* at 302.

ter" as imports and, consequently, their immunity from state taxation.

Although the Court's confession of error apparently spared us a discourse on the "original package" doctrine,[7] it could hardly fail to raise a number of questions. Some are historical. Are we assured that the Court, now fortified by "scholarly analysis,"[8] is correct in its confident assertion that "[n]othing in the history of the Import-Export Clause even remotely suggests that a nondiscriminatory ad valorem property tax which is also imposed on imported goods that are no longer in import transit was the type of exaction that was regarded as objectionable by the Framers"?[9] Others are jurisprudential. Was there any "reason" or "necessity" to overrule *Low v. Austin* since, as Mr. Justice White remarked, "None of the parties has challenged that case here, and the issue of its overruling has not been briefed or argued"?[10] And still others are of immediate practical importance. In delimiting the power of states to tax imports, should we continue to ask: "When does an import cease to be an import?"[11] or should we address other issues instead? Extended consideration of each of these questions may be warranted, but it is toward the last area of inquiry that this article is primarily directed.[12]

I. The Michelin Decision

A. THE FACTS

While most of the facts turned out to be largely beside the point, their brief recitation is necessary to an understanding of the issue the parties thought they were litigating.

---

[7] *Cf., e.g.,* Hooven & Allison Co. v. Evatt, 324 U.S. 652 (1945).

[8] 423 U.S. at 282.   [9] *Id.* at 286.

[10] *Id.* at 302. Although the "parties" may not have challenged *Low,* amici curiae surely did. See Amici Curiae Brief for the County of Los Angeles, pp. 19–42. And petitioner responded to the "arguments which ask this Court to overrule *Brown v. Maryland, Low v. Austin* and other decisions" by suggesting that "Congress, rather than this Court, is the appropriate tribunal to consider and pass on this group of arguments." Reply Brief for Petitioner, p. 2.

[11] The question is Professor T. R. Powell's. Powell, *State Taxation of Imports— When Does an Import Cease to Be an Import?* 58 Harv. L. Rev. 858 (1945).

[12] The historical issues have been explored at length elsewhere. See, *e.g.,* 1 Crosskey, Politics and the Constitution in the History of the United States 295–323 (1953); Early & Weitzman, *A Century of Dissent: The Immunity of Goods Imported for Resale from Nondiscriminatory State Personal Property Taxes,* 7 S.W.U.L. Rev. 247 (1975).

The Michelin Tire Corporation, a New York subsidiary of its
French parent,[13] operated as an importer and wholesale distributor
in the United States of automobile and truck tires and tubes manu-
factured in France and Canada. Michelin operated distribution warehouses for its products in various parts of the country. One such
warehouse was located in Gwinnett County, Georgia. Imported
tires and tubes were shipped to this warehouse in two ways. Approximately 75 percent, including all those imported from France,
were transported in sea vans, which are over-the-road trailers with
removable wheels. The vans were packed and sealed at the foreign
factory, hauled to a port where the wheels were removed, and loaded
on ships bound for the United States. At the port of entry, the vans
were unloaded, their wheels were replaced, and they were hauled
to the Gwinnett County warehouse, usually arriving within a week.
The remaining 25 percent of the tires and tubes were transported
from Canada in over-the-road trailers. They were packed and sealed
at the Canadian factory and delivered directly to the Gwinnett
County warehouse. Michelin owned none of the sea vans or trailers
in question and there was no intermediate distribution point for any
of the shipments.

The imported tires were packed into the sea vans and trailers in
bulk without otherwise being packaged or bundled. Upon arrival at
the warehouse, each van or trailer load of tires was unloaded, sorted
by size and style, and stored in the warehouse awaiting distribution
without further processing.[14] The imported tubes were individually
packaged in small boxes and were transported in the sea vans and
trailers in larger corrugated cartons. Upon arrival at the warehouse,
the shipments of tubes were unloaded, sorted, and segregated by size.
Most of the tubes were stored in the larger cartons, but some had
been removed from the cartons and held available for sale in small
quantities. Except for a few domestic tubes purchased by Michelin
when it was experiencing difficulty obtaining its imported tubes,[15]

---

[13] 2 DIRECTORY OF INTER-CORPORATE OWNERSHIP (WHO OWN WHOM IN AMERICA)
776 (Angel Comp. 1974).

[14] Both the United States Supreme Court, 423 U.S. at 280, and the Georgia Supreme Court, 233 Ga. at 713–14, made statements to the effect that at this point
the individual shipments ceased to be separate identifiable units. The tires were in
fact identifiable by serial number. 423 U.S. at 280.

[15] Record, pp. App. 29–30. "Domestic tubes are similarly packaged and similarly
handled at the warehouse." 233 Ga. at 714. On both tax dates in question, some domestic tubes were stored in the warehouse.

all the tires and tubes in the warehouse were imported from abroad and transported and stored in the manner indicated.

The Gwinnett County warehouse served as the distribution center for Michelin tires and tubes to franchised dealers in six southeastern states. All the tires and tubes in the warehouse were sold and distributed to such dealers, who numbered between 250 and 300. Orders from the dealers were filled without regard to the shipments in which the tires and tubes arrived in the United States or their place of manufacture. Orders varied in size, but they averaged 4,000–5,000 pounds per sale.[16] Delivery to the franchised dealers was by common carrier or customer pickup. No tires were sold directly to retail customers. Michelin paid a 4 percent federal duty on all of its imports.

In 1973, the tax commissioner and tax assessors of Gwinnett County, Georgia, assessed ad valorem property taxes against Michelin's inventory held in its warehouse on 1 January 1972 and 1 January 1973.[17] The assessments averaged about $10,000.[18] Alleging that all the tires and tubes located in its warehouse were immune from Gwinnett County property taxes under the Import-Export Clause, except for the imported passenger tubes that had been removed from their original shipping cartons,[19] Michelin filed a complaint in the Superior Court of Gwinnett County seeking declaratory and injunctive relief against enforcement of the tax.

B. THE STATE COURT PROCEEDINGS

It is apparent from the record that counsel for both the tax authorities and the taxpayer viewed Michelin's lawsuit as an oppor-

---

[16] An average shipment of tires on a sea van would weigh 23,000 to 25,000 pounds. Record, pp. App. 54.

[17] All real and personal property in Georgia, unless specifically exempted, is subject to taxation. GA. CODE ANN. § 92-101 (1974). The county is authorized to levy taxes for current expenses, accumulated debts, and for other county purposes. *Id.* at §§ 92-3702–17. The order assessing the county tax for the year must specify the percent levied for each specific purpose. *Id.* at § 92-3801. The county tax authority is obligated to have a statement prepared of the amount of tax required for county purposes for each year. *Id.* § 92-3709. The assessment also applies to property taxed by the state. *Id.* at § 92-3801. All tangible property is assessed at 40 percent of fair market value. *Id.* at § 92-5703. The tax rate is the aggregate of all lawful levies. CCH STATE TAX GUIDE (All States Unit) ¶ 20-354 (1974).

[18] Plaintiff's Complaint, ¶5, Record, p. App. 3.

[19] After its complaint was filed, Michelin discovered that some of the tubes it had claimed to be exempt were in fact of domestic origin and therefore not exempt. See Record, pp. App. 19–21. Michelin paid taxes on these tubes.

tunity to obtain guidance from the courts as to the scope of the
Import-Export Clause's prohibition against state taxes. Counsel for
the county stated to the trial court that:[20]

> a complete record would be built in this case . . . because we
> need direction in this particular matter. . . . [W]e have now,
> I believe—what four or five importers operating in the country
> [sic] . . . so its getting to be a mass-substantial amount of tax
> involved and we need some direction in how to handle this
> matter and that's really why we brought the matter to a head
> this way, to find out really where we stand.

Counsel for Michelin expressed similar sentiments.[21]

After a brief bench trial that established the record of virtually
undisputed facts, the court granted Michelin the requested relief.
The trial court's opinion recited the classic formulation from the
seminal case of *Brown v. Maryland*:[22]

> It is sufficient for the present to say, generally, that when the
> importer has so acted upon the thing imported, that it has be-
> come incorporated and mixed up with the mass of property in
> the country, it has, perhaps, lost its distinctive character as an
> import, and has become subject to the taxing power of the
> State; but while remaining the property of the importer, in his
> warehouse, in the original form or package in which it was
> imported, a tax upon it is too plainly a duty on imports to escape
> the prohibition in the constitution.

The court noted that this principle had been extended to immunize
imported goods from ad valorem property taxes. It construed the
facts in light of this principle:[23]

> The automobile and truck tires here involved while perhaps not
> in an original package are without doubt in the original form in
> which they were imported into this Country. Most tubes are
> in the original containers. Those tubes taken from the original
> containers have been included in inventory and tax paid on
> them.

And finally, while opining that "tires and tubes . . . placed in plaintiff's general inventory for the purpose of sale to its customers . . .

---

[20] Record, p. App. 25.   [22] 12 Wheat. 419, 441-42 (1827).
[21] *Id.* at 26.   [23] Petition for Certiorari, p. A-4.

should be taxed to the same extent as any other inventory of any other business in Gwinnett County, and the Court would so hold if supported by the law," it felt constrained "to bow to the authorities and hold that the automobile and truck tires in plaintiff's inventory are imports and until they have been sold are not subject to any ad valorem tax that may be levied against them by Gwinnett County."[24]

As anticipated, the county officials appealed to the Georgia Supreme Court. That court, evidently less impressed than the county tribunal by "the authorities," engaged in an analytic exercise that has typified opinions in this area ever since Chief Justice Marshall suggested that immunity of imports from state taxation may have something to do with "the original form or package" in which they are imported. Notwithstanding the admonition that "[i]t is a matter of hornbook knowledge that the original package statement of Justice Marshall was an illustration, rather than a formula, and that its application is evidentiary, and not substantive,"[25] the Georgia Supreme Court undertook a lengthy exegesis of the "original package" doctrine.

Through its opinion, a kaleidoscope of goods and packages was paraded before our eyes against an essentially[26] unchanging doctrinal backdrop. French champagne stored by the importer in a San Francisco warehouse, "whilst remaining in the original cases, unbroken and unsold," enjoyed immunity from state taxation.[27] European dry goods packed in separate parcels or bundles but exposed or offered for sale in opened shipping boxes did not.[28] An importer of hundred-pound bags of Chilean nitrate stored in an Alabama warehouse and kept in the original packages until sold enjoyed immunity from state taxation.[29] A wholesaler of fish caught in the Gulf of Mexico who is assessed by their weight after washing and reicing did

---

[24] *Ibid.*

[25] City of Galveston v. Mexican Petroleum Corp., 15 F.2d 208 (S.D. Tex. 1926).

[26] But see note 32 *infra.*

[27] Low v. Austin, 13 Wall. 29, 32 (1872) (ad valorem property tax), considered 233 Ga. at 716.

[28] May v. New Orleans, 178 U.S. 496 (1900) (ad valorem property tax), considered 233 Ga. at 716.

[29] Anglo-Chilean Nitrate Sales Corp. v. Alabama, 288 U.S. 218 (1933) (franchise tax), considered 233 Ga. at 717.

not.[30] Bales of Philippine hemp stored in an Ohio warehouse awaiting use in the manufacture of cordage and similar products enjoyed
immunity from state taxation.[31] Piles of foreign ore and plywood
awaiting use in manufacturing processes did not.[32]

At the same time, the opinion raised a host of theoretical questions bearing on the application of the doctrine. Are sea vans and
trailers considered to be the "original packages"?[33] Do unpackaged
imports enjoy an immunity different in scope from packaged imports,[34] and, in any event, how does one apply the doctrine to an
unpackaged import that never changes its "original form"?[35] And is
there a distinction between the application of the doctrine to goods
imported for use and goods imported for sale?[36]

---

[30] Gulf Fisheries Co. v. MacInerney, 276 U.S. 124 (1928) (license tax), considered
233 Ga. at 716–17.

[31] Hooven & Allison Co. v. Evatt, 324 U.S. 652 (1945) (ad valorem property tax),
considered 233 Ga. at 717.

[32] Youngstown Sheet and Tube Co. v. Bowers and United States Plywood Corp.
v. City of Algoma, 358 U.S. 534 (1959) (ad valorem property taxes), considered 233
Ga. at 717–18. The Court in Youngstown noted, inter alia, "Whatever may be the
significance of retaining in the 'original package' goods that have been so imported
for sale . . . goods that have been so imported for use in manufacturing are not
exempt from taxation, though not removed from the 'original package,' if, as found
here, they have been 'put to the use for which they [were] imported.'" 358 U.S. at
548. Whether Youngstown undermined the "original package" doctrine or merely
announced a rule for cases involving a manufacturer's "current operating needs,"
id. at 549, has been the subject of some discussion. See Justice Frankfurter's dissenting opinion, id. at 551–75. See also Dakin, The Protective Cloak of the Export-
Import Clause: Immunity for the Goods or Immunity for the Process? 19 LA. L.
REV. 747 (1959); Early & Weitzman, note 12 supra.

[33] Compare Volkswagen Pacific, Inc. v. City of Los Angeles, 7 Cal.3d 48 (1972)
(sea van constitutes "original package"), considered 233 Ga. at 719, with Garment
Corp. of America v. State Tax Comm'n, 32 Mich. App. 715 (1971) (sea van does not
constitute "original package"), considered 233 Ga. at 721.

[34] 233 Ga. at 723.

[35] See, e.g., E. J. Stanton & Sons v. Los Angeles County, 78 Cal. App.2d 181 (1947),
considered 233 Ga. at 719–20, where the California court waxed lyrical in approaching the problem: "A cargo of planks, timbers or logs imported from foreign lands
is surrounded by an invisible gossamer woven of law, custom and convention which
protects the merchandise from the local tax assessor only so long as it retains the
unbroken wrapper in which it entered the port. But when such cargo sheds its
invisible cover, even though in the warehouse of the importer, and is so sorted and
classified as to facilitate its sale . . . termination of immunity [is compelled]."
Id. at 187–88. See generally Trickett, The Original Package Ineptitude, 6 COLUM. L.
REV. 161 (1906).

[36] See note 32 supra.

The Georgia Supreme Court, while rejecting the argument that an ad valorem property tax does not fall within the prohibition of the Import-Export Clause,[37] had little difficulty in concluding that most of Michelin's inventory was constitutionally taxable. In its view, the unpackaged tires, once sorted, segregated by size and style, and commingled with other shipments had lost their status as imports and were subject to taxation. Not so, however, the packaged tubes in corrugated cartons, which retained their immunity under the "original package" doctrine:[38]

> This doctrine has been almost universally applied, in a mechanical way, for about 150 years. The great weight of authority makes a vast distinction between goods shipped in packaging, such as crates or cartons, and goods shipped in bulk. Packaged imports retain their status as imports, and are not subject to taxation. Bulk imports that have been mingled with other bulk imports, sorted, and arranged for sale do not retain their status as imports, and they are subject to taxation.

Unhappy with this disposition of the matter, Michelin petitioned the United States Supreme Court for certiorari. The Gwinnett County tax officials, apparently not wishing to challenge the application of the "original package" doctrine to Michelin's tubes that remained in the shipping cartons, did not cross-petition from the Georgia court's affirmance on this point. Thus, when the Supreme Court granted Michelin's petition, the only question presented was whether the Georgia Supreme Court was correct in holding that Michelin's tires were subject to Gwinnett County's ad valorem property tax, a question both parties framed in terms of the physical packaging, form, and arrangement of the tires.[39]

C. THE SUPREME COURT'S OPINION

The Supreme Court affirmed not on the ground that the state court had accurately drawn the line between tax-immune imports and goods that had become "incorporated and mixed up with the mass of property in the country,"[40] but on the ground that "Georgia's assessment of a nondiscriminatory ad valorem property tax

---

[37] 233 Ga. at 722.   [38] Id. at 723.

[39] Petition for certiorari, p. 2; Opposition to Petition for Certiorari, p. 2.

[40] Brown v. Maryland, 12 Wheat. at 441.

against the imported tires is not within the constitutional prohibi-
against 'laying any Imposts or Duties on Imports . . .' and that insofar
as *Low v. Austin*, 13 Wall. 29 (1872) is to the contrary, that decision
is overruled."[41] What induced the Supreme Court to discard *Low*
is a matter for speculation,[42] but its opinion in *Michelin* marks a
fundamental reexamination of the purpose and scope of the Import-
Export Clause's prohibition against state taxation of imports. In
contrast to its past opinions in this area, which have often been characterized by a mechanistic application of Marshall's "original package" language in *Brown v. Maryland* to determine whether the
goods under consideration had ceased to be "imports,"[43] the Court's
opinion explicitly refrained from addressing the question whether
Michelin's tires had lost their status as "imports."[44] Instead the Court
focused upon the nature of the exaction at issue to ascertain whether
it constituted a forbidden "impost" or "duty." Although the determination whether an exaction is an "impost" or "duty" would not
necessarily render academic the question whether the levy had been
imposed upon an "import,"[45] the Court's approach to the former
issue appears substantially to reduce the need for inquiring into the
latter.[46]

In returning to the original purposes of the constitutional prohibition against state taxation of imports, the Court identified three principal concerns of the Framers. First, "the Federal Government must
speak with one voice when regulating commercial relations with
foreign governments, and tariffs, which might affect foreign relations, could not be implemented by the States consistently with that
exclusive power."[47] Second, "import revenues were to be the major
source of revenue of the Federal Government and should not be
diverted to the States."[48] Third, "harmony among the States might

---

[41] 423 U.S. at 279.

[42] Conceivably, it was persuaded by the arguments of the California and Texas
brief amici curiae on this score. The importance of the question to states and localities may have been underscored by the submission of amici curiae briefs by
Kansas, Ohio, and Georgia, although these states did not argue that *Low* had been
wrongly decided.

[43] See cases cited at notes 27–32 *supra*.   [44] 423 U.S. at 279.

[45] The conclusion that a tax is not an "impost" or "duty" would obviate any inquiry into whether it had been imposed upon an "import." The opposite conclusion
would leave this issue open.

[46] See text *infra* at notes 76–99.   [48] *Ibid.*

[47] 423 U.S. at 285.

be disturbed unless seaboard States, with their crucial ports of entry, were prohibited from levying taxes on citizens of other States by taxing goods merely flowing through their ports to the inland States not situated as favorably geographically."[49]

Measured against these concerns, the Court could perceive nothing objectionable in a nondiscriminatory ad valorem property tax imposed on imports no longer in transit. It was "obvious" to the Court that such a tax could have "no impact whatsoever on the Federal Government's exclusive regulation of foreign commerce," because such a tax did not fall on imports "as such," could not be used "to create special protective tariffs or particular preferences for certain domestic goods," and could not be "applied selectively to encourage or discourage any importation in a manner inconsistent with federal regulation."[50] While the Court is on firm enough ground in making what amounts to little more than a tautological assertion that a nondiscriminatory tax does not have characteristics of a discriminatory tax, it is not altogether clear why it is so "obvious" that a nondiscriminatory state tax can have "no impact whatsoever" on the federal government's exclusive regulation of foreign commerce. If, for example, the Framers had intended that the federal government's plenary power over foreign commerce should extend to importers and their goods until the first sale in this country, the imposition of a variety of nondiscriminatory ad valorem property taxes by different states upon such goods prior to such sale might well be regarded as inconsistent with the constitutional plan, since they could subject importers and their goods to unequal economic and administrative burdens that could undermine federal control. Whether in fact the Import-Export Clause embodies such a design is, to be sure, a different question.[51] And it would be taking liberties with Marshall's language to so argue on the basis of his approval of counsel's contention in *Brown v. Maryland* that "the importer purchases, by payment of the duty to the United States, a right to dispose of his merchandise."[52]

---

[49] *Id.* at 285–86.   [50] *Id.* at 286.

[51] In this connection, one might want to consider whether the exception to the Clause's prohibition for those imposts and duties that are "absolutely necessary for executing [a state's] inspection Laws" provides grounds for challenging the imposition of other burdens on imports under the *inclusio unius exclusio alterius* principle.

[52] 12 Wheat. at 442. Counsel for Michelin did in fact so argue. Reply Brief for Petitioner, p. 3. Even if "the right to sell" is the "consideration for which the duty is paid," 12 Wheat. at 442, it hardly follows inexorably that the right includes a right to be free from a state's nondiscriminatory ad valorem property tax.

Nevertheless, the Court accomplishes nothing by overstating its case, and implicitly attributing to nondiscriminatory taxes virtues they may not possess.

The Court likewise found no inconsistency between the imposition of nondiscriminatory ad valorem property taxes by the states and the Framers' second purpose in committing exclusive power to the federal government to lay imposts and duties on imports: the protection of the federal government's major source of anticipated revenues. The Court's reasoning was in part definitional: "[I]f non-discriminatory ad valorem taxation is not in that category [of imposts and duties on imports], it deprives the Federal Government of nothing to which it is entitled."[53] In supporting its position that such taxes do not fall within the defined category, the Court again returns to the point that it regards as most critical, the nondiscriminatory character of the levies: "It should be emphasized . . . that they cannot be selectively imposed and increased so as substantially to impair or prohibit importation."[54] The impact that nondiscriminatory taxation might have on federal import revenues, "to the extent its economic burden may discourage purchase or importation of foreign goods,"[55] was, the Court now firmly asserts, merely an "incidental effect" the prohibition of which was not "even remotely an objective of the Framers."[56]

Nor, in the Court's view, would the imposition of nondiscriminatory ad valorem property taxes frustrate the third objective underlying the Import-Export Clause: preserving harmony and maintaining the free flow of imported goods among the states by preventing some states from exploiting their favorable geographic location by taxing goods destined for other states. Here the Court is a bit more tentative. It is no longer "obvious" that such levies could have "no impact whatsoever" on the stated purpose. Nor is it apparent that prohibition of such levies was not "even remotely an objective of the Framers." It is now by comparison to the exactions imposed by the states under the Articles of Confederation that such nondiscriminatory taxes "do not interfere with the free flow of imported goods."[57] In fact, the Court acknowledges that "allowance of nondiscriminatory ad valorem property taxation may increase the cost of goods purchased by 'inland' consumers"[58] but finds such taxation justified

---

[53] 423 U.S. at 286–87.   [55] *Id.* at 287.   [57] *Id.* at 288.

[54] *Id.* at 287–88.   [56] *Ibid.*   [58] *Ibid.*

in part by the countervailing consideration that it represents the "*quid pro quo* for benefits actually conferred by the taxing State" for which ultimate consumers rather than local taxpayers should pay.[59] Yet, in recognition of the possibility of a conflict between such taxes and this third purpose of the Import-Export Clause, the Court not only feels compelled to assure us that the purpose will still be secured under the Clause "merely by prohibiting the assessment of even nondiscriminatory property taxes on goods which are merely in transit through the State when the tax is assessed,"[60] but, as if harboring some doubts about the force of this prohibition, it allays further fears by reminding us that traditional Commerce Clause doctrine would likewise afford protection against interference with the free flow of goods.[61]

Indeed, the Court's gingerly treatment of this issue may have stemmed from its experience under the Commerce Clause. The Court had there developed a doctrinal limitation on the constitutionality of nondiscriminatory state taxes, the "multiple burdens" theory:[62]

> [T]he state may not impose certain taxes on interstate commerce, its incidents or instrumentalities, which are no more in amount or burden than it places on its local business, not because this of itself is discriminatory, cumulative or special or would violate due process, but because other states also may have the right constitutionally, apart from the commerce clause, to tax the same thing and either the actuality or the risk of their doing so makes the total burden cumulative, discriminatory or special.

The Court may well have sensed, though it was not willing to say so explicitly, that nondiscriminatory property taxes imposed on goods stored by an importer-wholesaler such as Michelin for distribution throughout the United States might in fact interfere with the free flow of imports among the states "by virtue of the cumulative impact of such taxes on the price of goods on their way to become part of a stock of goods for resale locally."[63]

---

[59] *Id.* at 289.   [60] *Id.* at 290.   [61] *Id.* at 290, n.11.

[62] International Harvester Co. v. Department of Treasury, 322 U.S. 340, 358 (1944) (Rutledge, J., concurring). See Hellerstein, *State Taxation of Interstate Business and the Supreme Court, 1974 Term: Standard Pressed Steel & Colonial Pipeline*, 62 VA. L. REV. 149, 150–51, n.6 (1976).

[63] Dakin, note 32 *supra*, at 766. *Cf.* CROSSKEY, note 12 *supra*, at 296, of the opinion that a nondiscriminatory property tax could not "entail any multiple burdening of

Having thus demonstrated that the objectives of the Import-Export Clause would not be served, except to the limited extent noted, by prohibiting nondiscriminatory ad valorem property taxes on imported goods, the Court turned to the text. Conceding that the Clause did not by its terms except nondiscriminatory taxes from its prohibition, the Court pointed out that it was equally clear that not every tax—but only "imposts or duties"—lay within its scope. Noting that the constitutional grant of power to Congress "to lay and collect Taxes, Duties, Imposts, and Excises"[64] supported a reading of the Import-Export Clause as not forbidding every tax which falls in some measure on imports, the Court drew upon Professor Crosskey's "persuasive demonstration"[65] that the words "imposts" and "duties" were understood in 1787 to be exactions upon imports or importation as such. Bolstered by its perusal of Crosskey's interpretation of the "True Meaning of the Imports and Exports Clause,"[66] the Court concluded that there was sufficient ambiguity in the language of the Clause to preclude a construction that would not further its objectives, as prohibition of nondiscriminatory ad valorem property taxation would not.

It remained only for the Court to explain the error of its previous ways. *Brown v. Maryland* was precisely the type of case to which the Import-Export Clause was directed. It involved a fee levied by a coastal state on importers for a license they were required to obtain before selling within the state. Since such a fee was equivalent to a discriminatory tax on the goods themselves, which fell squarely within the Clause's prohibition, it could not stand. Although the Court in *Brown* devised the celebrated "original package" test as an

---

'Imports and Exports,' except through the accidents of different tax-days upon transported goods, in the state of their origin and destination; and from any unfairness arising from this, the taxpayer ordinarily can escape by his own foresight and good management."

[64] U.S. CONST. Art. 1, § 8, cl. 1.   [65] 423 U.S. at 290–91.

[66] CROSSKEY, note 12 *supra*, at 295. Other aspects of Crosskey's views on the Import-Export Clause are inconsistent with existing constitutional doctrine. Crosskey believed that the Import-Export Clause applied to interstate "imports" as well as those shipped from abroad, *id*. at 296–304, a view apparently shared by Chief Justice Marshall. See Brown v. Maryland, 12 Wheat. at 449. But the Court rejected this interpretation in Woodruff v. Parham, 8 Wall. 123 (1868). Crosskey contended that "[t]he changed usage of "imports" and "exports," in modern times, has effectively concealed that the old tax barriers to trade between state and state were, in fact, specifically dealt with; it has therefore given to Justice Miller's strange opinion about the Imports and Exports Clause, in the *Woodruff* case, a wholly undeserved and increasing respectability." CROSSKEY, note 12 *supra*, at 323.

evidentiary tool for determining when imported goods had lost their status as imports and thus the protection of the Clause, this was but one of the situations in which it indicated that the prohibition would not apply. The other was when the particular state tax was not a proscribed "impost" or "duty," a point the *Michelin* Court had taken some pains to make and one which it was now prepared to find "clearly implied" in *Brown*.[67] In *Low v. Austin*,[68] however, the Court had, with "no analysis,"[69] ignored "the language and objectives of the Import-Export Clause, and . . . the limited nature of the holding in *Brown*,"[70] misread the "original package" doctrine as applying to a nondiscriminatory ad valorem property tax,[71] and held that such a levy fell within the scope of the Clause's prohibition.[72] *Low*, it followed, had been incorrectly decided and was therefore overruled.

Finally, there was the matter of disposing of the case the parties had litigated, which the Court accomplished in a brief paragraph. The Gwinnett County property tax was nondiscriminatory on its face and no contention was made that it was being discriminatorily applied. The only other inquiry indicated by the Court's analysis was whether the tires were still in transit. The record shed little light on this issue,[73] and the state courts had made no findings regarding it. The Supreme Court, apparently unperturbed by the fact that the parties had directed most of their attention to questions of packaging and had been given no opportunity to develop, in light of the Court's

---

[67] 423 U.S. at 298.   [69] 423 U.S. at 294.   [71] *Id.* at 282.

[68] 13 Wall. 29 (1872).   [70] *Id.* at 298.

[72] The Court added that the Court in *Low* had compounded its errors in misreading *Brown* by misreading Chief Justice Taney's views in *The License Cases*, 5 How. 504, 573 (1847), as well. 423 U.S. at 299–301. Taney had indicated his agreement with Marshall that "goods imported, while they remain in the hands of the importer, in the form and shape in which they were brought into the country, can in no just sense be regarded as a part of that mass of property in the State usually taxed for the support of the State government." 5 How. at 575. The *Low* opinion had seized upon this language in support of its conclusion. 13 Wall. at 33–34. Taney, however, had gone on to distinguish a tax on imports as such from a tax on all property owners, noting that "the importing merchant is liable to this assessment like any other citizen, and is chargeable according to the amount of his property, whether it consists of money engaged in trade, or of imported goods which he proposes to sell," 5 How. at 576. The Court in *Low* did not refer to this passage.

[73] There appears to be nothing in the record regarding the average length of time a tire remains in the Gwinnett County warehouse, a fact that would seem to have a critical bearing on the question whether the goods are in transit.

new wisdom, a factual record and legal arguments on the issue,[74] decided the question summarily:[75]

> Petitioner's tires in this case were no longer in transit. They were stored in a distribution warehouse from which petitioner conducted a wholesale operation, taking orders from franchised dealers and filling them from a constantly replenished inventory. The warehouse was operated no differently than would be a distribution warehouse utilized by a wholesaler dealing solely in domestic goods.

The Court's terse treatment of what turned out to be the critical factual issue in the case contrasts strikingly with its leisurely and discursive exploration of the historical issues raised. Whether this makes *Michelin* an uncertain guide to the future is the question to which I now turn.

II. State Taxation of Imports after Michelin

A. THE ANALYTICAL FRAMEWORK

In the wake of *Michelin*, courts confronting a taxpayer's claim under the Import-Export Clause that a state tax constitutes a prohibited "impost" or "duty" on "imports" will be operating in a new decision-making framework. Prior to *Michelin* the central aim of the vast majority of judicial inquiries into such a contention was to locate the imported goods in time and space in the context of their intended use to determine whether they had retained their distinctive character as imports.[76] While the nature of the exaction at issue was sometimes examined in the course of such an inquiry,[77] this was generally no more than a secondary consideration. *Michelin* suggests that these analytical priorities should be reordered.

A court's first task should henceforth be to determine whether the

---

[74] The parties had taken occasion to draw conflicting inferences from the record whether the "flow of import distribution" terminated at the Gwinnett County warehouse, *compare* Reply Brief for Petitioner, p. 9, *with* Brief for Respondent, p. 13, or whether the imported tires continued to "flow out from Michelin's warehouse to tire dealers scattered throughout six states." Reply Brief for Petitioner, p. 9.

[75] 423 U.S. at 302.

[76] See, *e.g.,* cases cited *supra,* at notes 27–35.

[77] See, *e.g.,* May v. New Orleans, 178 U.S. 496 (1900).

levy in question is in fact an "impost" or "duty" within the meaning of the Import-Export Clause. If it is not, no consequence attaches to whether the goods have lost their status as "imports." To
be sure, one could argue that if goods have lost their status as "imports," no consequence attaches to whether they have been subjected to an "impost" or "duty." But it seems clear that the purposes
of the Clause may be more faithfully served by pursuing the first line
of analysis rather than—or at least prior to—the second. As the
Court's opinion in *Michelin* demonstrates, one can rationally and
systematically examine the legality of a challenged levy in light of
the objectives of the Clause. By contrast, the Court's efforts over the
past 150 years to delineate the scope of the Clause's protection by
reference to whether goods had retained their status as imports have
met with limited success,[78] and, indeed, have led to the very error
that *Michelin* has sought to correct. Although it might be postulated
that the Court's past failures in this regard were due simply to the
lack of attention it paid to the purposes of the Clause and not to any
inherent weakness in the structure of its analysis, those purposes
seem capable of being more sensibly related to the character of an
exaction than to the character of imported goods.[79]

It should be emphasized that this initial inquiry is not to be narrowly limited to the textual question whether the exaction at issue
is an "impost" or "duty" as Professor Crosskey—and now, it seems,
the Court—have construed those terms. For even after strongly in-
timating that a nondiscriminatory ad valorem property tax did not
fall within the wording of the Import-Export Clause's prohibi-

---

[78] See Dakin, note 32 *supra;* Early & Weitzman, note 12 *supra;* Powell, note 11
supra; Trickett, note 35 *supra.*

[79] An attempt to restructure the inquiry in *Michelin* by focusing on the question
whether the tires retained their status as imports suggests some of the problems involved. Instead of asking whether a nondiscriminatory ad valorem property tax
would undermine the federal government's regulation of foreign relations, deprive
it of expected revenues, or interfere with the free flow of imported goods among
the states, one would ask whether a tax on tires stored in a Gwinnett County warehouse under the circumstances described above, see text *supra,* at notes 13–19, would
do so. Without referring to the nature of the exaction involved it is difficult to
devise an analytically satisfactory method of approaching the issue. One could,
perhaps, inquire whether such goods in their particular form and commercial context were goods of the type over which the federal government was intended to
have exclusive regulation, or from which it expected to derive revenue, or upon
which a state tax might interfere with the free flow of imported goods among the
states. Yet the form-and-commercial-context criterion provides a much less precise
basis for analysis than the words of a state tax statute.

tion,[80] the Court makes it clear that whatever ambiguity there might be in those terms,[81] a nondiscriminatory property tax imposed on goods no longer in transit is not forbidden by the Clause. The provision is not to be construed "to embrace taxation that does not create the evils the Clause was specifically intended to eliminate."[82]

The controlling question, then, at this stage of the analysis is whether a challenged tax disserves the underlying purposes of the Import-Export Clause. In theory, this could require an undertaking to determine whether the imposition of the tax at issue would threaten the federal government's exclusive regulation of foreign commerce, divert anticipated federal import revenues to the states, or interfere with the free flow of imported goods among the states.[83] As a practical matter, however, a court may accomplish the same thing by undertaking the more manageable task of determining whether the exaction discriminates against imported goods on the basis of their foreign origin. The answer to the latter question will provide the answer to the former, as the Supreme Court's own opinion reveals. For the Court appears in effect to have translated the former considerations into the single operational issue of discrimination. Thus, in determining whether a nondiscriminatory ad valorem property tax would offend the objectives noted above, the Court rooted its conclusion in the facts that "such a tax does not fall on imports as such because of their place of origin,"[84] "cannot be selectively imposed and increased so as substantially to impair or prohibit importation,"[85] and is not "directed solely at imported goods."[86]

If a court concludes that the levy at issue does not discriminate against imported goods on the basis of their foreign origin, the Supreme Court's opinion plainly indicates that there is still a further question to be considered, namely, whether the goods are still in transit through the state. The doctrinal basis for this inquiry is unclear. The Court suggests a number of times that the issue whether an exaction is an "impost" or "duty" within the meaning of the Clause can be determined simply by examining its terms and without regard to its application to particular facts, such as whether goods

---

[80] 423 U.S. at 290–94.

[81] Id. at 293.

[82] Id. at 293–94.

[83] Id. at 283–90.

[84] Id. at 286.

[85] Id. at 288.

[86] Ibid.

are in transit. Thus the Court states that "a nondiscriminatory ad valorem property tax is not the type of state exaction which the Framers of the Constitution or the Court in *Brown* had in mind as being an 'impost' or 'duty,' "[87] and that "prohibition of nondiscriminatory ad valorem property taxation would not further the objectives of the Import-Export Clause."[88] Yet, the Court unmistakably confines its holding to petitioner's tires which were "no longer in transit."[89] Moreover, it specifically observes that insofar as there is any conflict between the preservation of the free flow of imported goods among the states and the imposition of a nondiscriminatory ad valorem property tax, the Clause's purpose "may be secured merely by prohibiting the assessment of even nondiscriminatory property taxes on goods which are merely in transit through the State when the tax is assessed."[90] Whether the Court is saying that an exaction not otherwise an "impost" or "duty" becomes one when imposed upon goods in transit or, alternatively, that there is a "protected penumbra"[91] of guarantees beyond the explicit terms of the Clause that would bar such an exaction,[92] a court must consider this issue in examining a taxpayer's claim that a state tax is a prohibited tax on imports, if it has concluded that the levy does not discriminate against such goods.[93]

On the other hand, if a court concludes that a levy is in fact an "impost" or "duty," there remains in principle the question whether the levy has been imposed upon an "import." This would presumably trigger the application of the "original package" doctrine and related criteria for determining whether particular goods have retained their distinctive character as imports. Notwithstanding the Court's restructured approach to the underlying issue, it did nothing to discredit the evidentiary tests for drawing the line between "im-

---

[87] *Id*. at 283.

[88] *Id*. at 293. See also *id*. at 282, 286, 301.

[89] *Id*. at 302.

[90] *Id*. at 290.

[91] Griswold v. Connecticut, 381 U.S. 479, 487 (1965) (Goldberg, J., concurring).

[92] It is apparent that the Court finds this authority somewhere in the Import-Export Clause because it notes in the margin that such a levy "would also be invalid under traditional Commerce Clause analysis." 423 U.S. at 290 n.11. It may be worth recalling in this context that the Court explicitly declined to reach the question whether Michelin's tires had lost their status as imports, even while concluding that they were no longer in transit. See 423 U.S. at 279, 302.

[93] The criteria for making this determination are discussed *infra*, at notes 120–42.

ports" and "the mass of property in the country."[94] Nevertheless, in light of the Court's analysis of the nature of an "impost" or "duty" —now confined essentially to those taxes discriminating against imports by virtue of their foreign origin[95]—the range of application of these tests will be much more limited.[96] One could even contend that it would be a definitional impossibility to have an "impost" or "duty" that was not imposed upon an "import"—thus doing away altogether with the need for the various evidentiary tests. If the Court was in fact convinced by Crosskey's "persuasive demonstration that the words 'imposts' and 'duties' as used in 1787 had meanings well understood to be exactions upon imported goods as imports,"[97] the determination that a tax was an "impost" or "duty" would carry with it a rather strong implication that the goods in question were "imports." While the Court did not go this far, it is plain that the significance of those tests designed to aid in ascertaining when an import ceases to be an import has been greatly diminished. Moreover, the Court makes it clear that there is ample doctrinal authority to invalidate any tax effectively discriminating against imports regardless of mechanical distinctions based on the timing of the levy[98] or the form of the goods.[99]

B. DECISION-MAKING

Michelin teaches that nondiscriminatory ad valorem property taxes are not "imposts" or "duties" within the meaning of the Import-Export Clause, at least when the goods sought to be taxed are not in transit. At the same time, *Michelin* raises two key questions that will require judicial resolution on a case-by-case basis. First, whether other types of state taxes constitute "imposts" or

---

[94] *Brown,* 12 Wheat. at 441. Indeed, it reaffirmed them, but in the context of its revised analysis. 423 U.S. at 287, 296–97.

[95] But see text *supra,* at notes 87–92.

[96] Indeed, most cases in recent years involving challenges to state taxes as forbidden levies on imports have arisen under nondiscriminatory ad valorem property taxes. See notes 100–01 *infra.* Assuming no discriminatory application, an importer will most likely be limited to the claim that the goods are still in transit insofar as this category of exactions is concerned.

[97] 423 U.S. at 290–91; see also *id.* at 297–98.

[98] *Id.* at 288 n.7.

[99] *Id.* at 297.

"duties" as *Michelin* has construed those terms. Second, whether particular goods are "in transit."

1. *"Imposts" or "duties."* As the preceding discussion suggests, *Michelin* seems to provide both an analytical framework and substantive guidelines for determining whether particular state taxes are "imposts" or "duties." Although most cases in recent years involving state taxation of imports have arisen under nondiscriminatory ad valorem property taxes[100] and are thus specifically controlled in this respect by *Michelin*'s holding,[101] nonproperty taxes have been[102] and will no doubt continue to be the focus of such controversies. It may therefore be instructive to examine one or two earlier decisions of the Supreme Court involving challenges to nonproperty taxes under the Import-Export Clause to observe the application of *Michelin*'s new learning in this context. The two most recent Supreme Court cases involving successful challenges to nonproperty taxes on the grounds that the taxes violated the prohibition against laying "imposts" or "duties" on imports are *Anglo-Chilean Nitrate Sales Corp. v. Alabama*[103] and *Department of Revenue v. James B. Beam Distilling Co.*[104]

In the *Anglo-Chilean* case, the taxpayer, a New York corporation qualified to do business in Alabama, was engaged in the importation of nitrate through Mobile and other ports. The nitrate was brought into Mobile in hundred-pound bags and stored in a public warehouse in the original packages until sold and delivered to customers. The parties agreed that the "landing, storage and sale of the

---

[100] Of the Court's three latest opinions dealing with the question of state taxation of imports, two, *Michelin* and *Youngstown Sheet & Tube*, have involved nondiscriminatory ad valorem property taxes. The other, Department of Revenue v. James B. Beam Distilling Co., 377 U.S. 341 (1964), is considered *infra*, at notes 113–19. Over the same time period, the vast majority of state court cases dealing with state taxation of imports have likewise involved nondiscriminatory ad valorem property taxes. See, *e.g.*, CCH STATE TAX CASES [1958–75 Transfer Binders] (13 of 16 cases there reported dealing with state taxation of imports involve nondiscriminatory ad valorem property taxes).

[101] The reference to *Michelin*'s holding is not intended to embrace the question whether particular goods are in transit.

[102] See, *e.g.*, Volkswagen Pacific, Inc. v. City of Los Angeles, 7 Cal.3d 48 (1972) (franchise tax); Caterpillar Tractor Co. v. Department of Revenue, 47 Ill.2d 278 (1971) (use tax); Miehle Printing Press and Mfg. Co. v. Department of Revenue, 18 Ill.2d 445 (1960) (sales tax); Citroen Cars Corp. v. City of New York, 30 N.Y.2d 300 (1972) (franchise tax).

[103] 288 U.S. 218 (1933).   [104] 377 U.S. 341 (1964).

nitrate . . . [were] the only transactions in Alabama in which appellant is concerned."[105] Alabama's corporate franchise tax statute provided then, substantially as it does now, that "every corporation organized under the laws of this State . . . shall pay annually to the State an annual franchise tax of Two Dollars ($2.00) on each One Thousand Dollars of its capital stock"[106] and that "every corporation organized under the laws of any other state, nation, or territory, and doing business in this State . . . shall pay annually to the State an annual franchise tax of Two Dollars ($2.00) on each One Thousand Dollars of the actual amount of capital employed in this State."[107] Under the latter provision, Alabama assessed its franchise tax against Anglo-Chilean, measured by the value of its nitrate stored in Alabama.

The taxpayer challenged the exaction under both the Import-Export and Commerce Clauses, and the Supreme Court sustained the challenge on both grounds.[108] With regard to the former contention, the Court stated:[109]

> The right to import the nitrate included the right to sell it in the original bags while it remained the property of appellant and before it lost its distinctive character as an import. State prohibition of such sales would take from appellant the very rights in respect of importation that are conferred by the Constitution and laws of the United States. Alabama was powerless, without the consent of Congress, to tax the nitrate before such sales or to require appellant by the payment of occupation or franchise tax or otherwise to purchase from it the privilege of selling goods so imported and handled.

The question is whether such reasoning can survive *Michelin*. The answer is probably negative. The tax had none of the vices that the Court identified as characteristic of "imposts" and "duties." It did not fall on imports as such because of their foreign origin,

---

[105] 288 U.S. at 225.

[106] Section 53 of Act No. 163, Ala. General Acts, 1927, p. 176, now ALA. CODE tit. 51, § 347 (1958, Supp. 1973). The rate has been increased from $2.00 to $3.00.

[107] Section 54 of Act No. 163, Ala. General Acts, 1927, p. 176, now ALA. CODE tit. 51, § 348 (1958, Supp. 1973).

[108] It is questionable whether the Court's Commerce Clause analysis in *Anglo-Chilean* is consistent with modern precedents in this area. See Hellerstein, note 62 *supra*, at 176–92.

[109] 288 U.S. at 225–26.

but rather fell on all profit-making foreign corporations, regardless
of their business, and was measured by their capital employed in the
state regardless of its nature. It could not be selectively imposed and
increased so as substantially to impair or prohibit importation since
any increase would necessarily impinge equally on other foreign
corporations doing business in the state, whatever the nature of
their business. And it was not directed solely at imported goods as
is evident from the face of the statute. Furthermore, it was clear that
the Alabama taxing scheme did not discriminate against foreign corporations, although this fact in itself would not support an Import-
Export Clause objection however objectionable it might be under
the Commerce Clause. As Justice Frankfurter noted, the tax which
the Court struck down in *Anglo-Chilean Corp.* was a "non-discriminatory ta[x] which fell equally on imported and domestic goods
similarly situated."[110] A nondiscriminatory franchise tax imposed
upon all foreign corporations doing business in the state measured by
the value of the capital there employed is therefore not "the type of
state exaction which the Framers of the Constitution or the Court
in *Brown* had in mind as being an 'impost' or 'duty.' "[111] The possibility remains, however, that the tax would nonetheless be barred
under the Import-Export Clause on the basis of an 'in transit" or
equivalent[112] limitation.

In *James Beam*, a liquor distributor imported whiskey into the
United States from Scotland and stored it in a Kentucky warehouse
prior to sale on the domestic market. A Kentucky statute provided:
"No person shall ship or transport or cause to be shipped or transported into the state any distilled spirits from points without the state
without first obtaining a permit from the department and paying a
tax of ten cents on each proof gallon contained in the shipment."[113]
Pursuant to the statute, the Kentucky tax authorities required James
Beam to pay a tax of 10 cents on each proof gallon of whiskey it
had imported from Scotland. It was agreed that "the tax was collected while the whiskey remained in unbroken packages in the
hands of the original importer and prior to resale or use by the
importer."[114]

---

[110] *Youngstown Sheet & Tube*, 358 U.S. at 574 (Frankfurter, J., dissenting).

[111] 423 U.S. at 283.

[112] See text *infra*, at notes 120–42 and especially text at notes 140–42 and note 142.

[113] Quoted 377 U.S. at 342.   [114] 377 U.S. at 342.

The taxpayer contended that the Kentucky levy constituted a proscribed "impost" or "duty" on "imports." The critical issue in the case was whether the Twenty-first Amendment[115] had lowered the barriers of the Import-Export Clause with respect to state taxation of intoxicants.[116] In the course of an opinion holding that it had not, the Court stated:[117]

> The tax here in question is clearly of a kind prohibited by the Export-Import Clause. *Brown* v. *Maryland*. . . . As this Court stated almost a century ago in *Low* v. *Austin*, . . . a case involving a California *ad valorem* tax on wine imported from France and stored in original cases in a San Francisco warehouse, "the goods imported do not lose their character as imports, . . . until they have passed from the control of the importer or been broken up by him from their original cases. Whilst retaining their character as imports, a tax upon them, in any shape, is within the constitutional prohibition."

While it is apparent that this reasoning cannot survive *Michelin*, the result is not likely to be affected. In contrast to the tax at issue in the *Anglo-Chilean* case, the Kentucky levy had many of the earmarks of an "impost" or "duty." It fell on imports as such, although the statutory classification was broad enough to include out-of-state as well as foreign goods. It could be selectively imposed and increased to impair or prohibit importation, although, again, the impairment or prohibition would extend to out-of-state as well as foreign goods. And it was discriminatory on its face, directed solely at goods imported from abroad or out-of-state.[118] Under these circumstances, and in light of the undisputed facts relating to the status of the whiskey as an import, the conclusion that the Kentucky

---

[115] "The transportation or importation into any State, Territory, or possession of the United States for delivery or use therein of intoxicating liquors, in violation of the laws thereof, is hereby prohibited." U.S. Const. Amend XXI, § 2.

[116] The Court had "made clear in the early years following adoption of the Twenty-first Amendment that by virtue of its provisions a State is totally unconfined by traditional Commerce Clause limitations when it restricts the importation of intoxicants destined for use, distribution, or consumption within its borders." Hostetter v. Idlewild Bon Voyage Liquor Corp., 377 U.S. 324, 330 (1964).

[117] 377 U.S. at 343.

[118] Despite the fact that the statute was facially discriminatory, the suggestion has been made that it might not have been so in application since Kentucky imposed an equivalent tax on the manufacture of liquor. Note, *The Supreme Court, 1963 Term*, 78 Harv. L. Rev. 143, 239 n.16 (1964). The Court, however, showed no awareness of this fact. *Ibid.*

levy as applied in *James Beam* violated the Import-Export Clause would probably command a majority of votes in the Supreme Court today.[119]

2. *"In transit."* Unlike the guidance the Court's opinion provides for making the determination whether a tax is an "impost" or a "duty," it provides virtually no assistance with regard to the determination whether goods are still "in transit." The Court made only three brief references to this issue. It noted that the historical purposes of the Import-Export Clause did not embrace a nondiscriminatory ad valorem property tax imposed on imported goods that were "no longer in import transit";[120] that insofar as the Clause was designed to prevent the exactions of transit fees on the privilege of moving through a state, this purpose could be secured by prohibiting the assessment of such taxes on goods that were "merely in transit through the State when the tax is assessed";[121] and that Michelin's tires were "no longer in transit,"[122] having been stored in its warehouse to meet the demands of its wholesale operation.

It is conceivable, of course, that the Court provided no further guidance on this point because it felt none was necessary or useful. After all, the term is hardly new to the law,[123] and the question whether goods are in transit almost inevitably leads to nice distinctions between cases based on their particular facts about which generalizations are of little value. Nevertheless, because the *Michelin* opinion did not employ the term with complete consistency, the Court's failure to elaborate its discussion raises several issues.

The most important is whether the Court intended to draw a distinction between the generally accepted meaning of the term "in transit"—in the course of transportation from a specific origin to a

---

[119] One may not be able to determine whether a levy discriminates against foreign goods simply by examining the terms of a statute. Thus a tax upon a particular category of goods, which in fact are produced only abroad, though nondiscriminatory on its face may discriminate against such goods unless an equivalent tax is imposed on different but competing goods produced within the taxing state. See Note, *National Power to Control State Discrimination against Foreign Goods and Persons: A Study in Federalism,* 12 Stan. L. Rev. 355, 360–62 (1960). Such discriminatory taxes would seem to be vulnerable to attack under either the Import-Export Clause or the Commerce Clause. See *id.* at 364; text, *infra,* at notes 166–70. An instructive discussion of a closely analogous problem arising under the General Agreement on Tariffs and Trade appears in Dam, The GATT: Law and International Economic Organization 116–21 (1970).

[120] 423 U.S. at 286.

[121] *Id.* at 290.

[122] *Id.* at 302.

[123] See, *e.g.,* 80 A.L.R.2d 445 (1961).

specific destination—and its meaning in the context of importation. One could argue, on the basis of the Court's reference to goods *"in import transit,"* that the Court had in mind a broader concept of transport journey than is ordinarily associated with the shipment of goods from one point to another. Drawing on Chief Justice Taney's language in *The License Cases*,[124] quoted with approval by the Court in *Youngstown Sheet & Tube*[125] and cited with approval in *Michelin*,[126] one could further contend that such "import transit" must be deemed to continue until the goods reach the point where they are to be used, consumed, or sold:[127]

> The immense amount of foreign products used and consumed in this country are imported, landed, and offered for sale in a few commercial cities, and a very small portion of them are intended or expected to be used in the State in which they are imported. . . . And while they are in the hands of the importer for sale, in the form and shape in which they were introduced, and in which they are intended to be sold, they may be regarded as merely *in transitu*, and on their way to the distant cities, villages, and country for which they are destined, and where they are expected to be used and consumed, and for the supply of which they were in truth imported. And a tax upon them while in this condition, for State purposes, whether by direct assessment, or indirectly, by requiring a license to sell, would be hardly more justifiable in principle than a transit duty upon the merchandise when passing through a State.

On the basis of such reasoning and authority, one could make a case for the proposition that, whatever meaning "in transit" may have in other contexts, "import transit" continues until goods have reached the destination of their intended use, consumption, or sale whether or not they were stored or otherwise deliberately delayed en route.

There are, however, several reasons why such an interpretation of the Court's opinion should be rejected. First, judging solely by the Court's language in *Michelin* set forth above, there is no indication that it intended to draw the proposed distinction or to accord its single use of the term "import transit" any special significance. Second, *Michelin*'s reading of the purpose of the Import-Export Clause—to prohibit discrimination against imports—carries with it

---

124 5 How. at 575–76.

125 358 U.S. at 540 n.6.

126 423 U.S. at 290 n.10.

127 5 How. at 575–76.

no implication that it should be construed to justify discrimination in their favor; and to provide goods upon an import journey with protection not afforded similarly situated goods upon an interstate journey would permit the latter type of discrimination. Indeed, the Court's observation that such an assessment upon goods "in transit" would otherwise be invalid under traditional Commerce Clause analysis[128] affirmatively suggests that it did not intend to bestow upon imported goods in "import transit" an immunity from taxation unavailable to domestic goods in "interstate transit." Third, the Court in *Michelin* specifically cautions against misreading Taney's opinion in *The License Cases*,[129] and notes that Taney, consistently with the Court's own view, had made it "crystal clear that the prohibition applied only to state exactions upon imports *as imports*."[130] Finally, the Court's rejection in *Michelin* of the assertion that the tires were still in transit—in the flow of import distribution to their final destination at franchised tire dealers scattered throughout six states[131]—is further evidence that the term is not to be given an expanded reading in this context.

Even assuming that the Court did not intend to attribute any special meaning to the term "in transit" for purposes of the determination whether imports are immune from state taxation, there is still the question where one ought to look for guidance in applying it in this framework. A logical place to begin is with cases involving imports. But there is a dearth of relevant precedent—"the controversies in this Court over the meaning of [the Import-Export Clause] have numbered less than a dozen in our entire history"[132] and what precedent there is[133] may be somewhat suspect after *Michelin*.[134] Probably a more fruitful source of assistance are cases arising under the Commerce Clause, not simply because there are more of them[135]

---

[128] 423 U.S. at 290 n.11.

[129] 423 U.S. at 299–301. Admittedly, the specific language of the Court referred to was different from that quoted in the text, but the warning against drawing unwarranted inferences from Taney's opinion in light of his full views on the matter was not a narrow one. See also note 72 *supra*.

[130] 423 U.S. at 300.   [131] Brief for Petitioner, pp. 5–6, 10.

[132] *Youngstown Sheet & Tube Co.*, 358 U.S. at 553 (Frankfurter, J., dissenting).

[133] See, *e.g.*, The License Cases, 5 How. at 575–76.

[134] See text *supra*, at note 129.

[135] With respect to controversies arising under the Commerce Clause, the Court has noted: "This Court alone has handed down some three hundred full-dress opinions spread through slightly more than that number of our reports." Northwestern States Portland Cement Co. v. Minnesota, 358 U.S. 450, 457–58 (1959).

but more pertinently because the Court itself pointed to "traditional Commerce Clause analysis" as an alternative basis for finding that an assessment upon goods that are merely in transit would be constitutionally invalid.[136]

A leading case, *Minnesota v. Blasius*,[137] involving a state property tax, sets forth the governing principles:[138]

> [T]he States may not tax property in transit in interstate commerce. But, by reason of a break in the transit, the property may come to a rest within a State and become subject to the power of the State to impose a nondiscriminatory property tax. . . . The "crucial question," in determining whether the State's taxing power may thus be exerted, is that of "continuity of transit." . . .
>
> If the interstate movement has not begun, the mere fact that such a movement is contemplated does not withdraw the property from the State's power to tax it. . . . If the interstate movement has begun, it may be regarded as continuing, so as to maintain the immunity of the property from state taxation, despite temporary interruptions due to the necessities of the journey or for the purpose of safety and convenience in the course of the movement. . . . The question is always one of substance, and in each case it is necessary to consider the particular occasion or purpose of the interruption during which the tax is sought to be levied. . . .
>
> Where property has come to rest within a State, being held there at the pleasure of the owner, for disposal or use, so that he may dispose of it either within the State, or for shipment elsewhere, as his interest dictates, it is deemed to be a part of the general mass of property within the State and is thus subject to its taxing power.

A considerable amount of judicial energy has been devoted to the implementation of these principles, and there is consequently a substantial and apposite body of case law[139] to guide courts and state tax administrators[140] in determining whether imported goods are

---

[136] 423 U.S. at 290 n.11.   [137] 290 U.S. 1 (1933).   [138] *Id.* at 9–10.

[139] See, *e.g.*, 71 AM. JUR.2d §§ 245–47 (1973); 171 A.L.R. 283 (1947).

[140] In fact, the Washington State Department of Revenue instructed its county assessors that the determination whether goods are moving in foreign commerce should now be made under the same "physical movement" test as is used to determine the taxability of goods moving in interstate commerce. Washington Department of Revenue Property Tax Bulletin No. 76-2 (25 March 1976), reported in *Report Bulletin* No. 38, ¶ 38.4, P-H STATE AND LOCAL TAXES (All States Unit) (13 April 1976).

still "in transit." While the question whether goods are "in transit" is generally regarded as a limitation on property taxation,[141] it has its analogues in the context of nonproperty taxation where the issue may be whether there is a taxable "moment" or "event" in the state.[142] In short, the standards developed under the Commerce Clause should provide appropriate criteria for resolving the "in transit" issue under the Import-Export Clause.

C. THE IMPACT OF MICHELIN: WHO WANTS TO TAX IMPORTS?

The day after the *Michelin* decision was handed down, the New York Times carried a front-page story with the headline: "High Court Removes Curb on Nonfederal Import Tax . . . Justices Open Way for States, Cities and Counties to Increase Revenues."[143] Soon thereafter, the leading tax services reported what to many of their subscribers must have been the same gloomy message: "U.S. High Court Expands States' Right to Tax Imports";[144] "U.S. Supreme Court Ruling Broadens Power of States to Tax Imports."[145] Moreover, it was predicted that "many areas will revise their tax laws, to take fullest advantage of the implications of . . . [the] ruling."[146]

That *Michelin* has broadened the states' power to tax imports is indisputable. By narrowly defining "imposts" and "duties," the Court has paved the way for the imposition of nondiscriminatory state levies upon imports that were previously impermissible. And this is more than an abstract point of constitutional theory. The proposition that nondiscriminatory ad valorem property taxes upon goods no longer in transit fall outside the pale of the Import-Export Clause had a direct impact outside Gwinnett County upon litigation

---

[141] See, *e.g.*, *Blasius*, 290 U.S. 1; HARTMAN, STATE TAXATION OF INTERSTATE COMMERCE 73–79 (1953); *cf.* the excerpt from Chief Justice Taney's opinion in *The License Cases*, quoted in the text *supra*, at note 127.

[142] See, *e.g.*, Southern Pacific Co. v. Gallagher, 306 U.S. 167 (1939). Indeed, these decisions often rely on their property tax analogues. *Id*. at 177; Independent Warehouses, Inc. v. Scheele, 331 U.S. 70, 80 (1947); Nashville, C. & St. L. Ry. v. Wallace, 288 U.S. 249, 266 (1933). See HARTMAN, note 141 *supra*, at 138.

[143] N.Y. Times, 15 Jan. 1976, p. 1, cols. 1–2.

[144] *Report Bulletin* No. 27, ¶ 27.1, P-H STATE AND LOCAL TAXES (All States Unit) (20 Jan. 1976).

[145] *Report Letter* No. 209, p. 1, CCH STATE TAX CAS. REP. (All States) (10 Feb. 1976).

[146] N.Y. Times, 15 Jan. 1976, p. 20, col. 7.

involving not only *Michelin* itself[147] but other importers as well.[148] Furthermore, *Michelin* induced changes at the administrative level. The Indiana State Tax Board announced that *Michelin* would be interpreted to render imports subject to its property tax as of March 1976 and that the regulation pertaining to import exemptions would no longer be applicable.[149] The Ohio Tax Commissioner issued a bulletin advising county auditors to commence levying its personal property tax against all imports under specified conditions.[150]

Yet, not every state legislature or state tax authority jumped on the bandwagon to exercise its newly revealed tax power. The Maryland legislature enacted a law allowing counties and Baltimore City to exempt from taxation imports in the hands of the importer in their original package.[151] The South Carolina authorities assured taxpayers that *Michelin* would precipitate no change in that state's rule determining when imports acquire a taxable situs in the state.[152] And the Illinois Attorney General issued an opinion declaring that *Michelin* would have no effect on the state statute exempting from taxation certain personal property when stored in its original package in Illinois.[153]

More important than these isolated examples, however, is the plain fact that many states and their subdivisions have never sought to tax imports to the full extent that they were constitutionally permitted to do so. Thus over thirty-five states have enacted "free port" laws allowing goods to be stored in the state on a tax-free basis under specified conditions that would frequently exempt imports within

---

[147] Michelin Tire Corp. v. County of San Mateo, 57 Cal. App.3d 332 (1976).

[148] See, *e.g.*, City of Farmers Branch v. Matsushita Electric Corp. of America, 537 S.W.2d 452 (Tex. 1976), *cert. denied*, 97 S. Ct. 164 (1976); City of Farmers Branch v. American Honda Motor Co., 537 S.W.2d 454 (Tex. 1976), *cert. denied*, 97 S. Ct. 161 (1976); Sears, Roebuck & Co. v. County of Kings, 59 Cal. App.3d 446 (1976); Ralston Purina Co. v. County of Los Angeles, 56 Cal. App.3d 547 (1976); Japan Food Corp. v. County of Sacramento, 56 Cal. App.3d 442 (1976).

[149] Indiana State Tax Board Bulletin No. 76-27 (13 Feb. 1976), reported in *Report Bulletin* No. 44, ¶ 44.10, P-H STATE AND LOCAL TAXES (All States Unit) (25 May 1976).

[150] Ohio Tax Commissioner's Bulletin No. 244 to All County Auditors, reported in 37 STATE TAX REV. No. 11, p. 8 (16 March 1976).

[151] Maryland Laws 1976, Ch. 621 (S.B. 1042).

[152] Opinion of Attorney General No. 112 (April 1976), reported in *Report Bulletin* No. 1, ¶1.11, P-H STATE AND LOCAL TAXES (All States Unit) (6 July 1976).

[153] Opinion of Attorney General No. NP-1125 (15 July 1976), reported in *Report Bulletin* No. 5, ¶5.9, P-H STATE AND LOCAL TAXES (All States Unit) (3 August 1976).

the state's constitutional taxing power.[154] The purposes behind one such law were described as follows:[155]

> Sponsors of the bill assert that its enactment will be beneficial to Oregon because Oregon is so geographically situated as to be a natural distribution point for commerce which either originates in or is destined to Washington, California and overseas points. . . .
>
> SB 424 is designed to enhance Oregon's status as a distribution center and to stimulate the state's economy. Its sponsors feel that its enactment will improve Oregon's competitive tax position and divert commerce through the state which otherwise would not accrue to Oregon.

It is hardly likely, given the underlying rationale for such provisions, that *Michelin* will trigger their wholesale repeal or revision. In addition, several states, most significantly New York and Pennsylvania, no longer even levy tangible personal property taxes,[156] the principal source of contemporary controversy over the states' power to tax imports.[157] The narrow holding of *Michelin* would therefore have no impact on existing taxing provisions in these states, and it is improbable that it would single-handedly provide the necessary impetus for the reintroduction of such taxes in these jurisdictions.

On balance, it is unlikely that many state legislatures will rush to take "fullest advantage" of the doctrinal changes wrought by *Michelin*, but the decision is likely to affect the results in cases under litigation[158] and to create a climate in which the expectations of taxpayers and the determinations of tax administrators will redound to the benefit of the public fisc.

---

[154] CCH STATE TAX GUIDE (All States) ¶ 20-100 (Chart of State Free Port Law Requirements) (1967). To qualify for free-port exemptions, goods generally must satisfy some or all of the following conditions: They must have an out-of-state origin and/or destination; they must be stored in a public or other facility not owned by the consignee or consignor; and they must remain in their original packages. *Id.* Such exemptions would embrace interstate "imports" as well.

[155] Ore. Sen. Tax Comm., Description of S.B. 424, quoted in Weyerhaeuser Co. v. State Tax Comm'n., 244 Ore. 561, 565–66 (1966). The act was adopted by the Oregon Legislature as Oregon Laws 1959, ch. 659, p. 1390 and now appears as O.R.S. 307.810–50 (1975).

[156] The others are Delaware and Hawaii.

[157] See note 100 *supra*. But not the only source. See note 102 *supra*.

[158] See cases cited *supra*, at note 148. The California Legislature, however, has enacted a statute denying retroactive application of the *Michelin* decision to personal property tax assessments prior to the 1976–77 assessment year. California Laws 1976, Ch. 335 (A.B. 3061), reported in 37 STATE TAX REV. No. 31, p. 2 (3 August 1976).

III. Final Thoughts on the Implications of Michelin

"It would entail a substantial revision of the Import-Export Clause," the Court has said, "to substitute for the prohibition against 'any' tax a prohibition against 'any discriminatory' tax."[159] In *Michelin,* the Court in effect does just that by construing "Imposts or Duties on Imports" as levies discriminating against imports on the basis of their foreign origin.[160] The caveat that even a nondiscriminatory property tax may not be imposed on goods still in transit and the possibility that the Court may modify its views when dealing with other types of exactions[161] provide some basis for arguing that the Court's about-face may be less than 180 degrees. Nevertheless, the Court's reevaluation of the purposes underlying the Clause and its consequent restructuring of the constitutional analysis lay the groundwork for a more rational approach to future disputes over state taxation of imports than we have seen in the past.[162]

The Court's opinion also establishes a fairer basis for limiting the power of the states to tax imports. Although discrimination in favor of the importing process may be justifiable on the grounds that it was "part and parcel of the federal bargain,"[163] it does not commend itself as a matter of equity. As the Court itself noted in reference to the costs of governmental services, "there is no reason why an importer should not bear his share of these costs along with his competitors handling only domestic goods."[164] Although the Court's comment was directed to ad valorem property taxation—which it characterized as "the *quid pro quo* for benefits actually conferred by the taxing State,"[165] the point has equal force in connection with other types of levies if one is concerned with equalizing the state and local tax burden on foreign and domestic goods. It is important, of course, that care be taken to assure that the imposition of even a nondiscriminatory levy does not threaten to saddle imports with a

---

[159] Richfield Oil Corp. v. State Board of Equalization, 329 U.S. 69, 76 (1946).

[160] Beyond its frequent reiteration of the point that nondiscriminatory ad valorem property taxes fall outside of the purview of the Clause, the Court at times broadens its reference to "nondiscriminatory taxes" generally, 423 U.S. at 290, 298, and at one point states that the Clause "cannot be read to accord imported goods preferential treatment that permits escape from uniform taxes imposed without regard to foreign origin for services which the State supplies." *Id.* at 287.

[161] *Cf.* Powell, note 11 *supra,* at 867.

[162] See text *supra,* at notes 78–79.

[163] Powell, note 11 *supra,* at 867.

[164] 423 U.S. at 287.

[165] *Id.* at 289.

cumulative tax burden not borne by equivalent domestic products. *Michelin*'s "in transit" limitation seems fashioned to serve just this purpose. And as we have seen, there is nothing to prevent the states from according imports favorable tax treatment if they choose to do so as a matter of their own fiscal policy, Still, as a principle of constitutional adjudication under the Import-Export Clause, the non-discrimination criterion represents a salutary solution both to the problems it was designed to resolve and to the problems its interpretation has created—discrimination against domestic goods.

If *Michelin* replaces the physical/temporal criteria with the non-discrimination principle as the central focus of the inquiry into the power of the states to tax imports, it raises two further questions that I will address here only briefly.

The first is whether there remains any significant difference between the standards governing the validity of a state tax upon imports under the Import-Export Clause and those governing its validity under the Commerce Clause. With the obvious exception of cases affected by the Twenty-first Amendment,[166] it would appear that there does not. Under either rubric, discriminatory levies against imports would be struck down and nondiscriminatory levies sustained unless imposed on goods in transit. And there is no reason to believe that the criteria for determining whether a levy discriminates against imports or is imposed upon goods in transit would be any different under one clause than under the other.[167] To be sure, there is language in earlier cases that the "absolute want of power to tax imports . . . until they [have] completely lost their character as such"[168] was to be distinguished from the more limited Commerce Clause restraint which "dealt with no positive and absolute inhibition against the exercise of the taxing power, but determined whether a particular exertion of that power by a State so operated upon inter-

---

[166] See text *supra*, at notes 115–16 and note 116.

[167] See Cook v. Pennsylvania, 97 U.S. 566, 574 (1878) (tax discriminating against foreign goods sold at auction invalid under Import-Export and Commerce Clauses), cited with approval at 423 U.S. 288 n.7; *id*. at 290 n.11. Even assuming an identity between Import-Export Clause and Commerce Clause criteria with respect to the validity of a state tax on imported goods, there may be some basis for arguing that the test of reasonableness of state legislation in the foreign commerce area is generally more stringent than in the interstate commerce field. See Note, note 119 *supra*, at 358.

[168] American Steel & Wire Co. v. Speed, 192 U.S. 500, 521 (1904).

state commerce as to amount to a regulation thereof."[169] Nevertheless, if the absolute prohibition of the Import-Export Clause's ban
against taxing imports is limited to discriminatory levies or to levies
upon goods in transit—as *Michelin* indicates—and if the limited
prohibition of the Commerce Clause is absolute with respect to such
levies—as traditional Commerce Clause analysis indicates[170]—then
the suggested distinction no longer has substance in this context.

The second question concerns the implications of *Michelin* with
regard to analysis of controversies over the power of states to tax
exports. Just two Terms ago, the Court in *Kosydar v. National Cash
Register Co.*[171] emphatically reaffirmed the "settled doctrine"[172] that
the "essential question" in such cases is the "narrow one: is the property upon which a tax has been sought to be imposed an 'export' ";[173]
that the "essential problem" is therefore "to decide whether a sufficient commencement of the process of exportation has occurred so
as to immunize the article at issue from state taxation";[174] and that
this depends on the factual inquiry whether the article has begun
"its physical entry into the stream of exportation."[175] There was
not the slightest hint that Ohio's nondiscriminatory ad valorem property tax there at issue might not be an "impost" or "duty" within
the meaning of the Import-Export Clause. Indeed, three decades
earlier the Court had explicitly rejected the argument that "the history of the Import-Export Clause shows that it was designed to prevent discriminatory taxes and not to preclude the levy of general
taxes applicable alike to all goods."[176] And it declined to "read the
prohibition against 'any' tax on exports as containing an implied
qualification."[177]

Since *Michelin* fails even to acknowledge the existence of this line
of authority, it is hazardous to speculate on where the opinion leaves
it. While we should recognize that the problems of judicial inter-

---

[169] *Ibid*. See also Sonneborn Bros. v. Cureton, 262 U.S. 506, 509–13 (1923); *Hooven
& Allison*, 324 U.S. at 655–66; *Richfield Oil*, 329 U.S. at 75–78.

[170] Halliburton Oil Well Cementing Co. v. Reily, 373 U.S. 64 (1963); Minnesota
v. Blasius, 290 U.S. 1 (1933); HARTMAN, note 141 *supra*, at 67–70, 73–78, 144.

[171] 417 U.S. 62 (1974).   [173] *Id*. at 66.

[172] *Id*. at 71.   [174] *Id*. at 67.

[175] *Id*. at 71. See generally Abramson, *State Taxation of Exports: The Stream of
Constitutionality*, 54 N.C. L. REV. 59 (1975)

[176] *Richfield Oil*, 329 U.S. at 76.   [177] *Id*. at 78.

pretation associated with taxation of imports are not symmetrical with those associated with taxation of exports,[178] it would appear that the two approaches are analytically incompatible. Nevertheless, there are a number of reasons for believing that *Michelin* will not seriously disturb the framework for determining whether a levy is a prohibited state tax on exports. First, there may be some basis for arguing that the prohibition against state taxes upon exports was part of a "larger design"[179] that included the limitation upon Congress that "No Tax or Duty shall be laid on Articles exported from any State."[180] Considered as a whole, this "design" may be viewed as having effected a more extensive limitation upon the states' power to tax exports than was accomplished with respect to imports.[181] Second, in contrast to the decisions involving state taxation of imports which were described by Justice Frankfurter as "a confusing series of conflicting cases amidst which the States must blindly move in determining the extent of their constitutional power to tax,"[182] the Court's decisions involving state taxation of exports have been commendably intelligible and consistent.[183] The Court may be unwilling to abandon a rule whose simple "virtues" it has so recently admired.[184] Finally, whether or not the doctrinal disparity between *Michelin* and the export cases is reconciled, the ultimate inquiry in the vast majority of cases will not be substantially different. Assuming that the tax in question is nondiscriminatory, as most taxes are, decision will turn on whether the goods are in "import transit"[185] or in "the export stream"[186] which amounts to essentially—though not

---

[178] As a practical matter, it would seem to be considerably easier to identify goods that have come from abroad than those that are heading there. The former will frequently have characteristics that readily distinguish them from the mass of domestic goods while the latter will not. The different problems in identification may provide a plausible explanation—though not necessarily a theoretical justification—for the use of different approaches to the issue of state taxation of imports and exports.

[179] 329 U.S. at 77.

[180] U.S. CONST. Art. 1, § 9, cl. 5.

[181] 329 U.S. at 76–78.

[182] *Youngstown Sheet & Tube*, 358 U.S. at 553. (Frankfurter, J., dissenting.)

[183] Abramson, note 175 *supra*, at 81.

[184] Kosydar v. National Cash Register Co., 417 U.S. 62, 71 (1974).

[185] 423 U.S. at 286.

[186] *Kosydar*, 417 U.S. at 71.

precisely[187]—the same question asked at different ends of the journey.[188]

IV. Conclusion

A century ago, the Supreme Court held in *Low v. Austin* that a nondiscriminatory ad valorem property tax levied upon French champagne stored in its original package violated the prohibition against laying "any Imposts or Duties on Imports." Last Term in *Michelin*, the Court decided that the imposition of such a tax upon French tires was valid whether or not they were stored in their original packages, since the Framers of the Import-Export Clause never intended to include exactions of this type within its scope. Perhaps we "arrive where we started And know the place for the first time."[189]

---

[187] See note 178 *supra*.

[188] See note 139 *supra*.

[189] Eliot, *Little Gidding*, in The Complete Poems and Plays 145 (1952).

MARY CORNELIA PORTER

THAT COMMERCE SHALL BE FREE:
A NEW LOOK AT THE OLD
LAISSEZ-FAIRE COURT

Shortly before his death, Justice Black warned that the Supreme
Court's support of the "new" substantive due process and equal protection would lead, willy-nilly, down the path taken by the dis-
credited laissez-faire Court.[1] Some students of the Court agree.[2]
Wallace Mendelson, for instance, fears that the protection of judicially (and thereby subjectively) determined "fundamental rights"

Mary Cornelia Porter is Associate Professor of Political Science, Barat College,
Lake Forest, Illinois.

[1] The "new" due process and equal protection concepts cover a wide range of
cases and propositions. For examples of the proliferating literature on the subject
see: Goodpaster, *The Constitution and Fundamental Rights*, 15 ARIZ. L. REV. 479
(1973); Graham, *Poverty and Substantive Due Process*, 12 ARIZ. L. REV. 1 (1970);
Gunther, *In Search of Evolving Doctrine on a Changing Court: A Model for a
Newer Equal Protection*, 86 HARV. L. REV. 1 (1972); Michelman, *On Protecting the
Poor through the Fourteenth Amendment*, 83 HARV. L. REV. 1 (1969); Tribe, *Toward
a Model of Roles in the Due Process of Life and Law*, 87 HARV. L. REV. 1 (1973);
Tussman and tenBroek, *The Equal Protection of the Laws*, 37 CALIF. L. REV. 341
(1949). For purposes of this article, emphasis is on the rights of those generally con-
sidered least able "to take care of themselves," welfare recipients and debtors subject
to garnishment and replevin procedures. For discussion of such cases see: Rosenheim,
Shapiro v. Thompson: "The Beggars are Coming to Town," 1969 SUPREME COURT
REVIEW 303; PIVEN & CLOWARD, REGULATING THE POOR: THE FUNCTIONS OF PUBLIC
WELFARE ch. 10 (1971); Countryman, *The Bill of Rights and the Bill Collector:
Sniadach v. Family Finance Corp.*, 15 ARIZ. L. REV. 521 (1973).

[2] Lee, *Mr. Herbert Spencer and the Bachelor Stockbroker: Kramer v. Union Free
School District No. 15*, 15 ARIZ. L. REV. 457 (1973); Winter, *Poverty, Economic
Equality, and the Equal Protection Clause*, 1972 SUPREME COURT REVIEW 41.

of those whose economic, social, and political resources are minimal (welfare recipients, for example, and debtors) amounts, just as did the earlier protection of corporations, to "government by judiciary."[3] Those who have urged the additional responsibilities on the Court appear equally troubled, but for a different reason—believing they must have a rationale which permits approval of the new, and continued disapproval of the old, economic activism.[4]

Whatever the merits of the arguments, and justification for the anxieties, on either side, the fact remains that the Court is behaving in a traditional manner. In the first place, as Philip Kurland observes, it has always acted "as a centripetal force, [modifying] the Constitution in order to sustain the enhancement of national authority and the despoliation of state power."[5] And indeed, the Warren/Burger Court's cautiously extended solicitude for "the poor" is tendered at the expense of state initiative, state fiscal considerations, and state standards of fair play. In the second place the Court, as has been frequently noted, does respond, within the limitations of the judicial process, to the great imperatives of the times. Two articles in the *Yale Law Journal*, written more than thirty years apart, make the point most tellingly. The Supreme Court, given the nature of the American polity, wrote Max Lerner during the depths of the great depression, could not have avoided the economic controversies which it has been asked to mediate. For:[6]

> [C]apitalism pushes ultimately before the Court the clashes of interest that are attendant on the growth of any economic system, with the displacement in each successive phase of elements that had been useful in previous phases, with the antagonisms it generates among those who are bearing its burdens and the rivalry among those who are dividing its spoils. . . . If it be

---

[3] Mendelson, *From Warren to Burger: The Rise and Decline of Substantive Equal Protection*, 66 Am. Pol. Sc. Rev. 1226 (1972). Boudin's *Government by Judiciary* (1932) is a disapproving description of "laissez-faire" jurisprudence.

[4] Gunther and Tribe, note 1 *supra*. "Substantive equal protection . . . suffers from quite the same defects and has itself created some uneasiness even among its proponents. For that reason, we witness the tragicomic phenomenon of both Justices and commentators nervously seeking to distinguish between what they are doing and the rejected and reviled substantive due process of another era." Winter, note 2 *supra*, at 100.

[5] Kurland, Politics, the Constitution, and the Warren Court 58 (1970).

[6] Lerner, *The Supreme Court and American Capitalism*, 42 Yale L.J. 668, 685 (1933).

added to this that modern capitalism is perhaps the least organic system of economic organization the world has seen . . . and that the American social and political structure within which it operates is perhaps more sprawling and heterogeneous than that of any other major capitalist society, some notion may be had of the confusion of interests and purposes out of which it is the task of the Court to bring certainty and uniformity.

Nor, wrote Charles Reich in 1964, should the Court duck the constitutional issues posed by the positive, or what he calls the "public interest" state:[7]

> The most clearly defined problem posed by government largess is the way it can be used to apply pressure against the exercise of constitutional rights. A first principle should be that government must have no power to "buy up" rights guaranteed by the Constitution. . . . The courts in recent times have gone part of the distance toward this principle. . . .
>
> [T]he time has come for us to remember what the framers of the Constitution knew so well—that "a power over a man's subsistence amounts to a power over his will." We cannot safely entrust our livelihoods and our rights to the discretion of authorities, examiners, boards of control. . . . We cannot permit any official or agency to pretend to sole knowledge of the public good. . . . If the individual is to survive in a collective society he must have protection against its ruthless pressures. There must be sanctuaries or enclaves where no majority can reach. . . . [W]e must try to build an economic basis for liberty today. . . . We must create a new property.

Since the Court is not, as Justice Black and Professor Mendelson have said, embarking on an entirely uncharted course, and since the contemporary economic activism should not, within the context of Court history, be particularly surprising, another "exhumation"[8] of the first substantive due process era might be in order. And upon reexamination it can be claimed, I think, that the Court did not single-mindedly shelter "the interests." Such protection as it gave corporations was, in actuality, the Court's (necessarily prescribed) way of acting as a national regulatory agency. And it did the job tolerably well. So, while there may be other, and perfectly good, reasons for

---

[7] Reich, *The New Property*, 73 YALE L.J. 733, 779–87 (1964).

[8] For an earlier, and most illuminating, "exhumation" see McCloskey, *Economic Due Process and the Supreme Court: An Exhumation and Reburial*, 1962 SUPREME COURT REVIEW 34.

unease about the "new" property decisions, the commonly accepted interpretation of the "old" property-rights Courts' substantive record need not be among them.

What might, on the other hand, give pause is the extraordinary nature of the "laissez-faire" period's brand of judicial activism. For the Court went far beyond simply nay-saying legislatures and "assumed" congressional power. Less striking instances of judicial legislation have been condemned on the grounds that they take a toll, not only in the quality of the Court's work, but in political terms as well. Separation of powers and the viability of the federal system are jeopardized. Support and respect for the Court itself erodes.[9] If one accepts this argument, then it may be asked at what point in a series of activist rulings, be they from the Fuller, White, Taft, Hughes, or Warren Courts, is such a price exacted? And is it, after all, worth the candle? The "old" property-rights majorities, no less concerned with a perception of the public interest than are the proponents of the "new" judicial economic activism, never paused to ask. It is from this perspective, rather than from the "laissez-faire" Court's actual output, that the "new property" advocates—and their detractors—might take their bearings.

I. The Old Property-Rights Court: A Revisionist View

With few exceptions, most standard histories and accounts of the Court between the 1880s and 1940s assume a pro-business, anti-labor bias on the part of the majority.[10] The account is as follows: Shortly after the regulation of business "affected with a public interest" was sustained in the *Granger Cases*,[11] the Court, persuaded by the American Bar Association and Justices Field and Harlan, hinted that it would henceforth scrutinize state regulatory measures

---

[9] There is a vast literature in praise of judicial self-restraint. See, *e.g.*, Bickel, The Supreme Court and the Idea of Progress (1970); Kurland, note 5 *supra*.

[10] Kelly & Harbison, The American Constitution (1970 ed.); McCloskey, The American Supreme Court (1960); Swindler, Court and Constitution in the 20th Century: The Old Legality 1889–1932 (1969); Swisher, American Constitutional Development (1943); Wright, The Growth of American Constitutional Law (1942). For some specialized accounts see Jacobs, Law Writers and the Courts: The Influence of Thomas M. Cooley, Christopher G. Tiedeman and John F. Dillon upon American Constitutional Law (1954); Paul, Conservative Crisis and the Rule of Law (1960); Twiss, Lawyers and the Constitution: How Laissez-Faire Came to the Supreme Court (1942).

[11] Munn v. Illinois, 94 U.S. 113 (1877).

with greater care. By 1898 Justice Harlan had his day and, speaking for a unanimous Court, promulgated an elaborate (and altogether unworkable) formula for administratively and/or legislatively determined public utility rates.[12] In the meantime, having already forbidden states to regulate the charges of interstate carriers while traveling intrastate,[13] the Court struck down interstate rates established by the Interstate Commerce Commission,[14] decided against the government in its first antitrust prosecution,[15] and overruled one hundred years of precedent in the *Income Tax Case*[16] (most of this, it might be added, over the angry protests of the same Justice Harlan who was so eager to invalidate state regulatory measures).[17] On the labor scene the record was much the same. Eugene Debs remained in prison for his defiance of court orders to halt the Pullman strike;[18] the Danbury Hatters were advised that their labor boycott was in violation of the Sherman Anti-Trust Act;[19] and the *Lochner* decision[20] gratuitously guaranteed New York bakers their "liberty of contract" against legislative restriction of their hours of labor. The first "conservative crisis"[21] ended, so the tale continues, when the Court, impressed by the Brandeis brief, accepted the principle of economic and social regulation[22]—*Coppage v. Kansas*[23] and the *First Child Labor Case*[24] being significant exceptions—only to be suc-

---

[12] Smyth v. Ames, 169 U.S. 466 (1898).

[13] Wabash, St. L. & P. Ry. Co. v. Illinois, 118 U.S. 557 (1886).

[14] Texas & P. R.R. v. I.C.C., 162 U.S. 197 (1896); I.C.C. v. Alabama Midland Ry. Co., 168 U.S. 144 (1897).

[15] United States v E. C. Knight Co., 156 U.S. 1 (1895).

[16] Pollock v. Farmers' Loan & Trust Co., 158 U.S. 601 (1895).

[17] The literature on this great Justice is unaccountably meager. For a listing, and an effort to explain his apparently contradictory position in the economic cases, see Porter, *John Marshall Harlan the Elder and Federal Common Law: A Lesson from History*, 1972 Supreme Court Review 103.

[18] *In re* Debs, 158 U.S. 564 (1895).

[19] Loewe v. Lawlor, 208 U.S. 274 (1908).

[20] Lochner v. New York, 198 U.S. 45 (1905).

[21] The term is Paul's, note 10 *supra*.

[22] Muller v. Oregon, 208 U.S. 412 (1908).

[23] 236 U.S. 1 (1915). The decision invalidated a state statute which prohibited "yellow dog" anti-union contracts.

[24] Hammer v. Dagenhart, 247 U.S. 251 (1918), held that Congress could not prohibit the interstate shipment of goods produced by child labor. Four Justices dissented.

ceeded by another period of reaction. Finally, with the notorious "switch in time," the Court returned in the early 1940s to the principles of the *Granger Cases*.

There have been challenges to this presentation. It has been variously suggested that the picture is one-sided and exaggerated;[25] that the Court was less interested in thwarting reform than it was in preserving "competitive capitalism";[26] that *Lochner*, in fact, accurately reflects organized labor's preference for governmental neutrality in labor-management relations;[27] that the (misdirected) natural rights activism of Justice Field paved the way for the (well-directed) natural rights activism of Justice Douglas;[28] and, finally, that property rights are as worthy of judicial protection as civil rights.[29] This last proposition was recently articulated by the Court, when it invalidated a state wage garnishment law:[30]

> The right to enjoy property without unlawful deprivation, no less than the right to speak or the right to travel, is in truth a 'personal' right. . . . In fact, a fundamental interdependence exists between the personal right to liberty and the personal right in property. Neither could have meaning without the other.

There can be little doubt that a careful study of the wide range of cases decided during the first, and seminal, "laissez-faire" period does give rise to some skepticism about the usual characterization of the Court. So many stringent state economic regulations were sus-

---

[25] BETH, THE DEVELOPMENT OF THE AMERICAN CONSTITUTION, 1877–1917 esp. chs. 5 and 6 (1971); Jones, *Thomas M. Cooley and "Laissez-Faire Constitutionalism": A Reconsideration*, 53 J. AM. HIST. 751 (1967).

[26] Strong, *The Economic Philosophy of Lochner: Emergence, Embrasure and Emasculation*, 15 ARIZ. L. REV. 419 (1973).

[27] Mavrinac, *From Lochner to Brown v. Topeka: The Court and Conflicting Concepts of the Political Process*, 52 AM. POL. SCI. REV. 641 (1958).

[28] Karst, *Invidious Discrimination: Justice Douglas and the Return of the "Natural-Law-Due-Process Formula,"* 16 U.C.L.A. L. REV. 716 (1969).

[29] Learned Hand wondered why nobody "took the time to explain" why "property itself was not a 'personal right.' " McCloskey, note 8 *supra*, at 44, n.50. And Felix Frankfurter wrote: "Yesterday the active area . . . was concerned with 'property.' Today it is 'civil liberties.' Tomorrow it may again be 'property.' Who can say that in a society with a mixed economy, like ours, these two areas are sharply separated, and that certain freedoms in relation to property may not again be deemed, as they were in the past, aspects of individual freedom?" FRANKFURTER, OF LAW AND MEN 19 (Elman ed., 1956).

[30] Lynch v. Household Finance Corp., 405 U.S. 538, 552 (1972).

tained, many involving great expense to business,[31] that it is difficult
to claim that the court simply recorded a free enterprise predilection
of the majority. The Court beat a hasty, even unseemly, retreat from
its negative posture in the early ICC and Sherman Act cases and in
the *Income Tax Case* when Presidents Roosevelt and Taft began
vigorously to prosecute the trusts, and when Congress gave additional powers to the ICC and moved toward adoption of the Six-
teenth Amendment.[32]

There were other, equally prudent, modifications of earlier judicial positions. Consider *Allgeyer v. Louisiana*,[33] the decision which
elevated "liberty of contract" to the status of constitutional doctrine. The ruling invalidated a statute which regulated the sale of
marine and fire insurance policies. Five years later, with hardly a nod
to "liberty of contract," the Court sustained a similar statute.[34] Other
judicial shifts and turns will be discussed later. A "liberal" or a
"conservative" ruling often rested on the Court's view of its constitutional or statutory powers. For instance, rulings based on the
Eleventh Amendment refused[35] as well as granted[36] injunctions

---

[31] Commenting on regulatory legislation sustained by the Court, a contemporary
observer noted that "their cumulative effect [was] to impose vast expense upon
the [railroad] companies . . . ; [requiring] that [they] supply even at a loss enough
trains and adequate service." Swayze, *Judicial Construction of the Fourteenth
Amendment*, 26 HARV. L. REV. 1, 17 (1912). For decisions sustaining rate regulation,
see Chicago & Grand Trunk Ry. Co. v. Wellman, 143 U.S. 339 (1892); Budd v.
New York, 143 U.S. 517 (1892); Brass v. Stoeser, 153 U.S. 391 (1894). For decisions sustaining requirements that the railroads, at their own expense, provide for
public health, safety, and convenience, see Atchison, T. & S. Fe R. Co. v. Matthews, 174 U.S. 96 (1899); Mississippi Railroad Comm. v. Illinois Cent. R. Co., 203
U.S. 335 (1906); St. Louis Southwestern Ry. Co. v. Arkansas, 217 U.S. 136 (1910);
Chicago, R.I. & P. Ry. Co. v. Arkansas, 219 U.S. 453 (1911). For a comprehensive
listing of cases, see CORWIN, ED., THE CONSTITUTION OF THE UNITED STATES 1121–27
(1964).

[32] The Court reversed ICC rulings in: Texas & P. Ry. Co. v. I.C.C., 162 U.S. 197
(1896); I.C.C. v. Alabama Midland R.R., 168 U.S. 144 (1897); ruled against the
government in antitrust cases: United States v. E. C. Knight Co., 156 U.S. 1
(1895); Anderson v. United States, 171 U.S. 604 (1898); and struck down the income tax provision of the Wilson Act in Pollock v. Farmers' Loan and Trust Co.,
158 U.S. 601 (1895). And see Swift & Co. v. United States, 196 U.S. 375 (1905).
Illinois Central R. Co. v. I.C.C., 206 U.S. 441 (1907); I.C.C. v. Chicago, R.I. & P.
Ry. Co., 218 U.S. 88 (1910). *Pollock* was severely modified in Knowlton v. Moore,
178 U.S. 41 (1900); Flint v. Stone Tracy Co., 220 U.S. 107 (1911).

[33] 165 U.S. 578 (1897).

[34] Nutting v. Massachusetts, 183 U.S. 553 (1902).

[35] Fitts v. McGhee, 172 U.S. 516 (1899).

[36] Southern Pacific Co. v. Denton, 146 U.S. 202 (1892).

requested by corporations seeking to prevent state officials from enforcing rate regulation laws. Sometimes the Court sustained[37] and other times invalidated[38] state laws which banned corporations from doing business within a state unless they agreed not to avail themselves of a federal statute providing for the removal of suits from hostile state courts to friendly federal courts.[39] Justices Field, Brewer, and Peckham, considered to be the villains of the piece, sometimes rendered surprisingly liberal opinions and dissents in business regulation, antitrust, and labor cases.[40] Justices such as Harlan, Brown, and Holmes moved back and forth between the liberal and conservative ends of the judicial spectrum.[41] Except for *Lochner*, which was a five-to-four decision, and *Adair v. United States*,[42] the Court sustained all challenged labor legislation.[43] And

---

[37] Security Mutual Life Insurance Co. v. Prewitt, 202 U.S. 246 (1906).

[38] Southern Pacific Co. v. Denton, 146 U.S. 202 (1892).

[39] Removal Act of 1875, 18 Stat. 470. For the importance and ramifications of the Act, see FRANKFURTER & LANDIS, THE BUSINESS OF THE SUPREME COURT ch. 2 (1927).

[40] Justice Field: Missouri Pac. Ry. Co. v. Humes, 115 U.S. 512 (1885); Charlotte, C. & A. R. Co. v. Gibbes, 142 U.S. 386 (1892); Central R. Co. v. Keegan, 160 U.S. 259 (1895); Northern Pacific R.R. v. Hambly, 154 U.S. 349 (1894). Justice Brewer: Chicago & Grand Trunk Ry. Co. v. Wellman, 143 U.S. 339 (1892); Chicago, M. & St. P. Ry. Co. v. Tompkins, 176 U.S. 167 (1900); Adams Express Co. v. Ohio, 165 U.S. 194 (1897); Pullman's Palace Car Co. v. Pennsylvania, 141 U.S. 18 (1891); Atchison, T. & S. F. R. Co. v. Matthews, 174 U.S. 96 (1899). He dissented, with Field and Harlan, against the Court's refusal to compel a railroad company to put in stations at specified places, suggesting that the road's refusal to put in a station at Yakima, then the area's most populous center, was due to the road's interest in building up other commercial areas in its own interest. He also hinted that bribery might be involved. Northern Pacific R. Co. v. Dustin, 142 U.S. 492 (1892). Justice Peckham: United States v. Trans-Missouri Freight Assoc. 166 U.S. 290 (1897); Skaneateles Water Works Co. v. Skaneateles, 184 U.S. 354 (1902); Capital City Lt. & F. Co. v. Tallahassee, 186 U.S. 401 (1902); McCullough v. Virginia, 172 U.S. 102 (1898); Ludwig v. Western Union Tel. Co., 216 U.S. 146 (1910); Pullman Company v. Kansas, 216 U.S. 56 (1910).

[41] See Justice Brown's eloquent and angry dissent in Pollock v. Farmers' Loan & Trust Co., 158 U.S. 601, 686 (1895). Justice Holmes concurred in *Ex parte* Young, 209 U.S. 123 (1908), in which the Court, without the case being properly before it, invalidated a state rate schedule. He dissented in an important antitrust case won by the government. Northern Securities Co. v. United States, 193 U.S. 197, 364 (1904).

[42] 208 U.S. 161 (1908).

[43] Legislation limiting hours of labor: Holden v. Hardy, 169 U.S. 366 (1898); Atkin v. Kansas, 191 U.S. 207 (1903); Muller v. Oregon, 208 U.S. 412 (1908); legislation requiring employers to meet specified obligations toward their employees: St. Louis, Iron Mountain & St. P. Ry. Co. v. Paul, 173 U.S. 404 (1899); Knoxville Iron Co. v. Harbison, 183 U.S. 13 (1901); Dayton Iron & Coal v. Barton, 183 U.S. 23

it was during this period, when judges were supposedly averse to governmental interference in the market place, that the Court sustained a congressional prohibition against interstate sales of lottery tickets—thus sanctioning the first exercise of the national police power.[44]

The Court, as a matter of fact, upheld a large number of state regulatory measures.[45] The exceptions were those which controlled public utility rates, and these decisions can be "rationalized" on the ground that the Court was less interested in rate regulation per se than in assuring that regulated utilities would continue to attract the investment capital necessary for expanding and improving services to the public. Charles Warren put it this way:[46]

> As soon as the capitalists found that certain States would not allow them to earn interest on railroad investments, they refused to invest more money in those States. No new roads were constructed; the equipment that wore out was not replaced. While the rates at which wheat was carried to market remained low, a great deal of wheat did not get carried to market at all, owing to lack of the physical means of transportation. The Legislatures could prevent high charges, but they could not prevent deficient service.

Out-of-state financial owners and backers of the roads, who considered their investment jeopardized by rate regulation, could hardly follow the *Granger* suggestion that they "resort to the polls."[47] The alternative was to take their money elsewhere, or to persist in seeking the judicial redress denied by the *Granger* ruling. Eventually, of

---

(1901); legislation abolishing the common-law "fellow-servant" rule: Wilmington Star Mining Co. v. Fulton, 205 U.S. 60 (1907); Chicago, B. & Q. R. Co. v. McGuire, 219 U.S. 549 (1911); legislation providing for a day of rest (Sunday): Hennington v. Georgia, 163 U.S. 299 (1896); Petit v. Minnesota, 177 U.S. 164 (1900); National Safety Appliance Acts sustained in: St. Louis, Iron Mountain & Southern Ry. v. Taylor, 210 U.S. 281 (1908); Chicago, B. & Q. Ry. Co. v. United States, 220 U.S. 559 (1911); the Hours of Service Act sustained in B. & O. R. Co. v. I.C.C., 221 U.S. 612 (1911). While the Court invalidated the Federal Employers Liability Act, in the First Employers' Liability Cases, 207 U.S. 463 (1908), it sustained a similar, more precisely drawn statute in the Second Employers' Liability Cases, 223 U.S. 1 (1912).

[44] The Lottery Case, 188 U.S. 321 (1903).

[45] See note 31 *supra*. See also Minneapolis & St. L. R. Co. v. Minnesota, 193 U.S. 53 (1904); Nashville, C. & St. L. Ry. v. Alabama, 128 U.S. 96 (1888); Minneapolis & St. L. Ry. Co. v. Beckwith, 129 U.S. 26 (1889).

[46] 3 Warren, The Supreme Court in United States History 311 (1922).

[47] Munn v. Illinois, 94 U.S. 113, 134 (1877).

course, the Court, having previously agreed that the Due Process Clause of the Fourteenth Amendment protects corporations,[48] did provide a national forum for what were national grievances and national issues.

Stated differently, substantive due process, as it pertained to state regulation of intrastate public utility rates, served as a surrogate for the (then) inapplicable Commerce Clause.[49] The Court, by protecting the public securities market against the actions of parochial, however reform-minded, legislatures, broadened the scope of its traditional responsibility for maintaining a national free trade area. Another way of looking at it would be that just as the Court determines in Commerce Clause cases if challenged state legislation controls subject matter requiring a uniform national rule, so substantive due process provides the means for establishing a uniform national rule for rate regulation—a rule which would have the effect of stabilizing the expectations of those investing in state-regulated utilities.[50]

One may, with justification, protest such juggling of constitutional provisions. My response, not defense, is that the Court, cabined and cribbed as it is, has on other occasions reached for unlikely constitutional tools to do whatever it thought the public interest required. Chief Justice Marshall's Contract Clause[51] and the Warren/Burger Court's "right to privacy"[52] decisions provide examples. One may also contend that even though the Court did remove state impediments to interstate commerce, its rulings departed from generally accepted jurisprudential norms. For in Com-

---

[48] Santa Clara Co. v. Southern Pacific R. Co., 118 U.S. 394 (1886).

[49] There was never any question as to the constitutionality of state regulation of intrastate railroad charges. In Wabash, St. L. & P. Ry. Co. v. Illinois, 118 U.S. 557 (1886), the Court held that only Congress could regulate interstate rates. The following year Congress enacted the Interstate Commerce Act, 24 Stat. 379 (1887).

[50] "A . . . great mission of the Court is to maintain a common market of continental extent against state barriers . . . ." FREUND, ON LAW AND JUSTICE 57 (1968). In Cooley v. Board of Wardens, 12 How. 299, 319 (1851), the Court sustained a local regulation, which had the effect of interfering with interstate commerce, on the ground that the subject matter was local, not requiring a uniform national rule. For a comprehensive statement of the "Cooley doctrine," see Southern Pacific Co. v. Arizona, 325 U.S. 761, 766–70 (1945).

[51] Fletcher v. Peck, 6 Cr. 87 (1810); Dartmouth College v. Woodward, 4 Wheat. 518 (1819).

[52] Griswold v. Connecticut, 381 U.S. 479 (1965); Eisenstadt v. Baird, 405 U.S. 438 (1972); Roe v. Wade, 410 U.S. 113 (1973); Doe v. Bolton, 410 U.S. 179 (1973).

merce Clause cases the Court usually, and simply, invalidates the offending state legislation, leaving the rest up to Congress, which may or may not act. This was not so in the rate regulation cases, for here the Court not only cleared the channels of interstate commerce, but went the next step and fashioned the uniform national rule. Be this as it may, and without judgment as to what the Court should, or should not, have done, it is from this unique Commerce Clause perspective that substantive due process should be understood.

II. The Court and the Securities Market: Repudiation, Receiverships, and Rates

The Court's interest in public utility investments, developed to a sophisticated level in the rate regulation cases, actually began three decades earlier. The most dramatic example was provided by the municipal[53] and state debt repudiation cases which crowded the docket for over twenty years and which involved the Court in a long series of acrimonious struggles with state courts. The earliest cases in this category resulted from the railroad boom of the 1840s and 1850s when midwestern states authorized communities to vote the requisite taxes and issue bonds in aid of railroad construction. The enterprises were as often as not marked by foolishness on the part of the citizenry and fraud on the part of the railroad builders and speculators, and sometimes local officials as well. Many of the roads went into bankruptcy and were never completed. Some companies never started to build or never finished the spur vital to the town which had pledged its credit. The result was a heavy debt which was to have been paid out of the prosperity accruing from the benefits of the road. In the meantime the bonds had been sold to out-of-state and foreign purchasers. When it became evident that expectations had exceeded realities, local governments tried to get out from under their self-imposed tax burdens. While state courts were sympathetic, the Supreme Court turned a "face of flint"[54] toward the embattled farmers, insisting that obligations be met

---

[53] For a definitive discussion of cases, see Fairman, 6 History of the Supreme Court of the United States chs. 17 and 18 (1971). Also, Fairman, Mr. Justice Miller and the Supreme Court ch. 9 (1939). For further constitutional and legal implications of the cases, see Wendell, Relations between the Federal and State Courts 143–50 (1949). For the role played by Justice Harlan, see Porter *supra* note 17.

[54] Dillon, Law of Municipal Corporations 7 (1876).

despite empty treasuries and the willingness of local officials to go to jail rather than obey court orders to collect taxes. Public outcry was reflected in several unsuccessful congressional proposals to withdraw the cases from federal court jurisdiction.[55] At the same time, however, Congress vastly increased the federal judicial powers,[56] which may suggest a willingness to let the courts handle some of the problems attendant upon the (often unsavory) methods of financing the nation's railroad system.

The state debt cases, arousing equally strong popular reactions, presented the Court with the claims of aggrieved holders of bonds issued (often under equally questionable circumstances) by Reconstruction governments and repudiated by subsequent legislatures. Thanks to the ingenuity of legislatures and courts of the impoverished South, the Court had little choice but to hold that the Eleventh Amendment prohibited compelling state officers to pay interest due on the bonds.[57] Ultimately, however, the Court, engaging in a bit of legerdemain of its own, held that the states must make good on bonds worth "many millions of dollars," and which, the Court noted significantly, had "passed into the markets of the world."[58] Clearly, the cases, despite the constitutional and legal arguments upon which they were pegged—the Contract Clause, the Eleventh Amendment, the diversity jurisdiction—raised, in the mind of the Court, questions of national and foreign commerce.

The railroad receivership cases, fraught in the view of Justice Miller with "many evils,"[59] made the Court appear even more

---

[55] See Westin, *The Supreme Court, the Populist Movement and the Campaign of 1896*, 15 J. OF POL. 3, 7–9 (1953).

[56] Removal Act of 1875, *supra* note 39.

[57] The leading case is Louisiana v. Jumel, 107 U.S. 711 (1883). For background and discussion, see WARREN, note 46 *supra*, at 385–93; WOODWARD, THE ORIGINS OF THE NEW SOUTH 86–100 (1951). The bulk of the litigation came from Louisiana and Virginia. These states did not directly repudiate their debts (which the Contract Clause would prohibit), but either "scaled down" the amount of the debt, or made collection procedures so expensive and time-consuming that it was virtually impossible for bondholders to receive returns on their investments. Antoni v. Greenhow, 107 U.S. 769 (1883); *In re* Ayers, 123 U.S. 443 (1887).

[58] McCullough v. Virginia, 172 U.S. 102, 108 (1898). In the Virginia Coupon Cases, 114 U.S. 270 (1885), the Court was finally able to compel a state to make good on its obligations. Following this, Virginia enacted the "coupon crusher" laws. In *McCullough*, the Court, by exercising its independent judgment of common law, held, the highest state court to the contrary, that the statute incurring the debt was valid. Virginia officials were then ordered to pay interest due on the bonds.

[59] Barton v. Barbour, 104 U.S. 126, 137 (1881). The whole matter of railroad re-

solicitous toward capital. What often happened was that a railroad company declared bankruptcy and went into federal court to get itself a sympathetic receiver who would run the road on a business-as-usual basis. Next, the directors and stockholders, posing as "friendly" creditors, sued to settle their "claims" against the company. Genuine creditors, supplymen, and laborers, who tried to collect something on their bills, went away empty-handed. The Supreme Court, in the majority of these cases, condoned lower federal court practices.[60]

The public utility franchise cases, which were first heard in the 1880s, aroused the least controversy—possibly because the Court, as will be discussed later, practically reversed itself. The litigation began when municipalities began building their own water, gas, and electric plants,[61] thus effectively putting privately owned and managed companies, which held "exclusive" state grants, out of business—and effectively depriving investors of their dividends. In early cases the Court, approving injunctions to halt construction of municipal plants, indicated concern that states keep their "plighted faith" with those who had made "large investments."[62]

The rate regulation cases, involving questions of property valuation, were more complex. The valuation problem first surfaced in the *Railroad Commission Cases*.[63] Chief Justice Waite, while warning in dicta that charges so low as to be "confiscatory" would be in viola-

---

ceiverships was described as an "open scandal," filled with "injustice" and "abuse." Chamberlain, *New-Fashioned Receiverships*, 10 HARV. L. REV. 139, 148–49 (1896). For an illuminating discussion of the problems, see also Warren, *Federal and State Court Interference*, 43 HARV. L. REV. 345 (1930); FAIRMAN, MR. JUSTICE MILLER, note 53, *supra*, at ch. 10.

[60] Barton v. Barbour, note 59 *supra;* Hammock v. Loan & Trust Co., 105 U.S. 77 (1881); Quincy, M. & P. R. Co. v. Humphreys, 145 U.S. 82 (1892); Sage v. Memphis & Little Rock R. Co., 125 U.S. 361 (1888).

[61] "The parallel with the early days of railroads is striking. Electric utility promoters were commonly regarded as community benefactors who should be given incentives to invest in a risky and experimental industry. As a result, franchises of great prospective value were freely disposed of with little attempt to safeguard future community interests. . . . The way was open to abuse, and consumer complaints began to mount. It was charged that the utilities imposed excessive rates, overcapitalized their properties, and obtained exorbitant profits." FAINSOD, GORDON, & PALAMOUNTAIN, GOVERNMENT AND THE AMERICAN ECONOMY 70 (3d ed. 1959).

[62] New Orleans Gas Co. v. Louisiana Light Co., 115 U.S. 650, 673 (1885). See also St. Tammany Water Works v. New Orleans Water Works, 120 U.S. 64 (1887).

[63] Ruggles v. Illinois, 108 U.S. 526 (1883); Stone v. Farmers' Loan & Trust Co., 116 U.S. 307 (1886).

tion of the Fourteenth Amendment's Due Process guarantees, sustained the rates. But it is the Field-Harlan dissenting and concurring minority positions that are of import. They indicated that builders and backers of the roads would have thought twice about entering into such vast and expensive undertakings had they known that profits and returns would depend upon rates determined by railroad commissions whose members might be motivated more by political expediency than by expert knowledge of the intricacies of railroad management and finance. Shortly thereafter the Court did edge toward the Field-Harlan view, holding that with no way of estimating the "original" cost of a road, it would have to settle on a commission's judgment as to reasonable charges.[64]

The 1890s saw a change of emphasis. In the *First Minnesota Rate Case*[65] the Court ruled, according to most readings of the decision, that the ultimate determination as to the "reasonableness" of publicly established rates lay with the judiciary. A careful reading of Justice Blatchford's opinion,[66] however, elicits a more modest conclusion. He pointed out that since the statute which created the commission did not require notice and hearing before setting rates, it was up to the courts to supply the missing "machinery provided by the wisdom of successive ages for the investigation judicially of the truth of a matter in a controversy."[67] An administrative procedure, in other words, that did not provide for notice and hearing was arbitrary and thereby contrary to due process of law. On this ground, Justice Miller, no friend to the railroads, concurred separately.[68]

The Court's seriousness about proper administrative procedures

---

[64] Harlan and Field concurred separately in *Ruggles*, 108 U.S. at 535, 541; and dissented separately in *Stone*, 116 U.S. at 337, 342. In Dow v. Beidelman, 125 U.S. 680 (1888), the Court sustained a rate schedule which resulted in a payment of less than 2 percent of the road's bonded debt.

[65] Chicago, M. & St. P. Ry. Co. v. Minnesota, 134 U.S. 418 (1890).

[66] "The opinion of the Court was delivered by Mr. Justice Blatchford; but the line of argument bears the craftsmanship of Mr. Justice Brewer." Hamilton, *Due Process of Law*, in REED, ED., THE CONSTITUTION RECONSIDERED 182 (1938).

[67] 134 U.S. at 457.

[68] For Justice Miller's view of the federal system and his jaundiced view of the practices of railroad corporations, see FAIRMAN, MR. JUSTICE MILLER, note 53 *supra*, at chs. 8–10. "[I]t is necessary that the railroad corporations interested in the fare to be considered should have notice and have a right to be heard on the question . . . . For the refusal of the Supreme Court of Minnesota to receive evidence on this subject, I think the case ought to be reversed on the ground that this is a denial of due process of law." 134 U.S. at 461.

was evidenced by initial refusals to review legislatively determined rates,[69] and by the Court's willingness to sustain rates when public utilities were given an opportunity to present their case. In such circumstances judicial review was not necessary:[70]

> What this court said about the Minnesota statute can have no application . . . unless it be made to appear that the constitution and laws of California invest the municipal authorities of that State with power to fix water rates arbitrarily, without investigation, and without permitting the corporations . . . affected thereby to make any showing as to rates to be exacted or to be heard at any time or in any way upon the subject.

On the other hand, the Court, in dicta, also said that courts, not legislatures, make final determinations as to common-law standards of reasonable rates.[71] This yes and no attitude of judicial review of rates established directly by legislatures was untenable, and the Court moved toward a resolution in the *Texas Rate Case*.[72] Here the legislature, with an eye on the *Minnesota Rate Case* and the various judicial hints about "reasonable" rates, authorized a railroad commission to give notice, hold hearings, then fix rates which would be considered reasonable unless held otherwise by a court. These precautions were of no avail. The Court, adopting the Field-Harlan *Railroad Commission Cases* position, held that the rates, because of the commission's failure to take into account the costs of construction and returns to investors, were indeed unreasonable. And since the Court had shifted focus from process to substance, from the manner in which rates were fixed to the rates themselves, the way was clear to examine legislatively determined rates. This occurred just before the turn of the century in *Smyth v. Ames*.[73]

The litigation challenged Nebraska's Newberry Bill, passed after

---

[69] Budd v. New York, 143 U.S. 517 (1892); Brass v. Stoeser, 153 U.S. 391 (1894). In these cases the Court also noted that there was insufficient evidence to support the contention that the challenged rates were confiscatory.

[70] San Diego Land & Town Co. v. National City, 174 U.S. 739, 749 (1899). In San Diego Land & Town Co. v. Jasper, 189 U.S. 439, 441, 442 (1903), the Court reiterated this interpretation of the *First Minnesota Rate Case*.

[71] In the Railroad Commission Cases, Chief Justice Waite did not preclude judicial review of confiscatory rates. Stone v. Farmers' Loan & Trust Co., 116 U.S. 307, 331 (1886). In the Minnesota Rate Case, 134 U.S. 418 (1890), Justice Blatchford did not specifically order court review of commissioner-established rates.

[72] Reagan v. Farmers' Loan & Trust Co., 154 U.S. 362 (1894).

[73] 169 U.S. 466 (1898).

Populist gains in the 1892 election. It provided for the reduction of freight rates by almost 80 percent, but, mindful of previous Court rulings, the legislature conferred upon the state supreme court the duty of raising rates if the roads could prove existing rates to be unjust.[74] But, again, the state circumspection was futile. A unanimous Court found the rates unconstitutional on the grounds that they did not allow owners a "fair return" on the company's present value.[75] And in order to ascertain that value public rate-making bodies would henceforth be expected to take at least the following into account:[76]

> the original cost of construction, the amount expended in permanent improvements, the amount and market value of its bonds and stock, the present as compared with the original cost of construction, the probable earning capacity of the property under particular rates prescribed by statute, and the sum required to meet operating expenses.

The "*Smyth* rule," as it became known, raised more problems than it settled. Courts, commissions, legislatures, and the legal profession struggled for years with what Justice Frankfurter referred to as its "hodge-podge" components[77] until, in the early 1940s, a chastened Roosevelt Court got out of the public utility valuation business altogether.[78] These highlights overlook, as so many commentators have, the many cases which strongly suggest the Court's interest in public utility investments went beyond a concern for investors, and extended to the larger questions of the background and purposes of such investments. The Court not only assumed a duty to assure the continued flow of capital investment, but assumed a concomitant duty to protect only such investments as were made in utilities which were honestly financed, well-managed, and responsive to the public interest. Well enough aware of such phenomena as "watered stock," wild-cat finance schemes, and unscrupulous speculators, what the Court attended to was a reasonable securities market for business affected with a public interest.

---

[74] For background, see HICKS, THE POPULIST REVOLT ch. 5 (1931).

[75] 169 U.S. at 547.   [76] *Id*. at 546–47.

[77] F.P.C. v. Hope Natural Gas Co., 320 U.S. 591, 627 (1944). See Goddard, *The Evolution and Devolution of Public Utility Law*, 32 MICH. L. REV. 577 (1934).

[78] Power Commission v. Natural Gas Pipeline Co., 315 U.S. 575 (1942); *Hope Natural Gas*, note 77 *supra*.

III. Public Utility Investment Pro Bono Publico

After chiding the railroad lawyers for making the interests of their clients "the sole test" for determining the validity of the rates, Justice Harlan reminded the triumphant *Smyth* litigants that a:[79]

> railroad is a . . . corporation deriving its existence and powers from the State. [It] was created for public purposes. It performs a function of the State. Its authority to exercise the right of eminent domain and to charge tolls was given primarily for the benefit of the public. It is under governmental control.

That these words were not intended merely to placate the losers is attested by the Court's abrupt about-face in the municipal ownership cases. The Court, once it realized that municipal ownership was an idea whose time had come,[80] was, in the vast majority of these cases, positively eager to stress the "public purpose" and denigrate the private loss aspects of franchise revocation. Builders and backers of privately owned plants were told that they should have known that local governments do not, by implication, bargain away their inalienable powers of police.[81] In one instance when a city, despite specific assurances to the contrary, went ahead and built its own water plant, the Court advised stockholders of the private company that they would simply have to bear the resulting "hardship" as best they could:[82]

> It is said that the company could not possibly have believed that the city would establish waterworks to be operated in competition with its system, for such competition would be ruinous. . . . On the other hand, the city may . . . say that, having once thought of having its own waterworks, the failure to insert in that agreement a provision precluding it, in all circumstances and during a long period, from having its own separate system, shows that it was not its purpose to so restrict the exercise of its powers, but to remain absolutely free to act as changed circumstances or the public exigencies might demand.

---

[79] 169 U.S. at 544.

[80] For a discussion of the late nineteenth-century movement for municipal ownership of public utilities, see Fine, Laissez Faire and the General Welfare State ch. 10 (1969). For some cases, see note 40 *supra*.

[81] Lehigh Water Co. v. Easton, 121 U.S. 388 (1887); Stein v. Bienville Water Supply Co., 141 U.S. 67 (1891).

[82] Knoxville Water Co. v. Knoxville, 200 U.S. 22, 34–35 (1906).

"As the public demands." The idea appears and reappears as importunate suitors were turned out of Court, and, in language bordering on the suspicious to the scornful, warned not to trifle with *Smyth*, or its progenitor, *The Texas Rate Case*. There Justice Brewer had taken the pains, as had Justice Harlan in *Smyth*, to explain that there were circumstances which would indeed warrant, if not cry out for, tariffs such as those established by the state commission. Consumers, for instance, should not be asked to foot the bill for wasteful and incompetent management, for "enormous salaries," for building costs incurred "at a time when material and labor were at the highest price," or for railways "unwisely" constructed in localities where there was not "sufficient business to sustain a road."[83] However, upon examination of the facts of the instant case (and it should be pointed out that when companies did not present adequate evidence of earnings, the Court either sustained the challenged rates or dismissed the suit),[84] it appeared that the company had not only cut expenses to the bone, but had, over a ten-year period, voluntarily reduced tonnage rates. The road, which was in receivership, had not met operating expenses for three years. Investors, who had "never received a dollar's worth of dividends," had, "in order to make good the deficiency in interest . . . put their hands in their pockets and advanced over a million of dollars." Under such discouraging circumstances, worsened by the commission's rate schedule, "would," the Court asked, "any investment ever be made of private capital in railroad enterprises?"[85]

Few companies received such high marks for public spiritedness (or sympathy for a tale of woe). What a utility, for instance, was "pleased to call 'operating expenses' " might not include "exorbitant" salaries[86] or "injudicious expenditures."[87] What another might claim was "original cost" was, in a word, "inflated."[88] If investors expected "any dividends" it behooved them to look toward "prudent and honest management."[89] Otherwise they might be slated for a

---

[83] 154 U.S. at 412.

[84] Dow v. Beidelman, 125 U.S. 680 (1888); Chicago & Grand Trunk Ry. Co. v. Wellman, 143 U.S. 339 (1892).

[85] 154 U.S. at 411–12.

[86] Chicago & Grand Trunk Ry. Co. v. Wellman, 143 U.S. 339, 346 (1892).

[87] San Diego Land and Town Co. v. Jasper, 189 U.S. 439, 442 (1903).

[88] *Ibid.*   [89] 143 U.S. at 346.

"misfortune . . . which the Constitution does not require to be remedied by imposing unjust burdens upon the public."[90] Valuation, that troublesome concept, might not be based on costs incurred at a time of high prices, but on the "property at the time [it was] being used for the public."[91] A company which had foolishly "embarked upon a great speculation which has not turned out as expected" would have to settle on "more modest" valuations.[92] Excessive, fictitious, and other questionable forms of capitalization could not be absorbed by rates high enough to realize the profits necessary to pay dividends. "Bond and . . . stock issued under such conditions afford neither measure nor guide to the value of stock."[93]

What of returns on investments made in such soundly financed and managed companies which passed judicial scrutiny? Well:[94]

> stockholders [were] not the only persons whose rights or interests [were] to be considered. . . . The public [could not] properly be subjected to unreasonable rates in order simply that stockholders may earn dividends.

In one instance the Court wondered if shareholders in a water company really expected to be "forever entitled to eighteen per cent upon [the original] cost." Dashing such hopes, and sustaining rates based upon the calculations of a commission, the Court noted that "much of the capital was invested between twenty and thirty years ago, and to be able still to realize six per cent upon the money originally invested is more than most people are able to accomplish in any ordinary investment."[95]

The *Smyth* rule that utilities are "entitled to a fair return upon the capital invested" may have been, the Court said, "sound as a general

---

[90] Covington Turnpike Co. v. Sandford, 164 U.S. 578, 597 (1896). Cases decided prior to *Smyth* had considered questions of earnings, rates, returns, and valuation, and were, as was this one, referred to in *Smyth*, 169 U.S. at 544–45.

[91] San Diego Land & Town Co. v. National City, 174 U.S. 739, 757 (1899).

[92] San Diego Land & Town Co. v. Jasper, 189 U.S. 439, 447 (1903).

[93] City of Knoxville v. Knoxville Water Co., 212 U.S. 1, 11 (1909). In this case the Court noted that most of the stock "was issued to contractors for the construction of the plant, and the nominal amount of the stock issued was greatly in excess of the true value of the property furnished by the contractors . . . . It perhaps is unnecessary to say that such contracts were made by the company with persons who, at the time, by stock ownership, controlled its action."

[94] Covington Turnpike Co. v. Sandford, 164 U.S. 578, 596 (1896).

[95] Stanislaus County v. San Joaquin Canal & Irr. Co., 192 U.S. 201, 214, 216 (1904).

proposition," but only should "the conditions of the country . . . permit it." Each case, it was cautioned, would be "determined by its own considerations";[96] and indeed, as has gone entirely unnoticed, the Court, modifying the *Smyth* decree, advised the Nebraska State Board of Transportation that the Court did not lay down "any cast-iron rule covering each and every separate rate."[97] Permission was granted to lower rates selectively, as the situation warranted.

IV. Laissez-Faire in Perspective

Congressional power over commerce "is as broad as the need that evokes it."[98] What has been under discussion here is the exercise of judicial power to regulate commerce—and under a constitutional pseudonym at that. It is one thing for the Court, substituting its judgment for that of Congress, to invalidate federal legislation. It is one thing for the Court to strike down state laws which it deems to be interferences with interstate commerce. It is quite another thing not only to "free" interstate commerce, but then to go ahead and "usurp" a legislative function. While something akin to this occurred in such civil rights areas as reapportionment and busing to achieve integrated schools,[99] such operations are freakish as far as interstate commerce matters are concerned. And while I maintain that the Court has been unfairly accused of coddling vested interests, there should be no blinking the fact that it did move into a field which the Constitution specifically and unequivocally reserved to Congress. The Court arrogated the commerce power unto itself, going far beyond what is commonly understood as "government by judiciary." For as pertains to an aspect of interstate commerce, the Court did more than exercise a veto power. It ruled.

On the other hand, what the Court did in an unavoidedly haphazard way was not at all unlike what Senator La Follette tried to do in 1906 and what Congress did in 1920 when it ordered the Interstate Commerce Commission to ascertain the aggregate value of regulated roads and to determine what, upon that basis, would be a

---

[96] Minneapolis & St. L. R. Co. v. Minnesota, 186 U.S. 257, 268 (1902).

[97] Smyth v. Ames II, 171 U.S. 361, 365 (1898).

[98] See Carter v. Carter Coal, 298 U.S. 238, 328 (1936) (Cardozo, J., dissenting).

[99] Reynolds v. Sims, 377 U.S. 533 (1964); Swann v. Charlotte-Mecklenburg Board of Education, 402 U.S. 1 (1971).

fair return on investments,[100] and what it did in 1934 and 1935 when it legislated controls over the securities market in general[101] and the market in public utility securities in particular.[102] If one is able, then, to take the Court's extraordinary activism in stride, the first wave of laissez-faire jurisprudence and substantive due process may be viewed as something of a judicial holding action which made a contribution to national economic development. The Court did what it could to establish a national standard for public utilities regulation—a standard which would provide minimal assurances for necessary capital investment[103] as well as guidelines for consumer protection against unwarranted charges. By concerning itself with the relationship between public utility rate regulation and the continued flow of working capital to finance public services, the Court performed what may be described as an indispensable national function.

Scholars and judges who cannot be accused of harboring a laissez-faire bias subscribe, to some extent, and in some manner, to this view. Charles Beard, while severely criticizing the Court's "tenderness" toward "corporate rights," conceded that the power to nurture business growth "vested somewhere in the national government" was "essential to the continuance of industries and commerce on a national scale."[104] Justice Brandeis did not oppose the concept of a uniform valuation standard to be followed by regulatory commissions. On the contrary, his quarrel with *Smyth v. Ames* was that the rule was not very helpful. As a substitute for the "laborious and baffling task of finding the present value of the utility," he proposed the "prudent investment" method of valuation as a means of giving

---

[100] Transportation Act, 41 Stat. 456 (1920).

[101] Securities Exchange Act, 48 Stat. 881 (1934).

[102] Public Utility Act, 49 Stat. 803 (1935).

[103] Commentators have discussed the Court's focus on public utility investment. See, *e.g.*, DICKINSON, ADMINISTRATIVE JUSTICE AND THE SUPREMACY OF LAW 221 (1927): "It became increasingly clear . . . that the security of investments required the announcement of at least some more or less uniform guiding principles." The overriding and dominant valuation question was that the "rate must be high enough to give profit enough to make safe for investors the investment of a billion dollars a year in railroad stocks and bonds–fresh money for railroad extensions and improvements." Cook, *The Legal Legislative and Economic Battle over Railroad Rates*, 35 HARV. L. REV. 30, 33 (1921). My point is that the Court was equally concerned with consumer interests.

[104] BEARD, CONTEMPORARY AMERICAN HISTORY 87 (1914).

the "capital embarked in public utilities the protection guaranteed by the Constitution."[105] Harking back to the spirit of the *First Minnesota Rate Case*, Justices Frankfurter, Clark, Black, Brennan, and Chief Justice Warren have either claimed for the courts the final say in rate determinations or have protested against regulatory commissions behaving in ways that are "arbitrary and unreasonable . . . entirely outside of the traditional concepts of administrative due process."[106] And while the position of the Court now is that "he who would upset the rate order . . . carries the heavy burden of making a convincing showing that it is invalid because it is unjust and unreasonable in its consequences,"[107] the Court has not entirely abdicated responsibility for establishing standards. Investor and consumer interests must be "balanced" and returns on investments, ruled the Court in words reminiscent of the *Railroad Commission Cases* views of Justices Field and Harlan, "should be sufficient to assure confidence in the financial integrity of the enterprise, so as to maintain its credit and to attract capital."[108]

Professor Beard and the more recent members of the Court would undoubtedly be appalled to be associated with substantive due process. But in a real sense they may share a concern of their predecessors—a desire to preserve the very best aspects of capitalism. This meant, toward the end of the nineteenth century, maintaining a wary judicial outlook for excesses and abuses on the part of the captains of industry as well as their regulators. In a period of almost cataclysmic economic change, as Professor Lerner pointed out, great dislocations, and responses to those dislocations, occur. "Clashes of interests" revolve around the question of who is to share in and benefit from new forms of wealth—and how. The mid-nineteenth century American response to the problems associated with the extraordinarily rapid development of industrial capitalism and an interdependent national economy was—incongruously—state regulation. (The effective employment of the Interstate Commerce and Sherman Acts did not begin until the Progressive era.) This localized

---

[105] Southwestern Bell Tel. Co. v. Public Service Commission, 262 U.S. 276, 292 (1923) (concurring).

[106] Frankfurter, dissenting, in F.P.C. v. Hope Natural Gas Co., 320 U.S. 591, 625 (1944); Clark, Black, Brennan and Chief Justice Warren, dissenting, in Wisconsin v. F.P.C., 373 U.S. 294, 326 (1963).

[107] Hope Natural Gas Co., 320 U.S. at 602.

[108] *Id.* at 603.

reaction to new national demands was, perforce, inadequate; and, since it threatened the investment sources which made economic growth possible, self-defeating as well. The responsibility for averting this negative development, or, put more positively, the responsibility for encouraging continued investment belonged, in Professor Beard's words, "somewhere in the national government." That somewhere turned out, for many years, to be the Court.

V. Conclusion

The development of the "new" substantive due process and equal protection has raised, for some, the specter of the old laissez-faire Court, and, for others, the problem of reconciling (without the sacrifice of logic and precedent) espousal of judicial protection of "the poor" with antipathy toward judicial protection of corporations. Both opponents and proponents of the "new property" jurisprudence appear to agree that at one time Court decisions not only reflected the economic predilections of the majority, but brought the Court into disrepute. Neither group wishes a repetition, in form if not in kind, of this particular segment of judicial history.

Leaving aside the merits or demerits of the "new property" jurisprudence, the apprehensions of both groups may be off the mark. As some students of the Court again review the period in question, there is evidence that the characterization of the Court as "laissez-faire" is not entirely accurate. And, as I have tried to demonstrate, the Court was interested, primarily, in just one kind of "old property"— investments in public utilities. It is reasonable to assume that the "articulate major premise"[109] of these cases was that public utility investment was the lifeblood of an expanding national economy. The Court, by supervising state supervision of the utilities, established minimal and uniform guarantees for investors. Moreover, and this has been consistently ignored by critics of the laissez-faire Court, the Justices also strongly endorsed state efforts to protect the public. The Court, by balancing the interests of investors and consumers, turned itself into something of a federal regulatory agency. This was an extreme instance of "government by judiciary," for it went far beyond laying down judicial guidelines for state legislatures and administrative agencies, and extended to a lively judicial oversight of a vital element of the national economy.

---

[109] Holmes, dissenting, in Lochner v. New York, 198 U.S. 45, 76 (1905).

On the other hand, a justified condemnation might be tempered by taking the following into account. In the first place, the Court provided, as described by Robert McCloskey, for "the growth of entrepreneurial . . . freedom [which] helped to promote material progress . . . after the Civil War."[110] (Whether the result was, after all, desirable, cannot be assayed here.) In the second place, Congress took its bearings from *Smyth*. The Transportation Act of 1920 instructs the ICC to give "due consideration to all the elements of value recognized by the law of the land for rate-making purposes."[111] And whatever the problems created by *Smyth*, even those who have condemned the decision "as a major barrier to the effectiveness of public utility regulation,"[112] have also, unwittingly, conceded its salutory influence on the Transportation Act which:[113]

> taken as a whole, was a striking departure in railway regula-
> tion. Earlier laws had been dominated by a concern with rail-
> road abuses. . . . Abandoning this restrictive approach, while
> continuing the earlier mandate of "reasonable and just" rates,
> the legislation explicitly recognized the needs of the carriers
> for adequate revenue. By protecting the investor, it sought
> to stabilize railway credit and stimulate a flow of capital into
> the industry.

Finally, without making extravagant claims for the *First Minnesota Rate Case*, the Court did, in effect, warn against giving what Professor Reich calls unlimited "discretion" to public officials and agencies. The Court asked then, as advocates of the "new property" rights ask now, that "the machinery provided by the wisdom of successive ages for the investigation . . . of the truth of a matter,"[114] *i.e.*, notice and hearing, be made available to those whose property rights are affected or threatened by "authorities, examiners, boards of control."[115] That the property loss might be catastrophic for a welfare recipient deprived of benefits, and minuscule for a railroad corporation whose rates are regulated by the state, is beside the point. What is to the point is that the Court was aware, many years

---

[110] McCloskey, note 8 *supra*, at 48.

[111] § 15 (a) (4), 41 Stat. 489.

[112] Fainsod, Gordon, & Palamountain, note 61 *supra*, at 79.

[113] *Id*. at 269–70.

[114] Chicago, M. & St. P. Ry. v. Minnesota, 134 U.S. 418, 457 (1890).

[115] Reich, note 7 *supra*.

ago, of the dangers which the "public interest state" could pose to individual liberties. Justice Brewer's protestation (*obiter*, and in dissent in 1894) that the "paternalistic theory of government" was, to him "odious,"[116] has a hauntingly contemporary ring. The pervasive power of the welfare state, disquieting to conservatives, now troubles liberals as well.[117]

In sum, the old "laissez-faire" Court has been misunderstood and thereby disparaged. Its actual "transgressions" (if one takes this view) have, because of failure to comprehend its objectives, been overlooked. And while a reconsideration of this long dead past may seem, in Professor McCloskey's phrase, to be "mere bootless anti-quarianism,"[118] conventional interpretations of the "old" substantive due process are a reference for the "new." For this reason alone, it is instructive to grant the old "laissez-faire" Court its long overdue rehearing.

---

[116] Budd v. New York, 143 U.S. 517, 551 (1892).

[117] "The modern welfare state is a benevolent despot [that] retains the power to direct the behavior of recipients [of its benevolence]. Glasser, *Life under the New Feudalism*, 1 Civ. Lib. Rev. 27 (Winter/Spring 1974).

[118] McCloskey, note 8 *supra*, at 35.

SOTIRIOS A. BARBER

NATIONAL LEAGUE OF CITIES v. USERY: NEW MEANING FOR THE TENTH AMENDMENT?

If anything seemed settled in contemporary American constitutional law, it was the meaning of the Tenth Amendment. Chief Justice John Marshall stated, almost in the beginning, that the Amendment expressed no limitation on the powers of the national government. National powers were limited in number, but where they existed they were complete.[1] Others elaborated Marshall's theory by terming the Amendment a mere truism, not a rule of law specifying what the national government may not do, but a rule of construction directing the federal judiciary to answer questions of national authority by consulting the constitutional grants of power.[2] In the twentieth century the Court evolved a theory of national power which vitally affected our understanding of the Tenth Amendment. The new theory differed from Marshall's theory but was often confused with it. The new theory said the Constitution was flexible enough to accommodate virtually any policy not prohibited by expressed constitutional limitations, most notably those limitations of the Bill of

Sotirios A. Barber is Associate Professor of Political Science, University of South Florida.

[1] McCulloch v. Maryland, 4 Wheat. 316, 405–07 (1819).

[2] United States v. Darby, 312 U.S. 100, 124 (1941); STORY, COMMENTARIES ON THE CONSTITUTION OF THE UNITED STATES § 1900 (1833); Berns, *The Meaning of the Tenth Amendment*, in GOLDWIN, ed., A NATION OF STATES 130–32 (1961).

Rights.[3] The new theory of the Tenth Amendment combined what Marshall said about the completeness of national powers where they exist with what the modern Court said about the unlimited range of those powers. As a result the Tenth Amendment came to have no restrictive significance. It was considered a mere expression of sentiment whose time had passed with the growth of national power to meet national needs.

This view of the Tenth Amendment dominated constitutional thought in our time. But "living," "dynamic" constitutions being what they are, orthodoxies do not always impress judges. And in June 1976 the Supreme Court used a states'-sovereignty argument to invalidate a congressional act setting wage and hour standards for state employees.

I. National League of Cities v. Usery: An Overview

In *National League of Cities v. Usery*[4] five members of a bitterly divided Court discovered in the Tenth Amendment an "affirmative limitation" on the commerce power "akin to" limitations in the Bill of Rights, "running in favor of the States *as States*,"[5] and prohibiting congressional enactments threatening "the separate and independent existence" of the states as "sovereign political entit[ies]."[6] The existence of this states'-sovereignty limitation, said Mr. Justice Rehnquist for the Court, has been "consistently recognized" in the established constitutional doctrine of intergovernmental tax immunity.[7] Without the right to determine the hours and wages of employees performing "integral governmental functions" in fields like health, education, and police protection, "there would be little left" of a state's separate and independent existence.[8] On these grounds the Court invalidated three 1974 amendments to the Fair Labor Standards Act[9] and overruled its 1968 decision in *Maryland v. Wirtz*,[10] which had upheld earlier amendments of the act.[11] The combined effect of these amendments had been to extend to virtually

---

[3] Pritchett, The American Constitution 197–98 (1968); Reagan, The New Federalism 9–14 (1972); Berns, note 2 *supra*, at 141–44; *cf*. The Federalist No. 84.

[4] 96 S. Ct. 2465 (1976).   [7] *Id*. at 2467.

[5] *Id*. at 2467, 2469.   [8] *Id*. at 2473–74.

[6] *Id*. at 2470–71.

[9] 29 U.S.C. §§ 203 (d), 203 (s) (5), 203 (x).

[10] 392 U.S. 183 (1968).

[11] 29 U.S.C. § 203 (d), 203 (r), 203 (s), 207 (a) (2) (1964 ed.).

all state, county, and municipal employees federal minimum-wage and maximum-hours standards.

"But," protested Mr. Justice Brennan, "there is no restraint based on state sovereignty requiring or permitting judicial enforcement [of limitations on the commerce power] anywhere expressed in the Constitution; our decisions over the last century and a half have explicitly rejected the existence of any such restraint."[12] Intergovernmental immunity might have some validity in the area of taxation, Mr. Justice Brennan seemed to concede, but prior cases had clearly rejected its extension to the commerce power while declaring "unworkable" the distinction between essential and nonessential state functions.[13] The majority's decision was a mere *"ipse dixit* reflecting nothing but displeasure with a congressional judgment,"[14] and with a "portent . . . so ominous for our constitutional jurisprudence as to leave one incredulous."[15] The majority opinion "must astound scholars of the Constitution" by ignoring John Marshall's decision that "nothing in the Tenth Amendment constitutes a limitation on congressional exercise of powers delegated by the Constitution to Congress."[16]

Mr. Justice Stevens dissented separately although he made no legal points not contained in the Brennan dissent. One cannot tell whether he saw flaws in Mr. Justice Brennan's reasoning or whether he simply did not want to join an opinion with Brennan's tone. Mr. Justice Stevens disagreed with the wisdom of the FLSA amendments, but he could see no clear constitutional basis for the majority holding.[17] He could not identify a limitation on the national government's power over wages and hours of state employees that would not also invalidate such "unquestionably permissible" statutes as those requiring a state "to act impartially when it hires or fires the janitor, to withhold taxes from his pay check, to observe safety regulations when he is performing his job, to forbid him from burning too much soft coal in the capitol furnace, from dumping untreated refuse in an adjacent waterway, from overloading a state-owned garbage truck or from driving either the truck or the governor's limousine over 55 miles an hour."[18]

Mr. Justice Blackmun also had doubts: "I am not untroubled by

---

¹² 96 S. Ct. at 2477.

¹³ *Id*. at 2480.

¹⁴ *Id*. at 2483.

¹⁵ *Id*. at 2485.

¹⁶ *Id*. at 2479.

¹⁷ *Id*. at 2488.

¹⁸ *Ibid.*

certain possible implications of the Court's opinion—some of them suggested by the dissents."[19] Nevertheless, he concurred with the majority because "the result . . . here is necessarily correct," and because "it seems to me that it adopts a balancing approach, and does not outlaw federal power in areas such as environmental protection, where the federal interest is demonstrably greater and where state facility compliance with imposed federal standards would be essential."[20]

League of Cities would thus transport us from a regime which has sacrificed states' sovereignty for congressional supremacy to a regime in which the Court will balance states' rights against interests represented by Congress. One cannot read the several opinions of the case and be confident about its future. Without a doubt the decision will be roundly condemned by constitutional scholars. Solid constitutional ground for the holding will be difficult to discover. The decision departs from the expressed terms of the Constitution even as Mr. Justice Rehnquist himself previously understood those terms.[21] It virtually ignores contrary opinions by Chief Justice Marshall, enjoying in most quarters the status of founding documents. The decision seems in conflict with Mr. Justice Rehnquist's expressed views that judicial policy making is contrary to the language and intent of the framers.[22]

But while *League of Cities* will be easy to criticize we should be somewhat restrained by the fact that five reasonable individuals found its immediate result "necessarily correct." No question exists about the majority's disapproval of the FLSA amendments on economic grounds; the majority is quite open about that.[23] But the majority might have been motivated by something more. Something does seem wrong with the theory that the Tenth Amendment counts for nothing, and the majority may be understood as reacting to that theory. In what may be the most revealing part of his opinion Mr. Justice Rehnquist uses a footnote to say:[24]

---

[19] *Id.* at 2476.   [20] *Ibid.*

[21] Compare his statement that the Tenth Amendment contains "an express declaration" of a states'-sovereignty limitation, *id.* at 2470, with his statement in Fry v. United States, 421 U.S. 542, 557 (1975), that the Amendment does not "by its terms" restrict the commerce power, and also with his approval of Holmes's opinion in Missouri v. Holland, 252 U.S. 416 (1920), in Rehnquist, *The Notion of a Living Constitution*, 54 TEX. L. REV. 693, 694 (1976).

[22] See Rehnquist, note 21 *supra*.   [24] *Id.* at 2475 n.19.

[23] 96 S. Ct. at 2471–74.

The dissent leaves no doubt from its discussion . . . that in its view Congress may under its commerce power deal with the States as States just as they might deal with private individuals. We venture to say that it is this conclusion, rather than the one we reach, which is in the words of the dissent a "startling restructuring of our federal system."

Reexamining what the Tenth Amendment should have meant for the modern Court will hardly justify the errors of *League of Cities*, but it should enable us to recall a theory based on sound constitutional principle. This theory may in turn point the way to a truly constitutional accommodation of at least some of the values which form a part of the states'-rights tradition. The doctrine of *League of Cities* may not survive. The desire to live in real communities which enjoy a legal right to be different may well survive.

II. The Meaning of the Tenth Amendment

As already noted, the prevailing theory of the Tenth Amendment consists of two incompatible parts, one derived from the opinions of Marshall, the other mostly from twentieth-century cases. Marshall's theory that national power is plenary where affirmatively granted is consistent with constitutional language. Marshall's understanding of the Tenth Amendment, the enumeration of powers, and the enumeration of rights required two necessary tests for the constitutionality of congressional action: (1) whether an exercise of power was affirmatively authorized; (2) whether action otherwise permitted nevertheless contravened specific constitutional prohibitions. Marshall also recognized that even without specific prohibitions there were limits to the kinds of policy Congress could pursue.

The twentieth-century understanding eliminates the first of Marshall's tests. The manner in which it interprets clauses like the Commerce Clause, the Necessary and Proper Clause, and the General Welfare Clause has the effect of enabling Congress to do whatever it is not affirmatively prohibited from doing. The modern understanding is consistent neither with the language of the Tenth Amendment nor with the understanding the framers had of national power prior to and independently of the adoption of the Tenth Amendment.

A. THE LANGUAGE OF THE TENTH AMENDMENT

When the Tenth Amendment says powers not delegated are reserved to the states or to the people it does not say what specific powers are reserved. But given the historical context in which it was written the Amendment does imply that some powers are reserved. The Tenth Amendment thus expresses the negative or proscriptive implication of the acts of granting and enumerating the powers of government. This negative implication was admitted by the framers even before the Bill of Rights and the Tenth Amendment were adopted.[25] And if the Tenth Amendment is only a rule of construction addressed to the federal judiciary,[26] it should be treated as such. This is possible only if the enumeration of powers is read in a manner that preserves something of the implication that some matters are in some sense beyond the legal competence of the national government.

On the other hand, the enumeration of powers has a positive implication as well as a negative one. Granting powers implies the existence of functions government is expected to perform. If the Tenth Amendment is predicated on the idea of granting powers, it would would be illogical for the Amendment to defeat the positive implication of that idea. Marshall's opinion in *McCulloch v. Maryland*[27] contains a theory of national power which reconciles the negative and positive implications of the acts of granting and enumerating powers.

Marshall's opinion in *McCulloch* suggests that the notion of a governmental power should be construed with the theory that government is instituted to achieve desirable social results or ends.[28] Powers implicate ends to be pursued, even though enumerating powers implies the pursuit only of a limited number of ends. The following passage shows the relationship in Marshall's thinking between powers, ends, and enumerated powers:[29]

> [A]mong the enumerated powers . . . we find the great powers to lay and collect taxes; to borrow money; to regulate commerce; to declare and conduct a war; and to raise and support armies and navies. The sword and the purse, all the external relations, and no inconsiderable portion of the industry of the nation, are entrusted to its government. It can never be pre-

---

[25] THE FEDERALIST Nos. 45, 84.   [26] Berns, note 2 *supra*, at 130–32.

[27] 4 Wheat. 316 (1819).

[28] With the interpretation of Marshall stated here, compare Berns, note 2 *supra*, at 137–44; and CORWIN, THE COMMERCE POWER VERSUS STATES RIGHTS 213–23 (1936).

[29] 4 Wheat. at 407–08.

tended that these vast powers draw after them others of inferior importance, merely because they are inferior. Such an idea can never be advanced. But it may with great reason be contended, that a government, entrusted with such ample powers, on the due execution of which the happiness and prosperity of the nation so vitally depends, must also be entrusted with ample means for their execution.

The pattern of thought revealed by this passage is one of understanding formal powers of government in terms of desirable social results.

Marshall suggests that powers imply ends and are to be construed in terms of the ends they imply. This would explain Marshall's statement that "all the external relations . . . of the nation . . . are entrusted to its government." Of course, the explicit powers fall short of specifying all the foreign affairs powers.[30] But Marshall read explicit powers as pointing to certain ends, with those ends in turn implying the grant of other powers which Congress may employ as means to the ends. Thus, powers to raise armies, declare war, and other explicit powers point to the objective of national defense; this end in turn came to authorize establishment of an air force, an intelligence operation, and other instruments of national defense.[31] Because of the transcendent importance of such ends as national security and a prosperous national economy,[32] Marshall construed the Supremacy Clause and the Necessary and Proper Clause to deny state-sovereignty restrictions on the exercise of national power.[33] "Let the end be legitimate," said Marshall, "let it be within the scope of the constitution, and all means which are appropriate, which are plainly adapted to that end, which are not prohibited, but consist with the letter and spirit of the constitution, are constitutional."[34]

Marshall's approach seems consistent with common sense and basic constitutional principle. Neither government nor its institu-

---

[30] HENKIN, FOREIGN AFFAIRS AND THE CONSTITUTION 15–19 (1972).

[31] This approach would avoid Justice Sutherland's theory in United States v. Curtiss-Wright Export Corp., 299 U.S. 304 (1936), that the foreign affairs powers are inherent rather than granted powers. See also Jaffa, *The Case for a Stronger National Government*, in GOLDWIN, note 2 *supra*, at 118–19. Cf. the equivocation in Marshall's opinion in American Insurance Co. v. Canter, 1 Pet. 511, 542–43 (1828).

[32] FAULKNER, THE JURISPRUDENCE OF JOHN MARSHALL 20–33 (1968).

[33] 4 Wheat. at 412–21.   [34] *Id.* at 421.

tions and powers are ends in themselves. Only a desire for national security can explain or even make intelligible the grant of war powers to government. If national defense is the reason for armies and navies, it would be irrational to reject other needed instruments solely because they were not explicitly mentioned in the Constitution. "A government," says a famous passage in *The Federalist*,[35]

> ought to contain in itself every power requisite to the full accomplishment of the objects committed to its care . . . free from every other control but a regard to the public good and to the sense of the people.
>
> As the duties of superintending the national defense and of securing the public peace against foreign or domestic violence involve a provision for casualties and dangers to which no possible limits can be assigned, the power of making that provision ought to know no other bounds than the exigencies of the nation and the resources of the community.

But this does not mean the national government may pursue every policy it wants. Marshall insisted that the objectives of the national government were limited. He could not agree that the General Welfare Clause was a grant of power independent of the enumeration of specific powers in Art. 1, § 8.[36] At one point in his opinion in *McCulloch v. Maryland*, Marshall said:[37]

> Should congress, in the execution of its powers, adopt measures which are prohibited by the constitution; or should congress, under the pretext of executing its powers, pass laws for the ac-

---

[35] THE FEDERALIST No. 31.

[36] FAULKNER, note 32 *supra*, at 80. But one may still argue that Marshall's position on the General Welfare Clause amounted to the theory he thought he was rejecting. See Jaffa, note 31 *supra*, at 117–18. No real middle position exists between the theory that the General Welfare Clause is an independent grant of power to govern for the general welfare and the theory that it only authorizes taxing and spending for objects indicated by the specific grants of power elsewhere in Art. 1, § 8. The difference between taxing and spending for the general welfare and simply governing for the general welfare is a difference between governmental techniques, not objectives. Taxation was well understood as a regulatory technique at the founding, and what we know today about the regulatory powers of subsidy could have always been inferred from the disruptive effects of bribery on the performance of official functions. The well-known contradiction between decision and supporting theory in United States v. Butler, 297 U.S. 1 (1936), shows that the only theory compatible with the Tenth Amendment is that which understands the content of "general welfare" to be the objects indicated by the enumeration of powers. For the common sense of the matter, see THE FEDERALIST No. 41. See also text *infra*, at note 69.

[37] 4 Wheat. at 423.

complishment of objects not entrusted to the government; it would become the painful duty of this tribunal . . . to say that such an act was not the law of the land. But where the law is not prohibited, and is really calculated to effect any of the objects entrusted to the government, to undertake here to inquire into the degree of its necessity, would be to pass the line which circumscribes the judicial department, and to tread on legislative ground.

Thus, as long as Congress "really" pursues its authorized ends the courts should not question legislative judgments about the necessity of encroaching on the reserved powers of the states. But Congress might try to use its powers pretextually, and the courts should void such attempts. The reserved powers of the states will be protected to the extent that courts are willing to look beyond pretexts to the real purposes of Congress. If the Tenth Amendment is to be an effective rule of construction, courts must ensure that Congress pursues its authorized ends only.

B. THE DECLINE OF THE TENTH AMENDMENT

The proposition that the objectives of the national government are limited hardly settles all the problems of the Tenth Amendment. To begin with, there is no agreement on what the ends of the national government are. Were we guided by historical materials we might add the objects of the Civil War Amendments to the statement of *The Federalist*:[38]

> The principle purposes to be answered by union are these— the common defense of the members; the preservation of the public peace, as well against internal convulsions as external attacks; the regulation of commerce with other nations and between the States; the superintendence of our intercourse, political and commercial, with foreign countries.

But even with this enumeration of authorized objectives we would have to recognize that terms like "common defense" and "regulation of commerce between the states"[39] take their content largely from

---

[38] THE FEDERALIST No. 23.

[39] The Constitution, of course, speaks of commerce "among" the states, not "between." That this difference would have had no lasting effect on the scope of the commerce power is seen by what happened to the various forms of the state-line test. See PRITCHETT, note 3 *supra*, ch. 14.

specific and conflicting defense and economic policies. At best, these clauses authorize the pursuit of certain kinds of ends, without confining the government to certain specific ends. The authority to pursue commercial ends must be understood as broad enough, for example, to justify the debate between Hamiltonian and Jeffersonian economics.

History, however, is not the sole determinant of constitutional meaning; the rules of language also play their part. These rules are violated when the powers of government are used pretextually. Both Congress and the Court violate the Constitution when they say, for example, that a clause authorizing "commercial" ends authorizes purposes which they themselves perceive as "noncommercial." The very enunciation of the commerce power implies that somewhere noncommercial activities and purposes can be found. The noncommercial activities of one era may of course constitute the commercial problems of another. Congress should be free to regulate such activities under the Commerce Clause and related clauses when it does so for economic reasons. And if sometimes we cannot be sure what Congress's real purposes are, Congress may be given the benefit of the doubt—as long as power is not used in obviously pretextual ways. The Tenth Amendment was a meaningful rule of construction while the Court was willing to confine the national government to certain kinds of policies and as long as it would declare a pretext when it saw one. But when the Court is no longer willing to do these things, the Tenth Amendment becomes a dead letter.[40]

Many welcomed this result because the old Court used the Tenth Amendment against Congressional efforts to outlaw child labor[41] and to combat economic depression.[42] But it was not necessary to abandon the Amendment for the sake of these and other economic policies. The Court need only have recognized Congress's responsibility for the nation's economic health and Congress's right to use its taxing, spending, and commerce powers as long as it was doing so for economic reasons. That recognition, with Marshall's theory of

---

[40] REAGAN, note 3 *supra* at 9–14.

[41] Hammer v. Dagenhart, 247 U.S. 251 (1918); Bailey v. Drexel Furniture Co., 259 U.S. 20 (1922).

[42] Schechter Poultry Corp. v. United States, 295 U.S. 495 (1935); Carter v. Carter Coal Co., 298 U.S. 238 (1936).

the Tenth Amendment,[43] would have removed valid states'-rights objections to a wide range of economic policies, including efforts to govern labor conditions, wages and hours, prices and competitive practices, quality of products, and so on. Questions might have remained about child labor laws and social security legislation. But these questions could have been resolved in favor of national power without abandoning the Tenth Amendment because the problems involved were largely perceived as economic problems and because sometimes it is not possible to differentiate economic from noneconomic reasons, in which case judicial restraint is defensible.[44]

Real damage came to the Tenth Amendment when Congress was permitted to develop a national police power under its powers over commerce and taxation and when it was permitted to tax and spend for social objectives admittedly reserved to the states. No observer without a political or litigious stake could classify the Mann Act as economically motivated,[45] or the Lindbergh Act,[46] or the Civil Rights Act of 1964.[47] Congress has used the taxing power for purposes of regulating sales of sawed-off shotguns,[48] sales of marijuana,[49] and gambling.[50] Congress uses its spending power to improve recreational facilities in the states, for police and fire protection, to promote the arts, and even, through revenue sharing, to improve the political positions of state and local governments.[51] Such uses of federal power were either not justified in themselves or not rationalized by the Court in terms of the great national objectives of national defense, prosperity, racial justice, and fundamental civil liberties—

---

[43] Because Marshall's theory is not a static theory, it is not limited to what he saw as specific national concerns under the Commerce Clause in his day. See FRANK-FURTER, THE COMMERCE CLAUSE UNDER MARSHALL, TANEY AND WAITE 39–45 (1937).

[44] Thus, efforts on the part of the government to improve the political position of the poor in the Economic Opportunity Act of 1964 (78 Stat. 508) could have been held constitutional because of the lack of relationship between political power and poverty.

[45] Upheld in Hoke v. United States, 227 U.S. 308 (1913).

[46] Upheld in Gooch v. United States, 297 U.S. 124 (1936).

[47] Upheld in Heart of Atlanta Motel, Inc., v. United States, 379 U.S. 241 (1964); see note 53 *infra*.

[48] Upheld in Sonzinsky v. United States, 300 U.S. 506 (1937).

[49] Upheld in United States v. Sanchez, 340 U.S. 42 (1950).

[50] Upheld in United States v. Kahriger, 345 U.S. 22 (1953).

[51] REAGAN, note 3 *supra*, at 95–98.

as broad as these categories are. Instead, the court permitted these acts and others like them to reverse Marshall's means-end relationship. Encroachments on state powers were not really seen as means to authorized national ends; national powers became pretextual means in pursuit of ends reserved to the states. To protect such precedents, the Court fabricated a rule against scrutinizing congressional "motives,"[52] ending prospects for distinguishing pretext from reality and leaving only the affirmative prohibitions of the Constitution as effective limitations on congressional power.

Of course, a given social activity need not forever remain outside the legitimate scope of national power. Properly understood, the Tenth Amendment does not embody a static conception of power. It points to a limited number of authorized national objectives and to rules giving the national government supremacy when it pursues those objectives. It says, in effect, that when the national government acts for certain reasons, it may disregard the reserved powers of the states. But requiring the national government to give certain reasons when it seeks supremacy is requiring the government to tell the truth about its purposes. Pretextual uses of power may achieve desirable results, but they risk the government's reputation for integrity.[53]

No answer to this problem is found in the theory that the only reason Congress need give is that it deals with a "national problem" as opposed to a "local problem." A problem for the nation is that

---

[52] See Alfange, *Free Speech and Symbolic Conduct: The Draft-Card Burning Case,* 1968 SUPREME COURT REVIEW 1, 27–38; United States v. Kahriger, 345 U.S. 22, 37 (Frankfurter, J., dissenting). *Cf.* Fletcher v. Peck, 6 Cranch. 87, 130 (1810). Marshall's qualified statements in Fletcher are adequately explained by Alfange's distinction between the "motives" of individual legislators and the "purpose" or policy served by an enactment.

[53] Of course, one cannot be oblivious to the prudential uses of pretext, even in a democracy. The nation may not have been ready in 1964 for the Court to uphold the Civil Rights Act as an exercise of the Fourteenth Amendment. By upholding the act under the Commerce Clause the Court served one of the ends of modern democracy (racial justice) at the expense of procedural principles (truth) implicit in the idea of government by consent. One of the leading charges of the Antifederalists during the campaign for ratification was that the Constitution was a covert plan for consolidated government. If so, did that foreclose the utility of the plan for ends more important to the public than the preservation of states' sovereignty? The logic of ratification implies consent to means and ends. But suppose the sovereign people are simply unprepared to consent to the means necessary to achieve the ends they want? Suppose also a sovereign to be divided in other respects. Can the sovereign be fallible and truly "sovereign" at the same time? Consider Socrates' refutation of Thrasymachus in THE REPUBLIC, Book 1.

which is problematic to those who speak for the nation. The mere fact of congressional enactment is evidence enough that a national problem exists. The "national problem" approach denies the restrictive implication of the enumeration of powers. It places the entire burden of limiting government on rules like those of the Bill of Rights. In light of our constitutional history and philosophy, no pretext is greater.[54]

III. League of Cities: A Closer Look

A. MR. JUSTICE REHNQUIST'S MAJOR PREMISE

Mr. Justice Rehnquist begins his opinion by acknowledging that the wage-hour regulations would be within the scope of the Commerce Clause as applied to the "purely intrastate" activities of private business, so long as their activities affected commerce among the states.[55] He cites language from *United States v. Darby* upholding "regulations of commerce which do not infringe some constitutional prohibition," "[w]hatever their motive and purpose."[56] He also cites with approval language from *Heart of Atlanta Motel v. United States* stating that when Congress regulates private economic endeavor it may preempt state law.[57] With these citations Mr. Justice Rehnquist departs from the dual federalist position earlier in this century that rejected congressional power over purely intrastate activities while scrutinizing congressional purposes lest power be used pretextually.[58] He thus accepts the essentials of the twentieth-century theory that rendered the Tenth Amendment a rule with no effective meaning.

Nevertheless, concludes Mr. Justice Rehnquist, Congress may not extend wage-hour standards to state employees engaged in such "integral governmental functions" as fire and police protection, sanitation, public health, education, and recreation.[59] The Constitution, he argues, guarantees the "separate and independent existence" of the states as "sovereign political entit[ies]."[60] And the Tenth

---

[54] The Federalist No. 84; Lincoln, *Message to Congress in Special Session*, 4 July 1861, in Basler, ed., Abraham Lincoln: His Speeches and Writings 604–05 (1962); Kansas v. Colorado, 206 U.S. 46 (1907); *cf.* Berns, note 2 *supra*, at 141–44.

[55] 96 S. Ct. at 2469.

[56] *Id.* at 2467, citing 312 U.S. at 115.

[57] *Id.* at 2469, citing 379 U.S. 262.

[58] See, *e.g.*, cases cited *supra*, at note 41.

[59] 96 S. Ct. at 2473–74.

[60] *Id.* at 2470–71.

Amendment prevents the "utter destruction" of states' sovereignty by imposing an "affirmative limitation" on the commerce and taxing powers "akin" to limitations imposed by constitutional guarantees of individual rights.[61] Congress does not violate the Tenth Amendment by displacing state authority over private activity. It does violate the amendment by displacing a state's authority over the hours and wages of its own employees.[62]

The governing premise of Mr. Justice Rehnquist's argument is that the Constitution prevents the utter destruction of the states as sovereign political entities. If the Constitution guarantees a measure of states' sovereignty, he is entitled to believe that somewhere in the Constitution a corresponding judicial handle can be found. If no other can be found except the Tenth Amendment, established doctrines may have to be modified, including doctrines as sacrosanct as Chief Justice Marshall's. And if it is somewhat arbitrary to conclude that control of a state's employees is more essential to its sovereignty than governing private activities within its borders,[63] sovereignty over state employees may be the only thing left to claim at this late date in the advance of national power. Thus, everything in Mr. Justice Rehnquist's opinion turns on the proposition that the Constitution prevents the utter destruction of the states as sovereign entities. And one of the few flaws in Mr. Justice Brennan's powerful dissent is his failure to deny this proposition in an unequivocal way.

Mr. Justice Brennan seems to deny the proposition at a few points in his opinion by quoting language from authorities like Marshall and Chief Justice Stone about the import of the Supremacy Clause and the diminution of state sovereignty "to the extent," in Stone's words, "of the grants of power to the federal government."[64] But at other points he seems to agree that the Constitution prevents the utter destruction of state sovereignty.[65] He strengthens this impression by outlining two ways in which the Constitutional guarantee would be honored: by confining the national government to a limited number of objectives[66] and by guaranteeing the states'

---

[61] *Id.* at 2469–70.   [62] *Id.* at 2475–76.

[63] *Id.* at 2485 (Brennan, J., dissenting).

[64] *Id.* at 2476–77, 2485, quoting from United States v. California, 297 U.S. 175, 184 (1936).

[65] 96 S. Ct. at 2478.   [66] *Ibid.*

participation in the formation of national policy.[67] The difficulty is that neither of these two methods effectively guarantees state sovereignty. The majority, therefore, can think that Mr. Justice Brennan believes the guarantee is there, but that he is unable to show an effective way to honor it. His failure may in some measure justify the majority's invention of what they hope is a more effective way to honor a guarantee that they believe is admitted by all.

For Mr. Justice Rehnquist a state is not a "sovereign entity" simply by virtue of the fact that its representatives participate in national policy making. Mr. Justice Brennan unsuccessfully argues that "the States are fully able to protect their own interests" through such participation, and that "[d]ecisions upon the extent of federal intervention under the Commerce Clause into the affairs of the States are in that sense decisions of the States themselves."[68] The majority aptly responds by citing cases in which the Court had invalidated congressional limitations of presidential authority notwithstanding the President's approval.[69] Mr. Justice Rehnquist might have argued more generally that the Constitution prescribes an arrangement of offices and powers envisioning certain entities making certain kinds of decisions in certain ways. Persons in office are not free to diminish the power of their offices as they might waive their constitutional rights as individuals. Office implies duty. And the judiciary should have ways of maintaining the constitutional arrangement of offices and powers just as it has ways of helping maintain other parts of the "supreme Law." If, therefore, the Constitution guarantees states' sovereignty, the Court should maintain that guarantee in spite of the states' participation in its denial.

Mr. Justice Brennan purports to see a way for the judiciary to protect states' sovereignty in remarking, "Of course, regulations that this Court can say are not regulations of 'commerce' cannot stand ... and in this sense" the Court can "prevent ... 'the utter destruction of the State as a sovereign political entity.' "[70] This approach presupposes effective limits on the commerce power. But as the modern Court understands the commerce power and national power generally, the only limits to be found lie in affirmative constitutional prohibitions. By his citations Mr. Justice Brennan himself indicates

---

[67] *Id.* at 2486.

[68] *Ibid.*

[69] *Id.* at 2469 n.12.

[70] *Id.* at 2478.

concurrence with the modern view that the distinction between interstate and intrastate economic activities is no longer meaningful,[71] that the Commerce Clause may be employed as a national police power,[72] and that the Court is not to question congressional motives in "regulating commerce."[73] The states have no guarantee of sovereignty under this conception of national power.

Nor would the states have a guarantee of sovereignty under the correct understanding of national power. The states find guarantees of existence and participation in such constitutional provisions as those dealing with voter qualifications, presidential electors, the amending process, and representation in Congress. But participation and existence are not to be confused with sovereignty. Mr. Justice Rehnquist sees this very clearly when he refutes Mr. Justice Brennan's argument that the states are adequately protected by participation in national policy making. Sovereignty is not the right to join in; it is the right to go one's own way. At best, the states have this right only as long as Congress does not diminish it for the sake of authorized national objectives. "Sovereignty" held on such conditions is not sovereignty.

B. THE PROBLEM OF CONSTITUTIONAL PRINCIPLES

Of course, the fact that both sides shared a premise does not constitute adequate defense of Mr. Justice Rehnquist's conclusions about states' sovereignty. These conclusions contravene constitutional language and tradition, and we must now see how Mr. Justice Rehnquist supports them. His strategy, basically, is counter-assertion, not argument. He relies on dicta whose meaning and authority are in dispute. At no point does he confront Marshall's arguments in behalf of national sovereignty. And if we try to extract a principled constitutional argument from his citations we emerge with something no one could defend in the open.

The first example of Mr. Justice Rehnquist's approach is his use of a dictum from *Maryland v. Wirtz* that the Court has "ample power to prevent . . . 'the utter destruction of the State as a sovereign political entity.' "[74] Mr. Justice Brennan shows it to be quoted

---

[71] *Id*. at 2477–78, citing *e.g.*, Wickard v. Filburn, 317 U.S. 111 (1942).

[72] *Id*. at 2477, citing Katzenbach v. McClung, 379 U.S. 294 (1964).

[73] *Ibid.*, citing United States v. Darby, 312 U.S. 100 (1941).

[74] *Id*. at 2469–70, citing 392 U.S. 196.

out of context and at variance with other parts of the opinion, including its principal thrust[75]—things to be expected from the fact
that the majority opinion had just announced the overruling of
Wirtz. Mr. Justice Rehnquist uses a footnote from *Fry v. United
States* which contains a statement that the Tenth Amendment "expressly declares the constitutional policy that Congress may not
exercise power in a fashion that impairs the States' integrity or their
ability to function effectively in a federal system."[76] Mr. Justice
Brennan is persuasive in arguing that this could only mean "Congress may not invade state sovereignty by exercising powers not
delegated to it." He points out that *Fry* itself upheld presidentially
imposed wage ceilings on state employees.[77] Mr. Justice Rehnquist
also uses Chief Justice Chase's language in *Texas v. White* concerning "an indestructible Union, composed of indestructible
States,"[78] a citation "puzzling to say the least," according to the
Brennan opinion, in view of that case's affirmation of congressional
power to form a new state government under the Guarantee
Clause.[79]

The closest Mr. Justice Rehnquist comes to the kind of precedent
he needs is language from cases in the area of intergovernmental
tax immunity. The doctrine of federal tax immunity originated in
McCulloch v. Maryland as Marshall invalidated a state tax on a
branch of the national bank, invoking national supremacy and remarking that the power to tax was "power to destroy."[80] Later
Courts, seeking first to protect the states from the Radical Recon-
structionists and later to protect the interests of private property,
made the immunity reciprocal in behalf of the states. The doctrine
reached ridiculous lengths in the 1920s when it was used to protect
private profits derived from doing business with government. It
declined sharply in the late 1930s as a result of the Roosevelt appoint-
ments, but it did not collapse altogether. Modern cases are still
thought to protect from federal taxation such things as a state-house,
other state property, and the tax revenues of a state.[81] Mr. Justice
Rehnquist employs these remnants of the immunity doctrine as

---

[75] *Id.* at 2478 n.3, citing 392 U.S. 196–97.

[76] *Id.* at 2470, quoting 421 U.S. 547 n.7.

[77] *Id.* at 2478–79 n.4.

[78] *Id.* at 2470, quoting Texas v. White, 7 Wall. 700, 725 (1869).

[79] 96 S. Ct. 2481 n.8.   [80] 4 Wheat. 431.

[81] Pritchett, note 3 *supra*, at 240–45.

evidence for a states'-sovereignty limitation on the commerce power.[82] Just as some state functions are protected by the tax-immunity doctrine, he reasons, power over wages and hours of state employees in such "traditionally afforded" services as fire and police protection, health, sanitation, and recreation is a power or function "essential" to the separate and independent existence of the states.[83]

Mr. Justice Brennan argues that prior Courts had all but abandoned as unworkable the distinction between "essential" and "nonessential" state functions for tax-immunity purposes, and that in any event prior Courts had clearly declined to extend the immunity doctrine from the taxing power to the commerce power.[84] Nevertheless, he is unwilling altogether to deny a state-sovereignty limitation on the taxing power, [85] and Mr. Justice Rehnquist inevitably says: "The asserted distinction . . . escapes us. Surely the federal power to tax is no less a delegated power than is the commerce power . . . . [The tax immunity] is derived from the sovereignty of the States and the concomitant barriers which such sovereignty presents to otherwise plenary federal authority."[86] Brennan never adequately addresses this point, preferring instead to argue that the distinction between essential and nonessential functions is unworkable and that it will lead to overruling even more of the Court's prior decisions, consequences the majority denies.[87] The essential-state-function test seems meaningless and unworkable for Mr. Justice Brennan largely because of the discretion it allows the judiciary. But this is hardly a sufficient reason for refusing to apply constitutional doctrine, as he concedes when referring to the right of the Court to assess the reasonableness of a "legislative judgment respecting what is 'commerce.' "[88] Mr. Justice Rehnquist's challenge survives: If the taxing power can be limited by an essential-state-function test, why not the commerce power?

Mr. Justice Brennan indicates he considered it,[89] but he was unwilling to make the argument that the doctrine of reciprocal tax immunity was simply wrong. It has no explicit support in *McCulloch v. Maryland*, and it is inconsistent with Marshall's theory

---

[82] 96 S. Ct. 2467, 2470.

[83] *Id*. at 2471, 2474.

[84] *Id*. at 2480–81.

[85] *Id*. at 2480.

[86] *Id*. at 2470 n.14.

[87] *Id*. at 2483–85; *compare* 2483 n.11 *with* 2475 n.18.

[88] *Id*. at 2485–86.

[89] *Id*. at 2481 n.7.

of national supremacy.[90] Marshall's remark about the "power to destroy," if applied in behalf of the states, should speak only to their existence, not their sovereignty. The national taxing power, and every other national power, must stop short of such affirmative limitations as are implied by provisions for state representation in the national government, participation in the amending process, and so on. As with the other national powers the taxing power should have been used only for authorized national ends. But in the pursuit of those ends no national power should have been subjected to a states'-sovereignty limitation.

Mr. Justice Rehnquist does not try to defend a state-sovereignty limitation beyond this dubious extension of the faded doctrine of intergovernmental tax immunity. He does not confront John Marshall's theory of national supremacy. This is the most severe defect of the Rehnquist opinion, not simply because of Marshall's authority, but because confronting Marshall's theory might have put Mr. Justice Rehnquist in touch with basic constitutional principles and inspired the kind of reasoning those principles require. If we are to read into the Tenth Amendment a limitation on national power in behalf of state sovereignty, we must be able to answer a question Mr. Justice Rehnquist fails to raise: Does the Constitution imply that state governments are entrusted with ends more important to Americans than those of economic prosperity, national defense, fundamental civil liberties, and racial justice? It would have been rational—although unconstitutional in the legal and cultural senses[91]—to argue that something like educational excellence (an end reserved to the states) was more important than economic health (entrusted to the national government), and that a state-sovereignty limitation existed on those grounds. But this is not the kind of argument he makes. Beyond the value of state sovereignty itself he gives no reason for the *League of Cities* holding. Intentionally or not, his argument suggests state sovereignty is an end in itself, for, by his theory, should a clash occur between state sovereignty over its employees and what Congress says is necessary for the nation's economic health, the latter must give way.

The idea that government is an end in itself is clearly repugnant to our constitutional philosophy, yet Mr. Justice Rehnquist points

---

[90] See Bradley, J., dissenting, in Collector v. Day, 11 Wall. 113, 128 (1871).

[91] FAULKNER, note 32 *supra*, at 33–38.

to this conclusion by the manner in which he limits the implication of *League of Cities*. The Rehnquist opinion opens by reaffirm-
ing *United States v. Darby*[92] and its approval of the Fair Labor
Standards Act as applied to private economic activity.[93] He ap-
proves the Commerce Clause as a federal police power by his citation
of *Heart of Atlanta Motel v. United States*.[94] Later he insists that
Fry v. United States[95] is undisturbed by *League of Cities*, because the
freeze on state salaries upheld in *Fry* was narrowly designed to meet
an economic emergency.[96] Also undisturbed by *League of Cities* are
the holdings of *United States v. California*,[97] subjecting a state-oper-
ated railroad to federal taxation because the railroad operation was
not an "integral" or traditional state function,[98] and *Case v. Bowles*[99]
upholding as an exercise of the war power federal price controls on
a state transaction.[100] Mr. Justice Rehnquist assures us further that
League of Cities might have reached a different result had Congress
pursued its aims through the spending power.[101]

Construing these statements in light of *League of Cities* and in
terms of the ends they involve, we would have the following constitutional principles: (1) national security is constitutionally more
important than state sovereignty (*Bowles*); (2) avoiding economic
collapse is more important that state sovereignty (*Fry*); (3) national prosperity is more important than state sovereignty over
(*a*) private economic activity (*Darby*), (*b*) noneconomic activity
with economic effects (*Heart of Atlanta*), and (*c*) nontraditional
or nonessential state functions (*United States v. California*); but
(4) state sovereignty over those employees engaged in essential
state functions is constitutionally more important than national
prosperity (*League of Cities*), although (5) the states may elect
not to actualize this value in exchange for federal funds.

The only way to rationalize this set of would-be constitutional
principles is to see states' sovereignty over state employees as an end

---

92 312 U.S. 100 (1941).   97 297 U.S. 175 (1936).

93 96 S. Ct. at 2467.   98 96 S. Ct. at 2475 n. 18.

94 379 U.S. 241 (1964).   99 327 U.S. 92 (1946).

95 421 U.S. 542 (1975).   100 96 S. Ct. at 2475 n.18.

96 96 S. Ct. at 2474–75.

101 Id. at 2474 n.17. Note also the statement here that one of the factors distinguishing *Fry* was that "the Economic Stabilization Act operated to reduce the pressures
upon state budgets rather than increase them." *Id.* at 2475.

in itself—a value second only to national defense and the avoidance of economic crisis. "State sovereignty" in this scheme would also be a value higher than constitutionalism itself, for office in a constitutional regime implies duty, and the states seem free to alienate their sovereignty for federal funds.[102]

No one, of course, could knowingly intend these conclusions. But they are the principles of Mr. Justice Rehnquist's opinion. Mr. Justice Blackmun's brief concurrence makes more sense: The Court simply "adopts a balancing approach, and does not outlaw federal power in areas . . . where the federal interest is demonstrably greater."[103] But Mr. Justice Blackmun's is not a states'-sovereignty position. The power he claims is power for the federal judiciary, logically and historically quite contrary to what a true states' righter would have claimed. Mr. Justice Blackmun makes no effort to couch his conclusion in constitutional principle.

IV. CONCLUSION: BEYOND LEAGUE OF CITIES

We might ask in conclusion whether states' sovereignty can find a place in constitutional theory. States' sovereignty might have appeared meaningful while the Tenth Amendment was an effective rule of construction. But even assuming there really was such a period, states' sovereignty was always conditioned on compatibility with national power, and conditional sovereignty is not sovereignty. As for returning to the Tenth Amendment, it seems far too late to confine the national government to a limited number of authorized ends. Real sovereignty for the states was never consistent with the Constitution, and it is no longer likely that it can be restored on a conditional basis.

Nevertheless, values of community autonomy were always a part of the states'-rights tradition, and it may be possible to find a place for some of these values in the Bill of Rights. Freedom of association comes to mind immediately as a possible basis for community rights through recognition of the rights of individuals to live in small, voluntary communities (small because voluntary) organized, say, on religious or ideological grounds. Two decisions of 1976 sug-

---

[102] In Buckley v. Valeo, 424 U.S. 1, 290 (1976), Mr. Justice Rehnquist joined the Court's most recent reaffirmation of the putative theory of United States v. Butler, 297 U.S. 1 (1936).

[103] 96 S. Ct. at 2476.

gest both the possibilities and the problems. In one case the Court reaffirmed the rights of religious organizations to make and enforce rules governing religious doctrine, the status of their clergy, and control of their property free of review by civil courts beyond such questions as fraud or bad faith for secular purposes.[104] In another, freedom of association to the extent of racial discrimination in non-sectarian private schools was held no barrier to legislation under the Thirteenth Amendment.[105] Some freedoms of association are protected; some are not. The same would be true of voluntary communities grounded in the freedom to associate.

The old states'-rights theories were destroyed by the triumph of Hamiltonian economics, increased commitments to the Civil War Amendments, and the nationalization of the Bill of Rights. Should a Hamiltonian order prove unworkable in the future, values other than property may yet become the bases for new communities. On the enormously problematic assumption that our institutions will survive such a change, the Supreme Court would confront the task of deciding which communities to protect and why. These decisions would not be decentralized as they were under the old doctrines of states' sovereignty. They would be made by the Court, under the Bill of Rights, with the aim of reconciling new bases for community with whatever set of national values survives. The task the Court would face is mind boggling, of course, but no more so than other tasks of the future. And if *League of Cities* makes us pessimistic in some respects, it shows in others that there are many rooms in the house of our Constitution.

---

[104] Serbian Eastern Orthodox Diocese for the United States of America and Canada v. Milivojevich, 96 S. Ct. 2372 (1976).

[105] Runyon v. McCrary, 96 S. Ct. 2586 (1976).

DAVID P. CURRIE

THE SUPREME COURT AND FEDERAL JURISDICTION: 1975 TERM

During the 1975 Term the Supreme Court decided a number of issues respecting the jurisdiction and powers of the federal courts. By no means are all of these decisions of earth-shaking significance in their impact upon that jurisdiction, much less upon the world at large; but individually and in the aggregate they cast a good deal of light on the Court's craftsmanship and on the Justices' views of their institutional position. This article will take the form of a catalog, as the best means for exposing both the individual deficiencies and the institutional flaws.

I. CASES AND CONTROVERSIES

A. STANDING

Simon v. Eastern Ky. Welfare Rights Org.[1] was a challenge by indigents to a revenue ruling allowing charitable tax status to hospitals that offered only limited services to indigents. The opinion by Mr. Justice Powell contains no fewer than seven explicit references to the constitutional requirement that the plaintiffs be injured by the action they attack. These observations were quite unnecessary, since the action was brought under the Administrative Procedure

David P. Currie is Professor of Law, The University of Chicago.

[1] 426 U.S. 26 (1976).

Act, which itself requires that the plaintiffs be "adversely affected."[2]
But they further dim the prospects for survival of the universal-
standing provision of the Clean Air Act, which authorizes "any person" to sue to require the administrator of the Environmental Protection Agency to perform a nondiscretionary duty.[3]

Standing was denied in *Simon*. It was "purely speculative" that
the revenue ruling was responsible for the hospitals' limitation of
services, and "the complaint suggests no substantial likelihood that
victory in this suit would result in respondents' receiving the hospital treatment they desire."[4] Two Justices, concurring on other
grounds, disagreed.

The majority rested primarily upon *Linda R.S. v. Richard D.*,[5]
which held the mother of an illegitimate child could not challenge
the constitutionality of a statute construed to impose criminal non-
support penalties only in the case of legitimate children:[6]

> [I]f appellant were granted the requested relief, it would result
> only in the jailing of the child's father. The prospect that prose-
> cution will . . . result in payment of support can, at best, be
> termed only speculative.

The two cases are strikingly parallel, and both impose a highly
restrictive notion of what it takes to satisfy the injury requirement.
As the two dissenters, Justices White and Douglas, observed in
S. v. D,. the whole purpose of the criminal law was to induce fathers
to support their children: "I had always thought our civilization has
assumed that the threat of penal sanctions had something more than
a 'speculative' effect on a person's conduct."[7] Similarly, the purpose
of charitable tax advantages is to encourage private charity by offering financial inducements, and it seems reasonable to assume, as Congress did, that some people will be influenced accordingly.

The Court has not insisted in the past that injury be absolutely
certain in order to support standing. It has allowed preenforcement
challenges to the validity of criminal provisions despite the possibility that the plaintiff might decide not to break the law or the

---

[2] 5 U.S.C. § 702.

[3] 42 U.S.C. § 1857h-2. I have discussed this issue in some detail elsewhere. Currie,
Judicial Review under the Federal Pollution Laws, shortly to be published. I shall
not repeat the discussion here.

[4] 426 U.S. at 42, 45–46.   [6] *Id*. at 618.

[5] 410 U.S. 614 (1973).   [7] *Id*. at 621.

prosecutor not to enforce it.[8] It has allowed a taxpayer to challenge expenditures although it was possible that if he won Congress might find other uses for the money than reducing taxes.[9] It has upheld the standing of students to attack a rate increase for recyclable materials on the basis of allegations that the increase might discourage recycling, which in turn might deplete local natural resources and cause littering in local parks.[10] Needless to say, the Justices disagreeing in *Simon*, Justices Brennan and Marshall, who had written *S. v. D.*, invoked this last decision.

Surely at some point the probability of injury can become so slim that it will not support standing, and drawing the line is a highly subjective exercise. But I think the Court was unnecessarily stingy in both *Simon* and *S. v. D.* When substantial inducements are offered or penalties threatened in plain legislative attempts to influence conduct, the pressures to conform seem sufficiently great to satisfy the injury requirement's purposes of assuring the adversary presentation and avoiding litigation of merely academic significance.

On the other hand, in *Hynes v. Mayor and Council of Borough of Oradell*,[11] an action by persons proposing to campaign for political election, to speak with political candidates, and to canvass for them, the Court in an opinion by Chief Justice Burger struck down as unconstitutionally vague an ordinance provision requiring registration by persons soliciting for a "recognized charitable cause." This was done quite without explanation, over the solitary dissent of Mr. Justice Rehnquist, who pointed out the lack of any allegation that this provision affected any plaintiff. Other terms of the challenged law did apply to the plaintiffs, but the principle of severability ought to make clear that the invalidity of a law as to one group of persons will not in most cases invalidate it as to another. The plaintiffs simply had nothing to gain from a decision that the charitable provision was too vague,[12] except the judgment the Court gave to them.

---

[8] *E.g.*, Steffel v. Thompson, 415 U.S. 452 (1974).

[9] Flast v. Cohen, 392 U.S. 83 (1968).

[10] United States v. Students Challenging Regulatory Agency Procedures, 412 U.S. 669 (1973).

[11] 425 U.S. 610, 621 (1976).

[12] *Cf.* McGowan v. Maryland, 366 U.S. 420 (1961), refusing to allow store employees to argue that Sunday closing laws were unconstitutional as applied to unidentified Sabbatarians.

The Court had no difficulty with the injury requirement in holding, in *Singleton v. Wulff*,[13] that doctors had standing to challenge
a state statute denying medicaid payments for nontherapeutic abortions. "If the physicians prevail," wrote Mr. Justice Blackmun,
"they will benefit, for they will then receive payment for the abortions" they had performed and would perform.[14] No one disagreed.
But there were four dissents from the further holding that the doctors could assert not only their own rights but those of their patients.
Mr. Justice Stevens, whose vote was necessary to a majority judgment, concurred specially. He agreed that Mr. Justice Blackmun's
reasons for this holding were adequate because the plaintiffs had
asserted rights of their own as well and had standing to do so. Why
this mattered he did not say; perhaps it reflects a new doctrine of
pendent standing whose justifications should have been made clear.

Two factors, said Mr. Justice Blackmun for four members of the
Court,[15] determine whether a litigant may assert the rights of others:
"the relationship of the litigant to the person whose right he seeks
to assert" and "the ability of the third party to assert his own
right."[16] The relationship between doctor and patient was a close,
confidential one, and there were "several obstacles" to the woman's
assertion of her own right: "She may be chilled from such assertion
by a desire to protect the very privacy of her decision from the
publicity of a court suit,"[17] and her suit may be mooted by the birth
of her child. *Doe v. Bolton*[18] had allowed a doctor prosecuted for
performing an abortion to assert his patient's rights, and "we decline to restrict . . . *Doe* to its purely criminal context."[19]

The opinion does not contend that existence of a confidential
relationship alone would suffice, conceding that even in such a case
"the reasons for requiring persons to assert their own rights will
generally still apply" absent "some genuine obstacle to such assertion."[20] Yet, as pointed out in Mr. Justice Powell's dissent,[21] the
Blackmun opinion "virtually concedes . . . that the two alleged 'ob-

---

[13] 96 S. Ct. 2868 (1976).   [14] *Id.* at 2873.

[15] He was joined by Justices Brennan, Marshall, and White.

[16] 96 S. Ct. at 2874–75.   [18] 410 U.S. 179 (1973).

[17] *Id.* at 2875.   [19] 96 S. Ct. at 2876.

[20] *Id.* at 2875.

[21] Joined by the Chief Justice and Justices Stewart and Rehnquist.

stacles' to the women's assertion of their rights are chimerical,"[22] for the opinion recognizes that privacy can be protected by suing under a pseudonym and that *Roe v. Wade*[23] held birth does not moot an abortion case.

Doe v. Bolton did allow a doctor to attack an abortion law, but the opinion was concerned solely with whether he must await a concrete threat of prosecution. It nowhere said he could assert any-one's rights but his own. Moreover, the "criminal context" of *Doe*, lightly dismissed by Mr. Justice Blackmun, had figured prominently in the earlier *Griswold v. Connecticut*,[24] where a doctor had been allowed to assert his client's right to contraceptive advice: "Cer-tainly the accessory should have standing to assert that the offense which he is charged with assisting . . . cannot constitutionally be a crime."[25]

Griswold would have provided both the nearest precedent and the best argument for the Court's position in *Singleton*. Even if the particular unseemliness of permitting a criminal conviction under an invalid statute did not extend to the mere withholding of money payments, the *Griswold* opinion relied heavily on the conclusion that "the rights of husband and wife . . . are likely to be diluted or adversely affected"[26] unless they could be asserted by those on whose professional assistance they relied. Since the statute in *Sin-gleton* apparently provides for payment directly to the doctor, he may be unwilling to perform an abortion unless he can collect from the government in court. The woman's ability to assert her own right to privacy therefore may not be sufficient to assure that she can exercise it. The argument for third-party standing is thus very much the same as if there were legal or practical obstacles to her asserting her rights at all, but the Court did not make it.

B. MOOTNESS

Franks v. Bowman Transp. Co.[27] was a class action seeking relief for racial discrimination in employment. By the time the case reached the Supreme Court the sole issue related to the appropriate-ness of an award of seniority for victims of discrimination, and the

---

[22] 96 S. Ct. at 2880.

[23] 410 U.S. 113 (1973).

[24] 381 U.S. 479 (1965).

[25] *Id.* at 481.

[26] *Ibid.*

[27] 424 U.S. 747 (1976).

sole representative of the plaintiff class in court had been determined to be ineligible for such relief in any event since he had been
discharged for cause. Yet the Court, in an opinion by Mr. Justice
Brennan, refused to hold the case moot. Other members of the class
still had an interest in the outcome, and *Sosna v. Iowa*[28] had held it
immaterial that "the named representative no longer had a personal
stake."[29] "No questions are raised," the Court added, "concerning
the tenacity and competence of [the plaintiff's] . . . counsel in pursuing [the case] . . . before this Court."[30]

This final remark is startling indeed. Surely the Court did not
mean to suggest that hereafter the existence of a case or controversy
will be determined by a subjective and tedious inquiry into the
tenacity and competence of counsel, or that the engagement of a
tenacious and competent lawyer will be an adequate substitute for
what until now has been said to be the constitutional requisite of a
litigant with a stake in the outcome. The Court's gratuitous remark
must be viewed as an unfortunate makeweight.

Sosna v. Iowa, on which the Court relied, was an attack upon a
durational residency law which the representative plaintiff had satisfied before the case reached the Supreme Court. Jurisdiction was
sustained:[31]

> [T]he case before us is one in which state officials will un-
> doubtedly continue to enforce the challenged statute and yet,
> because of the passage of time, no single challenger will remain
> subject to its restrictions for the period necessary to see such a
> lawsuit to its conclusion. . . . A case such as this, in which . . .
> the issue sought to be litigated escapes full appellate review at
> the behest of any single challenger, does not inexorably be-
> come moot by the intervening resolution of the controversy
> as to the named plaintiffs.

Sosna was the logical outgrowth of a line of cases, commencing
with *Moore v. Ogilvie*,[32] relaxing the mootness doctrine in nonclass
actions because otherwise the time required for litigation would
effectively insulate the challenged provision from judicial review.
This policy consideration, of course, is simply irrelevant, since it
makes the case no less moot. Article III has been long held to forbid

---

[28] 419 U.S. 393 (1975).

[29] 424 U.S. at 753.

[30] *Id.* at 756.

[31] 419 U.S. at 400–01.

[32] 394 U.S. 814 (1969).

the decision of moot cases;[33] if that means some laws cannot be attacked, that ought to be just too bad. Given *Moore*, however, no hanky-panky about class actions ought to have been necessary to justify the result in *Sosna*. The Court did say *Moore* alone was not dispositive, since in that case "the defendants . . . could be expected again to act contrary to the rights asserted by the particular named plaintiffs,"[34] while in *Sosna* the residency requirement was no longer a bar to the representative. But the Court did not base *Moore* upon an imminent threat that the law would be applied to the same plaintiff again.[35] If it had, no distortion of the law of mootness would have been necessary, and indeed there was no allegation that the plaintiffs meant to take similar action in the future.[36] Nevertheless, in *Sosna* the Court went on to say that upon certification of a class action "the class . . . acquired a legal status separate from the interest asserted by" the representative and that the requisite controversy "may exist . . . between a named defendant and a member of the class represented by the named plaintiff, even though the claim of the named plaintiff has become moot."[37]

The Court in *Franks* thought *Sosna* totally dispositive: "nothing in our *Sosna* . . . opinion holds or even intimates that the fact the named plaintiff no longer has a personal stake in the outcome of a certified class action renders the class action moot unless there remains an issue 'capable of repetition, yet evading review.' "[38] After saying, however, that mootness as to the representative was not fatal in a case where "the issue . . . escapes full appellate review at the behest of any single challenger," the *Sosna* opinion continued:[39]

---

[33] *E.g.*, Golden v. Zwickler, 394 U.S. 103 (1969).   [34] 419 U.S. at 399.

[35] "The burden . . . remains and controls future elections. . . . The need for its resolution thus reflects a continuing controversy . . . ." 394 U.S. at 816.

[36] *Id.* at 819 (dissenting opinion).   [37] 419 U.S. at 399, 402.

[38] 424 U.S. at 1259.

[39] 419 U.S. at 401–02. At first glance the use of the term "plaintiff's" in the last sentence might be thought ambiguous enough to embrace unnamed class members. But the preceding sentences leave no substantial doubt that the Court meant the doctrine just announced—that mootness as to the representative alone is not fatal—was limited to cases in which the issue would otherwise evade review. In support of its contrary reading, the *Franks* opinion noted that *Sosna* had "cited with approval" two lower court decisions relaxing mootness requirements in class actions not involving issues evading review. But all the Court said in citing them was that "this" —meaning that mootness as to the representative is not fatal when the issue would evade review, for it is to this sentence that the relevant footnote is appended—"has been the prevailing view in the circuits." The careless citation of cases not squarely in point can hardly overcome the highly specific language of the opinion itself.

[T]he same exigency that justifies this doctrine serves to identify its limits. In cases in which the alleged harm would not dis-
sipate during the normal time required for resolution of the
controversy, the general principles of Art. III jurisdiction require that the plaintiff's personal stake in the litigation continue
throughout the entirety of the litigation.

Questions of precedent aside, *Franks* gives us a class with no representative, a lawyer with no client. Of course there were live controversies between the absent class member and the defendant, but
the wrong person was asserting them. If my neighbor is bitten by a
tiger, I cannot sue on his behalf; nor may I sue if twenty neighbors
are bitten, even if I employ the magic words "class action." Rule 23
of the Federal Rules of Civil Procedure itself makes this clear. Such
an action may be brought only by "one or more members of a
class," not by a stranger. Nor is this limitation a mere foible of the
rulemakers. One lacking an interest in the outcome lacks standing
to sue. Moreover, only when there is an identity of interest between
the representative and the class are the policies satisfied that justify
permitting one person to represent the interests of others, for only
then is there a reasonable assurance of adequate representation, and
only then does judicial efficiency dictate that the claims of the class
should be adjudicated along with the pending claim of the representative.

The existence of the mootness doctrine is proof enough that
standing to sue is important not only at the outset but throughout the
proceeding, as are its underlying policy concerns of adversary
presentation and the avoidance of unnecessary litigation. In *Franks*
the named party had lost his standing; his case was moot; he was no
longer a proper party to represent anyone. Unless a remaining member of the class was substituted, there was no controversy before the
Court, and the action should have been dismissed as moot.

II. Independence of Judges

Mathews v. Weber[40] unanimously upheld a district court
order referring social security cases to federal magistrates for oral
argument and a recommendation. The statute, designed to unburden
busy judges, authorizes them to use magistrates not only as special
masters "pursuant to . . . the Federal Rules of Civil Procedure"

---

[40] 423 U.S. 261 (1976). (Mr. Justice Stevens did not participate.)

but also to perform "such additional duties as are not inconsistent with the Constitution and laws of the United States."[41] Because the referred cases are decided solely on the basis of the administrative record, and because the judge is free to ignore the magistrate's recommendation, the Chief Justice reasoned, the reference was within the authority conferred by the statute. Nor was it significant that Civil Rule 53 provided that references to masters were to be made only in "exceptional" cases: The magistrate was not serving as a master since his findings were not given the force of the clearly erroneous test prescribed for those made by masters. *Wingo v. Wedding*,[42] which had held magistrates could not hold evidentiary hearings in habeas corpus cases, was distinguished as based upon an interpretation of the habeas statute to guarantee a hearing before a judge.

All this seems quite correct. Moreover, while the Court disclaimed any need to deal with the constitutional question, the same factors that brought the reference within the statute would appear to satisfy any constitutional doubts. Article III's guarantee that the "judicial power" be vested in judges with life tenure and irreducible salary seems amply met so long as such judges retain the right of independent decision. A more difficult statutory question would arise, in light of *Wingo*, if magistrates were assigned to conduct civil trials instead of simply reviewing administrative records. For *Wingo*, notwithstanding its reliance on the habeas corpus statute, stressed the importance of a judge's assessment of oral testimony and concluded that "listening to a recording" was not a satisfactory substitute for presiding at the hearing.[43]

III. Appellate and Collateral Review

A. APPEAL

In *Thermtron Products, Inc. v. Hermansdorfer*,[44] a trial judge had remanded a removal case to the state court for the patently improper reason that he was too busy to hear it. The Court of Appeals held it was without power to review his decision, since 28 U.S.C. § 1447 (d),

---

[41] 28 U.S.C. § 636(b).   [42] 418 U.S. 461 (1974).

[43] *Id.* at 474.

[44] 423 U.S. 336 (1976). (Justices Rehnquist and Stewart and the Chief Justice dissented; Mr. Justice Stevens did not participate.)

with an inapplicable exception for civil-rights cases, flatly states that "an order remanding a case to the State court from which it was removed is not reviewable on appeal or otherwise." The Supreme Court, in an opinion by Mr. Justice White, reversed over three dissents. The statute permits remand only of cases removed "improvidently and without jurisdiction."[45] The prohibition on review, the Court decided, applied only to remand orders purportedly entered on the grounds specified by the statute. There was nothing in the language of the review provision to suggest this narrow construction. Anyone reading it would think it applied to all remand orders. Moreover, the policy against review applies just as strongly regardless of the reason for remand: Congress decided that the cost of unreviewable erroneous remands was worth the saving of time and energy in appellate review.

The Court's sole attempted justification was that a predecessor section appeared to tie together the provisions for remand and for review: The court should remand if the case was "improperly removed," and an order "so remanding" was not reviewable.[46] The present version, according to the House Report, was intended to preserve "the former law."[47] But "so remanding" can as easily mean "remanding to a state court" as "remanding for the above reason," and the policy against review applies equally whatever the reason for remand. The Supreme Court apparently never had the opportunity to rule on the earlier form of the statute, but twice it uttered dicta expressly declaring the review prohibition applicable to "all" remand orders.[48] This history does not justify what the Court did to the plain language and policy of the statute in *Thermtron*.[49]

City of New Orleans v. Dukes[50] unanimously entertained an appeal from a Court of Appeals decision invalidating a grandfather clause in a municipal ordinance and remanding for a determination of severability. 28 U.S.C. § 1254(2) gives the Supreme Court appeal

---

[45] 28 U.S.C. § 1447 (c).   [46] 28 U.S.C. § 71 (1946).

[47] H. R. REP. No. 352, 81st Cong., 1st Sess. 15 (1949).

[48] Morey v. Lockhart, 123 U.S. 56, 58 (1887); Employers Reinsurance Corp. v. Bryant, 299 U.S. 374, 381 (1937).

[49] *Thermtron* has already begun to bear fruit. The Fifth Circuit in *In re* Southwestern Bell Tel. Co., 535 F.2d 859, 860 (1976), reviewed an order remanding for lack of diversity jurisdiction because the question was "purely a legal one." Not even *Thermtron* justifies this disposition.

[50] 96 S. Ct. 2513 (1976). (Mr. Justice Stevens did not participate.)

jurisdiction when a federal court of appeals has held a "State statute" unconstitutional. The holding that an ordinance is a "statute" for this purpose, while highly debatable as an original matter in terms of language and policy,[51] is not new.[52] Nor would it have been disturbing had the Court simply held that § 1254(2) allowed the Court to review interlocutory judgments, since the statute does not say the judgment must be final. Instead the per curiam opinion declared that the case satisfied "any 'finality' test":[53] The sole question remaining for decision was one of state law; the outcome of the severability question "will not moot a difficult constitutional issue";[54] "the ruling on remand is not one which would be subject to further review in this Court";[55] and a reversal of the Court of Appeals would put an immediate end to the proceedings.

Much of this may be sound policy, although I fail to see why the severability ruling could not be taken to the Supreme Court.[56] But for the Court to hold the Court of Appeals decision "final" is another story. Once upon a time the Court held that a final judgment was one that "ends the litigation on the merits and leaves nothing for the court to do but execute the judgment."[57] An appellate decision sending the case back for further proceedings was sensibly held not to be "final."[58] But the Court has departed so far from the clear meaning of the statutes limiting review to "final" judgments[59] that it regularly reviews interlocutory ones on the basis of an almost ad hoc balancing of competing policies,[60] and it does so in the face of carefully drawn statutes making interlocutory rulings reviewable under narrowly specified circumstances.[61] *Dukes* is just one more instance in this well-established pattern; one can scarcely be surprised, but one can scarcely be pleased either.

---

[51] See King Mfg. Co. v. Augusta, 277 U.S. 100 (1928) (Brandeis & Holmes, JJ., dissenting).

[52] See, *e.g.*, Doran v. Salem Inn, Inc., 422 U.S. 922, 927 n.2 (1975).

[53] 96 S. Ct. at 2516.   [54] *Ibid.*   [55] *Ibid.*

[56] 28 U.S.C. § 1254(1) grants the Court power to review "any civil or criminal case" in the courts of appeals.

[57] Catlin v. United States, 324 U.S. 229, 233 (1945).

[58] See Southern Pac. Co. v. Gileo, 351 U.S. 493, 495–96 (1956).

[59] 28 U.S.C. §§ 1257, 1291.

[60] See, *e.g.*, Cox Broadcasting Corp. v. Cohn, 420 U.S. 469 (1975).

[61] 28 U.S.C. § 1292(a), (b).

B. HABEAS CORPUS

In 1963, in *Fay v. Noia*,[62] the Supreme Court held that a procedural default in state court—there the failure to appeal from conviction—did not preclude a federal court from considering a
coerced-confession claim on habeas corpus unless the petitioner had
"deliberately" bypassed his state-court remedies: "Whatever residuum of state interest there may be under such circumstances is
manifestly insufficient in the face of the federal policy . . . of
affording an effective remedy for restraints contrary to the Constitution."[63] In *Francis v. Henderson*[64] the petitioner had failed to
make a timely challenge to the composition of his grand jury and
sought to raise the issue by habeas corpus. There was no suggestion
of a deliberate bypass. Mr. Justice Stewart's opinion for the Court,
holding the issue could not be raised, did not say *Noia* had been
wrongly decided. It did not say *Noia* was distinguishable. It did not
bother to mention what *Noia* had held.[65] But Mr. Justice Brennan's
dissent gave ample notice of what *Noia* had decided.

The Court relied instead upon *Davis v. United States*,[66] which
had held that a federal prisoner's failure to make a timely grand-jury
challenge was fatal to his attempt to secure post-conviction relief
under 28 U.S.C. § 2255. The state requirement that an issue be raised
before trial served the same interests as the federal, the Court said.
And "surely considerations of comity and federalism require that
. . . [federal courts] give no less effect to the same clear interests
when asked to overturn state criminal convictions."[67] But *Davis*,
as the *Francis* dissent observed, was based upon a Federal Rule of
Criminal Procedure that was as binding on federal courts as if it were
an Act of Congress: "We believe that the necessary effect of the
congressional adoption of Rule 12(b) (2) is to provide that a claim
once waived pursuant to that Rule may not later be resurrected,
either in the criminal proceeding or in federal habeas, in the absence
of the showing of 'cause' which that Rule requires."[68] There was
no such rule applicable to the state-court prosecution in *Davis*. The

---

[62] 372 U.S. 391 (1963).   [63] *Id.* at 433–34.

[64] 425 U.S. 536 (1976). (Justices Marshall and Stevens did not participate.)

[65] *Id.* at 539.   [67] 425 U.S. at 541.

[66] 411 U.S. 233 (1973).   [68] 411 U.S. at 242.

issue, as in *Noia*, was the interpretation of the habeas corpus statute in light of conflicting state and federal interests.

In *Stone v. Powell*[69] the Court, with Justices Brennan, Marshall, and White dissenting, explicitly balanced competing interests in holding that a state convict's claim of unreasonable search and seizure was not cognizable on federal habeas corpus petition when the state courts had provided a full and fair opportunity to litigate the claim. Since the "evidence sought to be excluded is typically reliable,"[70] recognition of such a claim "often frees the guilty";[71] and there is no reason to assume that the deterrent purpose of the exclusionary rule would be furthered by permitting the issue to be raised collaterally as well as in the original criminal proceeding. The same argument could have been used to justify the deference to the state forfeiture rule in *Francis*. Any defect in the composition of the grand jury raised no doubt as to the petitioner's guilt, which had been determined after a fair trial before a proper jury; any interest in providing a collateral federal forum was accordingly quite slim.

This argument is by no means new; it had been squarely rejected by a divided Court in *Kaufman v. United States*[72] in 1969, which held a federal convict could raise the search-and-seizure issue collaterally. The Court acknowledged this in *Stone*, noting that *Kaufman* was essentially overruled "to the extent" it "did not rely upon the supervisory role of this Court over the lower federal courts."[73] The "plethora" of other precedents invoked by the dissent, however, was less impressive; for while the Court had often heard search claims made by state prisoners seeking federal habeas, it had discussed the issue only in *Kaufman*.

Mr. Justice Brennan's dissent did make one policy argument: Habeas is necessary because "institutional constraints totally preclude any possibility that this Court can adequately oversee whether state courts have properly applied federal law."[74] This does not meet the majority's contention that the purpose of the exclusionary rule can be adequately served without overseeing the state courts in every case. The dissent's principal argument, however, was that the Court had ignored the plain words of the statute giving habeas

---

[69] 96 S. Ct. 3037 (1976).

[70] *Id*. at 3050.

[71] *Ibid*.

[72] 394 U.S. 217 (1969).

[73] 96 S. Ct. at 3045 n.16.

[74] *Id*. at 3066.

corpus jurisdiction. For when a state court convicts after admitting the fruits of an unconstitutional search "the defendant has been placed 'in custody in violation of the Constitution.' "[75]

The majority's response was less than clear. It began by noting that the Court had limited habeas corpus to questions of "jurisdiction" in the face of similar language under the 1867 act. It then cited *Fay v. Noia,*[76] which had recognized in dictum the authority of a district judge to deny relief when the petitioner had deliberately bypassed his state-court remedies because "discretion is implicit in the statutory command that the judge . . . 'dispose of the matter as law and justice require,' 28 U.S.C. § 2243."[77] Concluding that "the Constitution does not require . . . federal habeas corpus relief" under the circumstances, the Court cautioned that its decision "does not mean that the federal court lacks jurisdiction over such a [search] claim, but only that the application of the [exclusionary] rule is limited to cases in which there has been both such a showing [no chance for full and fair litigation] and a Fourth Amendment violation."[78]

Perhaps the theory is that, while the statute gives jurisdiction, it does not require that relief be granted. Whether habeas is an appropriate remedy for a search violation is left to the courts. But in saying that an application for the writ shall be entertained "only on the ground that [the applicant] . . . is in custody in violation of the Constitution or laws or treaties of the United States" the statute can easily be read to imply that such custody constitutes an adequate ground for relief. The Court never said why it should not be so read. Though history demonstrates that the Court has not always allowed habeas relief when there was a constitutional flaw in the original proceedings—even *Brown v. Allen,*[79] much relied on by the dissent for its view of the statute, held relief precluded by failure to take a timely state appeal—it falls short of providing an adequate statutory explanation. To "dispose of the matter as law and justice require" need not impart a free-wheeling authority to determine the scope of the writ. It may mean that relief should be

---

[75] *Id.* at 3059, citing 28 U.S.C. § 2254(a).   [76] 372 U.S. 391 (1963).

[77] *Id.* at 438. Similar language was also quoted from *Francis v. Henderson.*

[78] 96 S. Ct. at 3046, 3052 n.37.   [79] 344 U.S. 443 (1953).

granted if the grounds prescribed elsewhere in the statute are established. Perhaps the Court meant that the petitioners' custody did not violate the Constitution. Whether it did depends upon whether their convictions should be set aside, which in turn depends upon whether the errors they asserted were cognizable on habeas corpus. The statute need not be read to require relief for every constitutional violation at or before trial,[80] but the *Stone* opinion is obscure on this important issue, leaving the dissent's argument largely unanswered, and thereby failing to persuade.

IV. PENDENT JURISDICTION

In *Aldinger v. Howard*[81] the Court held six to three that pendent jurisdiction over a county could not be exercised in an action against county officers for deprivation of constitutional rights. The reason, according to Mr. Justice Rehnquist, was that Congress in enacting the statute creating a cause of action against public officials[82] had deliberately refused to extend it to local governments themselves.

The Court conceded that the considerations of judicial economy underlying other applications of pendent jurisdiction[83] would be served by joining the county, and its conclusion that the statute precludes doing so was a glaring non sequitur. As Mr. Justice Brennan observed in his dissent, which Justices Marshall and Blackmun joined, Congress's explicit reason for not creating local-government liability was the conviction that " 'Congress had no constitutional power to *impose any obligation* upon county and town organizations.' "[84] The exercise of pendent jurisdiction over state-law claims imposes no federal-law obligations upon local governments and is wholly consistent with the congressional concern. Indeed, the House manager of the bill expressly acknowledged that state laws making local governments liable could be enforced in federal courts "under the ordinary restrictions as to jurisdiction."[85]

---

[80] See Hart, *Foreword: The Time Chart of the Justices,* 73 HARV. L. REV. 84 (1959).

[81] 96 S. Ct. 2413 (1976).   [82] 42 U.S.C. §1983.

[83] See United Mine Workers v. Gibbs, 383 U.S. 715 (1966).

[84] 96 S. Ct. at 2425.

[85] CONG. GLOBE, 42d Cong., 1st Sess. 794 (1871).

V. Sovereign Immunity

A. SUITS AGAINST THE UNITED STATES

Before 1960 the Suits in Admiralty Act, which gives consent to suits against the United States arising out of certain maritime transactions, applied only to cases concerning a "merchant vessel" or "tugboat."[86] A separate statute, the Public Vessels Act, consented to suits arising from the operation of a "public vessel."[87] In 1960 Congress omitted from the Suits in Admiralty Act both the requirement that a vessel be involved and the language requiring that the ship be "employed as a merchant vessel" or "tugboat."[88]

In *United States v. United Continental Tuna Corp.*[89] the Supreme Court held that the Suits in Admiralty Act still did not apply to a collision involving a Navy destroyer. Mr. Justice Stewart's dissent, like the opinion of the court below,[90] made the obvious points: The current statute contains no language excluding public vessels, and explicit words creating such an exclusion were conspicuously removed in 1960. Moreover, in an earlier case the United States had argued, and the Supreme Court had affirmed in dictum, that the 1960 amendment had extended the Suits in Admiralty Act to public vessels.[91]

All this notwithstanding, Mr. Justice Marshall made a persuasive case for the Court's conclusion. Congress, the Court pointed out, has never expressly repealed the Public Vessels Act, and to read the one statute to include public vessels would render essentially nugatory the limitations in the other. Those limitations include a reciprocity provision for suits by foreign nations, which was at issue in the *Tuna* case; a restriction on subpoenas to the crew; provision for a stay in time of war when the suit would interfere with naval operations; and a prohibition on prejudgment interest.[92]

Mr. Justice Stewart argued that no "significant" interest was

---

[86] 46 U.S.C. § 742 (1958).

[87] 46 U.S.C. § 781.

[88] 74 Stat. 912 (1960).

[89] 425 U.S. 1621 (1976).

[90] 499 F.2d 774 (9th Cir. 1974).

[91] Amell v. United States, 384 U.S. 158, 164 (1966); see Brief for the United States there, at p. 9 n.1.

[92] 46 U.S.C. §§ 784, 785; 10 U.S.C. §§ 7721–30; 46 U.S.C. § 782.

served by any of these provisions. The essence of reciprocity was satisfied, he said, because the United States could have sued the private plaintiff in this case; the courts would probably protect national security against crew subpoenas or stay proceedings even in the absence of the Public Vessels Act; prejudgment interest is discretionary, and the sums awarded are "not large." That the United States may sue foreign individuals, however, does nothing to aid the American injured by a foreign public vessel, which was the aim of the reciprocity provision,[93] and discretion may sometimes be exercised in favor of prejudgment interest. More basically, whether Mr. Justice Stewart was right or not as to the importance of the limitations in the Public Vessels Act, Congress clearly thought them important enough to legislate; it is not for the Court to treat them as meaningless.

Mr. Justice Stewart also observed that there still could be cases in which only the Public Vessels Act applied, because it alone allows suit in "any district" when the ship and the plaintiff's residence and principal business are all outside the United States.[94] But to restrict the act to such a narrow class of cases is to leave it such a small sphere of operation that the question is essentially the same as if it had been totally repealed. Moreover, these venue provisions suggest a strong argument against Mr. Justice Stewart's position, for no reason appears why Congress might have wished to preserve the public-vessel limitations only when the plaintiff and the ship are outside the United States.

Further, the Court said, legislative history showed that the omission of the "merchant" language was designed to serve a different and narrower purpose than to bring all public-vessel cases within the Suits in Admiralty Act. The Senate Report, as the Court observed, leaves no doubt that the problem to which the 1960 amendment was addressed was the existing uncertainty over whether a maritime action against the United States should be filed in a district court or in the Court of Claims. The Suits in Admiralty Act and the Public Vessels Act, which authorized suit in the district courts, had been held not to include all maritime claims. Maritime contract claims outside those statutes and for over $10,000 had to be brought

---

[93] The statute forbids suit by an alien unless his government "under similar circumstances allows nationals of the United States to sue in its courts." 46 U.S.C. § 785.

[94] 46 U.S.C. §§ 742, 782.

in the Court of Claims under the Tucker Act.[95] Thus the Senate Committee said:[96]

> The purpose of the amendments is to make as certain as possible that suits brought against the United States . . . can be originally filed in the correct court. . . . The serious problem, and the one to which this bill is directed, arises in claims exceeding $10,000 where there is uncertainty as to whether a suit is properly brought under the Tucker Act on the one hand or the Suits in Admiralty or Public Vessels Act on the other.

Elimination of the requirement that the vessel be "employed as a merchant vessel" removed uncertainty over the proper forum when it was argued, as in cases noted in the Senate Report, that the ship was neither a public vessel nor employed as a merchant vessel, for example, when it was in drydock and thus not employed at all. And the sole reference in the Report to confusion over whether a vessel was "merchant" or "public" was expressly made in the context of the Tucker Act and the applicable forum:[97]

> If [a vessel is] a "merchant vessel," under the Suits in Admiralty Act exclusive jurisdiction is in the district court in admiralty. If a "public vessel," jurisdiction may be either in admiralty under the Public Vessels Act or under the Tucker Act, depending on the nature of the claim. It will be recalled that a claim under the Tucker Act exceeding $10,000 must be brought in the Court of Claims.

Mr. Justice Stewart argued that the legislative history was "ambiguous," showing only that "Congress was concerned with more than one problem."[98] But he cited nothing to counter the Senate Report, which quite unambiguously shows only a single problem with which Congress was concerned, namely, avoiding uncertainty as to the proper forum in maritime actions against the United States —a purpose that did not require bringing public vessel cases within the Suits in Admiralty Act, since both statutes provide for suit in the same forum.

The Public Vessels Act thus can reasonably be read to limit the

---

[95] 28 U.S.C. §§ 1346(a) (2), 1491.

[96] S. REP. No. 1894, 86th Cong., 2d Sess. 2, 3 (1960).

[97] *Id.* at 3. The Court explained that certain contract claims involving public vessels had been held outside the Public Vessels Act. 425 U.S. at 180.

[98] *Id.* at 183.

broad language of the Suits in Admiralty Act, as the Court held. The fault in this case is Congress's, not the Court's. A careful legislature would have specified that the Suits in Admiralty Act does not apply to cases within the Public Vessels Act, unless the latter was to be repealed.

B. SUING STATE OFFICERS

In 1974 *Edelman v. Jordan*[99] held that sovereign immunity forbade a federal court to order a state officer to pay money from the treasury for past wrongs, and lower courts have differed as to whether the *Edelman* rationale applied to attorneys' fees.[100] But in *Fitzpatrick v. Bitzer*[101] the Court without dissent allowed both these forms of relief in an action under the employment-discrimination provisions of the Civil Rights Act of 1964.[102]

Mr. Justice Brennan's special concurrence was based upon his disagreement with *Edelman;* Mr. Justice Stevens's on a refusal to extend that decision to a case in which payment would be made from "separate and independent pension funds."[103] Since those funds would be reimbursed with state money, it is hard to see why this should make any difference. It would seem that Mr. Justice Stevens is not too happy with *Edelman.* Mr. Justice Rehnquist's opinion for the Court, however, took a novel tack:[104]

> [W]e think the Eleventh Amendment, and the principle of state sovereignty which it embodies, . . . are necessarily limited by the enforcement provisions of § 5 of the Fourteenth Amendment. . . . When Congress acts pursuant to § 5, not only is it exercising legislative authority that is plenary within the terms of the constitutional grant, it is exercising that authority under one section of a constitutional Amendment whose other sections by their own terms embody limitations on state authority. We think that Congress may, in determining what is "appropriate legislation" for the purpose of enforcing the provisions of the Fourteenth Amendment, provide for private suits against States or state officials which are constitutionally impermissible in other contexts.

---

[99] 415 U.S. 651 (1974).

[100] See, *e.g.,* Jordon v. Gilligan, 500 F.2d 701 (6th Cir. 1974), denying attorneys' fees; Souza v. Travisono, 512 F.2d 1137, 1140 (1st Cir. 1975), allowing them as "incidental" to the grant of appropriate substantive relief.

[101] 96 S. Ct. 2666 (1976).

[102] 42 U.S.C. §§ 2000e *et seq.*

[103] 96 S. Ct. at 2673.

[104] *Id.* at 2671.

This reasoning could easily be applied to permit similar relief in all suits under 42 U.S.C. § 1983 to enforce rights under the Fourteenth Amendment.[105] If it is, the inroads of *Fitzpatrick* upon *Edelman* will be quite considerable.

What I have quoted is essentially all there is to the Court's opinion, and it is little more than a bare conclusion. One might have thought that § 5, like other grants of legislative authority, was meant to be subject to the limitations imposed by other parts of the Constitution. I would not read it to empower Congress to authorize cruel and unusual punishments for violators of the Fourteenth Amendment. That the Amendment itself limits state sovereignty merely poses the question and does not answer it. So do other constitutional limitations such as the Contract Clause, which has been held limited by sovereign immunity.[106] The argument that the purposes of the Fourteenth Amendment cannot be met unless states can be sued was equally applicable to the Contract Clause cases and was decisively rejected.[107] That the Fourteenth Amendment came after the Eleventh is not decisive. As the Court insisted in another opinion this Term, repeals by implication are not favored.[108] As the Contract Clause cases show, the two Amendments can stand together; and the Court cited no legislative history to demonstrate that repeal was intended. There may be sound arguments in support of the Court's conclusion, but we have yet to see them.

VI. Amount in Controversy

28 U.S.C. § 1331 gives the district courts jurisdiction over federal-question cases only if the amount in controversy exceeds $10,000. Among the many exceptions to the amount requirement is 28 U.S.C. § 1343(3), which basically gives jurisdiction without regard to the amount in controversy, of actions to redress the deprivation of constitutional rights "under color of any State law." In

---

[105] The 1964 Act is somewhat more explicit in authorizing such relief than is § 1983. The former provides for "such affirmative action as may be appropriate," specifically including back pay, while the latter makes the defendant "liable to the party injured in an action at law, suit in equity, or other proper proceeding for redress."

[106] *E.g.*, Louisiana v. Jumel, 107 U.S. 711 (1883).

[107] *Id.* at 746. (Harlan, J., dissenting.)

[108] Radzanower v. Touche Ross & Co., 426 U.S. 148, 154 (1976).

Examining Bd. of Engineers v. Flores de Otero[109] the Court held this provision applied to a suit challenging the validity of a statute of Puerto Rico.

Puerto Rico is not, in any technical sense, a "State." It was once a territory; it has become a largely self-governing "Commonwealth."[110] It has never been admitted to the Union; it elects no congressional delegation; its citizens do not vote for president. In *Hepburn v. Ellzey*[111] the Court construed the word "State" in the statute giving diversity jurisdiction to mean "the members of the American confederacy," excluding the District of Columbia.[112] A majority followed this holding in construing the words of the Constitution with respect to diversity of citizenship.[113] The Court has also held that Puerto Rico itself is not a "State" for purposes of § 1254, which allows an appeal as of right to the Supreme Court from a court of appeals decision holding a "State statute" unconstitutional,[114] and that the District of Columbia is not a "State" within § 1343's substantive analogue, 42 U.S.C. § 1983.[115]

But the Court has not held that the word "State" must invariably be limited to the States of the Union. In *Hepburn* itself the Court conceded that the term can bear a broader meaning embracing any "distinct political society."[116] The decision there that the District was not a "State" for diversity purposes was based upon conclusions that the word had been used "as used in the constitution," and that it had a single meaning throughout that document. The exclusion of Puerto Rico statutes from the Supreme Court appeal provision was derived from a "practice [however unjustified] of strict construction of statutes authorizing appeals"[117] and by negative inference from the existence of an explicit provision for review of decisions of the Puerto Rico Supreme Court.[118] And the District was held outside § 1983 because of the congressional "assumption that the Federal Government could keep its own officers under control"[119] without

---

[109] 96 S. Ct. 2264 (1976). (Mr. Justice Stevens did not participate.)

[110] 48 U.S.C. § 731 *et seq.*   [111] 2 Cranch 445 (1805).

[112] *Id.* at 452.

[113] National Mut. Ins. Co. v. Tidewater Transfer Co., 337 U.S. 582 (1949).

[114] Fornaris v. Ridge Tool Co., 400 U.S. 41, 42 n.1. (1970).

[115] District of Columbia v. Carter, 409 U.S. 418 (1973).

[116] 2 Cranch at 452.   [117] 400 U.S. at 42 n.1.

[118] 28 U.S.C. § 1258.   [119] 409 U.S. at 430.

such legislation—an assumption that the Court explicitly said did not apply to the territories because of their practical freedom from direct federal control. Indeed, in 1974 the Court, without dissent, held Puerto Rico was a "State" for purposes of 28 U.S.C. § 2281, which required a three-judge district court to enjoin enforcement of "State" statutes on constitutional grounds, because the purpose of that law embraced Puerto Rico.[120] Unlike the territories, the Commonwealth enjoys a degree of sovereignty and self-government entitling it to special consideration when invalidation of its laws is at issue.

Thus the precedents establish, as might be expected, that whether Puerto Rico is a "State" depends upon the context and the purpose of the particular law being construed. Acknowledging this, the Court in *Flores de Otero* relied chiefly on the history of § 1343. As originally enacted, both the substantive and the jurisdictional provisions of the Civil Rights Act referred only to actions under color of "state" law. In 1874 the two were separately codified and only the former amended to include the territories. But there was no reason to think Congress meant to create a right without a forum in which to vindicate it, and therefore § 1343 should be read to include the territories. This conclusion was buttressed by statutes giving the Puerto Rico district court the same jurisdiction exercised by other district courts, which included jurisdiction to enforce § 1983. Since there was no indication that the creation of the Commonwealth was intended to take Puerto Rico outside the statute, § 1343 applies to Puerto Rico. The Court added that the purpose of § 1343 applied to the Commonwealth. Unlike the District of Columbia, and to an even greater extent than the territories, which § 1983 expressly reaches, Puerto Rico is outside any alternative scheme of direct federal control.

There are several difficulties with this argument. First, whatever its reason, Congress did leave the territories out of the jurisdictional provision while including them in what later became § 1983. Just such a distinction was given weight in holding Puerto Rico not a "State" for purposes of appeal to the Supreme Court. Moreover, the jurisdiction of the general district courts, conferred on the Puerto Rico court by special statute, was only that given by the present § 1343(3), namely, to enforce § 1983 with respect to actions under

---

[120] Calero-Toledo v. Pearson Yacht Leasing Co., 416 U.S. 663 (1974).

color of "state" law. Further, even if the creation of the Commonwealth was not expressly meant to reduce jurisdiction in civil rights cases, the special Puerto Rico statute the Court relied on is no longer on the books. Jurisdiction must now be found within § 1343 itself.

Nonetheless I think the result can be challenged only by accepting the discarded argument that "State" must be construed to mean the members of the Union unless there is clear evidence that a broader construction was intended. There is an appeal to this position. Congress was pretty clearly thinking of the constituent states when it enacted the Civil Rights Act, as it was when legislating about diversity jurisdiction, Supreme Court appeals, and three-judge district courts. For the Court to expand these laws to embrace other political units that come within their purpose is a little like holding that wolves are "dogs" within a leash law because the policy of the law applies to wolves as well. Nevertheless, given the three-judge decision, the meaning of "State" is to be determined according to the purpose of the statute; and the Court seems quite right that the purpose of § 1343 is applicable to Puerto Rico.

VII. THE TAX INJUNCTION ACTS

26 U.S.C. § 7421(a), with exceptions not here material, provides that "no suit for the purpose of restraining the assessment or collection of any tax shall be maintained in any court by any person." Supreme Court disrespect for this statute has a long history. In *Miller v. Standard Nut Margarine Co.*,[121] the Court held the statute merely codified the equity principle that the collection of taxes would not be enjoined absent "special and extraordinary circumstances sufficient to bring the case within some acknowledged head of equity jurisprudence."[122] Retreating from this extreme position, the Court in *Enochs v. Williams Packing & Nav. Co.*[123] held it improper to grant an injunction solely on the ground that legal remedies were inadequate. But even this opinion added in dictum that the statute was inapplicable "if it is clear that under no circumstances could the Government ultimately prevail."[124]

The statute contains no such exception. The weakness of the Government's case does not render a suit any the less one to restrain

---

[121] 284 U.S. 498 (1932).   [123] 370 U.S. 1, 6, 7 (1962).
[122] *Id*. at 509.   [124] *Id*. at 7.

the collection of a tax. The Court argued that if the Government clearly cannot win, "the central purpose of the Act"—assuring the United States "prompt collection of its lawful revenue"—"is inapplicable."[125] The logic of this argument would make the statute inapplicable whenever the taxpayer is entitled to prevail on the merits, which would destroy the act entirely. As in the case of the three-judge-district-court requirement,[126] the statute seems concerned with the possibility of an erroneous trial-court decision against the Government; the interim injury to the revenue cannot be remedied by appellate reversal. That a district judge must find not only that the government is wrong but that it is "clear that under no circumstances" could it prevail may make such an error less likely, but it does not remove the danger. The Court's exception gives the district judge power to interrupt the collection of "lawful revenue" simply by attaching the label "clear" to his conclusion that the taxpayer is right on the merits. Moreover, whether or not the policy of the Act would have justified an exception for cases in which the taxpayer was clearly right, Congress made no such exception.[127] It is for the Court to follow the statute, not to amend it.[128]

Last Term, in *Commissioner v. Shapiro*,[129] the *Enochs* dictum was applied and arguably extended. The sole item in the record bearing on the Government's chances of success was a deficiency notice in which the Government, giving figures but no explanation, declared that the challenged assessment was based upon "unexplained bank deposits" and upon the failure to report income from "activities as a dealer in narcotics."[130] The trial court dismissed the

---

[125] *Ibid.*

[126] 28 U.S.C. § 2282. See Currie, *The Three-Judge District Court in Constitutional Litigation,* 32 U. Chi. L. Rev. 1, 7–9 (1964).

[127] Much the same exception has been read into 28 U.S.C. § 2281, with equally little justification. Bailey v. Patterson, 369 U.S. 31 (1962). See Currie, *supra* note 126, at 64–66.

[128] The Court in Commissioner v. Shapiro, *infra* at 129, attempted to justify its application of the *Enochs* dictum as an effort to avoid the serious due process question that would arise if the statute were read to forbid an injunction without requiring a showing that the Government had an arguable case. Cf. Fuentes v. Shevin, 407 U.S. 67 (1972). But surely there are limits to what one may legitimately do to the plain words and policy of a statute in the interest of avoiding constitutional questions.

[129] 424 U.S. 614 (1976).   [130] *Id.* at 621 n.4.

request for injunction, the Court of Appeals reversed and remanded,[131] and the Supreme Court affirmed. *Enochs*, Mr. Justice
White declared, had said the decision whether the Government
could prevail was to be based upon "information available to the
Government at the time of the suit."[132] Since no one knows what
information the Government has unless it is disclosed, "it is obvious
that the Court . . . intended some disclosure by the Government."[133]
Therefore the Court of Appeals was correct in remanding for an
examination of "the facts on which the Government bases its
claim."[134]

The Court disclaimed any intention to place the burden of proof
on the Government. It was consistent with *Enochs* "to place the burden of producing evidence with the taxpayer,"[135] and to require the
Government to provide the information through discovery. While
the record in *Shapiro*, however, failed to establish that the Government had an arguable basis for its claim, it equally failed to establish
that it had not. The Court thus seems to have held that a request for
discovery requires the Commissioner to present information sufficient to provide such an arguable basis. The difference between this
and putting the burden of proof on the Commissioner is slight indeed. *Shapiro* appears to expand significantly the number of cases
in which the *Enochs* exception can be invoked.

It is difficult, however, to see how a taxpayer can ever show there
is no factual basis for the claim unless he can obtain information from
the Government as to its reason for making it. Thus the holding
that the Commissioner upon proper request must justify the assessment appears to be the logical consequence of *Enochs*, for the Court
surely did not mean to disable the taxpayer from bringing himself
within the exception it explicitly recognized. The basic fault lies
with the *Enochs* dictum itself.

In *Federal Energy Administration v. Algonquin SNG, Inc.*,[136] the
Court announced another exception to the Anti-Injunction Act. The
suit attacked oil-import license fees imposed by the President under
the Trade Expansion Act of 1962.[137] In a footnote by Mr. Justice

---

[131] 499 F.2d 527 (D.C. Cir. 1974).

[132] 424 U.S. at 627.

[133] *Ibid.*

[134] 499 F.2d at 535.

[135] 424 U.S. at 628 n.10.

[136] 96 S. Ct. 2295 (1976).

[137] 19 U.S.C. § 1862(b).

Marshall the Court without dissent held that § 7421 applied only to "taxes assessable under the Internal Revenue Codes of 1954 and 1939."[138] No reasons were given. No precedent was cited. Apparently there was none. The Court had once in dictum said the statute applied to "internal revenue taxes,"[139] but it did not say explicitly that other taxes were excluded. In later cases the Court considered the application of the act to oleomargarine[140] and grain-future[141] taxes without saying whether or not they were parts of the Internal Revenue Code; both cases were found within the exemption for "exceptional circumstances." The question was an open one.

The language of the statute is apparently all-encompassing. It bars injunctions against the collection of "any tax." The purpose to prevent erroneous interruption of the revenue seems equally applicable regardless of which title of the Code a particular tax is placed in. The act does not apply to penalties, but not every tax intended in part to discourage consumption is a penalty.[142] The Court's dictum that the act applies only to federal taxes,[143] supported somewhat by its codification among federal tax laws, has since been confirmed by the enactment of a separate provision dealing with state tax laws.[144] The best support for the Court's narrow construction comes from 26 U.S.C. § 7851(a) (6), which the opinion cites without explanation: "The provisions of subtitle F [which contains the anti-injunction statute] ... shall be applicable with respect to any tax imposed by this title [i.e., the 1954 Internal Revenue Code]"; and chapter 76 (also containing the injunction ban) applies to "taxes imposed by the Internal Revenue Code of 1939." This section does not explicitly say the ban applies to no other taxes, and as I have argued neither its language nor its policy suggests such a limitation. But the Court's interpretation of § 7851 is at least plausible.

28 U.S.C. § 1341 in equally absolute terms provides that "the district courts shall not enjoin" the assessment or collection of state

---

[138] 96 S. Ct. at 2302 n.9.

[139] Pacific Steam Whaling Co. v. United States, 187 U.S. 447, 452 (1903). The holding was that there was no controversy subject to appellate review.

[140] Miller v. Standard Nut Margarine Co., 284 U.S. 498 (1932).

[141] Hill v. Wallace, 259 U.S. 44 (1922).

[142] Miller v. Standard Nut Margarine Co., 284 U.S. 498 (1932).

[143] State Railroad Tax Cases, 92 U.S. 575, 613 (1875).

[144] 28 U.S.C. § 1341.

taxes if there is a "plain, speedy and efficient" state-court remedy. Section 1341 was obviously designed as a limitation on the jurisdiction granted by other statutes, since otherwise it would have no scope of operation at all. Yet in *Moe v. Confederated Salish & Kootenai Tribes*[145] the Court unanimously held § 1341 did not apply to an action brought under 28 U.S.C. § 1362, which gives the district courts jurisdiction of "all civil actions" brought by certain Indian tribes and arising under federal law. Use of the word "all," the Court conceded, was not conclusive. The general federal question statute, which is clearly limited by § 1341, similarly speaks of "all" civil actions.[146] Mr. Justice Rehnquist's argument was straightforward. Section 1362 was intended to give tribes the right to sue whenever the United States could sue on their behalf, and the Court had already held that § 1341 did not apply to actions brought by the United States.[147]

The absolute language of § 1341 is no barrier to this conclusion. Section 1362 is equally absolute and to the opposite effect, and one or the other must yield unless one takes the unsatisfyingly technical position that § 1341 limits the substantive powers of the Court and not its jurisdiction. The argument based on legislative history, however, does not tell the full story. While the Court quoted the House Report's general statement that § 1362 would provide "the means whereby the tribes are assured of the same judicial determination whether the action is brought in their behalf by the Government or by their own attorneys,"[148] it omitted mentioning that the one clear purpose of the statute was to eliminate the jurisdictional amount:[149]

> The district courts now have jurisdiction over cases presenting Federal questions brought by the tribes when the amount in dispute exceeds $10,000. Enactment of this bill would merely authorize the additional jurisdiction of the court over those cases where the tribes are not able to establish that the amount in controversy exceeds that amount.

Whether Congress would also have wanted to remove the impediment of §1341 in Indian cases is quite unclear. The federalism con-

---

[145] 425 U.S. 463 (1976).   [146] 28 U.S.C. § 1331.

[147] Department of Employment v. United States, 385 U.S. 355 (1966).

[148] H. R. Rep. No. 2040, 89th Cong., 2d Sess. 2–3 (1966), 2 U.S. Code Cong. & Admin. News 3147 (1966).

[149] *Id.* at p. 1, 2 U.S. Code Cong. & Admin. News 3146 (1966).

cerns underlying that provision are of a quite higher order than the docket considerations that produced the jurisdictional amount. Moreover, the language chosen is more conducive to holding that the statute merely removes the amount requirement than to holding it removes all impediments that do not apply to the United States. For the amount limitation, unlike the tax injunction ban, is not independently imposed upon jurisdictional grants by a separate section. To give jurisdiction without mentioning the amount clearly suffices to remove that limitation, while it leaves the question of tax injunctions in doubt. Moreover, the Court's reasoning is not limited to § 1341; it would also, for example, free tribal suits from the restrictions of § 2283 respecting injunctions against state court proceedings, because that has been held inapplicable to suits by the United States.[150] Given Congress's explicitly narrow intention to eliminate the jurisdictional amount and the sweeping consequences of the Court's reasoning, I am not at all sure the Court was justified in holding that the generally expressed desire to give the tribes themselves the right to sue when the Government could sue for them demonstrates that § 1362 removes all obstructions to federal court authority that do not apply to the United States.

VIII. Abstention

Boehning v. Indiana State Employees Ass'n[151] was an action challenging the constitutionality of procedures for the dismissal of state employees. The Supreme Court unanimously agreed with the district court that the case should be held pending resort to a state court for determination of state law. As the per curiam opinion noted in describing the district court's holding, "the controlling state statutes, as yet unconstrued by the state courts, might require the hearing demanded by respondent and so obviate decision on the constitutional issue."[152]

This quite commonplace application of the unpedigreed[153] abstention doctrine is of interest only as a further indication of the Court's failure to articulate consistent principles respecting applicability to Civil Rights Act cases[154] of doctrines limiting the exercise of federal

---

[150] Leiter Minerals, Inc. v. United States, 352 U.S. 220 (1957).

[151] 423 U.S. 6 (1975).   [152] Ibid.

[153] See Currie, Federal Courts 647–54 (2d ed. 1975).

[154] 42 U.S.C. § 1983.

jurisdiction. The typical abstention case is a Civil Rights Act case brought to redress the alleged deprivation of constitutional rights under color of state law. Since the Court has assured the right to return to federal court for ultimate decision of the federal question,[155] abstention generally seems only to make access to the federal forum more delayed and more expensive, which one might still have thought inconsistent with the congressional policy "to interpose the federal courts between the States and the people, as guardians of the people's federal rights."[156] More drastic in terms of its destructive effect upon the rights to a federal forum is the doctrine of *Younger v. Harris*,[157] which except in extraordinary circumstances forbids federal injunctions against state court criminal proceedings. Not only is federal consideration postponed, as in abstention. Even if the prosecution results in custody so that some of the federal issues may be litigated on federal habeas corpus,[158] not all of them may be,[159] and there are severe limitations on federal-court freedom to determine the facts for itself[160] as it would have done in an original action.

Moreover, if the defendant is merely fined, or if the state proceeding is a civil one of the "quasi-criminal" type the Court has recently held also falls within *Younger*,[161] the sole federal forum is the Supreme Court, which may often refuse certiorari and which the Seventh Amendment bars from independent determination of the facts.

All these inroads into the authority apparently granted by the Civil Rights Act might arguably be justified by countervailing policies of respect for state interests such as were enunciated in *Younger* and in the abstention cases.[162] The difficulty is in reconciling them with the Court's apparently absolute rule, never explained, that state administrative remedies need not be exhausted in civil-rights cases.[163] Similar policies of federalism and of avoiding unneces-

---

[155] England v. Louisiana State Bd. of Medical Examiners, 375 U.S. 411 (1964).

[156] Mitchum v. Foster, 407 U.S. 225, 242 (1972).

[157] 401 U.S. 37 (1971).　　　　　　[158] 28 U.S.C. § 2241.

[159] See Stone v. Powell, text *supra*, at notes 69–80.

[160] 28 U.S.C. § 2254(d).　　　　[161] Huffman v. Pursue, Ltd., 420 U.S. 592 (1975).

[162] *E.g.*, Railroad Comm. v. Pullman Co., 312 U.S. 496 (1941).

[163] See *e.g.*, Hochman v. Board of Educ., 534 F.2d 1094 (3d Cir. 1976), citing, inter alia, flat statements to that effect in Wilwording v. Swenson, 404 U.S. 249, 251 (1971); Preiser v. Rodriguez, 411 U.S. 475, 494 (1973); and Steffel v. Thompson, 415 U.S. 452, 472–73 (1974).

sary constitutional questions underlie the exhaustion doctrine.[164] And, at least where state law does not attempt to give binding force to administrative findings supported by substantial evidence, exhaustion, like abstention and unlike *Younger*, leaves the federal court free to determine for itself both the law and the facts relevant to the federal claim.

In *Examining Board of Engineers v. Flores de Otero*[165] the Court unanimously made clear what some had suspected[166] on the basis of *Wisconsin v. Constantineau:*[167] that the abstention doctrine does not apply when the ambiguous state law that might serve to avoid the federal question is a general constitutional provision analogous to the federal. If the challenged state statute is ambiguous, the Court will order abstention;[168] so, too, if there is ambiguity in a state constitutional provision directed narrowly to the subject matter and without federal analogy.[169] *Constantineau* nowhere explicitly drew such a distinction. Although the state in that case had a due process provision that might arguably have invalidated the challenged action, the complaint had not invoked it and nobody had argued its ambiguity justified abstention. All the policies underlying abstention apply equally when the ambiguity is in a general provision of the state constitution: avoidance (1) of unnecessary federal constitutional questions; (2) of friction in striking down state action; and (3) of possible error in construing state law.[170] The Court's only justification was that abstaining on the basis of an ambiguous general provision of the state constitution "would convert abstention from an exception into a general rule."[171] But that should be no cause for misgivings. If the doctrine itself is sound, it should be applied to all cases within its purpose. Perhaps the Court's unprincipled limitation of abstention indicates a healthy disaffection with the doctrine itself. If so, it would be more consistent to abolish abstention altogether.

---

[164] See Eisen v. Eastman, 421 F.2d 560 (2d Cir. 1969); FRIENDLY, FEDERAL JURISDICTION: A GENERAL VIEW 100–01 (1973).

[165] 96 S. Ct. 2264 (1976).   [166] *E.g.,* FRIENDLY, note 164 *supra,* at 93.

[167] 400 U.S. 433 (1971).

[168] Boehning v. Indiana State Employees Ass'n, *supra,* at notes 151–52.

[169] Reetz v. Bozanich, 397 U.S. 82 (1970) (fishing rights); Harris County Comm'rs Court v. Moore, 420 U.S. 77 (1975) (tenure of local officers).

[170] 312 U.S. at 500–01.   [171] 96 S. Ct. at 2279.

Colorado River Water Conservation Dist. v. United States[172] was an action by the United States under 28 U.S.C. § 1345 for a declaration of its rights to the use of water from certain Colorado streams. Holding that the McCarran Amendment,[173] which allows the United States to be made a defendant in state water-rights proceedings, did not deprive the court of jurisdiction, and that the abstention doctrine did not apply, the Supreme Court over three dissents nevertheless held the action should be dismissed and the Government required to present its claims in an ongoing state court proceeding.

Abstention, Mr. Justice Brennan decided, was not the proper course. There was no constitutional question to avoid and no unsettled issue of state law. Nevertheless, and despite the "virtually unflagging obligation of the federal courts to exercise the jurisdiction given them," dismissal was proper in the interest of " 'conservation of judicial resources and comprehensive disposition of litigation.' "[174] While the McCarran amendment did not deprive the federal court of jurisdiction, it did express a policy of "avoidance of piecemeal adjudication of water rights in a river system."[175] Colorado had "established a single continuous proceeding for water rights adjudication which antedated the suit in District Court,"[176] and the United States had been made a party to that proceeding. The Court also found significant that nothing much had been done in the federal court prior to the motion to dismiss; that the federal court was three hundred miles from the state court on the scene; that the United States had participated in similar state court proceedings elsewhere; and that there was "extensive involvement of state water rights occasioned by this suit naming 1,000 defendants."[177]

Justices Stewart, Blackmun, and Stevens dissented. Dismissal would not avoid piecemeal adjudication. The state court would have to conduct a separate proceeding to determine the Government's rights. The state court had not yet taken any action on those claims either. Distance was irrelevant in this age of "easy transportation," especially since live testimony was unlikely to be necessary and since the federal court could sit at the situs. Participation in similar proceedings could not constitute a waiver. The presence

---

[172] 424 U.S. 800 (1976).

[173] 43 U.S.C. § 666.

[174] 424 U.S. at 817.

[175] *Id*. at 819.

[176] *Ibid*.

[177] *Id*. at 820.

of numerous defendants merely meant all necessary parties were before the federal court. Dismissal was particularly inappropriate since "the issues involved are issues of federal law" and since some of the Government claims were made on behalf of Indians, who are traditionally "free from state jurisdiction and control.' "[178]

The dissent had the better of the argument. Mr. Justice Brennan never challenged the dissenters' accurate description of the state court proceedings. His naked assertion that the dismissal would avoid piecemeal adjudication thus stands rebutted and without support. State courts are closer to the situs of most lawsuits arising outside the major metropolitan areas, but that has never before been thought to justify a refusal to exercise federal jurisdiction. Forum non conveniens was invoked when the action should have been brought in some other federal district,[179] not to deny a federal forum altogether, and the argument is wholly destroyed by the ability of the federal court to sit in the same town as the state court. Participation in other proceedings is simply irrelevant. Just what "involvement of state water rights" the Court had in mind is not clear. The Government's principal claim was for a declaration of its reserved rights under federal law, and the Court had already said federal adjudication would not impair state policy. That dismissal in this case would not jettison extensive prior federal proceedings is not sufficient to justify it; it has never been the rule that federal courts must dismiss all actions in which nothing has been done by the time a similar proceeding is filed in state court.

Thus, even as a simple matter of policy the Court's arguments fail to support its decision in favor of dismissal. Moreover, dismissal seems basically inconsistent with the same opinion's holding that the district court had jurisdiction: The McCarran amendment does not deprive the court of jurisdiction, but its policy requires that jurisdiction not be exercised. Beyond this lies a more basic objection to the Court's free-wheeling willingness to order federal courts to decline jurisdiction that Congress has given. The Court used to say that when a statute gave jurisdiction a court could not refuse to exercise it. "We have no more right to decline the exercise of jurisdiction which is given, than to usurp that which is not given."[180] The absten-

---

[178] *Id.* at 825–26.   [179] Gulf Oil Corp. v. Gilbert, 330 U.S. 501 (1947).

[180] Cohens v. Virginia, 6 Wheat. 264, 404 (1821); see also Wilcox v. Consolidated Gas Co., 212 U.S. 19, 39–40 (1909).

tion doctrine is basically in conflict with this principle; so is forum non conveniens. The former doctrine, however, generally preserves the right to return to federal court, and the latter to sue in federal court elsewhere. Moreover, most of the time the Court at least has been fairly careful to confine the cases in which jurisdiction will not be exercised within relatively narrow and specific categories. *Colorado* compounds the uncertainty and the insult to congressional policy by basing dismissal simply on a preference for the state forum in the particular case. The Court could have derived considerable support from three prior decisions deferring to state court proceedings on ad hoc grounds outside the traditional categories of abstention,[181] but it would have been preferable to put a stop to the practice altogether.

IX. VENUE

The Securities Exchange Act allows suits where the transaction occurred, or where "the defendant is found or is an inhabitant or transacts business."[182] The National Bank Act allows suits against national banks where the bank is "established."[183] *Radzanower v. Touche Ross & Co.*[184] was an action against a national bank under the Securities Exchange Act. The majority opinion, by Mr. Justice Stewart, invoked hoary maxims of statutory construction. "Repeals by implication are not favored,"[185] and "a specific statute will not be controlled or nullified by a general one."[186] Thus the National Bank Act had not been modified by the later Securities Exchange Act, and its narrow venue provision governed. While this holding would further the purposes of the bank statute—to promote the banks' "convenience" and "to prevent interruption in their business that might result from their books being sent to distant counties"— it would not frustrate the purposes of the Securities Exchange Act because suing where the bank is established "is hardly an insurmountable burden in this day of easy and rapid transportation."[187]

---

[181] Langnes v. Green, 282 U.S. 531 (1931); Brillhart v. Excess Ins. Co., 316 U.S. 491 (1942); Scott v. Germano, 381 U.S. 407 (1965). *Colorado* cited only *Brillhart*, and only for the proposition that the avoidance of piecemeal litigation could be considered.

[182] 15 U.S.C. § 78aa.

[183] 12 U.S.C. § 94.

[184] 426 U.S. 148 (1976).

[185] *Id.* at 154.

[186] *Id.* at 153.

[187] *Id.* at 156.

The Court's analysis of statutory policy is built upon sand. How-ever unimportant broad venue may be today, Congress plainly thought it important in enacting the Securities Exchange Act; and the decision forces its policy to give way. Moreover, if the Court is right that the difficulty of litigating in a distant forum is a matter of no concern, then an opposite decision would not significantly impair the policy of the bank statute either. Mr. Justice Stevens's dissent demolished the argument based on canons of construction. There was no reason to conclude that the bank statute was the more spe-cific, as one statute applied to a single class of litigant and the other to cases under a single law. And the Court's maxim was coun-tered by "the rule that the more recent of two conflicting statutes shall prevail."[188]

The dissent attempted to get out of the box by finding no con-flict between the two statutes: The bank act does not say actions may be brought only where the bank is established, and it should not be read as if it did. Prior holdings that banks may not be sued in state courts other than those enumerated in the venue statute,[189] Mr. Justice Stevens argued, should be distinguished: It was unlikely that Congress meant to allow states "to subject national banks to the potential harassment of defending litigation in places other than the county or city where the bank was located," but this reasoning did not apply to federal courts since they "could only entertain such litigation against national banks as Congress might authorize."[190] But litigation in a distant court is no less burdensome just because the court is federal, and an implicit limitation on federal bank venue was necessary if general venue statutes were not to impose such a bur-den on national banks. The precedents holding the bank statute exclusive cannot be distinguished.

This leaves us where we started, with two inconsistent statutes and no good way to chose between them. Cases must, however, be decided. The Court would have looked better if it had simply made an explicit policy choice instead of cloaking its decision in trans-parent efforts at statutory construction.

---

[188] *Id*. at 159–60.

[189] *E.g.*, Mercantile Nat'l Bank v. Langdeau, 371 U.S. 555 (1963).

[190] 426 U.S. at 161.

X. Federal and State Law

In *Day & Zimmermann, Inc. v. Challoner*,[191] the Fifth Circuit Court of Appeals in a diversity case had refused to follow the choice-of-law rule of the forum state because "we could not apply the law of a jurisdiction that had no interest in the case."[192] The Supreme Court, per curiam, unanimously reversed, quoting from *Klaxon Co. v. Stentor Elec. Mfg. Co.*:[193] "The conflict of laws rules to be applied by the federal court in Delaware must conform to those prevailing in Delaware's state courts."

While one may argue that *Klaxon* does not capture the essence of the choice-of-law process in the context of the policy underlying deference to state law in diversity cases,[194] there can be no doubt that *Klaxon* demanded the Court's result in *Challoner*. A more interesting question, nowhere discussed, is whether the Texas choice-of-law rule was unconstitutional in prescribing application of the law of a disinterested jurisdiction, for on occasion the Supreme Court has held such an application deprived a litigant of property without due process.[195] As that question belongs in the realm of conflict of laws, I shall not pursue it further here.

XI. Conclusion

The Court's 1975 federal jurisdiction decisions are thus a mixed bag. Those respecting the Suits in Admiralty Act and the powers of magistrates I think well reasoned and correctly decided. That concerning standing to attack charitable tax status I think exposes the relevant considerations and reaches a result on which reasonable people can differ. So, in general, does the opinion on habeas corpus for search claims, although it does not deal adequately with the language of the statute. The opinion on Puerto Rico and the Civil Rights Act has its weaknesses but generally addresses the right questions. The opinion excluding import fees from the tax-injunction statute at least cites a statutory provision that arguably

---

[191] 423 U.S. 3 (1975).   [192] 512 F.2d at 80.

[193] 313 U.S. 487, 496 (1941), quoted at 423 U.S. at 4.

[194] See CURRIE, note 153 *supra*, at 846.

[195] *E.g.*, Home Ins. Co. v. Dick, 281 U.S. 397 (1930).

supports the conclusion. The decisions respecting final judgments, abstention in civil-rights-act cases, choice of law in diversity actions, and the Government-can't-win exception to the tax-injunction act basically follow precedents earlier established. If these were the whole story, there would be no basis for concern.

In holding the ambiguity of a state equal protection clause does not justify abstention, however, and in deciding that Congress may override sovereign immunity under the Fourteenth Amendment, the Court gave essentially no supporting argument at all. In relegating determination of federal water rights to a state court, it failed to substantiate its central conclusion, rebutted by the dissent's description of the state system, that to do so would avoid piecemeal litigation. In allowing standing to challenge a provision that did not affect the plaintiffs it did not advert to the issue. In deciding between conflicting venue statutes, in denying pendent jurisdiction over counties in civil-rights cases, and in upholding a doctor's standing to assert patients' rights it made arguments that were patently fallacious, and in the last case it refuted them itself. In allowing Indians to obtain injunctions against state taxes it omitted critical legislative history. Its misuse of precedent respecting failure to raise grand-jury objections and mootness of class actions was glaring. In allowing review of a remand order it disobeyed an unmistakable direction of Congress.

The opinions just noted bespeak, in my judgment, a distressing lack of craftsmanship in the legal arts. It is the function of judicial opinions to explain and to persuade. Naked conclusions, transparently fallacious arguments, and the failure even to advert to important issues can only impair the respect in which the Court is held and thus weaken its institutional position. More disturbing than the mere appearance of a few poorly crafted opinions is the fact that in so many of them the defects were plainly pointed out by dissenting Justices. One can only conclude that the writer of the inadequate opinion simply did not care. Disturbing, too, is the lack of candor in dealing with precedent and with legislative history. One ought at the very least to be able to rely upon the representations of the Justices. Perhaps most distressing of all is the clear disinclination shown in the *Thermtron* case, as in earlier decisions respecting final judgments and tax injunctions, to obey congressional mandates with which the Justices disagree—an attitude irreconcilable with the basic precepts of a democratic government.

That most of the cases in which these traits were exhibited were unimportant only makes matters worse. One can understand, if not condone, stretching things when great policies are at stake. But the willingness of Justices to engage in such practices in order to assure that a few more routine diversity cases are heard, or when, as in the grand-jury and doctor-standing cases, perfectly acceptable alternative arguments would have led to the same result, suggests that disrespect for Congress's authority and disregard for candor in opinion writing are deeply ingrained indeed. Nor is the problem confined to a few of the Justices. The unfortunate opinions noted in the preceding paragraphs were written by six different Justices. The Justice who protested loudly against distortion of the appeal statute in *Thermtron* left out the damaging legislative history in *Moe;* the Justice who called attention to the abuse of precedent in *Francis* abused it himself in *Franks.* The three who wrote none of these opinions joined several of them. I conclude that the federal jurisdiction decisions of the 1975 Term reveal a widespread lack of concern for candor and craftsmanship in the writing of opinions and a distressing unwillingness to allow Congress to legislate within its clear authority.

ROBERT J. GLENNON JR. and

JOHN E. NOWAK

A FUNCTIONAL ANALYSIS OF
THE FOURTEENTH AMENDMENT
"STATE ACTION" REQUIREMENT

I. Introduction

The problem of defining "state action" continues to haunt constitutional adjudication and legal literature. Few doubt that the Bill of Rights and the Fourteenth Amendment apply only to those acts which are somehow connected to governmental or "state" action.[1] But there are no generally accepted formulas for determining when a sufficient amount of government action is present in a practice to justify subjecting it to constitutional restraints. Although several tests for finding state action have emerged from Supreme Court decisions,[2] none is adequate to predict whether state action will be found in a new case. The lack of predictability

---

Robert J. Glennon, Jr., is Associate Professor of Law, Wayne State University. John E. Nowak is Associate Professor of Law, University of Illinois.

[1] This article is concerned with the "state action" requirement of the Fourteenth Amendment arising from the phrasing of § 1 which reads "no State shall" deprive persons of certain rights. The problem is the same for any provision or Amendment which has similar wording or "requirement." The analysis remains the same for Amendments that are phrased in terms of action by the United States, although the requirement is now one of "governmental" action. The Bill of Rights applies directly only to the federal government so that "federal governmental action" is required. See Columbia Broadcasting System v. Democratic Nat'l Comm., 412 U.S. 94 (1973).

[2] These "tests" are summarized and examined in Part III of this paper.

stems from the Court's repeated insistence that state action depends in each case on "sifting facts and weighing circumstances."[3]

In three decisions during the 1975 Term, the Justices effectively removed any semblance of meaning from the state action requirement. They completed a process of converting the doctrine into a decisional tool that masks a judicial balancing of private interests. In *Hudgens v. N.L.R.B.*[4] the Court used the doctrine to insure that private property would not be subject to the strictures of the First Amendment. Yet the Justices ruled, in *Hills v. Gautreaux*,[5] that suburbs could be forced to accept integrated low-income public housing although the suburbs played no part in causing racial discrimination in city housing. These cases may be read as indicating that state action will be found only if the Justices see little merit in the claim of a defendant to the free use of private property. The Justices did not distinguish these cases by some formal quantitative test of the amount of government activity connected to each alleged violation.

The death knell for formal state action theories rang at the end of the Term in *Runyon v. McCrary*.[6] In *Runyon* the Court held that 42 U.S.C. § 1981[7] prohibited racial discrimination by private schools. Because that provision is based on the Thirteenth Amendment, there is no state action or color of law requirement for its application.[8] The Court's previous decisions that gave expansive

---

[3] Burton v. Wilmington Parking Authority, 365 U.S. 715, 722 (1961).

[4] 424 U.S. 507 (1976).   [5] 425 U.S. 284 (1976).

[6] 96 S. Ct. 2586 (1976).

[7] 42 U.S.C. § 1981: "All persons within the jurisdiction of the United States shall have the same right in every State and Territory to make and enforce contracts, to sue, be parties, give evidence, and to the full and equal benefit of all laws and proceedings for the security of persons and property as is enjoyed by white citizens, and shall be subject to like punishment, pains, penalties, taxes, licenses, and exactions of every kind, and to no other."

[8] Section 1983 is the general civil statute implementing the Fourteenth Amendment. It incorporates the state action requirement by referring to action taken under the "color" of state authority. The statute reads as follows: "Every person who, under color of any statute, ordinance, regulation, custom, or usage, of any State or Territory, subjects, or causes to be subjected, any citizen of the United States or other person within the jurisdiction thereof to the deprivation of any rights, privileges, or immunities secured by the Constitution and laws, shall be liable to the party injured in an action at law, suit in equity, or other proper proceeding for redress."

readings to statutes based on that Amendment[9] made it no surprise that the Justices were ready to outlaw private racial discrimination under these statutes.[10] But it is important to note how this reading of § 1981 may affect Fourteenth Amendment analysis. Any type of racial discrimination that can be deemed a refusal to contract is now illegal and, not incidentally, judicially controllable. On the basis of past decisions, one can expect that most forms of serious discrimination may be so characterized. This may eliminate the need to bring § 1983 suits against private individuals under which plaintiffs have to show that defendant's racial discrimination was perpetrated under color of state law.

It is probable that only cases involving racial discrimination of a lesser impact—primarily in social contacts—will continue to be brought under the Fourteenth Amendment and related statutes. In those cases the Court may carve out an exception to the ban against racial discrimination for certain personal associations which have no tangible impact on members of a racial group.[11]

In *Hudgens* and *Gautreaux* the Court made it clear that when a Fourteenth Amendment claim is countered by a private individual's claim to freedom of action, there is no test that can be used to predict the outcome of the case. When the Justices decided to integrate the suburbs, their earlier decision prohibiting inter-district school busing in the absence of discriminatory acts by the suburbs posed no barrier to them.[12] A slightly different "sifting facts and weighing circumstances" disclosed enough government action to distinguish the cases. Similarly, when the majority decided that union access to

---

[9] See, *e.g.*, Johnson v. Railway Express Agency, 421 U.S. 454 (1975); Tillman v. Wheaton-Haven Recreation Assn., 410 U.S. 431 (1973); Sullivan v. Little Hunting Park, Inc., 396 U.S. 229 (1969); Jones v. Alfred H. Mayer Co., 392 U.S. 409 (1968).

[10] Justices Powell and Stevens joined the decision because they felt it was required by the earlier decisions. 96 S. Ct. at 2601, 2603.

Although it is beyond the scope of our discussion the reader is advised to note the wide prohibition of discrimination against white persons provided by § 1981 as the Court has recently interpreted that statute. McDonald v. Santa Fe Trail Transportation Co., 96 S. Ct. 2574 (1976).

[11] The relationship of the *McCrary* decision to previous rulings on the permissibility of private social discrimination is examined at notes 72–74 *infra*.

[12] The Court distinguished Milliken v. Bradley, 418 U.S. 717 (1974), on very technical grounds. The justification for treating these cases in this category, as well as the discussion of the distinction and the substantive differences in the cases are set out at notes 98–113 *infra*.

private property should be determined by economic factors rather than constitutional guarantees they did not hesitate to overrule recent cases to reach that result.

The cumulative effect of these cases is to end any possibility of a meaningful role for formal state action tests. By removing all major claims of racial discrimination from the state action area, by recognizing them under § 1981, the Justices will be able to rule on the presence of state action solely on the basis of their desire to protect certain individual freedoms. In these remaining state action cases they will seek to balance the alleged constitutional deprivation against the right to private property or freedom of association. The majority's view of how to strike the balance, rather than the examination of government connections to the alleged violation, will determine the outcome of the state action decision.

II. State Action Revisited

While the determination of state action depends on a case-by-case analysis, the Court's development of tests has led to the widespread belief that state action is a unitary concept. Under this unitary concept the only issue is whether sufficient state contact(s) factually do or do not exist. If the Court finds a sufficient quantum of state connection(s) to a particular activity, then that activity is subject in theory to the limitations of the Fourteenth Amendment, even though performed by a private party. Under this traditional theory of state action both the value of the challenged practice and the nature of the complainant's asserted rights are irrelevant.

It was this classic view of state action that the Supreme Court reaffirmed in *Hudgens v. N.L.R.B.* In *Hudgens,* warehouse employees of a shoe company struck the company and picketed both the warehouse and its retail stores. When they picketed the retail store in the North DeKalb Shopping Center, the manager of the center ordered them to leave or face arrest for criminal trespass. The employees left and their union subsequently filed an unfair labor practice charge against the owner of the shopping center with NLRB. The Court refused to impose the restraints of the First and Fourteenth Amendments on the employer, finding that the employees did not enjoy a First Amendment right to picket on the shopping center property.

Hudgens was the most recent of a trilogy of shopping center cases raising state action issues. In 1968, in *Amalgamated Food Employees Union Local 590 v. Logan Valley Plaza, Inc.*,[13] the Court upheld the right of labor pickets to protest a store's nonunion policy by picketing the privately owned shopping center. Four years later, however, in *Lloyd Corp. v. Tanner*,[14] the Court refused to require the proprietors of a shopping center to permit demonstrators to distribute antiwar leaflets. The Court overruled *Logan Valley* in *Hudgens* because five of the eight participating Justices saw no principled way to distinguish *Logan Valley* from *Lloyd*.[15]

It seems evident that *Logan Valley* would not have been overruled if a majority of the Court had perceived a principled method for harmonizing the cases. Indeed, five of the Justices indicated that when the *Lloyd* opinion was written it was not meant to overrule *Logan Valley*.[16] But, given the traditional state action theory, *Lloyd's* effort to distinguish *Logan Valley* seemed to rest "upon rather attenuated factual differences."[17]

The Court's analysis is accurate only if one adheres to the traditional all-or-nothing theory that has become increasingly difficult to accept. While the Warren Court repeatedly found the requisite amount of state connection(s) in virtually every private practice whose constitutionality was contested,[18] the past few years have witnessed a series of decisions in which the Court has declined to find state action in challenged private practices.[19] The inability

---

[13] 391 U.S. 308 (1968).   [14] 407 U.S. 551 (1972).

[15] 424 U.S. at 518. Mr. Justice Stewart's opinion for the Court was joined by Chief Justice Burger and Justices Blackmun, Powell, and Rehnquist. In a separate concurrence Mr. Justice Powell also asserted that *Logan Valley* and *Lloyd Corp.* were incompatible. See *id*. at 523–24.

[16] *Id*. at 517–18. Mr. Justice Powell, the author of the *Lloyd* opinion, indicated that his attempt to distinguish *Logan Valley* had not been a subterfuge for overruling it, but that now in *Hudgens* he thought *Lloyd* and *Logan Valley* could no longer coexist. The Chief Justice joined his opinion. *Id*. at 523–24. Mr. Justice White was of the belief that the two cases were distinguishable. *Id*. at 524–25. Justices Marshall and Brennan, dissenting, thought the cases were compatible, but if one was to be overruled, it should be *Lloyd*. *Id*. at 534–43.

[17] *Id*. at 524 (Powell, J., concurring).

[18] The only major recent decision on state action in which a majority of the Justices found state action and held it valid was Evans v. Abney, 396 U.S. 435 (1970). In Bell v. Maryland, 378 U.S. 226 (1964), the Justices split on the issue in such a manner that there was no determination of the presence of state action in the challenged exclusion from public restaurants. See notes 60–65 *infra*.

[19] See Moose Lodge No. 107 v. Irvis, 407 U.S. 163 (1972); Lloyd Corp. v. Tanner, 407 U.S. 551 (1972); Columbia Broadcasting System v. Democratic Nat'l Comm., 412

to explain these cases in terms of the unitary concept has prompted some commentators to conclude that the Burger Court is unfairly restricting the concept or is less disposed to protect civil liberties.[20] Additionally, the unitary concept has made commentators, judges, and litigants "actor focused": in any particular context a single entity or person either always possesses or always lacks the requisite contact to government which renders any of the entity's actions subject (or not subject) to constitutional restraint. Viewed in light of this focus, the Court's recent decision in *Jackson v. Metropolitan Edison Co.*[21] has immense implications. A majority of the Justices found that a utility company's termination of service for alleged nonpayment by the customer lacked sufficient state action to subject the company to the strictures of the Due Process Clause of the Fourteenth Amendment. If one adheres to the traditional, unitary concept this ruling would indicate that the utility company lacks sufficient contacts with the state to subject any of its acts to constitutional restraints.[22] Such a conclusion raised the specter of the Court sanctioning the company's termination of service on the basis of race or political affiliation. The Court eliminated this possibility, however, in *Runyon v. McCrary*, when it applied § 1981 to all refusals to contract on the basis of race. If a utility company (or any business) refused service because of the customer's race, relief could be granted under § 1981. Still unanswered is the serious question as to the applicability of the Fourteenth Amendment to such cases in the absence of legislation.

We think that the Court would not allow significant racial discrimination by private parties even in the absence of § 1981. Nor do we find anything in the *Jackson* or *Hudgens* decisions which indicates that the current Justices are less receptive to civil liberties claims. Instead, these decisions show only the falsity of the traditional, unitary concept of state action. It is our thesis that the Court

---

U.S. 94 (1973); Jackson v. Metropolitan Edison Co., 419 U.S. 345 (1974); Hudgens v. N.L.R.B., 424 U.S. 507 (1976). See also, Milliken v. Bradley, 418 U.S. 717 (1974). Our reappraisal of the state action concept will show that *Millikin* should be regarded as a state action decision. See text *infra*, at notes 98–113.

[20] See, *e.g.*, Black, *Civil Liberties in Times of Economic Stress*, 1976 ILL. L.F. 559, 561; Note, *State Action and the Burger Court*, 60 VA. L. REV. 840 (1974).

[21] 419 U.S. 345 (1974).

[22] *Cf. id.* at 373–74 (Marshall, J., dissenting). Restraints deriving from constitutional provisions not requiring state action would still be possible.

decides state action cases by balancing the values which are advanced or limited by each of the conflicting private rights. If true, this thesis leads to two important conclusions regarding current criticism of the Court. First, it is unfair to say that the Justices are less sympathetic to individual liberties without recognizing that the recent cases present different conflicts of individual rights and these conflicts require a new and careful balancing of interests. Second, one must reject the actor-focused, narrow interpretation of *Hudgens* and *Jackson*. The determination that a particular activity of a person (or company) is not proscribed by the Fourteenth Amendment has little meaning for the question whether other actions of that person so endanger fundamental constitutional values that they are prohibited by the Amendment.[23]

While there were some early suggestions that a balancing process was central to state action decisions, these suggestions were made primarily in terms of finding private, racially discriminatory actions unconstitutional.[24] This concept of balancing was never expanded to account for all state action decisions; the traditional, unitary concept has gone essentially unchallenged.[25]

---

[23] *Cf. Hudgens*, 424 U.S. at 541 (Marshall, J., dissenting).

[24] For an excellent exposition of a balancing test for state action issues relating to racial discrimination, see Black, *"State Action," Equal Protection and California's Proposition 14*, 81 HARV. L. REV. 69 (1967). For a use of a balancing test which focuses on the need for the exercise of "national power," including congressional action, see Van Alstyne & Karst, *State Action*, 14 STAN. L. REV. 3 (1961). For early suggestions of a general balancing test but with a primary focus on questions concerning racial discrimination, see Henkin, *Shelley v. Kraemer: Notes for a Revised Opinion*, 110 U. PA. L. REV. 473 (1962); Horowitz, *The Misleading Search for "State Action" under the Fourteenth Amendment*, 30 So. CALIF. L. REV. 208 (1957); Karst & Horowitz, *Reitman v. Mulkey: A Telophase of Substantive Equal Protection*, 1967 SUPREME COURT REVIEW 39. Judge Friendly proposed a balancing test as a limited alternative to open ended state action rulings. See FRIENDLY, THE DARTMOUTH COLLEGE CASE AND THE PUBLIC-PRIVATE PENUMBRA 17–19, 30–31 (1960). For provocative questions speculating on the utility of a balancing approach, see GUNTHER, CASES AND MATERIALS ON CONSTITUTIONAL LAW 916–19 (9th ed. 1975).

[25] Three recent articles have employed the unitary concept quite correctly in traditional terms, but with little indication of the possibility of using a principled balancing test in this area. See Quinn, *State Action: A Pathology and a Proposed Cure*, 64 CALIF. L. REV. 146 (1976); Note, *State Action: Theories for Applying Constitutional Restrictions to Private Activity*, 74 COLUM. L. REV. 656 (1974); Note, *The Supreme Court, 1974 Term*, 89 HARV. L. REV. 49, 139–51 (1975). See also Henely, *Property Rights and First Amendment Rights: Balance and Conflict*, 62 A.B.A. J. 76 (1976). For a defense of a quantitative test and an attack on the use of a balancing test to determine state action, see Winter, *Poverty, Economic Equality, and the Equal Protection Clause*, 1972 SUPREME COURT REVIEW 41, 44–52.

III. A Functional View of State Action

Two distinct types of cases arise under the Fourteenth Amendment. The first involves what we call "official governmental action." In these cases the Court is asked to review some specific act of a branch of government that was done with formal authority.[26] When such an action is challenged under the Amendment there is no problem of determining whether the challenge relates to a "state" deprivation or denial of a right. The Court need determine only the ability of the government to act upon an individual in a certain manner.

The second type of case is one that does not involve official governmental action. In these cases one party claims the denial of a right secured by the Fourteenth Amendment by the act of another nongovernmental party. Under traditional analysis these cases require an initial determination of the existence of state action in the challenged act. Conventional wisdom dictates that the activities of private persons are subject to review under the Amendment if, but only if, the state has positively acted in some way so that the otherwise private person and the state have become one. Indeed, commentators supporting this traditional theory have left the impression that the Fourteenth Amendment by its own terms is applicable only when the state has acted in some positive manner.[27] The language of the Fourteenth Amendment, however, does not refer to the existence of acts of commission by state governments as being a prerequisite to the application of its substantive restrictions. The Amendment reads that "no State shall make or enforce . . . deprive . . . or deny" certain rights. It says nothing about what state action (or inaction) will constitute a "making or enforcing," "depriving" or "denying."

When a case involves a challenge to a practice that is not an official governmental action, it only appears that there is an additional issue regarding state action. There is but a single ultimate

---

[26] This category includes all legislative acts, executive or agency decisions, or judicial rulings of any level of "government." For the constitutionality of judicial rulings (which should be distinguished from a determination of state action), see text *infra*, at notes 52–65.

[27] See, *e.g.*, Winter, note 25 *supra*, at 52; Note, *Developments in the Law—Equal Protection*, 82 Harv. L. Rev. 1065, 1069–70 (1969).

issue in both types of cases: does the Amendment proscribe the challenged practice?[28] The additional issue in the private practice case merely provides another way of answering the ultimate question. Under traditional theory a holding that no state action is present is a separate ruling from a decision on the constitutionality of the challenged practice. But the consequence of such a ruling is authorization to continue the challenged practice. In other words, such a ruling produces a decision that the private activity is consistent with the principles of the Fourteenth Amendment. Despite traditional doctrine, it can readily be seen that a ruling on the presence of state action is a decision on the merits of the underlying constitutional claim. Therefore, a judicial decision focusing on the existence of state action has nothing to do with whether a challenged practice is subject to review under the Amendment. It is merely the Court's chosen manner of determining whether the challenged nongovernmental act is compatible with the substantive guarantees of the Amendment. This realization does not end the state action concept. Instead it leads to a clearer understanding of the concept as a part of the basic guarantee of the Fourteenth Amendment. The Amendment does not require the judiciary to determine whether a state has "acted," but whether a state has "deprived" someone of a guaranteed right.

It should be clear that a state may be connected to the asserted deprivation by its tolerance of the challenged practice as well as by its positive acts. To illustrate, assuming that a right to do something is protected by "due process," how may a state "deprive any person" of that right? Obviously it could do so in three formally different but substantively similar ways. First, it could act to end the right by simply outlawing activities involving exercises of that right. Second, it could create or explicitly approve activities by some nongovernmental entities which would limit or eliminate the right. Third, observing that absent laws to the contrary, a practice of some nongovernmental persons will exist in a form which limits or eliminates the right, the state could do nothing. Despite traditional theory it seems hard to contend that the state has done less "depriving" of the right in the third alternative. The state has acted to set a priority between the

---

[28] Throughout this article we use the phrase "challenged practice" to denote the action of the private party which is alleged to violate the Amendment. In other words, a "challenged practice" is the activity which is the focus of the state action decision.

two conflicting private rights if the challenged practice is lawful within the state. If the practice limits the existence of the right and the practice is lawful, then the state has at some point chosen to define the challenged practice as the superior right. This is true whether the state has explicitly authorized the challenged practice or simply allowed it to exist. The only difference is that in the latter alternative the state has legitimated the practice through its common law rather than by specific statutory enactment.

When nongovernmental acts are challenged under the Fourteenth Amendment the complainant is claiming that the state has deprived him of some right by granting a legal preference to the challenged practice. In each case the exercise of the asserted right must in fact be limited by the existence of the practice; and the practice must be lawful or there would have been no need for challenging the practice under the Amendment.

What must be determined is whether the deprivation or denial of the asserted right violates the Amendment. The determination must be made as to whether the Amendment guarantees individuals the ability to exercise that right free of the limitation arising from the existence of the challenged practice, since the right and the practice cannot coexist. If the right is guaranteed by the Amendment the state is not permitted to maintain a legal system which legitimates or tolerates the challenged practice. The Amendment's granting of the right directly to individuals would place the state under a duty to protect its existence, and its failure to do so would constitute a deprivation of the right by an act of omission.[29] In this situation the Amendment remedies the state's failure to protect the right by making the challenged practice unconstitutional, thus insuring the existence of a legal system which prefers the right above the challenged practice.

It is crucial to remember that all cases, other than those in which an official government action is challenged, really involve a battle for supremacy between the asserted rights of private persons. State law in some manner has preferred the right to engage in the challenged practice to the full exercise of the asserted right. A court is

---

[29] This is similar to the concept of acts by omission which has long been recognized in tort and criminal law analysis. See PROSSER, LAW OF TORTS § 56 (4th ed. 1971); LaFAVE & SCOTT, CRIMINAL LAW 182–91 (1972). Consider also the Court's recognition of Congress's "positive inaction" regarding baseball's exemption from the antitrust laws. Flood v. Kuhn, 407 U.S. 258, 283 (1972).

now asked to reverse that preference, which requires that it determine whether the state's setting of priorities is compatible with the Fourteenth Amendment. The established "standards of review" for determining the legitimacy of official acts of government are not appropriate for a determination of the values of nongovernmental activities.[30]

If a court finds under traditional analysis that state action is present in a challenged activity, the nongovernmental act is treated as if it were the act of government. This is a fiction of the unitary concept of state action. The state government is not the real party in interest because no official act of government has been challenged. Whether or not state action is found to be present in the challenged practice, it is a person other than the government who wishes to continue engaging in that practice. The fiction performs a disservice because there may exist some positive value in allowing individual freedom to engage in the activity. Disregarding the private nature of the practice and using the standards derived for testing official governmental acts would result in failing to consider the value of that freedom.

Confronted with a conflict between individual rights, the court must determine whether the Fourteenth Amendment dictates a preference for one over the other. The court must balance the relative merits of permitting the challenged practice to continue against the limitation which it imposed on the asserted right. If the value of the right clearly outweighs the value of the challenged practice, the Amendment proscribes the practice. If the importance of the right is not clearly greater than that of the challenged practice, the effect of the practice on the right does not violate the Amendment.[31] The impact of the practice on the asserted right is in

---

[30] These standards are based upon the role of the judiciary in reviewing the official acts of other branches of government (or of the state governments). Thayer, *The Origin and Scope of the American Doctrine of Constitutional Law*, 7 HARV. L. REV. 129 (1893); Choper, *The Supreme Court and the Political Branches: Democratic Theory and Practice*, 122 U. PA. L. REV. 810 (1974). On the nature and definition of standards of review under the Fourteenth Amendment, see, Gunther, *In Search of Evolving Doctrine on a Changing Court: A Model for a Newer Equal Protection*, 86 HARV. L. REV. 1 (1972); Nowak, *Realigning the Standards of Review under the Equal Protection Guarantee—Prohibited, Neutral, and Permissive Classifications*, 62 GEO. L. J. 1071 (1974).

[31] The requirement is phrased so that the asserted right should clearly outweigh the challenged practice, since the judiciary in close cases should respect the preference set by the legislature.

accordance with the Amendment, not because state action is missing, but because it is permissible for the state to prefer the challenged practice rather than the asserted right.

The Supreme Court's decisions on state action reflect how the judicial balancing of rights functions to sort out those private activities whose collision with other rights makes them constitutionally infirm. While the balancing has nothing to do with finding a minimum quantum of state activity, the process of sorting out proscribed activities has occurred under the guise of a formalistic search for an undefined minimum amount of state acts. In practice, when the challenged practice deserved state protection the Court has ruled that state action is lacking, declaring in effect that the practice is compatible with the Fourteenth Amendment. When the harm to protected rights outweighed the value of the challenged practice, the Court has found sufficient state action, which made easy a final ruling of unconstitutionality.[32]

IV. The Balancing Test of Earlier Cases

Review of the major state action theories and cases will show that adopting a balancing test does not lead to rejecting the state action concept. Instead, the balancing approach clarifies the nature of the state action requirement beyond the current "sifting facts and weighing circumstances" standard. It is our position that the Court need only openly address the function of the state action requirement in order to clarify its past use of a balancing test.

A. THE "PUBLIC FUNCTION" CONCEPT

"Public function" cases clearly demonstrated the use of a balancing approach by the Court in determining the existence of state action. The traditional view of these cases has been that a state may not delegate or allocate the operation of its essential functions to private parties so as to remove those operations from the limitations of the Constitution.[33] The concept is hollow, however, because it affords no help in determining what powers or functions may not

---

[32] The only major state action decision of the Court where state action was found and the challenged practice was upheld was Public Utilities Comm'n v. Pollak, 343 U.S. 451 (1952).

[33] See Note, *The Supreme Court, 1974 Term*, note 25 *supra*, at 143.

be delegated. But both the theory and the results in the prior cases are compatible with a balancing of rights approach. Under the balancing approach the question is whether it is permissible for the state to define the rights of private persons so as to allow the challenged practice to exist. In "public function" cases the importance and public nature of the challenged practice will tend to maximize the harm done to an individual by the person who controls that activity while diminishing the importance of unfettered individual control of the activity.

The public function doctrine originated in *Marsh v. Alabama*.[34] In *Marsh* the Court found that the owners of a "company town" could not prohibit a Jehovah's Witness from distributing leaflets in the privately owned business district even though the message was not related to the function of the district. Variations on this problem were presented to the Court in *Logan Valley*, *Lloyd*, and most recently in *Hudgens*.

In all four cases there existed the use of trespass laws to exclude would-be speakers from privately owned business areas. In each case there would seem to be a similar delegation of state authority to establish privately owned business districts and to enforce that establishment through the use of trespass laws. It must be acknowledged that the ability to use the trespass laws to enforce the private nature of the property is absolutely irrelevant to the state action determination. Part of the basic definition of any state property right is exclusiveness of use,[35] and the ability of the owner to use trespass laws is a necessary part of his property right. Thus the question is whether the state can define property rights so as to establish a truly privately owned shopping district.

One might attempt to distinguish *Marsh*, as the *Hudgens* majority did, on the basis that the state had delegated a larger number of functions and powers to the company which owned the entire area. The majority opinion by Justice Black in *Marsh*, however, made it clear that the rights of the would-be pamphleteer were being balanced against those of the property owner.[36] Essential to the deci-

---

[34] 326 U.S. 501 (1946).

[35] See POSNER, ECONOMIC ANALYSIS OF LAW 12 (1972). For an excellent exposition of the economic theory behind such property rights, see Demsetz, *Toward a Theory of Property Rights*, 57 AM. ECON. REV. 347 (Proceedings Issue, May, 1967), reprinted in MANNE, THE ECONOMICS OF LEGAL RELATIONSHIPS 23–26 (1975).

[36] 326 U.S. at 509.

sion was the Court's determination that freedom of speech was in a preferred position vis-à-vis private ownership of so wide a spectrum of property interests. Thus *Marsh* cannot be explained on pure delegation theory.

The *Logan Valley* and *Lloyd* cases would appear to involve exactly the same amount of "delegation" of power by a state. Yet the different results depend on the relatedness of the speech to activities within a shopping center. In refusing to find state action in *Lloyd* the Court relied on two distinguishing factors that seem to have no bearing on the role of the state. First, the majority relied on the fact that there was available an alternative forum, because the shopping center was surrounded by public streets and sidewalks where handbills might be distributed.[37] Second, the handbills had no relation to the purposes and business of the shopping mall. In contrast, *Logan Valley* concerned the labor practices of a particular store in the shopping center and the picketing aimed to influence customers of that store.[38] Additionally, the majority in *Lloyd* emphasized that the right of private property was a factor counseling the Court to move slowly before imposing a burden on the proprietors of the mall.[39]

The *Hudgens* majority correctly recognized that these factors are specious distinctions, at least in terms of traditional state action theory. The problem is that they do not measure any significant difference in the role of the state in delegating authority to the property owners. The distinguishing factor of the "alternative forum" clearly has nothing to do with the activities of local government. If there was state action in *Logan Valley*, the availability of an alternate forum should not justify a decision that state action is not present in a similar shopping center. In either case the role of the state is identical. The second factor, that the speech was unrelated to the purposes of a shopping center, lacks any significance in measuring the state's role in excluding the speaker. *Logan Valley* and *Lloyd* differ on the nature of the speech involved: labor picketing versus antiwar leafleting. Yet the substance of the expression in no way measures the character of the state's participation. Similarly, constitutionally recognized private property rights were also pres-

---

[37] 407 U.S. at 566.

[38] *Id.* at 563–66.

[39] *Id.* at 567–70.

ent in *Logan Valley* and therefore do not help to identify why the state action determination is different in *Lloyd*.

Measured by traditional state action theory, these factors are irrelevant as standards for measuring the amount of state activity. Thus, to the *Hudgens* majority, "the reasoning of the Court's opinion in *Lloyd* cannot be squared with the reasoning of the Court's opinion in *Logan Valley*."[40] Believing the factors were not principled distinctions, the Court chose to follow *Lloyd* and to overrule *Logan Valley*. We believe, to the contrary, that the Court in *Lloyd* was employing a balancing approach in distinguishing *Logan Valley* and that a balancing of rights can be principled.

The issue, again, is whether private conduct in this kind of state action case should be limited by the strictures of the Fourteenth Amendment. In *Logan Valley* and *Lloyd* the constitutional rights of speech and property collided, demanding a balancing of interests by the Court. Since the value of property was relatively constant in each case, the Court's resolution depended on the differing degree of harm to the right of free speech. Was the damage to speech severe enough to insist that the right of property tolerate the expression? The *Lloyd* majority concluded that it was not. The majority employed a balancing approach:[41]

> It would be an unwarranted infringement of property rights to require them to yield to the exercise of First Amendment rights under circumstances where adequate alternative avenues of communication exist. Such an accommodation would diminish property rights without significantly enhancing the asserted right of free speech.

The Court reached this conclusion, at odds with *Logan Valley*, because preferring the rights of private property did not occasion as substantial a burden on free speech. Whether the speech relates to activities within the shopping center is crucial in determining the degree of harm which each speaker suffers from exclusion from the property. The effectiveness of alternative modes and sites for communication is inversely proportional to the degree to which the speech relates to activities on the premises. Because the labor dispute in *Logan Valley* related to the actual use and practices of the store in the center, no other site would be nearly as effective for commu-

---

[40] 424 U.S. at 518.   [41] 407 U.S. at 567.

nicating this message to the public. Where the speech has no particular relationship to activities within the shopping center, however, the speakers suffer no substantial harm by exclusion so long as there are alternative avenues available for them to reach the public.

In *Lloyd* the division between majority and minority rested partially on how, rather than whether, to balance interests. Mr. Justice Marshall's dissent, expressing the views of four Justices, specifically embraced a balancing approach:[42]

> We must remember that it is a balance that we are striking—a balance between the freedom to speak, a freedom that is given a preferred place in our hierarchy of values, and the freedom of a private property owner to control his property. When the competing interests are fairly weighed, the balance can only be struck in favor of speech.

His quarrel with the majority stemmed from the appropriate weight assigned variables used in the balancing test. While agreeing with the balancing technique, the dissenting Justices disagreed as to the weight assigned to First Amendment rights and as to the dangers of the challenged practice to those rights.

The *Hudgens* Court's failure to follow the *Lloyd* analysis produced two unfortunate results. First, the *Hudgens* majority aspired to bring clarity to a confusing area of the law. The clarity will be short-lived, however, for the confusion stems from the shopping center cases only because they are part of the larger confusion surrounding state action. The rigid *Hudgens* precept will provide no illumination for these related problems. Second, the Court may have slighted important First Amendment rights. The Court should have asked how critical it was for the warehouse employees to obtain access to this retail store. Surely, picketing retail rather than wholesale outlets would more effectively communicate to the public their grievances. And the mall, which was totally enclosed, does not suggest a viable, alternative forum. On the other hand, with a warehouse and nine retail outlets, it is possible there was no need to rely on this outlet, in a privately owned shopping center, in order to express labor dissatisfaction.

Other "public function" cases also illustrate the use of a balancing of interests. Consider the "white primary" cases,[43] especially *Terry*

---

[42] 407 U.S. at 580 (Marshall, J., dissenting).

[43] This series of decisions related to successive attempts to exclude black voters

v. *Adams*,[44] which was the most difficult case. The Court held that the Jaybird Democratic Association violated the Fifteenth Amendment by excluding blacks from participating in its "pre-primary" election.[45] Because the winners in the Jaybird election traditionally ran unopposed, this pre-primary was tantamount to election.[46] The problem was that the Jaybird group was a voluntary association whose pre-primary election was not administered by the state. How then did the state delegate a public function sufficient to warrant finding state action? While no opinion commanded majority support, one opinion stressed that the Jaybird primary had become "an integral part, indeed the only effective part, of the elective process that determines who shall rule and govern in the county."[47] Another emphasized "when a state structures its electoral apparatus in a form which devolves upon a political organization the uncontested choice of public officials, that organization itself, in whatever disguise, takes on those attributes of government which draw the Constitution's safeguards into play."[48] The problem with each explanation is that the state took no affirmative steps to grant the Jaybirds effective control; the decisive cast to the Jaybird elections developed informally.

The *Terry* decision is better understood as a ruling that the state's tolerance of the pre-primary violated the Fifteenth Amendment's guarantee to members of all races of a meaningful opportunity to participate in the elective process. Therefore, "for a state to permit such a duplication of its election processes is to permit a flagrant abuse of those processes to defeat the purposes of the Fifteenth Amendment."[49] Delegation was unnecessary; it was simply impermissible for the state to tolerate the existence of a practice which eliminated meaningful exercise of the franchise by blacks.

Justice Frankfurter's concurring opinion explicitly recognized the futility in searching for positive state delegation as the sine qua non to applying the Fifteenth Amendment to private conduct: "The evil

---

from primary elections. See Nixon v. Herndon, 273 U.S. 536 (1927) (law excluding blacks from primary held unconstitutional); Nixon v. Condon, 286 U.S. 73 (1932) (delegating power to party committee to exclude minorities held unconstitutional); Grovey v. Townsend, 295 U.S. 45 (1935) (convention's exclusion of blacks upheld); Smith v. Allwright, 321 U.S. 649 (1944) (*Grovey v. Townsend* overruled); Terry v. Adams, 345 U.S. 461 (1953) (private "pre-primary" held unconstitutional).

44 345 U.S. 461 (1953).   47 *Id*. at 469.

45 *Id*. at 469.   48 *Id*. at 484 (Clark, J., concurring).

46 *Id*. at 463.   49 *Id*. at 469 (Black, J.)

here is that the State, through the action and abdication of those whom it has clothed with authority, has permitted white voters to go through a procedure which predetermines the legally devised primary."[50] To insist on affirmative delegation would insulate the Jaybirds' conduct and approve undermining the vote of blacks. Thus it can be seen that adoption of an open balancing approach would clarify the nature of those decisions so that they could be used more easily in resolving similar problems.

B. STATE COMMAND OR ENCOURAGEMENT

Under traditional theory, those activities of private parties which the state commands or encourages entail sufficient state action to be reviewed under the Fourteenth Amendment. There can be no doubt that the official command of action by the legislature constitutes reviewable state action; there is no real state action issue in such cases.[51] The encouragement issue occurs in two forms: the problem of judicially "ordered" results and the problem of determining the sufficiency of state encouragement. Both of these problems arise, however, only because the Court has failed openly to adopt the balancing approach. When viewed in functional terms, the encouragement cases show the Court balancing the right to be free of some form of public or semipublic discrimination against various types of property rights.

In *Shelley v. Kraemer*[52] the Court found that specific enforcement by the state court of racially restrictive covenants in property conveyances violated the Fourteenth Amendment. In the later case of *Barrows v. Jackson*[53] the Court determined that the award of damages to adjacent homeowners for breach of such a covenant also violated the Amendment. These opinions did not hold that judicial orders enforcing private decisions imbue those decisions with sufficient state action to review them as the acts of government. Such a unitary state action decision would mean that a member of a racial minority who barged into a private home could not be convicted of

---

[50] *Id.* at 477 (Frankfurter, J., concurring).

[51] This "issue" would simply be another way of stating that the actions of the legislative or executive branches which have the effect of law are reviewable by a court.

[52] 334 U.S. 1 (1948).

[53] 346 U.S. 249 (1953).

trespass if the prosecuting property owner was a bigot.[54] Yet the difference between that hypothetical case and the *Shelley* or *Barrows* results is not explainable if one adheres to the unitary concept of state action. Both situations challenge the judicial enforcement of a private, racially discriminatory decision.

The results in these cases are, however, compatible with the balancing approach. In *Shelley* the Court was forced to determine whether the state could so define property rights as to prefer the interest of a former owner of property over the current owner's desire to sell to a member of a racial minority and the injury done to members of a minority race by restrictive covenants. The involvement of the state judiciary was the minimum involvement required for the protection of any state-defined property right.[55] The state action which violated the Fourteenth Amendment was the decision not to foreclose the effectiveness of restrictive covenants or (for those still addicted to positive act language) the definition of rights in private property which legitimized the use of such covenants.

The recognition that the mere involvement of a state judiciary, or the use of trespass laws in protection of property rights, does not automatically establish state action illustrates how difficult were the decisions which the Court had to make in the "sit-in" cases.[56] In these cases peaceful protesters sought access to goods and services in privately owned restaurants which segregated on the basis of race. It is important to note that in each case the Court found some state command or encouragement of the decision to segregate or prosecute. Yet the degree of state encouragement of the racially discriminatory acts was slim at best.

The Court struck down the trespass convictions of sit-in demonstrators in *Lombard v. Louisiana*[57] because city officials, prior to the demonstration, had condemned sit-ins and stated that the city was prepared to enforce its laws. To the Court, "the city must be treated

---

[54] At no time has the Court indicated that it would support such a result, see text *infra*, at notes 60–62.

[55] See note 35 *supra*.

[56] In this series of cases the Court overturned the conviction of "sit-in" demonstrators at otherwise public restaurants which discriminated on the basis of race. See Peterson v. Greenville, 373 U.S. 244 (1963); Lombard v. Louisiana, 373 U.S. 267 (1963); Robinson v. Florida, 378 U.S. 153 (1964).

[57] 373 U.S. 267 (1963).

exactly as if it had an ordinance prohibiting such conduct."[58] If state action were a unitary concept these statements by city officials should insulate persons protesting in a private home. Would the Court hold that a private homeowner could not rely on trespass laws to exclude black demonstrators because city officials stood ready to enforce the law? Under a balancing test the difference would be that a person's right to be left alone in the privacy of his home outweighs any harm either to the sensibilities of the demonstrators or the effectiveness of their protest.[59]

The traditional theory accounts for the split of opinion and curious turn of the Court in *Bell v. Maryland*.[60] A decision on the merits in *Bell* would have determined whether the state was under a duty to prohibit segregation in certain "public" facilities. The central issue in the case was the ability of the state to define property rights so as to prefer property ownership over the injury done to members of a minority race who are denied services in businesses otherwise open to the public. While the Court ducked the merits by reversing the conviction on other grounds, six Justices faced the substantive issue. An opinion by Justice Douglas, representing the views of only two Justices, would have prohibited the discrimination by the restaurant owner regardless of the existence of positive action by government officials.[61] Yet even Douglas apparently would distinguish business from personal prejudice:[62]

> The property involved is not, however, a man's home or his yard or even his fields. Private property is involved, but it is property that is serving the public. . . . The problem with which we deal has no relation to opening or closing the door of one's home. The home of course is the essence of privacy, in no way dedicated to public use, in no way extending an invitation to the public.

The clear inference is that Douglas would uphold the homeowner's right to exclude blacks by invoking the state's trespass law. Yet the invocation of the same state trespass law would produce different constitutional results depending on the circumstances in which the

---

[58] *Id*. at 273.

[59] See Black, note 24 *supra*, at 101–02.   [60] 378 U.S. 226 (1964).

[61] It was sufficient for Douglas that the restaurant owner's bias was effected by his use of the courts to enforce his property rights. *Id*. at 259–60.

[62] *Id*. at 252–53.

property owner seeks state aid. Since the state's role is identical in both cases, how can one case find state action and the other not? Douglas's *Bell* opinion recognized the presence and value of counter-vailing constitutional rights: private property, privacy, and freedom of association. While property rights are present in both cases, the business property owner invites a greater degree of state control by virtue of opening his property to the public. Similarly, he minimizes his expectation of privacy and unfettered right to associate by al-lowing anonymous patrons to enter freely. By contrast, the private homeowner has not acted to open his property to use by third per-sons. Thus, Douglas seems to have adopted a balancing approach for resolving state action questions in regard to these conflicting private rights.

Black's dissent would elevate the property right of the restaurant proprietor over the rights of members of a racial minority seeking service.[63] Although he reached an opposite conclusion on the merits, his opinion seems to balance the conflicting rights almost as openly as Douglas did. To reach his conclusion, Black needed to distinguish *Shelley*. He relied on two grounds which further undercut the tra-ditional theory of state action. First, in *Shelley* the Court found state action because the state ruling upholding the restrictive cove-nant interfered with a federal statutory right: the 1866 Civil Rights Act protecting the right to own property.[64] But the role of the state is unaffected by the presence or absence of a federal statute. Sec-ond, Black distinguished *Shelley* as concerning two willing parties to the transfer of land, whereas in the sit-in case the owner re-mained unwilling to deal with the minority members.[65] Again, this factor does not help identify a difference in state action in any quan-titative sense. The distinctions make eminent sense, however, if Black was balancing the freedom of association against differing property rights. The distinctions indicate that Black would protect the rights of the restaurant owner in *Bell* because he saw a greater hardship on property rights and a lesser burden on minority inter-ests than was present in *Shelley*.

The split of opinions in *Bell* and the recognition of the balancing test allow us to reevaluate the Court's decision in *Moose Lodge No. 107 v. Irvis*.[66] In *Moose Lodge* the majority held that there was in-

---

[63] See *id*. at 318.

[64] *Id*. at 330.

[65] *Id*. at 331.

[66] 407 U.S. 163 (1972).

sufficient state action connected with a private social club to review the club's racially restrictive policies under the Fourteenth Amendment. This case provides an apt contrast to the sit-in cases because the Court permitted the Lodge to use the trespass laws to enforce its exclusive property rights and discriminatory practices.[67]

After the Warren Court's substantial efforts to eliminate segregated restaurants, it seemed highly reactionary for the Burger Court to allow even a private club to serve food and drink on a segregated basis. The methodology of the decision, however, is simply an application of a balancing test that was developed during the Warren Court years.[68] The Court has always recognized an associational interest in private clubs, whether political organizations or country clubs.[69] The Court has never indicated that it is impermissible for a state to define property rights in order to allow this type of association to exist. It is only when such an association causes some harm to a member of the excluded race, beyond the emotional harm of being refused admittance into the club, that the state may not tolerate the practice of the private club. If even that slight psychological harm were enough to offset the values in association, then the use of a trespass law by a homeowner to evict a black whom he had refused to invite to dinner could not be tolerated under the Amendment. Even Douglas would not find the harm done someone by the refusal to invite him into a private home enough to offset the associational and property interests of the home owner.

The question in *Moose Lodge* was whether there was any harm to members of the minority race by the existence of the segregated club in Harrisburg, Pennsylvania. The majority and minority parted company on this issue because the majority saw no lessening of the ability of blacks to obtain food and drink in Harrisburg owing to the existence of the club.[70] By contrast, one of the dissent's key points was that the granting of the liquor license to this club re-

---

[67] If this is not true the decision in *Moose Lodge* is meaningless. The association and property rights are worthless unless they encompass an enforceable right to exclusivity. See note 35 *supra*.

[68] This is not to say that the balancing approach would have been applied to reach the same result. While the methodology was the same it is hard to believe that the Court, in the heyday of the Warren era, would have subscribed to the *Moose Lodge* decision.

[69] See N.A.A.C.P. v. Alabama, 357 U.S. 449 (1958); Bell v. Maryland, 378 U.S. 226, 242 (1964) (Douglas, J.).

[70] 407 U.S. at 176.

duced the number of licenses which could be granted to nondiscriminatory groups and thereby lessened the availability of drinks to members of the minority race and others who wish to drink in an integrated bar.[71] Thus the central issue for both majority and dissent was to balance the interests of the two private parties. The test was not a new or restrictive one; the Justices merely disagreed on the impact of the practice and on how to apply the balancing test.

The balancing test in these cases has produced two results. In cases where racial discrimination had a substantial economic or political impact state action would be found and the discrimination eliminated. But, if the racial discrimination related to purely social contacts which did not have such an effect, no state action would be found and the practice would be allowed to continue. These results mirror the application of § 1981 as it was interpreted last Term. In *Runyon v. McCrary*[72] the Court held that § 1981 prohibited refusals to contract on the basis of race. In holding that § 1981 rendered invalid the establishment of segregated private schools the majority found no interest in the parents or schoolchildren which could offset the command of racial equality.[73] Thus it is probable that the statute will apply with full force to all the commercial refusals to contract which have been the subject of the state action decisions. Yet the Court was careful to note that the case did not involve the issue of "the right of a private social organization to limit its membership on racial or any other grounds."[74] The majority's citation of *Moose Lodge* in connection with this statement clearly implied that the results of the Fourteenth Amendment cases will not be altered by § 1981. Instead, social discrimination will simply be held outside the purview of § 1981, which prohibits only refusals to contract. Any substantial form of racial discrimination may be termed a refusal to contract and made illegal under that statute. Thus we will have the same decisional results, even though the state action test is formally eliminated when the litigation is based on § 1981.

C. THE JOINT CONTRACT–SYMBIOTIC RELATIONSHIP "TEST"

While a few authors have made heroic attempts to separate a variety of specialized tests for state action depending on the type of

---

[71]See *id*. at 182–83.

[72] 96 S. Ct. 2586 (1976).

[73] *Id*. at 2596–98.

[74] *Id*. at 2592.

contracts or control between government and the challenged practices,[75] these tests have never been adopted by the Court. Indeed,
very few cases at the Supreme Court level have involved such an
issue. Most decisions included in this category concern governmental grants of funds,[76] government compulsion or encouragement of
specific activities, or delegation of public functions.

In a few cases, the Supreme Court has found state action on the
basis of the control, contacts, or entanglement of the private practice and some official branch of government. No refinement of this
contact concept ever took place in the decisions of the Court. In
these decisions, although the private actor could not be tied to
the state by any of the more specific tests, a majority of the Justices
had found sufficient connections to hold the actor accountable by
"sifting facts and weighing circumstances."[77] This "joint contacts–
sifting facts" standard, however, was never more than an informal
justification for balancing the interests of the private parties. The
leading "joint contact" cases show a consistent pattern of Court
assessment of the public impact of the challenged practice, followed
by a balancing of the worth of that practice against the asserted
private right that it limits.

In *Public Utilities Commission v. Pollak*[78] the Court upheld a transit company's practice of broadcasting radio programs in the buses
and streetcars in Washington, D.C. While the Court seemed to find
that the high degree of regulation made the transit company subject
to constitutional restraints, it found that the practice was permissible.
Since the majority was certain that the practice was compatible
with the Constitution, the Justices spent little effort assessing the
quantity or quality of contacts between the transit company and the
city. Indeed, their treatment of the issue was so cavalier that it is not
clear whether they found government action or merely assumed it
arguendo.[79] The Court clearly found that the freedom of operation

---

[75] See, *e.g.*, Note, note 25 *supra*, 74 COLUM. L. REV. 656.

[76] The problem of direct aid to private activities is dealt with in text at notes 88–
93 *infra*.

[77] Burton v. Wilmington Parking Authority, 365 U.S. 715, 722 (1961).

[78] 343 U.S. 451 (1952).

[79] This point was made by the majority in Jackson v. Metropolitan Edison Co.,
419 U.S. 345, 356 n.16. (1974): "See [Public Utilities Comm'n v. Pollak], 343 U.S. at
462. At one point the Court states: 'We find in the reasoning of the court below

of the bus company outweighed any asserted private right to be free from this intrusion. The case is unique in that it is the only major opinion of the Court to strike the balance in favor of the challenged private practice without masking the decision behind the ruling that there was insufficient state action involved.

The Court's decisions on the permissible use of property devised to a city for a racially segregated park also demonstrate the use of the balancing test under the "contacts" standard. In *Evans v. Newton*[80] the Court determined that the continued segregation of a park devised by Senator Bacon to the town of Macon, Georgia, violated the Fourteenth Amendment. While the Court mentioned the past and present contacts between the city government and the operation of the park, the opinion clearly forbade the continued existence of the park on a segregated basis even if the city immediately terminated all activities in relation to its operation.[81] The opinion strongly indicated that the associational interests in a "private park" were of less value than associational interests in a private school or a private golf club, and therefore state action would be found more readily in the operation of the park.[82]

The balancing approach emerged clearly in *Evans v. Abney*[83] when the Court allowed the same land to revert to the heirs of Senator Bacon when the trust failed. It is certain that the differing determinations of state action could not have been based upon the quantity or history of acts involving the city with the park, since the degree of past association and involvement was the same in both cases. With the change of title, the weight shifts radically between the two fact situations. In *Newton* the balance was between the worth of private ownership of a park which is otherwise open to the public and the injury inflicted upon members of racial minorities who are publicly excluded from that area. In *Abney*, by contrast, the balance was between those who had private property rights to

---

a sufficiently close relation between the Federal Government and the radio service to make it necessary for us to consider those Amendments.' *Ibid*.

"Later, the opinion states: 'We, therefore, find it appropriate to examine into what restriction, if any, the First and Fifth Amendments place upon the Federal Government . . . *assuming* that the action of Capital Transit . . . amounts to sufficient Federal Government action to make the First and Fifth Amendments applicable thereto.' *Id.*, at 462–463. (Emphasis added.) The Court then went on to find no constitutional violation in the challenged action."

[80] 382 U.S. 296 (1966).   [82] *Ibid*.

[81] *Id*. at 301–02.   [83] 396 U.S. 435 (1970).

the land for personal use and members of a racial minority desiring to use the land as a public park. It is hard to find an affirmative obligation by the state in *Abney* to redress past injustice by depriving the current property holders of any use of the land. Thus it was permissible for the state to define property rights to allow the heirs of Senator Bacon sole use of the land—so long as it was no longer used as a segregated public facility. *Abney* also reinforces the important point that judicial involvement with a particular private practice will not necessarily result in a finding of state action. If state action were really determined by searching for a certain quantity of state involvement, the decision in *Abney* could not stand simultaneously with that in *Shelley v. Kraemer.*

The classic "joint contact–symbiotic relationship" case is *Wilmington Parking Authority*. The Court found that a private restaurant which leased space in a government parking facility violated the Fourteenth Amendment by refusing service to members of racial minorities. Although the restaurant did not receive direct aid from the government, was not under its literal command, and was not performing a governmental function, it did receive some benefit from its location.[84] Thus, the challenged private practice was the use of property in public to make a profit from physical proximity to the government offices. Balanced against this private practice was the exclusion of racial minorities from an otherwise public retail establishment which was most convenient to persons using government facilities. The private practice being a less "worthy" or pristine form of property ownership and the discrimination being at least as serious as was present in the *Bell v. Maryland* situation, the balance was easily struck against the restaurant owner.

The Court's decision in *Reitman v. Mulkey*[85] was the last of the "multi-reasoned" findings of state action. The majority found that a California constitutional amendment which repealed open housing legislation and inhibited the passage of similar legislation violated the Fourteenth Amendment. The majority did not explain, however, whether the finding of state action related to the encouragement of racial bias in land transactions, the total "delegation" of control of

---

[84] It would appear that this was expected to be an ongoing and profitable business owing to its proximity to the government office. This conclusion is justified by the nature of the lease and the investments in the resturant. See 365 U.S. at 719.

[85] 387 U.S. 369 (1967).

land transactions to private parties, or simply the public withdrawal and reversal of previous aid to those seeking homes on a nondiscriminatory basis. The decision seems hard to justify in terms of future hypothetical refusals to sell homes to blacks because of the passage of Proposition 14. The case makes sense, however, as Professor Black has pointed out, if we disregard all state activities relating to future property sales and merely look at the effect of the California constitutional revision.[86] What was really to be judged in *Reitman* was the decision to impede minority members' access to legislative remedies, which was accomplished by specific constitutional amendment. There was no difficult problem in terms of either state activity or a balance of interests; the only difficult aspect of *Reitman* was the Court's inability to state openly that it would not allow state governments effectively to create a super-majority requirement for the passage of laws which would assist members of a racial minority.[87] The Court effectively balanced the right of the current populace of California to have guaranteed freedom from open housing laws against the burden on racial minorities from being denied access to the legislature for redress of their problems.

This analysis of *Reitman* shows not only the Court's use of a balancing approach, but also the problems caused by masking decisions on the merits under the guise of technical state action rulings. The inability to understand *Reitman* and the other "control-relationship" cases stems from the Court's failure openly to balance the interests and its reliance on formalistic state action language to hide the reasoning behind its decisions.

D. STATE ACTION CASES NOT COMMONLY THOUGHT OF AS SUCH

The unitary concept of state action has so effectively diverted attention from the underlying reasons for the Court's decisions that it is easy to miss the similarity between state action cases and related

---

[86] See Black, note 24 *supra*.

[87] Professor Black states the conclusion as follows: "[W]here a racial group is in a political duel with those who would explicitly discriminate against it as a racial group, and where the regulatory action the racial group wants is of full and undoubted federal constitutionality, the state may not place in the way of the racial minority's attaining its political goal any barriers which, within the state's political system taken as a whole, are especially difficult of surmounting, by comparison with those barriers that normally stand in the way of those who wish to use political processes to get what they want." *Id*. at 82.

cases concerning the constitutionality of official government actions. This misuse of the state action concept has left the Court without a framework for making decisions in at least two areas. Cases involving governmental subsidies to private parties and the prohibition of de jure segregation in the public schools both present state action issues. In the former, a court must assess the legitimacy of state action which aids a person whose activities allegedly would violate the Amendment if the government performed them. In the latter, the existence of state action in separating schoolchildren by race must be determined. These are state action cases in our terms for they involve the constitutional resolution of conflicting private rights. If our balancing of rights approach is correct it should be equally applicable to these problems.

1. *Public funding cases.* In cases involving the acts of a party or entity that receives a governmental subsidy, there may be a tendency to assume either too much or too little on the basis of traditional theory. For example, let us assume that an otherwise private school which receives a $5,000 yearly state grant discriminates on the basis of race. If a black student sues to gain admission to the school, does the financial support by the state automatically establish his right to entry? If a court finds that the single grant is insufficient to establish state action so that the student can gain admission, does this ruling imply that the grant can continue? The traditional state action concept leads one to believe that there must be a single answer to both questions, but the questions have almost nothing to do with each other. The school's right to exist is certainly greater than its claim to state funds, and minority citizens are more injured by payments from tax revenues to such schools than from denial of admittance alone. Thus, a court could decide that the school could continue to discriminate on the basis of race since the associational right of its teachers, students, and parents outweighed the rights of the minority citizens, while simultaneously finding that the state grant must be stopped as a prohibited form of aid to racial segregation. Courts have produced this dichotomy of results in cases concerning racially restrictive private social clubs. The Supreme Court found that the Moose Lodge had a right to exist as a racially restricted voluntary association. Both before and after that decision, however, lower federal courts have held that such clubs cannot receive any tax exemption which is the functional equivalent of a subsidy.[88]

---

[88] See Pitts v. Dep't. of Revenue, 333 F. Supp. 662 (E.D. Wisc. 1971) (three-

The Supreme Court has used such an approach to determine the permissibility of state subsidies to private schools. In *Board of Education v. Allen*,[89] the Court upheld a New York law that provided free textbooks to all students, including those attending religious schools. In so doing the majority rejected a claim that the law violated the Establishment Clause by aiding religion. A later case, *Norwood v. Harrison*,[90] concerned a similar Mississippi textbook program which lent books to students attending racially discriminatory schools. Assuming that state action is a unitary concept, if the program did not constitute state aid to sectarian schools, it should not constitute state aid to the racially discriminatory schools, since in each case the role of the state was to provide books. In *Norwood*, however, the Court honestly admitted that these cases differed because the sectarian school was concerned with the exercise of a right specifically recognized by the Constitution. As to the sectarian schools, "the transcendent value of free religious exercise" permitted some state support.[91] As to the segregated schools:[92]

> [A]lthough the Constitution does not proscribe private bias, it places no value on discrimination as it does on the values inherent in the Free Exercise Clause. Invidious private discrimination may be characterized as a form of exercising freedom of association protected by the First Amendment, but it has never been accorded affirmative constitutional protections. . . . However narrow may be the channel of permissible state aid to sectarian schools, . . . it permits a greater degree of state assistance than may be given to private schools which engage in discriminatory practices that would be unlawful in a public school system.

The Court had held previously that the minimal associational rights of the segregated school could not offset the harm to those excluded by race. When the state gave substantial aid to segregated schools, it hurt blacks both by diverting otherwise available state funds and by seemingly placing public approval on segregation. The use of the balancing approach to determine this state action issue was evident in the Court's dictum which approved the state's providing the seg-

---

judge district court); McGlotten v. Connally, 338 F. Supp. 448 (D.D.C. 1972) (three-judge district court, opinion by Judge Bazelon); Falkenstein v. Dep't. of Revenue, 350 F. Supp. 887 (D. Ore. 1972) (three-judge district court), *app. dismissed*, 409 U.S. 1099 (1973). Both decisions in *Falkenstein* came after the *Moose Lodge* decision.

[89] 392 U.S. 236 (1968).   [91] *Id*. at 469.
[90] 413 U.S. 455 (1973).   [92] *Id*. at 469–70.

regated school with "generalized services"—such as electricity, side-walks, fire and police protection.[93] While the state action is not materially different from providing textbooks, the impact on private rights varies substantially. Denying these minimal services would all but preclude parents and children from exercising their freedom of association to establish a private school. Further, the harm to blacks from providing "generalized services" is minimal both as to the cost and as to public approval—since the service extends to all in the community there is no appearance of special state support.

The Court followed the *Norwood* rationale in *Gilmore v. City of Montgomery*[94] by holding that a city could not grant temporary, exclusive use of public facilities to racially segregated groups. The majority opinion indicated, however, that private groups might be granted a nonexclusive use so long as the facilities remained open for general use. A nonexclusive use would be similar to providing "generalized services," whereas any additional state activities would implicate the state in discrimination, thus damaging the rights of blacks. Mr. Justice White's concurring opinion exposed the Court's resolution of the state action problem as a balancing approach. As noted by the Justice, state action is not an issue when parks and recreational facilities are owned by the city.[95] The issue is whether the official loan of city property to racially segregated groups violates the Fourteenth Amendment. The Court distinguished between exclusive and nonexclusive use, not because the amount of state action varied, but because equal protection condemns only action which gives significant aid to segregated groups. In Part III of the majority opinion, Mr. Justice Blackmun made plain that the private groups possess rights of association which the state may not deny.[96] The starting point must be unfettered use of public facilities by all groups. At some point, however, the right of association collides with the right to be free from racial discrimination. At that point the value in freedom from discrimination outweighs the value in association.[97] Again, it is important to note that the recent interpretation of § 1981 in *Runyon v. McCrary* will have the effect of adopting identical rules on the legality of private racial discrimination.

2. *The school desegregation and "inter-district" relief cases.* To

---

[93] *Id.* at 465.

[94] 417 U.S. 556 (1974).

[95] *Id.* at 581–82.

[96] *Id.* at 575.

[97] *Ibid.*

date, the Supreme Court has found that only de jure segregation in public schools violates the Fourteenth Amendment. While this is not often thought of as a state action determination, the de facto–de jure distinction presents a state action decision in pristine form. The Court has held that certain acts of commission by public officials are prerequisite to finding that patterns of segregated attendance constitute a prohibited racial classification. This is simply a decision that there is no state action connected to the racial separation that justifies a judicial change of the attendance patterns absent acts of commission by the government.

The use of a balancing test to determine the presence of sufficient state action for remedial purposes was demonstrated in *Milliken*. In this case a majority of the Justices determined that interdistrict relief in the form of student reassignment and busing could not include students from school districts which were not found to have engaged in de jure segregation.[98] The determination in *Milliken* was that in the absence of positive acts designed to cause racial segregation a school district is immune from interference by federal courts in the name of desegregation. The state is always involved in segregated school districts, however, as the drawing of school district lines is subject to the power of the state government.[99] This is true of every type of de facto segregation, for it would always be within a state's prerogative to dismantle school districts within its boundaries and restructure them so as to create a truly integrated school system. Yet the Court has been reluctant to embrace such sweeping power, in part because other constitutional interests would suffer. In *Milliken* the property and association rights of suburban residents, and the educational interests of suburban children who resided in districts which did not actually discriminate, were held to outweigh the interests of the city children to attend integrated schools. While only adumbrated in the cases, it would appear that the Court was balancing the interests of parents and students in having locally controlled schools against the harm done to members of the minority race by the failure to have integrated schools. When the actions of the relevant school officials constitute "active" discrimination against

---

[98] The majority opinion by Chief Justice Burger noted at the outset that the question was limited to this problem of imposing relief on districts where there was no finding that those districts "committed acts" of discrimination. 418 U.S. at 721.

[99] *Id.* at 793–97 (Marshall, J., dissenting).

members of the racial minority, the balance changes. Now the members of the minority race have been harmed by intentional exclusion, the harm which the Court in *Brown v. Board of Education*[100] found both in fact and philosophy to outweigh any interest of school officials, parents, or students.

The conclusion that the Court has balanced the interests of the parties in the school segregation cases seems to be supported by its earlier decision in *Keyes v. School District No. 1.*[101] In *Keyes*, the court-ordered, city-wide desegregation was based on the school officials' intentional segregation of one area. The Supreme Court upheld this even though it placed a burden on residents in those areas previously unaffected by the school officials' actions. *Keyes* differs from *Milliken* in that the countervailing interests are less compelling. In the single district situation children are bused to other schools in the same district, rather than to a completely different school system. Unlike comparisons between school districts, the schools of a single system presumably are of comparable quality.[102] Additionally, the associational interests of the members of the majority race who do not want to integrate should be given less weight in the single district situation. Responsibility for the district officials' segregative acts are properly attributable to residents of the district which elected them. Thus, the balance should be struck in favor of the minority race student whenever officials of the district have engaged in segregative acts.[103]

This view of the school desegregation cases was reinforced by the Court's reasoning in its most recent "interdistrict" relief case. In *Gautreaux* the Justices had to decide whether a federal court could

---

[100] 347 U.S. 483 (1954).   [101] 413 U.S. 189 (1973).

[102] If the claim were that white children were bused to inferior schools in the black area, that would only confirm the substantive claim that the white majority relegated blacks to poorer schools. In this posture the Court would not give weight to the claimed harm to the quality of the children's education. *Cf.* Norwood v. Harrison, 413 U.S. 455, 463–67 (1973).

[103] Another decision illustrating this principle of responsibility is Wright v. Council of the City of Emporia, 407 U.S. 451 (1972). The Court refused to permit Emporia to withdraw its students from county schools. The county was under an existing school desegregation order and Emporia, a newly created city, had been covered by that order. While the new city might legitimately desire to establish its own schools, the Court overturned the withdrawal. The chain of responsibility, hence the justification for imposing a burden, was stronger than in *Milliken*. Emporia residents participated through the electoral process in investing county officials with the power to discriminate.

order the Department of Housing and Urban Development (HUD) to locate public housing in the metropolitan area around Chicago, Illinois. In previous years the Chicago Housing Authority (CHA) had contributed to racial segregation in Chicago through its low-income housing-site selection and tenant-assignment practices. In federal court suits against CHA and HUD it was determined that HUD had violated the Fifth Amendment and the Civil Rights Act of 1964 by supporting the CHA practices.[104] The district court, however, refused to order HUD to do more than establish a city-wide desegregation plan.[105]

The Court of Appeals for the Seventh Circuit, in an opinion by Justice Tom Clark, held that a metropolitan plan was required to remedy effectively the racially discriminatory public-housing system within the city. His opinion found that in *Milliken* the Supreme Court had balanced the competing interests and had concluded that for equitable reasons the federal courts should not abridge political subdivisions in school desegregation suits.[106] Clark reasoned that there was no equitable barrier to an interdistrict remedy since the interest of suburban residents in living in an area without public housing was less important than the interest in the educational experience of their children.[107]

The Supreme Court affirmed the Court of Appeals decision while rejecting its reasoning. In an opinion by Mr. Justice Stewart, the majority stated that *Milliken* imposed a basic limitation on the equity power of federal courts based on the concept that court-ordered remedies must be "commensurate with the constitutional violation to be repaired."[108] Of course, this in substance (if not form) does no more than reaffirm the de facto–de jure distinction as a state action problem. Thus Mr. Justice Stewart found that an interdistrict remedy could be ordered in this case since HUD had authority to act throughout the metropolitan area.[109] The Justice neglected to mention that since HUD could be invloved in all such housing suits, the Seventh Circuit was, in substance, correct in finding *Milliken* inapplicable to such cases.

Perhaps realizing that this was a purely formal change in Clark's reasoning, Mr. Justice Stewart characterized the decision on how far

[104] 448 F.2d 731 (7th Cir. 1971).

[105] 363 F. Supp. 690 (N.D. Ill. 1973).

[106] 503 F.2d at 934–36.

[107] *Id*. at 936–39.

[108] 425 U.S. at 294.

[109] *Id*. at 296–300.

a court could go in ordering HUD to disregard local and suburban governments as a "more substantial question."[110] Actually, it was the only question. Despite the federal-action, commensurate-remedy rhetoric, the case comes down to a question of how great a burden can be placed on a community which has not been directly implicated in a constitutional violation.

The Court decided that HUD could operate under its statutory authority to place low income housing in suburban areas as long as the actual program did not undercut "the role of those governments in the federal housing assistance scheme.[111] In effect, an order would place public housing in the suburbs as long as it did not violate the legitimate local interests in land use and city planning.[112] While the Court could claim a formal distinction between *Milliken* and *Gautreaux* in that the former case required more direct action on local government units, this balancing of localized interests undercuts the premise that the prior actions of HUD were the actual basis for judicial intervention. Instead it appears that the Court realized that in housing actions the rights of suburban property owners can be adequately protected without totally eliminating interdistrict remedies for violations of the rights of minority citizens in a large city.

Unfortunately, the Court's formal rejection of a balancing test[113] makes the result beyond comprehension. At least temporarily we must pretend that the fact that a federal agency is formally involved in all housing cases, but not in any school cases, makes a meaningful distinction in the ability of federal courts to impose remedies for constitutional violations in those cases. The lack of an open balancing test in the formal state action cases leaves the Court without a theoretical background for explaining the distinctions in these cases. The traditional concept of state action causes confusion of opinions whenever the Court must balance the rights of nongovernmental parties.

---

[110] *Id*. at 300.   [111] *Id*. at 301.

[112] "[T]he local governmental units retain the right to comment on specific assistance proposals, to reject certain proposals that are inconsistent with their approved housing-assistance plans, and to require that zoning and other land use restrictions be adhered to by builders . . . . The remedial decree would neither force suburban governments to submit public housing proposals to HUD nor displace the rights and powers accorded local government entities under federal or state housing statutes or existing land use laws." *Id*. at 305–06.

[113] *Id*. at 294.

E. THE NEW CHALLENGE TO STATE ACTION—THE "PUBLIC ACTOR"
   CASES

All went well with the hidden balancing test for a period of time.
It was not difficult to pretend that the Fourteenth Amendment was
an "all or nothing" restriction on nongovernmental actions when
the Court continually faced "all or nothing" fact situations. The
earlier state action cases presented fairly simple fact situations which
cried out for protection of some fundamental value of the Fourteenth
Amendment. Finding a lack of value in private decision-making relating to restrictive covenants, company towns, and trespass prosecu-
tions of peaceful sit-in demonstrators is not hard. It was easy, therefore, for the Court to pretend that there was a single standard under
the Fourteenth Amendment which any practice involving state
action had to live up to, regardless of its private nature. The Court
had no occasion to expound a sophisticated balancing test which gave
preference to private decision-making while fully protecting the
substantive rights guaranteed by the Amendment.

The myth could not last. One day the Court would face the
question whether a certain type of nongovernmental decision-maker
(rather than a single decision) was to be considered the equivalent
of a government agency. If the case called for the answer "sometimes," the traditional state action concept would be proved worthless. If state action is a unitary, quantitative concept the decision-
maker should either always possess or always lack the requisite
contacts with the government regardless of the particular action. A
decision that only some actions of the private decision-maker were to
be treated as strictly as those of the government would require an
open balancing of the value in each challenged practice against the
harm which it caused. Any attempt to employ the traditional doctrine to achieve this result would lead to hopeless confusion. Just
such an attempt led to the array of opinions in *C.B.S. v. Democratic
National Committee.*

In *C.B.S.* the Court had to decide whether a television or radio
station's refusal to accept editorial advertising was consistent with
the First Amendment. Chief Justice Burger, with the concurrence
of Justices Stewart and Rehnquist, found that there was no "governmental action" connected with this refusal and so the practice
need not be reviewed under the First Amendment.[114] The result

---

[114] 412 U.S. at 114–21.

clearly involved the Justices balancing the First Amendment interests of the station operators against the interests of would-be advertisers. The Chief Justice found important First Amendment values being fostered by the decision to leave members of the broadcast media, insofar as possible, free of regulation and in a position similar to that of newspapers and magazines.[115] On the other side of the scale, the detriment to those whose advertisement was refused by a station is not severe, since they have the opportunity to induce other stations to accept their message or to use alternative means of communication. While the Chief Justice did not find the First Amendment required this freedom for individual station owners, he ruled that the balance was one which Congress was free to strike in this way.[116]

It is interesting that three of the concurring Justices did not need to find an absence of governmental action in order to uphold the decision of Congress and the FCC allowing private broadcasters to refuse editorial advertising.[117] This fact reinforces the conclusion that the Justices merely balanced the interests of the parties rather than searched for a degree of government connection with the broadcasters' decisions.

While the balancing of interests analysis best explains the result reached by the Justices, their opinions indicate a hopeless state of confusion in dealing with the governmental action issue. Chief Justice Burger's opinion, which took the position both that the government was not connected with the licensee's decision and that the government's approval of such practice is permissible,[118] was hardly a clear ruling on the presence of government action. Mr. Justice Stewart indicated that if sufficient government action were found, the broadcast licensee would have to be treated as a government owned and operated station.[119] His position is the ultimate error of traditional state action analysis. Even if one takes the position that the action is reviewable under the First Amendment, under no circumstances can one justify disregarding the private nature of the operator of the broadcast station. To do otherwise would result in terminating freedom of individual media operations under the

---

[115] *Id.* at 120–21.   [116] *Id.* at 117–19.

[117] 412 U.S. at 146 (White, J., concurring); *id.* at 147 (Blackmun, J., joined by Powell, J.).

[118] *Id.* at 119, 121, 122–23.   [119] *Id.* at 139–41.

Amendment which guarantees their freedom. Mr. Justice Stewart felt that to avoid this result the Court must avoid any review of the licensee's practices.[120] The Justice failed to appreciate that other decisions of the private licensee might damage other individual rights to such an extent that the licensee's actions would be incompatible with the First Amendment. For example, if the same stations decided to broadcast only programs which attacked the character of racial minorities, the right of the minorities to reply or receive another remedy would be a substantial issue. Assuming no further contacts between the government and the station than were present in *C.B.S.*, it would seem that Mr. Justice Stewart would have to find that such acts were not constitutionally reviewable. Such a position seems to be unlikely as well as unsupported by prior decisions.

The "public actor" problem arose again in *Jackson v. Metropolitan Edison Co.*[121] A majority of the Justices used traditional state action language in making a determination that a specific act of a public utility did not violate the Fourteenth Amendment. Only one act of the utility was at issue—the termination of service without a hearing after a dispute as to payment and following notice to the customer. The majority opinion carefully tested only the relationship of the government to the failure of the company to give a full pretermination hearing.[122] Its conclusion that state action was not present should only be viewed as the determination that this specific practice did not violate any important rights protected by the Fourteenth Amendment. The utility asked for the right to protect its property by being able to terminate service during the dispute and following notice to the customer. Requiring a hearing prior to termination would require the company to provide a service to the user even though there was little hope of payment, an extended provision of credit and service which would result in increased cost to other customers. The plaintiff's "right" to due process was infringed to the extent that there was no prior hearing afforded her and no final termination notice provided. Since the utilities tariff required the company to give reasonable notice of asserted nonpayment of bills, the infringement of the "right" was simply the lack of a com-

---

[120] *Ibid*.

[121] 419 U.S. 345 (1974).

[122] *Id*. at 354, 358–59.

pany initiated procedure to guarantee against the chance of error.[123] Balanced against this was the utility's right of private property and the general public interest in low rates and efficient service. The Court easily struck the balance on behalf of the utility.

While this reasoning justifies the result, the opinion is subject to a broader and less justifiable interpretation. Because it is written against the history of a unitary state action theory it might be interpreted as a ruling that no action of this utility (or any utility?) would be reviewable under the Fourteenth Amendment. The dissent[124] and at least one commentator[125] reached this conclusion and attacked the majority opinion on the basis that it failed to consider the total relationship between the utility and the government. These criticisms assume that in the future the majority would approve a wide variety of egregious practices by utilities. The ability of the company to refuse or terminate service based on some other basis, however, such as the customer's race or political views, was not an issue in the case. The opinion tested only the permissibility of the termination practice, not practices which infringed upon other, more substantial rights. There is no reason to believe that the majority would continue to strike the balance for the utility where more serious injury was done to individual rights and the fundamental values of the Amendment.

While the *Jackson* decision thus posed no real danger to civil liberties, it showed the ultimate folly of traditional state action theory. The result of the case may be justified but the implications of the opinion were frightening in opening the door to racial discrimination. After *Jackson* it was imperative that the Court clarify the meaning of the state action requirement by addressing the functions and purposes of the Fourteenth Amendment. An honest functional analysis by the Court would lead to an end of formalism and confusion.

The Court refused to confront openly the Fourteenth Amendment problem. Instead, the Justices in *Runyon v. McCrary* merely

---

[123] The Court of Appeals for the Seventh Circuit in an opinion by Judge (now Mr. Justice) Stevens had taken the position that even if state action were found in such a practice there was no cognizable infringement of any right guaranteed by the Fourteenth Amendment. Lucas v. Wisc. Elect. Power Co., 466 F.2d 638 (7th Cir. 1972).

[124] 419 U.S. 369–70, 371–74 (Marshall, J., dissenting).

[125] Note, note 25 *supra*, 89 HARV. L. REV. at 150–51.

transferred the prohibition of any significant racial discrimination to the Thirteenth Amendment. The expansive reading of § 1981 is a questionable way of avoiding the difficult state action questions which were raised by prior decisions. The Court is now able to outlaw all significant private racial discrimination by finding it to be a refusal to contract based on race. This "refusal to contract" concept may well be easier to manipulate than was the state action requirement. There is no indication, however, that the results in any given case are likely to change. Racial discrimination with any important impact will be prohibited, while purely social discrimination will be tolerated. All the Court has done in this instance is to trade one kind of label for another. The only major benefit of the trade is that the racial fears of the *Jackson* decision have been laid to rest.

V. Conclusion—Something for Everyone

Adopting a functional view of state action requires only the recognition that it is merely a tool for separating out those nongovernmental activities whose existence so impairs certain fundamental values that they are proscribed by the Constitution. This sorting is done by a balancing process that weighs the value of a challenged nongovernmental practice against the harm it does to a given right and the value of that asserted right. While this process is no different from that which the Supreme Court has used in its state action decisions, it serves to clarify past decisions. The recognition of the balancing test, however, leaves us with differing conclusions for differing persons. As this comment has only identified the basic process, each reader is fairly entitled to ask, "Where do I go from here?" Like the balancing process itself, the conclusion differs in terms of the functions of the reader.

A. THE CONGRESS

The power granted to Congress under § 5 of the Fourteenth Amendment has nothing to do with state action analysis. The Court has used the basic balancing test to determine when the unexecuted provisions of the Constitution void certain practices. This requires a judicial balancing of interests. When the Congress acts it has determined that the national interest in the values represented in § 1 require further protection. The balance between this national interest

and the interest of private parties is totally different. The history of
the Amendment[126] and the deference due the decision of a coordi-
nate branch of government argue strongly for allowing Congress so
to act unless it is clearly depriving a regulated individual of a fundamental right which itself has substantial constitutional recognition.[127]

B. LAWYERS AND THEORISTS

It is the function of the bar and those who seek to "enlighten"
the judiciary to help explore and clarify the balancing test of state
action. We must be careful not to assume results in any given case on
the basis of formalistic state action tests. Instead, it is incumbent upon
us to evaluate closely the competing interests in state action cases
before advocating specific results. It is especially important that
counsel in such cases provide the courts with clear information so
that the judiciary may accurately evaluate the competing interests
and strike a proper balance of the private rights.

C. STATE AND LOWER FEDERAL COURTS

So long as the Supreme Court retains the state action concept,
lower courts must remember formally to rule on it in appropriate
cases. Lower courts, however, ought not to rest their decisions only
on the basis of formalized tests and the easy assumptions of the unitary theory. Instead, lower courts should honestly address the need
to balance the conflicting private rights. After determining the relative values and the impairment done to each by differing results,
lower courts should strike the balance openly in their opinions so
that their decisions can be understood and evaluated.[128]

---

[126] tenBroek, Equal under Law 202-05 (1965).

[127] Six Justices expressed this view in dictum in United States v. Guest, 383 U.S.
745, 782 n.6 (1966) (Brennan, J., concurring). For an examination of a balancing
test which relates to the testing of congressional regulation of private activity, see
Van Alstyne & Karst, note 24 *supra*.

[128] Some perceptive lower courts have gingerly moved toward a balancing test.
See Lopez v. Henry Phipps Plaza South, Inc., 498 F.2d 937 (2d Cir. 1974) (Friendly,
J.); Wahba v. New York University, 492 F.2d 96, 100 (2d Cir. 1974) (Friendly, J);
Adams v. Southern California First National Bank, 492 F.2d 324, 333 (9th Cir. 1974);
Grafton v. Brooklyn Law School, 478 F.2d 1137, 1142 (2d Cir. 1973) (Friendly, J.);
Greco v. Orange Memorial Hospital Corp., 513 F.2d 873 (5th Cir. 1975); Golden v.
Biscayne Bay Yacht Club, 521 F.2d 344 (5th Cir. 1975), rev'd en banc, 530 F.2d 16
(5th Cir. 1976); cf. Jackson v. The Statler Foundation, 496 F.2d 623, 629 (2d Cir.
1974).

D. THE JUSTICES OF THE SUPREME COURT

There is nothing wrong with a state action concept and we do not advocate its termination. It is necessary to sort out those private activities whose existence so endanger Fourteenth Amendment values that the Amendment itself forbids them. State action is a good term for describing this sorting function and the results decided upon by the Court. But the concept does not have any intrinsic meaning as a formalized test. The writing of opinions using such a test and focusing on the quantity of state action present in a given case only obscures the decisional process. It is now necessary to admit that in all cases where official government acts are not the subject of review the Court is forced to balance the conflicting rights of private persons. The honest and open balancing of those rights in terms of Fourteenth Amendment values can only benefit the development of constitutional theory. The reduction in confusion of interpretation will result in greater guidance for the resolution of other conflicts and greater respect for the decision-making process. So long as state action decisions remain hidden behind a unitary concept there will be confusion of interpretation and the appearance of unfairness caused by mechanically applied formalistic tests.

BARBARA LERNER

WASHINGTON v. DAVIS: QUANTITY, QUALITY AND EQUALITY IN EMPLOYMENT TESTING

> *Between the idea/And the reality*
> *Between the motion/And the act*
> *Falls the Shadow*
>   T. S. Eliot

I. EMPLOYMENT TESTING CASES: AN ILLUSTRATION OF IMPLEMENTATION PROBLEMS

It is the promise and not the reality of equality that is the Warren Court's legacy.[1] The relative poverty and joblessness of black Americans as a group remains a fact of contemporary life,[2] despite the intense and sustained legal assault on inequality set in motion by the *Brown* decision of 1954,[3] and by the passage of Title VII of the Civil Rights Act of 1964.[4] In this context, it seems help-

---

Barbara Lerner is a practicing psychologist in Chicago and a third-year student in The Law School, The University of Chicago.

[1] Critics and admirers of the Warren Court both seem to agree on this point. See, *e.g.*, BICKEL, POLITICS AND THE WARREN COURT (1965); COX, THE WARREN COURT 6 (1968); KURLAND, POLITICS, THE CONSTITUTION, AND THE WARREN COURT 98 (1970); SAYLER, BOYER & GOODING, eds., THE WARREN COURT (1969).

[2] U.S. DEP'T OF COMMERCE, BUREAU OF THE CENSUS, THE SOCIAL AND ECONOMIC STATUS OF THE BLACK POPULATION IN THE UNITED STATES, 1973 (1974).

[3] Brown v. Board of Education, 347 U.S. 483 (1954).

[4] 42 U.S.C. §§ 2000e *et seq.*

263

ful to recall Professor Freund's reminder of "the always comforting advice of Mr. Justice Holmes that we need education in the obvious more than investigation of the obscure."[5] Comfort aside, education in the obvious often seems to provide the best illumination of the obscure.

The following two statements are offered as relevant examples of the obvious. Detailed analyses of them may serve to shed a few rays of light on some of the shadowed areas of equal protection. First. The relative poverty and joblessness of black Americans is, in major part, a function of employment discrimination and of educational inequality and of the relationship between the two. Second. From this it follows that effective remedial action requires a balanced and directed two-pronged attack on both problems.

The thesis of this article is that efforts at legal implementation of the equal protection promise have become unbalanced and misdirected in relation both to schooling and employment. An altered approach is needed. It is needed to increase the odds on implementing the promise at all, and to do so without violence to other ideals which help to insure that equal status in this particular society will continue to be worth the cost of its attainment. Here the focus will be on employment discrimination rather than on educational discrimination, but the two are inextricably intertwined.

It seems a gross and dangerous oversimplification to expect aggressive enforcement of employment antidiscrimination laws alone to solve black unemployment woes, thus ignoring the heavy contribution of inadequate educational preparation to the vocational problems of many black Americans. Yet, many equal rights advocates seem to be doing just that,[6] charging ahead with sweeping attacks on qualitative employment standards instead of mounting a direct attack on the gross inequalities in schooling which make a sizable percentage of the black population as well as very large numbers of poor people of all races less able to meet those standards than their more affluent competitors.

---

[5] Freund, The Supreme Court of the United States 172 (1961).

[6] See, e.g., Blumrosen, Black Employment and the Law (1971); Cooper & Sobol, Seniority and Testing under Fair Employment Laws: A General Approach to Objective Criteria of Hiring and Promotion, 82 Harv. L. Rev. 1598 (1969); Stacy, Title VII Seniority Remedies in a Time of Economic Downturn, 28 Vand. L. Rev. 487 (1975); Note, Employment Testing: The Aftermath of Griggs v. Duke Power Company, 72 Colum. L. Rev. 900 (1972); Note, Legal Implications of the Use of Standardized Ability Tests in Employment and Education, 68 Colum. L. Rev. 691 (1968).

Oversimplification, along with imbalance and misdirection, is also apparent in direct attacks on educational inequality. School segregation, rightfully held illegal in 1954, quickly became the sole focus of legal attacks on educational inequality. The Warren Court's approach, here as in other equal protection areas, tended to combine strong rhetoric with simple arithmetic.[7] The sad fact is that this approach has not succeeded in significantly reducing de facto segregation, much less eliminating it,[8] and the cost has been high.[9] Massive busing and redistricting have increased racial tension and decreased the amount of money and energy available for efforts to achieve a more equal quality of education by improving the schooling offered to the most deprived American schoolchildren, black and white.

Despite disappointing results, there are many who still seem to worry only about the strength of the Burger Court's commitment to equality and not about the efficacy of its predecessor's approach to implementation.[10] These people will, perhaps, be heartened by the recent decision in *Runyon v. McCrary*[11] holding, pursuant to civil rights law,[12] that exclusion of minorities is illegal in private as well as in public schools. Those who think that a reexamination of the old approach is in order can, perhaps, take more comfort in two other very recent decisions. Both concerned employment discrimination and both suggest that the Burger Court will approach problems in that area with more respect for the complexities involved than the Court has thus far shown for the problems of educational discrimination.

---

[7] See, *e.g.*, Casper, *Jones v. Mayer: Clio, Bemused and Confused Muse*, 1968 SUPREME COURT REVIEW 89; Dixon, *The Warren Court Crusade for the Holy Grail of "One Man–One Vote,"* 1969 SUPREME COURT REVIEW 219; Kurland, *Equal Educational Opportunity: The Limits of Constitutional Jurisprudence Undefined*, 35 U. CHI. L. REV. 583 (1968).

[8] See New York Times Annual Education Survey for 1968, (*1969*), the last year of the Warren Court, 23 Feb. 1969, p. 1, col. 1; *compare* New York Times Annual Education Survey for 1974, 12 May 1974, p. 1, col. 2; 13 May 1974, p. 24, col. 1, twenty years after the *Brown* decision.

[9] See Kaplan, *Equal Justice in an Unequal World: Equality for the Negro—The Problem of Special Treatment*, 61 Nw. L. REV. 363, 401 (1966). See also *id.* at 380, where a similar point is made regarding the high cost and low benefits of similar approaches to the problems of employment discrimination.

[10] Liberal court-watchers of this stripe are often referred to as "result-oriented," but an objective appraisal of empirical results suggests that "rhetoric-oriented" may be a more apt designation.

[11] 96 S. Ct. 2586 (1976).   [12] 42 U.S.C. § 1981.

In *McDonald v. Santa Fe Trail Co.*,[13] Mr. Justice Marshall, speaking for a unanimous Court on this point, held that Title VII forbids employment discrimination against whites as well as against blacks and other special groups. The other major employment discrimination case decided the same month, *Washington v. Davis*,[14] was an employment testing case, the third such case to reach the Court. It seems to mark the start of a major shift in the Court's approach in this area and will be discussed in detail below, along with its two predecessors, *Griggs v. Duke Power Co.*[15] and *Albemarle Paper Co. v. Moody*.[16] These three employment testing cases will provide the primary analytic material for this paper for three reasons.

The Burger Court's decision in *Griggs*, like the Warren Court's decision in *Brown*, represented a bright beginning in a new area. In *Griggs* the Court began the long, complex, and delicate process of articulating workable standards for deciding whether and when a job testing requirement violates Title VII of the Civil Rights Act, and how the act itself relates to the Equal Protection Clause. Speaking for a unanimous bench of eight,[17] Chief Justice Burger said: "If an employment practice which operates to exclude Negroes cannot be shown to be related to job performance, the practice is prohibited."[18] From almost any point of view, there is little cause to find fault with that general holding or with the Court's three other broadly applicable rules in *Griggs*: (1) The appropriate focus in Title VII actions is on the objective consequences of employment practices and not simply on the subjective motivations of those who institute them. (2) The burden of proof for showing discriminatory consequences is on the plaintiffs in these cases. And (3) once plaintiffs have done so, the burden shifts to the defendants to prove that an employment practice having these effects is in fact job-related.

Shadows in the background had to do with the Court's definition of discriminatory effects via the pool-of-applicants standard and with its definition of job-relatedness in terms of test-specificity for the particular job in question. These shadows were only background phenomena in *Griggs* because the definitions articulated there were appropriate ones, given the particular facts of that case. Unfortunately, the Court said nothing to differentiate these narrowly appro-

---

[13] 96 S. Ct. 2574 (1976).

[14] 426 U.S. 229 (1976).

[15] 401 U.S. 424 (1971).

[16] 422 U.S. 405 (1975).

[17] Brennan, J., did not participate.

[18] 401 U.S. at 431.

priate holdings from the broadly stated ones suggested in the preceding paragraph, nothing to give a clear warning that the particular
definitions used in *Griggs* should be limited to cases with facts similar to those in *Griggs*. Background shadows quickly became fore-
ground darkness as lower courts across the land applied the *Griggs*
definitions to cases arising out of vastly different factual contexts,
making the burden of proving discriminatory effects weightless, and
the burden of proving job-relatedness onerous, at times impossible.

Distress over these results was apparent in *Albemarle*, where a
deeply divided Court reconfronted the same questions it had faced
in *Griggs* four years earlier. Mr. Justice Stewart, speaking for a
majority that had shrunk to four,[19] reaffirmed the *Griggs* pool-of-
applicants standard and added a quite gratuitous and rather Kafka-
esque analysis of the defendant's statistical data on the job-relatedness of its tests. Actually, the factual context of *Albermarle* was
similar enough in essential respects to that of *Griggs* to mandate a
similar decision, divergent concurrences and partial dissents notwithstanding.

Facts in both cases were, however, dissimilar enough to those in
the growing list of federal trial and appellate court cases to warrant
some clear distinctions. None was made. Instead, the majority spoke
as if *Griggs* and *Albermarle* were indistinguishable from other Title
VII cases and their divided brethren spoke as if *Griggs* and *Albermarle* were distinguishable from each other, but their distinctions
were not developed to the point where they could command a
significant consensus.

The turnabout came in *Washington v. Davis*, where intent to discriminate—the subjective motivational factor that was played down
in *Griggs*—reemerged not only as a relevant factor but as a key element which plaintiffs must prove in order to establish a prima facie
constitutional case of discriminatory effect. *Griggs* was not overruled. Mr. Justice White, speaking for the most part for six members of the Court,[20] distinguished *Griggs* on the ground that it was a

---

[19] Stewart, J., was joined by Douglas, Brennan, and White, JJ. Separate concurring
opinions were filed by Justices Marshall and Rehnquist; Blackmun, J., concurred in
the judgment only. Burger, C.J., concurred in part and dissented in part. Mr.
Justice Powell did not participate.

[20] Stewart, J., joined in Parts I and II of the White opinion; Stevens, J., filed a
separate concurring opinion, and Brennan, J., filed a dissenting opinion in which
Marshall, J., joined.

Title VII case, whereas *Davis* was an Equal Protection Clause Case. In a temporary, technical sense, this was true. Plaintiffs in *Davis* were would-be police officers of the District of Columbia and, at the time when their action was filed, Title VII did not apply to government employers, an omission which Congress remedied with an amendment to the Civil Rights Act of 1964,[21] passed in 1972, four years before *Washington v. Davis* was decided.

Thus, whatever utility this distinction may have in other areas where equal protection is at issue, it seems foredoomed to obsolescence in the realm of employment discrimination. More important, Mr. Justice Stevens was surely right in cautioning that "the line between discriminatory purpose and discriminatory impact is not nearly as bright, and perhaps not quite as critical, as the reader of the Court's opinion might assume."[22] With or without the element of intent, however, the stubborn problem of setting reasonable standards for proof of employment discrimination remains. So, too, does the equally difficult and key problem of establishing reasonable standards for proof of job-relatedness.

Davis solves neither problem, but it does suggest that the Court is struggling to shift the balance between the two standards so as to reduce the gross disproportion in the burdens of proof heretofore placed on defendants as contrasted with plaintiffs. Hereafter, it is unlikely that plaintiffs will be able to stride into court virtually unencumbered, or that defendants will appear bowed down under impossible weights. The danger, of course, is that the balance will swing too far the other way. Implementation of the ideal requires a centering that takes due account of the resources of each party, and of the needs of both for clarity and consistency.

II. Discriminatory Effects: Internal Promotion versus
    External Hiring Situations

The important understanding is that *Griggs* and *Albemarle* represent the same type of case while *Davis* represents a significantly different type of case and, therefore, requires a different standard for proof of discriminatory effects. The Court seems to have understood this but it failed clearly to elucidate the distinction. The Court

---

[21] Equal Employment Opportunity Act of 1972, 42 U.S.C. § 2000e *et seq.*
[22] 426 U.S. at 254.

is hardly alone in this failure. Both types of cases have been repeatedly litigated in the federal courts[23] and discussed in the law
reviews;[24] clear distinctions between them have almost never
emerged.[25] Thus, to the extent that there is a meaningful difference
between the Supreme Court and at least some of the circuit courts
here, it has to do with process and direction rather than with results.
The high court appears to be searching for distinctions that some
of the lower courts and their academic celebrants have not yet seen.

The trouble is that a search, however painstaking, is likely to
yield little or nothing to even the most far-seeing, if they are looking
in the wrong place. This is simply not an area in which legal theory
can order the facts. Rather, it is the facts which are primary here
and which must be allowed to lead and guide the needed developments in legal theory.[26] Looking to the facts first of *Griggs* and

---

[23] Cases similar to *Griggs* and *Albemarle* insofar as plaintiffs were incumbent
employees challenging the alleged discriminatory impact of tests on job promotion
or retention include, *e.g.*, Douglas v. Hampton, 512 F.2d 976 (D.C. Cir. 1975); Rogers
v. International Paper Co., 510 F.2d 1340 (8th Cir. 1975); Walston v. County School
Board, 492 F.2d 919 (4th Cir. 1974); Brito v. Zia Co., 478 F.2d 1200 (10th Cir. 1973);
Chance v. Board of Examiners, 458 F.2d 1167 (2d Cir. 1972); Allen v. City of
Mobile, 466 F.2d 122 (5th Cir. 1972).

Cases similar to *Davis* insofar as plaintiffs were rejected applicants challenging
the alleged discriminatory impact of tests on hiring include, *e.g.*, Smith v. Troyan,
520 F.2d 492 (6th Cir. 1975); Coopersmith v. Roudebush, 517 F.2d 818 (D.C. Cir.
1975); Boston Chapter NAACP v. Beecher, 504 F.2d 1017 (1st Cir. 1974); Morrow
v. Crisler, 491 F.2d 1053 (5th Cir. 1974); Vulcan Soc. of N.Y. City Fire Dept. v.
Civil Serv. Comm'n, 490 F.2d 387 (2d Cir. 1973); Cooper v. Allen, 467 F.2d 836 (5th
Cir. 1972); Castro v. Beecher, 459 F.2d 725 (1st Cir. 1972); Carter v. Gallagher, 452
F.2d 315 (8th Cir. 1971).

Cases in which there is a simultaneous challenge to the impact of tests on both
internal promotion and external hiring are also common, *e.g.*, Pettway v. American
Cast Iron Pipe Co., 494 F.2d 211 (5th Cir. 1974); Guardians Ass'n of the N.Y.C.P.
Dept., Inc. v. Civil Serv. Comm'n, 490 F.2d 400 (2d Cir. 1973); Harper v. Kloster,
486 F.2d 1134 (4th Cir. 1973); Bridgeport Guardians, Inc. v. Members of Bridgeport
C.S. Comm'n, 482 F.2d 1333 (2d Cir. 1973); United States v. Georgia Power Co.,
474 F.2d 906 (5th Cir. 1973); Pennsylvania v. O'Neill, 473 F.2d 1029 (3d Cir. 1973).

[24] See, *e.g.*, Bernhardt, *Griggs v. Duke Power Co.: The Implications for Private
and Public Employers*, 50 Tex. L. Rev. 901 (1972); Cooper & Sobol, note 6 *supra;*
Wilson, *A Second Look at Griggs v. Duke Power Company: Ruminations on Job
Testing, Discrimination, and the Role of the Federal Courts*, 58 Va. L. Rev. 844
(1972); Winter, *Improving the Economic Status of Negroes through Laws against
Discrimination: A Reply to Professor Sovern*, 34 U. Chi. L. Rev. 817 (1967); Note,
72 Colum. L. Rev. 900, note 6 *supra;* Note, 68 Colum. L. Rev. 691, note 6 *supra;*
Developments in the Law, *Employment Discrimination and Title VII of the Civil
Rights Act of 1964*, 84 Harv. L. Rev. 1109 (1971).

[25] For the exception that proves the rule, see Blumrosen, *The Duty of Fair Recruitment under the Civil Rights Act of 1964*, 22 Rutgers L. Rev. 465, 468 (1968).

[26] There is nothing new about this suggestion; it is as old as the common law

Albemarle and then of *Davis*, the obvious and paramount distinction is that plaintiffs in *Griggs* and *Albemarle* were incumbent employees seeking on-the-job promotions. They were not a large, shifting, ill-defined, potentially limitless and endlessly manipulable group of would-be employees, as in *Davis*. That, in essence, is why the pool-of-applicants standard that the Court developed in *Griggs* was appropriate proof of discriminatory effects in that case and in *Albemarle*, and why it was utterly inappropriate when applied to the *Davis* case.

When the Court in *Griggs* said that Title VII prohibits, without proof of job-relatedness, the use of tests that "operate to disqualify Negroes at a substantially higher rate than white applicants,"[27] the "applicants" it was talking about were the fourteen incumbent black employees in the Duke Power Company's ninety-five-man work force at its Dan River steam plant in Draper, North Carolina. This plant had a long history of overt racial segregation and discrimination, the effects of which were still strikingly manifest in the hierarchical positions of the company's labor force, as well as in its overall racial makeup. Thirteen of fourteen black employees had long been and still were locked into positions at the bottom of the wage and status hierarchy. That is why they all applied for promotion when the bars of segregation were finally removed, and why they charged discrimination when they were denied promotion on the basis of tests that their white co-workers had not had to take to attain their promotions. The situation in *Albemarle* was similar.

Plaintiff-respondents in *Davis*, however, were not employees at all. They were representatives of a class of rejected black applicants denied jobs as police officers for the District of Columbia. They alleged that the police department had violated their right to equal protection by selecting all applicants on the basis of a written test of verbal ability, which they had failed.

The petitioners in *Washington v. Davis* were Walter Washington, the black mayor of the District of Columbia, and his police chief. Chief Wilson earned the ignominy of being sued for discriminatory hiring by instituting an aggressive affirmative action

---

itself and is thought by many to constitute both its essence and the dynamic of its development. See LEVI, AN INTRODUCTION TO LEGAL REASONING (1949), for the classic modern restatement of this view.

[27] 401 U.S. at 426.

program aimed at recruiting black officers, a program which district court Judge Gesell, who found for petitioners, justly described as "a model nationwide."[28] The program was a model one, not merely for the good motives of those who instituted it, but for the positive results it had achieved in creating and maintaining an integrated police force—a superior record explicitly recognized and commended as such not only by Judge Gesell, but also by appellate court Judge Robinson[29] who, paradoxically, found the practices by which they had achieved these results to be discriminatory.

Under a *Griggs* pool-of-applicants standard, it was irrelevant that, since Chief Wilson took office in August of 1969, 44 percent of all new officers hired were black.[30] So, too, was the fact that the figures had risen "dramatically"[31] since Chief Wilson took over, and that they continued to rise during his tenure: 55 percent of the officers hired between January and September of 1970 were black,[32] and the figures may well have risen since.

No matter; under the pool-of-applicants standard, all of this is irrelevant. The only relevant fact is that the challenged test was one which "operate[d] to disqualify Negroes at a substantially higher rate than white applicants,"[33] and there is little question that Test 21 did just that, given a pool of applicants that was 72 percent black,[34] thanks to Chief Wilson's earnest and successful efforts to recruit blacks. Between 1968 and 1971, 57 percent of black applicants from within the District of Columbia area failed the test, compared to a failure rate of only 13 percent among nonrecruited white applicants from the same area.[35] This pass-fail ratio in the pool of applicants was sufficient, in and of itself, to prove a discriminatory effect for Court of Appeals Judges Robinson and McGowan who concurred in reversing District Court Judge Gesell's finding for the plaintiffs.

More disheartening is the fact that the case did not turn at either the district or the appellate court level on the question of discriminatory effects. A case that should have been decided without ever reaching the question of job-relatedness was twice decided on that

---

[28] 348 F. Supp. at 18.

[29] 512 F.2d at 961.

[30] 348 F. Supp. at 16.

[31] *Ibid.*

[32] 512 F.2d at 961, n.32.

[33] 401 U.S. at 426.

[34] 512 F.2d at 961, n.32.

[35] *Id.* at 958.

basis and by four different judges. Judge Gesell called plaintiff's showing of discriminatory effects "minimal" but accepted it as "sufficient to shift the burden."[36] Judge Robb, who agreed with Judge Gesell, dissenting from his appellate court brethren did so, like Judge Gessell, by finding Test 21 to be job-related,[37] a conclusion which Judges Robinson and McGowan rejected. In fact, as Mr. Justice White indicated[38] and as will be shown later, Test 21 is sufficiently job-related, but that is not the point.

The point is that employers who succeed in opening up new opportunities for large numbers of qualified blacks ought not to be subjected to the humiliating and onerous burden of proving that they are justified in hiring on a discriminatory basis when they have not, in fact, done so.[39] Neither Title VII nor the Equal Protection Clause can reasonably be construed to guarantee that unqualified blacks receive treatment equal to that accorded qualified blacks. Both the 1960s legislation and the 1860s Amendment were intended to insure that qualified black applicants receive treatment equal to that accorded qualified white applicants. Suspicion about the validity of qualification standards should and does arise in many situations where an employer claims that there are few or no qualified blacks for him to hire. It has but should not arise when he seeks, finds, and hires sufficient numbers of qualified blacks.

Use of pass-fail ratios among the pool of applicants as the standard for proof of discriminatory effects in external hiring situations all but guarantees that unhappy result. Two brief hypotheticals, eschewing technically appropriate but abstruse probabilistic statistics and using only simple arithmetic calculations, may serve to illustrate the point, highlighting the irrationality of the pool-of-applicants standard in external hiring situations:

a) Assume that employer A has one hundred job openings for which he recruits from a metropolitan area with a labor force that is 40 percent black and 60 percent white. One thousand blacks and one hundred whites apply. Since he can hire only one hundred people, he must select from among the eleven hundred applicants on some basis. After much thought, study, and professional consultation, he decides to use Test B and to set his cut-off score at point C.

---

[36] 348 F. Supp. at 16.   [37] 512 F.2d at 966.   [38] 426 U.S. at 250–51.

[39] See SOVERN, LEGAL RESTRAINTS ON RACIAL DISCRIMINATION IN EMPLOYMENT 124 (1966).

Eighty blacks and twenty whites obtain scores above the cut-off point and are hired. Blacks are thus employed at a rate double their percentage of the labor force of the area of recruitment and they outnumber white employees by a ratio of four-to-one. Yet, because 20 percent of white applicants were hired as compared to only 8 percent of black applicants, this employer is, by the pool-of-applicants standard, guilty of discriminatory hiring.

b) Assume that employer X also has one hundred job openings and that he, too, recruits from a greater metropolitan area with a labor force that is 40 percent black and 60 percent white but, this time, one thousand whites and one hundred blacks apply. Using Test Y and cut-off point Z, this employer selects and hires eighty whites and only twenty blacks. Blacks are here employed at a rate which is only half that of their percentage of the labor force of the area of recruitment; white employees outnumber them by a ratio of four-to-one. This employer is not, however, in violation of Title VII on the basis of the pool-of-applicants standard because he has accepted a percentage of black applicants which is more than double the percentage of accepted white applicants. He may, however, be guilty of reverse discrimination on the basis of the pool-of-applicants standard.

Readers tempted to dismiss the foregoing as idle speculation should take note of Judge Robinson's statement in *Davis*: "If the examination had no disparate effect, one would expect approximately 72% rather than 55 or 56% of the successful applicants to be black"[40] (because 72 percent of the applicants were black).

Reliance on pass-fail ratios in external hiring situations has another major disadvantage. It gives men of ill will a virtual hunting license, enabling them to blast away, legally, at men of objectively demonstrated good will. The open season thus created is a year-round phenomenon because the pool of applicants is an endlessly manipulable sample. Chief Wilson's success in raising the percentage of black applicants through his affirmative action recruitment program amply demonstrates that it can be manipulated for good reasons. A little reflection should make it apparent, even to readers with no scientific training, that such a sample can just as easily be manipulated for bad ones, *e.g.*, to institute unsavory strike suits.

Even assuming utter purity of motive on the part of all plaintiffs

---

[40] 512 F.2d at 961, n.32.

—and all plaintiffs' attorneys—in these situations, the pool-of-applicants standard incorporates the intellectually indefensible assumption that everyone who applies for a particular job would actually accept it, were it offered to him. As the *Davis* case clearly illustrates, this is simply not true. Forty-eight percent of black applicants who passed the test failed to show up for work; 49 percent of the successful white applicants did likewise.[41]

These are only some of the many severe drawbacks inherent in the use of pass-fail ratios among the pool of applicants as the standard for proof of discriminatory effects in external hiring situations. Others will be discussed later. Here, the focus is on the fact that many courts and many law review commentators have insisted that this standard is often or even always preferable to its major alternative: the percentage of blacks actually hired. The obvious problem with the latter standard is the difficulty of defining what constitutes a sufficient percentage, and the obvious question raised is, sufficient in relation to what? The typical legal answer has been, sufficient in relation to the racial composition of the general population. Courts and commentators, unaware of the flaws in the pool-of-applicants standard, have been quick to point out the defects of this answer.[42]

The most obvious objection is that it would necessitate quota hiring in certain situations, something that is thought by many to fly in the face of congressional intent. Perhaps, but if so, that provides no basis for preferring the pool-of-applicants standard to the percentage hired standard. Rather, it provides a basis for rejecting both. This is so because the pool-of-applicants standard also mandates quota hiring, the only difference being that under the latter standard the quota is determined in relation to the racial makeup of the pool of applicants rather than on the basis of the racial makeup of the general population.

---

[41] *Ibid*. The fact that the figures are nearly identical for both races in this case should not delude the reader into assuming that they will necessarily be the same or even very similar in other cases. Most distinguishable cultural groups tend to have distinguishable cultural preferences for particular sorts of work and, as discriminatory barriers to employment crumble, these preferences may manifest themselves more rather than less clearly.

[42] See, *e.g.*, Chance v. Board of Examiners, 330 F. Supp. 203, 214 (S.D. N.Y.), *aff'd*, 458 F.2d 1167 (2d Cir. 1972). See also Cooper & Sobol, note 6 *supra* at 1664; Note, *supra* note 6, 72 Colum. L. Rev. 909–12, 919; Developments in the Law, note 24 *supra*, at 1136.

The solution to this apparent dilemma is to recognize that quota hiring is not always an evil, nor is it necessarily a practice which violates congressional intent, if established on a proper basis.[43] The trick is to find the proper basis. The racial makeup of the pool of applicants does not and cannot provide a proper basis in all situations; neither do general population figures because, as was pointed out in *Chance*, there are jobs where candidates "must meet preliminary eligibility requirements as to education and experience that are not possessed by most of the general population."[44] This is certainly true, but it is no solution to retreat to the pool-of-applicants standard in all cases because, while there is some reason to believe that the members of the pool of applicants constituted by incumbent employees would meet these requirements with a higher frequency than the general population, there is little or no reason to believe that the members of the pool of applicants in an external hiring situation would do so.

One final hypothetical will serve to illustrate the point here. Assume that fifty white and fifty black clerk-typists all pass the same entry level test of typing speed and accuracy and are hired as Clerks I in 1976. Assume that in 1980, all of them apply for promotion to Clerk II. If forty whites and only four blacks are promoted, the probability that prejudice—rather than random chance or differential qualifications—accounts for the difference would be high. The probability is high precisely because the two incumbent groups were initially comparable; that is why they were hired.

By contrast, in external hiring situations there is no good reason to assume that any two groups of applicants are comparable to each other, or that either is fairly representative of any larger group de-

---

[43] Senator Joseph S. Clark said "quotas are themselves discriminatory," 110 CONG. REC. 7218 (1964). He and his fellow floor manager, Senator Clifford S. Case, expressed similar sentiments in a jointly submitted Interpretative Memorandum of Title VII of H.R. 7152, 110 CONG. REC. 7213 (1964). The type of quotas they seem to have had in mind, however, were the sort that courts are currently enforcing by using the pool-of-applicants standard in external hiring cases. It is at least doubtful that they would reject out of hand the kinds of quotas to be suggested here. Quotas which require only that (1) if an employer rejects applicants of a particular race, sex, religion, or nationality consistently enough to result in a group of actual employees which differs to a statistically significant extent from the "minority's" percentage of the qualified labor force of the area of recruitment, then (2) he should be required to make some demonstration that such discriminatory impact is either (*a*) a function of factors beyond his control or (*b*) justified on some nondiscriminatory basis.

[44] 330 F. Supp. at 214.

fined by race, sex, religion, or ethnicity.[45] The basic problem here is one of sampling, and the key point is that external applicants do not constitute or even approximate either a matched or a random sample. Instead, they constitute a sample which is biased in uncontrolled and uncontrollable ways, negating any likelihood of valid generalizations about the abilities of employees or about the proclivities of employers.

General population figures are also unsuitable as a basis for generalizations about employment practices, but for a different reason. Here, the problem is not biased data but irrelevant data. General population figures have only limited relevance because the percentage of blacks—or of any other group—in any given area at any given time bears only the most inexact of relationships to the number of employable people in that group. This follows because general population figures for any group include very young and very old members of that group, and the relative distribution of the very young and the very old within any one group can and often does vary dramatically from the distributions within other groups in the same area at the same point in time.[46]

---

[45] One particularly egregious and unfortunate consequence of the failure to recognize this fact is a widespread tendency to underestimate considerably the intellectual performance of black Americans relative to white Americans. Inequality of opportunity has produced a differential, but its magnitude is nowhere near the size of the discrepancies reported in the legal literature on the basis of biased applicant samples. Using intelligence test scores as an example, studies based on more representative samples of both populations indicate that black and white test score distributions have about the same size standard deviation and a difference between means which approximates one standard deviation. In less technical terms, this means that the overlap is far more impressive than the difference as shown, for example, by the fact that 15–20 percent of blacks score above the white mean and the same proportion of whites score below the black mean.

[46] Differential birth rates, life expectancies, and migration patterns in various racial and ethnic groups are some of the more important factors accounting for such variations, and socio-economic status tends to interrelate with all three of those factors in complex ways. See, e.g., United States v. City of Chicago, 411 F. Supp. 218, 233 (N.D. Ill. 1976): "The evidence shows that . . . [i]n 1970 the male population of Chicago was 60.1% white, 32.1% black and 7% Spanish, while the male labor force was 67% white, 25.8% black, and 7.2% Spanish. Furthermore, the male labor force for the greater metropolitan Chicago area for 1970 was 86.5% nonblack and 13.5% black." The figures for the city proper provide an illustration of the difference between general population figures and labor force figures, showing that in this case, blacks constitute nearly one-third of the population but only about one-fourth of the labor force. The figures for the greater metropolitan area raise doubts about the reality of the alleged discrimination, since the black male hiring rate for 1971 was 10 percent, differing from the labor force of the area by only 3.5 points. Judge Marshall, however, was unimpressed by these figures because he

In short, the problem raised in *Chance* is only a subspecies of the much larger problem of sampling. Thus defined, the problem may be larger and more general but it is not nearly so difficult. Indeed, it becomes quite manageable as soon as one begins to focus, as any competent scientific researcher would, on the racial makeup of the labor force of the area of recruitment, narrowing the lens further, when necessary, to pinpoint the percentage of blacks in the labor force of the area of recruitment who possess the requisite special qualifications, *e.g.*, degrees in law, medicine, or psychology, for jobs that require them.

Quotas based on meaningful sample statistics of this sort are, arguably, reasonable ones, at least in the abstract. Intelligently applied, they can be reasonable in actual practice as well. Here, the key point is that quotas need not force each employer to hire a percentage of blacks equal to or even approximately equal to the proportion of even the qualified black workers in the labor force of the area of recruitment. People do not, by choice or by chance, distribute themselves with mathematical precision, and the goal, after all, is equality, not uniformity.[47] To implement the goal of equality, the appropriate standard for proof of discriminatory effects in external hiring would be evidence that a particular employer has a labor force with a racial makeup significantly different from that of the qualified labor force of the area of recruitment. The common, uniformly accepted, scientific criterion for statistical significance is at the .05 level, meaning that the probability of the distribution in question occurring by chance would be only five times out of one hundred trials or test-runs.

Federal courts have repeatedly recognized and adopted this standard of significance for proof of the job-relatedness of employment tests. They have not adopted it for proof of discriminatory effects in

---

was convinced on the basis of *Albemarle* that "[t]he primary inquiry is whether 'the tests in question select applicants for hire or promotion in a racial pattern significantly different from that of the pool of applicants.'" *Id*. at 234.

[47] The forces of uniformity, marching under the banner of equality, as Professor Kurland has warned us with haunting eloquence, have profoundly destructive implications for other values heretofore shared by civilized men, and for objectives which are "of the essence of a democratic dream." See KURLAND, THE PRIVATE I: SOME REFLECTIONS ON PRIVACY AND THE CONSTITUTION 38 (1976). See also KURLAND, note 1 *supra*, at 169: "Those too young to remember what happened to Europe immediately prior to World War II, as country after country fell under the thrall of equality, may yet find the allegory of Orwell's *Animal Farm* instructive and frightening."

hiring, although it is equally applicable to both problems and its consistent application would eliminate the grossest of the disparities in the burdens assigned to plaintiffs as contrasted with defendants in employment discrimination cases.

Clearly, the adoption of such a standard would protect many employers from unjustified accusations and the resultant expense and embarrassment. Would it also shield others from justified charges of discriminatory hiring by imposing a burden on plaintiffs so heavy as to constitute a barrier to the redress of legitimate grievances? In ordinary situations it hardly seems likely. Meaningful statistical data of the sort described above are usually readily available, and free. Statistics compiled by the U.S. Census Bureau and by the Department of Labor are the obvious starting points. In many, perhaps most cases, they will be end points as well. In others, statistical data routinely compiled and published by professional schools and organizations may also be necessary, e.g., to obtain needed data on the number of qualified minority group members in particular employment areas. Problems can, of course, arise with regard to a particular employer's definition of his area of recruitment. Such problems, however, are essentially the same in any situation where gerrymandering of lines is an issue, and the courts have much experience in handling such problems.[48]

The topic of deliberate gerrymandering raises the larger question of discriminatory intent. As previously noted, the Supreme Court in *Davis* held that intent was a key factor in Equal Protection Clause cases but not—or at any rate, not yet—in Title VII cases. The suggestion here is that intent is relevant to both Equal Protection and Title VII cases, but not to bar the doors of the federal courts to plaintiffs in legitimate cases where discriminatory effects are clear but subjective intent is impossible to prove. Rather, it would seem preferable to use discriminatory intent to open the doors of the courts and to ease the burden and length of the trial for both plaintiffs and judges in cases where discriminatory intent is objectively demonstrable. In such cases, proof of discriminatory intent on the part of the employer should be sufficient, in and of itself, to shift the burden of proof for the job-relatedness of his employment test or any other employment qualification to him.

---

[48] See, *e.g.*, Gomillion v. Lightfoot, 364 U.S. 339 (1960); Wright v. Rockefeller, 376 U.S. 52 (1964); Taylor v. McKeithen, 407 U.S. 191 (1972).

Conversely, where intent to discriminate is absent but a discriminatory impact is shown in terms defined herein, the presumption of discrimination should also arise, but reasonableness would seem to require that it be a rebuttable one. Thus, compelling evidence that objectively adequate steps were taken to advertise the availability of the jobs in question to all potentially qualified employees and to encourage them to apply should suffice to disprove a charge of discriminatory hiring.

III. JOB RELATEDNESS: SIMPLE, REPETITIVE TASKS VERSUS COMPLEX VARIED ONES

Duality is the basic theme. Here, the fundamental distinction being urged is that between two types of jobs, one involving the sorts of tasks at issue in *Griggs,* the other involving the sorts of tasks at issue in *Davis.* Once again, the proposal is that there is a need for different standards of proof, this time for the job-relatedness of tests in each situation. In this area, courts and commentators have not tended to lump all types of cases together as they did with internal promotion and external hiring cases. Alas, the distinctions drawn explicitly have too frequently been based on schooling and status,[49] not on an analysis of the tasks actually required of workers in various occupational categories.

The fundamental distinction referred to is the one between jobs involving the performance of a small number of simple, repetitive tasks and jobs involving the performance of a large number of complex and varied tasks. In an ideal world, the correlation between job status and job complexity might, perhaps, be very high. In the real world, it is very low. The strong reality relationship in contemporary America is that between schooling and status. Jobs requiring many years of schooling tend to have high status; jobs requiring relatively little in the way of formal education tend to have low status. But the relationship between years of schooling required and job complexity is quite modest. Most jobs requiring many years of schooling are, in fact, complex but the converse is not true: some jobs requiring little formal education are quite simple; many others are very complex indeed.

---

[49] See, *e.g., Chance,* 330 F. Supp. at 213–14, and authorities cited in notes 59–61, and 84 *infra.* See also Note, note 6 *supra,* 72 COLUM. L. REV. at 917–19.

The two types are, in truth, only points at different ends of a continuum, not discrete entities, but in the interest of initial clarity, the focus will be on gross differences at or near the extremes, rather than on subtle gradations. For that purpose, *Griggs* seems to offer at least some reasonably good examples of jobs calling for the performance of simple, repetitive tasks. Plaintiffs in *Griggs* were employed at a plant which was organized into five operating departments: (1) labor; (2) coal handling; (3) operations; (4) maintenance; and (5) laboratory and tests. The Court noted that the tests and educational requirements instituted by the company to govern transfers from one department to another "were adopted . . . without meaningful study of their relationship to job-performance ability,"[50] and, on that basis, held that they were not job-related and struck them down.

This conclusion was probably correct, but it is difficult to be certain, since neither the company nor the Court had anything much to say about the specific nature of the jobs in question. As a result, data are not adequate for definitive analysis. Nonetheless, it seems reasonable to assume that workers in the coal-handling department, like workers in the labor department, performed simple, repetitive tasks. This was probably true of at least some jobs in some, perhaps all, of the other departments as well, particularly in light of the fact that promotion within each department was mainly a matter of seniority. From the point of view of employees in general, the major differences between these jobs was probably salary: the highest paying jobs in the labor department paid less than the lowest paying jobs in any of the other departments. From the point of view of black employees, two additional facts were also crucial. Prior to the effective date of Title VII of the Civil Rights Act of 1964, black workers were restricted to the labor department. Until 1955, when the company's personnel policies first began to change, there were no formal requirements for transfers from one department to another—for white employees.

From a purely abstract, psychometric point of view, the similarities among all or most of these jobs is what is striking. Because the tasks involved are simple, repetitive ones, successful job performance is relatively easy to define and measure in ways that virtually every

---

[50] 401 U.S. at 431 (1971).

reasonable person would consider fair, accurate, thorough, and objective. Certainly, it is unlikely that it would be any more diffi- cult to do that for higher paying jobs in the coal-handling depart- ment than for lower paying jobs in the labor department. Coal is, after all, a more-or-less fungible item, and what the company wants, presumably, is to have so many tons of it shoveled or otherwise moved from one place to another at certain intervals in a certain manner. Given equivalent tools, materials, and working conditions, it is easy enough to compare one man's job performance with that of another in terms of amount, rate, and whatever accuracy of handling may be required. It is also easy enough to repeat these measurements at periodic intervals in order to obtain a fair sample of each man's work over time, so as to measure his output reliably.

Criterion validity alone thus poses no problem in this situation. Indeed, it is hard to see why any educational requirement or test is needed at all. A work-sample might not only be fairer to the em- ployees, but cheaper and more efficient for the employer as well. High school diplomas and tests of general intelligence and mechanical aptitude like those used by the Duke Power Company[51] might be relevant, but only if promotion to jobs involving complex, varied tasks is at issue, or could reasonably be expected to become so in the near future. If no such promotion possibilities existed, employees with high scores on general intelligence and/or mechanical aptitude tests might, in fact, be predicted to perform less ably and reliably over time than low scorers. Such a prediction would be based on the hypothesis that, absent counteracting motivation (*e.g.*, from desperate financial need for the job), boredom and frustration would be expected to reach higher levels in such employees, resulting in lower morale. Low morale often has demonstrably adverse effects on the job performance of employees, white or black. In short, pure criterion validity of this simple sort is the obvious psychometric choice for the validation of any screening device—test or nontest— for hiring or promotion when simple, repetitive tasks are at issue.

The appellate court in *Davis* insisted upon the same standard of proof for the job-relatedness of the tests used in that case to select

---

[51] The Wonderlic Personnel Test and the Bennett Mechanical Comprehension Test. See BUROS, ed., 7 MENTAL MEASUREMENTS YEARBOOK ## 401 and 1049 (1972 ed.), for critical reviews of both tests and a complete list of published references pertaining to each.

police officers for the District of Columbia. It noted that the test used, Test 21, "was developed by the Civil Service Commission for general use throughout the federal service as a measure of verbal ability, rather than specifically to measure the full range of skills required to perform the tasks of a police officer."[52] It went on to note that the district court had held that defendants had met their burden of proof of job-relatedness by finding "that Test 21 is exonerated [of its alleged discriminatory effects] by a direct and reasonable relationship to the requirements of the Department's police training program."[53] The appellate court concluded: "We deem that insufficient, and finding Test 21 not otherwise demonstrated to be job related, we hold that appellees have not met their burden."[54]

In psychometric terms, the District of Columbia Court of Appeals held, as it had in *Douglas v. Hampton*,[55] decided the same day, "that construct validity may be considered only after a showing that it is infeasible to undertake proof of empirical validity."[56] "Empirical validity" is Judge Robinson's name for criterion validity, as he explained in the *Douglas* case:[57]

> Three techniques for proving the validity of testing procedures have been judicially and professionally noted. "Empirical" validity is demonstrated by identifying criteria that indicate successful job performance and then showing a correlation between test scores and those criteria. "Construct" validity is proven when an examination is structured to determine the degree to which applicants possess identifiable characteristics that have been determined to be important to successful job performance. "Content" validity is established when the content of the test closely approximates the tasks to be performed on the job by the applicant.

Specific consideration of the adequacy of these definitions of basic psychological concepts and of the judicial understanding which underlies them will be deferred until after an examination of the example provided by the *Davis* case. But as I have already posited, there are two basic types of jobs, simple, repetitive ones and complex, varied ones, and the relationship between schooling and status on the one hand, and job complexity on the other is modest

---

[52] 512 F.2d at 958.

[53] *Id.* at 959.

[54] *Ibid.*

[55] 512 F.2d 976 (D.C. Cir. 1975).

[56] *Id.* at 986.

[57] *Id.* at 984.

overall and approaches the vanishing point in relation to many complex jobs.

The job at issue in the *Davis* case, police work, is a good illustration. It is an extremely complex task, yet the usual requirement for it is only a high school degree. Sometimes, not even that much education is required.[58] Increasing the educational requirements and making them job-specific would probably solve the immediate legal problem faced by police administrators like those involved in the *Davis* case. Courts have had no difficulty in finding the requirement of a J.D. for the practice of law,[59] an M.D. for the practice of medicine,[60] or a D.D.S. for the practice of dentistry[61] to be job-related and/or reasonable, without requiring any validation evidence whatsoever. Thus, requiring a Ph.D. in police science or criminology would probably be upheld, although requiring a high school degree might not be, because the fact that it is not, in and of itself, job-specific has led some courts to wonder if it is really a necessary requirement for the job.[62]

A Ph.D. requirement for police work would, of course, eliminate many more minority group applicants—and since higher education is expensive, poor people generally—than would Test 21 or any other test in common use by American police departments. The trouble with such an approach, discriminatory effects aside, is that not all complex tasks are best learned in academic environments. Nonetheless, complex jobs do require complex skills and, since some selection method is necessary in any situation where applicants outnumber openings, police departments should, in fairness, try to select people who possess some of those skills, or at least the capacity to learn them in a realistically feasible amount of time.

---

[58] See REPORT OF THE PRESIDENT'S COMMISSION ON LAW ENFORCEMENT, THE CHALLENGE OF CRIME IN A FREE SOCIETY (1967).

[59] Lombardi v. Tauro, 470 F.2d 798 (1st Cir. 1972).

[60] Dent v. West Virginia, 129 U.S. 114 (1889).

[61] Graves v. Minnesota, 272 U.S. 425 (1926).

[62] In Morrow v. Crisler, 491 F.2d 1053 (5th Cir. 1974), a troubled court sitting en banc struggled with this very question, faced with a situation in which gross racial imbalance was clear. As of 11 February 1974, the Mississippi Highway Patrol had 543 white patrolmen and only 5 blacks. *Id*. at 1064. All the judges agreed that affirmative action was necessary, but there was little agreement on the question of waiving the requirement of a high school diploma. The tentativeness and variety of answers reached, expressed in six thoughtful, separate opinions, suggest the difficulties inherent in the question.

Selection of this sort can be a very difficult business, because while some of the complex skills needed can be easily specified and objectively measured, others do not readily lend themselves to such treatment. Among the most easily specifiable and measurable of the requisite skills for police work is the one Test 21 was designed to measure: verbal ability. District Court Judge Gesell may not be a psychologist, but his explanation of the reasons why it is a relevant skill was quite cogent:[63]

> Study of the syllabus of the training course readily demon-
> strates the intricacy of police procedures, the emphasis on
> report writing, the need to differentiate elements of numerous
> offenses and legal rulings, and the subtleties of training required
> in behavioral sciences and related disciplines. Daily the signifi-
> cance of these skills demanding reasoning and verbal and
> literacy skills is borne out in the crucible of the criminal trial
> court. Law enforcement is a highly skilled professional service.
> The ability to swing a nightstick no longer measures a police-
> man's competency for his exacting role in this city.

This is, in fact, a partial, preliminary job analysis, and a good one, focusing first on the relation between the test and the training program, and then on the relationship both bear to at least one key ele-
ment of the actual job, testifying against criminal defendants, in the actual job setting in which it is performed, "the crucible of the crim-
inal trial court." At the appellate court level, Judge Robb's dissent was similar, but focused more heavily on the content of the test, the construct underlying it, and the relevance of both to a variety of specific tasks policemen are called upon to perform in their daily work.[64] Presumably, it was these sorts of analyses that Judge Robinson referred to when he said: "The common sense theory of validity espoused by the dissent is clearly an inadequate response to appel-
lants' proof of racially disproportionate impact."[65]

In fact, the analyses of Judges Gesell and Robb have a great deal in common with what a competent professional psychologist would do in beginning to analyze a job and the relevance of a particular training program to the demands of that job, and of a particular test

---

[63] 348 F. Supp. at 17.

[64] 512 F.2d at 966. See also the copy of Test 21 which Judge Robb attached as an appendix to his dissent, *Id*. at 967–76.

[65] *Id*. at 965.

to either or both. Perhaps what was troubling to Judge Robinson is the fact that while some level of verbal ability is obviously a necessary skill for a police officer, it is hardly a sufficient one. A degree of physical courage is certainly required as well. So is judgment in a wide variety of tense social and interpersonal situations, to name only two additional variables on what could turn out to be quite a long list. Test 21 does not purport to measure either courage or judgment, nor is there any reason to assume that what it does purport to measure—verbal ability—would correlate with either to any significant degree. Yet both seem at least as relevant to police work as the verbal ability needed to read and understand the law and apply it in investigating and arresting suspects, writing reports about these activities, and testifying in court with respect to evidence and how it was obtained.

The question then becomes, is its limited coverage of requisite skills a good reason for rejecting Test 21 as not sufficiently job-related? An appropriate answer depends, in part, upon how the test was being used. In the District of Columbia police department, it was used as a screening device in initial hiring to establish what was thought to be a minimum threshold level on one key element necessary for satisfactory job performance. The cut-off point chosen to reflect this minimum level was 50 percent: applicants were given an eighty-item test and required to answer at least forty items correctly.[66] All applicants who did so were accepted into the recruit training program and, when necessary, given special tutoring to insure that they mastered the program, graduated, and became police officers.[67] Only applicants who got less than 50 percent were rejected.

Assuming the appropriateness of the cut-off score, the result was that no one who could learn to perform the job adequately in a practicable amount of time was eliminated, but some applicants who, for various other reasons, will also fail to perform the job adequately were not excluded. In more technical language, use of such a relevant but limited criterion means that there will be no false negatives but an unknown and potentially sizable number of false positives. Obviously, this is not ideal in terms of ultimate efficiency, but the question at issue is whether it is unfair in light of the probable fact that

---

[66] *Id*. at 966.   [67] *Id*. at 963.

no one who can successfully perform the job has been eliminated.

Before answering that question, legal readers would do well to consider some of the implications of an affirmative answer, and some of the difficulties in attempting to measure and evaluate other relevant characteristics like courage and judgment. A good way to do this is to think about the procedures used in choosing candidates for admission to law schools, or, for that matter, in selecting Supreme Court Justices, and judicial clerks. Law schools also use a test which is basically a measure of verbal ability, the LSAT,[68] but few of them establish a cut-off score thought to represent the minimum level of verbal ability necessary for successful performance in law school and thereafter, and then accept everyone above the cut-off point, as the police department did. Instead, law schools often select the highest scorers out of their pool of applicants, sometimes discriminating between successful and unsuccessful candidates on the basis of test score differences as small as one or two points out of a potential range of eight hundred points. Grading in law schools is usually similar, and at least some judges select students for prestigious judicial clerkships by preferring, for example, students with a 78.4 grade average over students with a 78.2 average.

Psychometrically, such distinctions are not merely dubious; they are meaningless. Tests of physical attributes sometimes discriminate with such exquisite fineness, but no professionally developed mental ability, aptitude, or achievement test does, even when applied to sample groups of highly diverse individuals, and no reputable test manufacturer claims that they do. The odds that the totally unvalidated, amateur-designed tests used within law schools on groups of students pre-selected for homogeneity of verbal and reasoning ability do so are very close to zero.

The point is not that tests cannot discriminate meaningfully between candidates for admission to law schools or between students in law schools. The point is that most such tests can make meaningful distinctions of a relatively gross sort and some of them can make meaningful distinctions of a relatively fine sort. As a result, the psychometrically responsible and intelligent way to use such tests is to establish cut-off points between categories of individuals, ignoring intra-category differences, as the District of Columbia police de-

---

[68] See Buros, note 51 *supra*, at # 1098, for critical reviews and published references of the LSAT.

partment did. Of course, it is possible and, in many situations, desirable to create more than two categories. One of the most psychometrically sophisticated of older psychological tests, the Wechsler Adult Intelligence Scale, creates seven categories, ranging from Very Superior to Defective.[69] Demonstrably meaningful categories of a similar sort can be established for lawyers as for policemen. Exquisite fineness of measurement within categories is not possible at this point. More importantly, to attempt it is unnecessary, irrelevant, and potentially quite harmful and counterproductive.

This is so because while a certain level of verbal facility and reasoning ability may be necessary for adequate performance as a policeman, a lawyer, or a judge, beyond that level the differences between superior and inferior workers are a function of other characteristics. Focusing people's energies on the meanly competitive task of scrounging about for an extra half-point advantage on an exam can be demeaning and demoralizing. It is conducive to the development of a fierce but intellectually contentless competition at the expense of intellectual depth, originality, or character. Ex hypothesi, it may well serve to eliminate from the upper echelons of the legal profession many people of superior ability who pursue intellectual enlightenment rather than points and, as a result, earn grades which, on the average, could be predicted to be slightly lower than those earned by the single-mindedly opportunistic.

Looking at the selection of Supreme Court Justices, it might be reasonable to assume that candidates Carswell and Haynsworth were rejected because some members of the bar felt that they were not in the same intellectual category with accepted Justices like Powell and Rehnquist. It would not, however, be reasonable to say that, for example, William Rehnquist will make a better justice than Lewis Powell because his law school grades were slightly higher, assuming purely for the sake of argument that they were, and that both men attended the same law school at the same time, taking exactly the same courses from the same professors simultaneously.

Given intellectual and verbal ability adequate to the task, the differences between outstanding and mediocre Supreme Court Justices are, in all probability, like the differences between outstanding and mediocre policemen, a function of characteristics like courage —in the cases of judges, moral rather than physical courage—and

---

[69] *Id.* at #429.

social judgment.[70] Justices Powell and Rehnquist may be superior to candidates Carswell and Haynsworth in these areas as well, but it is much more difficult to tell, for the same reason that such differences are more difficult to define, measure, evaluate, or test in policemen. While there is considerable agreement about the relevance of those qualities, there is much less agreement about their manifestations.

Did the Warren Court, for example, display the first quality, the second, both, or neither? Eminent legal scholars who have devoted their lives to studying the Supreme Court have disagreed, profoundly. A psychological consultant might point out that some of that disagreement could be more apparent than real, a function of the fact that different scholars may reach different conclusions because they are focusing on different aspects of the Warren Court's work. Thus, he might suggest that it would be helpful to select specific decisions in specific areas for a group of expert Court-watchers to focus on, e.g., school desegregation cases, and might try to make the task more manageable and the comparisons more meaningful via the method of selecting "critical incidents" within each area, e.g., the decision in *Brown v. Board of Education.*

He might sharpen the focus still more by asking all the legal experts, now converted into experimental subjects, to assume: (1) that *Brown* stands for the principle that de jure segregation in public schools is inherently unequal and thereby violates the Equal Protection Clause, and (2) that de facto segregation in such schools is also inherently unequal and that the constitutionally required remedy is massive redistricting and busing to achieve integration.

In some work situations, such an approach helps. In this one, it probably would not. Eminent legal scholars seem to have viewed the decision in *Brown* as an instance of moral courage and sound judgment; others have wondered whether it was not an instance of poor judgment and/or inadequate reasoning.[71] Is the problem, as some courts have suggested in related contexts, that psychology is a de-

---

[70] See Freund, N.Y. Times, 26 Nov. 1971, p. 23, cols. 2–3; Kurland, *The Appointment and Disappointment of Supreme Court Justices,* 1972 LAW AND THE SOCIAL ORDER 183.

[71] *Compare, e.g.,* Wechsler, *Toward Neutral Principles of Constitutional Law,* 73 HARV. L. REV. 1, at 31–34 (1959), *with* Bickel, *The Passive Virtues,* 75 HARV. L. REV. 40, at 48–51 and 78–79 (1961).

veloping science? It seems unlikely. No amount of psychological sophistication and measurement expertise is likely to eliminate this disagreement because it is not artifactual but intrinsic. It arises from the stubborn, irreducible fact that reasonable men of good will, focusing on the same problems, knowing the same facts, having the same type of training and the same degree of experience, expertise, and intelligence, reach different conclusions.

Arguably, this example is unfair, because a most controversial area has been focused upon, controversial in the legal profession as well as in society at large. If school segregation and other areas of hot controversy are put to one side and if more narrowly technical legal questions are focused upon, it should be possible to eliminate much of the disagreement between legal experts. Still, some disagreement is likely to remain. Some scholars will persist in giving one answer while their fellows give another. Is it possible to test which answer is right against some criterion?

Here, a range of possible choices opens up. One possibility would be to eliminate all items on which legal experts disagree and to include only items on which there is concurrence among them, requiring unanimity, as is done with juries. Another alternative would be to require only a majority, as is the case for Supreme Court and electoral decisions. A third option would be to set some statistical in-between point, selected on the basis of probability theory and current developments in test and measurement theory, e.g., judging the significance of concurrence via the Spearman-Brown prophecy formula.

Instead of pondering statistical formulas, the legal reader might find it more profitable to consider some of the grosser implications of such choices. First, the problem of validity: the elimination of controversial cases may also have eliminated all or most questions of moral choice and social judgment, making the resultant test or criterion invalid as a measure of either. Putting that basic question aside and hanging onto the noncontroversial items, if unanimity is adopted as the criterion for their inclusion, the list is likely to be very short. More importantly, all the hard cases will be eliminated. Anything less and the implicit assumption is that the majority is probably right, the minority wrong. Often that is the best that can realistically be done, in law as in psychology. Yet it seems advisable to be wary of such procedures. Chief Justice Taft was rarely a minority of one;[72] Justice Black frequently was.[73] Was Taft a better Justice than Black? Times change, and men's opinions with them.

The relevance of all this to the *Davis* case is that the problems in developing a measure of criterion validity adequate to a complex and varied job requiring decision-making in situations where reasonable men disagree is, in essential respects, the same, whether the decisions are made by judges in law courts or by police officers on the streets. In both situations, the difficulties involved in establishing criterion validity are truly formidable ones.

Interestingly, lawyers who insist that police departments must either establish such validity for their selection methods or forgo them altogether do not seem even to consider applying comparable standards to the means used to select and evaluate attorneys and judges. Perhaps they are simply being inconsistent, telling employers outside the legal profession, "Do as we say, not as we do." Perhaps, however, they are acting on the basis of unstated assumptions about the inherent difficulty of the jobs in question, *e.g.*, assuming that the judge's job is intrinsically more difficult than the policeman's, and that it is therefore fair and reasonable to demand criterion validity for selection methods in one group and no validity at all for selection methods in the other. Such assumptions have neither an empirical nor a compelling logical basis. They appear to be a function of ignorance of police work combined with deference to men and jobs with high status and unjustified disparagement of men and jobs with low status.[74]

Such attitudes would be rationally justifiable only if job complexity bore a consistent logical relationship to job status. It does not and has not. The fact that dull men with little training can and do perform police work does not prove that it is an intellectually undemanding task any more than the fact that dull men trained only as barbers once did surgery proves that surgery is an intellectually easy job. Most judges are probably brighter and better trained than most policemen, not because they "need" to be in any task-intrinsic sense,

---

[72] Chief Justice Taft dissented in only 20 cases and wrote only 4 dissenting opinions while on the Supreme Court.

[73] See Kurland, *Hugo Lafayette Black: In Memoriam*, 20 J. Pub. L. 359 (1971).

[74] Professor Kaplan has suggested that such unstated assumptions may be especially common among proponents of employment preference for blacks: "one can be more comfortable advocating preference if he considers the type of work unimportant." See Kaplan, note 9 *supra*, at 372.

but because society has been generally unwilling to accept a level of judicial performance as low as it once accepted from surgeons and as it now accepts from policemen—at least in some countries, our own included. Is this because judicial work is more important, if not more difficult, than police work? Perhaps, but then again, perhaps not.

The point of the foregoing is to suggest that criterion validity—the sort of validity which Judge Robinson declared by judicial fiat to be superior to all other forms of validity in all job-testing situations—becomes awesomely complex or fraught with danger when applied to complex varied jobs. Of course it is possible to oversimplify matters, as some industrial psychologists employed by management have tended to do, by taking the position that pleasing the particular employer in each job situation is, in and of itself, a sufficient measure of job performance. From this point of view only, criterion validity in the form it typically takes in complex job situations—supervisors' ratings of on-the-job performance—is both the best and the only measure needed for complex as well as for simple jobs. For most psychologists, however, such an approach confuses success, of a sort, with excellence, and involves serious risks of immediate unfairness to employees and long-term inefficiency for businesses, their owners, and their managers.

More thoughtful and even-handed professional appraisals confront the fact that too often a particular employment supervisor may have poor judgment and/or poor data on his employee's work performance, *e.g.*, as in police work where much of the officer's work is done out in the field, far from supervisory eyes. The potential here for ratings that are not only wrong but seriously discriminatory is obviously enormous, and much greater than the potential for unjustified discrimination on the basis of tests. There are, however, ways of reducing, if not eliminating, the potential for bias here, but care is needed to distinguish methods which actually reduce bias from those which merely teach supervisors how to rationalize it to avoid the appearance but not the reality of unfairness. The proper utilization of a construct validity approach is one of the most promising ways psychology has developed for moving beyond criterion validity and providing a needed check on the misconceptions and abuses that reliance on criterion validity alone can foster in complex situations.

To expound adequately upon all these matters would require a book, and several have already been written.[75] One of these is especially good and up to date, Anastasi's *Psychological Testing*. The American Psychological Association's efforts,[76] on the other hand, are misleading for the nonprofessional. Certainly, the very intelligent and conscientious legal laymen who have read the APA's materials appear to have emerged with numerous misconceptions about what psychology's mainstream position is on a variety of key issues.[77] Other misconceptions about the ideas most psychologists subscribe to seem to have come from reliance on materials prepared by psychologists representing various subspecialties with special slants on, and/or special stakes in, various issues. Still others stem from perusal of the *Equal Employment Opportunity Commission Guidelines*. The major problem here, as Mr. Justice Blackmun pointed out in *Albemarle*, is that these guidelines "have never been subjected to the test of adversary comment."[78] Chief Justice Burger made the same well-taken point: "they are not federal regulations which have been submitted to public comment and scrutiny as required by the Administrative Procedure Act."[79]

---

[75] *E.g.*, ANASTASI, PSYCHOLOGICAL TESTING (4th ed. 1976); CRONBACH, ESSENTIALS OF PSYCHOLOGICAL TESTING (3rd ed. 1970).

[76] See, *e.g.*, American Psychological Association, Task Force on Employment Testing of Minority Groups, *Job Testing and the Disadvantaged*, 24 AM. PSYCHOL. 637 (1969); Cleary, Humphreys, Kendrick, & Wesman, *Educational Uses of Tests with Disadvantaged Students*, 30 AM. PSYCHOL. 15–41, 88–96 (1975); Deutsch, Fishman, Kogan, North, & Whiteman, *Guidelines for Testing Minority Group Children*, 20 J. SOC. ISSUES 127 (1964); *The Responsible Use of Tests: A Position Paper of the AMEG, APGA, and NCME*, 5 MEASUREMENT & EVAL. IN GUIDANCE 385 (1972); Fincher, *Personnel Testing and Public Policy*, 28 AM. PSYCHOL. 489 (1973); Flaugher, *Some Points of Confusion in Discussing the Testing of Black Students*, in MILLER, ed., THE TESTING OF BLACK STUDENTS: A SYMPOSIUM 11 (1974).

[77] Some of the most common misconceptions appear to stem from a failure to recognize the fact that the APA STANDARDS FOR EDUCATIONAL AND PSYCHOLOGICAL TESTS (1974) (APA Standards), contains recommendations for professional test developers as well as for test users, and that the standards appropriate for the former are not appropriate for the latter. Still others derive from an overreliance upon and uncritical acceptance of psychometric analyses and conclusions contained in two references that are frequently cited in legal articles on employment testing: Cooper & Sobol, note 6 *supra;* KIRKPATRICK, EWEN, BARRETT & KATZELL, TESTING AND FAIR EMPLOYMENT (1968). For more recent data and/or more psychometrically sophisticated comments on various aspects of these publications, see, *e.g.*, ANASTASI, note 75 *supra;* Bray & Moses, *Personnel Selection*, 23 ANNUAL REV. PSYCHOL. 551, 553 (1972); and Ruch, *Critical Notes on "Seniority and Testing under Fair Employment Laws" by Cooper and Sobol*, 7 IND. PSYCHOL. 13 (1970).

[78] 422 U.S. at 449.

[79] *Id.* at 452. See also United States v. Georgia Power Co., 474 F.2d 906, 914 n.8 (5th Cir. 1973).

There are, however, at least nine misconceptions about psychological testing that seem most prevalent among law review contributors, judges, and members of the EEOC.[80] These misconceptions are set out below in italics, grouped under three main subject headings. Each misconception is followed by a correction in ordinary type, summarizing mainstream psychology's position on the relevant issues.

A. MISCONCEPTIONS ABOUT "CULTURAL BIAS" AND ABOUT GENERAL INTELLIGENCE AND APTITUDE TESTS

1. *That all tests on which minority performance is currently depressed are ipso facto culturally biased and invalid and that such bias can and should be eliminated, either by discarding all items which differentiate between groups or by using different scoring formulas for minority group members.*

"Cultural bias" is a phrase or slogan which obscures meaning more often than it clarifies it. In fact, culture is, in essence, simply another name for experience and all human behavior is a product of the interaction between experience and genetic endowment. Differences in the experiential backgrounds of individuals or groups are inevitably manifest in test performance as in virtually all other samples of human behavior. As long as these differences are relevant to the abilities and skills a test purports to measure, they not only will but should affect test scores.

Eliminating such differences from test scores tends to lower test validity and to obscure the need for corrective measures to remedy experiential deficits. Poverty, prejudice, and racism tend to limit access to experience, thereby producing experiential deficits. Concealing evidence of their existence by altering test scores will neither remove arbitrary barriers, remedy the deficits they produce, nor advance the cause of equality. Such an approach is like "breaking a thermometer because it registers a body temperature of 101°"[81] or "like the ancient practice of killing the messenger who brought bad news to the emperor."[82]

---

[80] For legal source materials representing some or all of these misconceptions, see, *e.g.,* Davis v. Washington, 512 F.2d 956 (D.C. Cir. 1975); Douglas v. Hampton, 512 F.2d 976 (D.C. Cir. 1975); *EEOC Guidelines on Employee Selection Procedures,* 29 C.F.R. § 1607; Cooper & Sobol, note 6 *supra;* Wilson, note 24 *supra;* Note, 72 COLUM. L. REV. 900, note 6 *supra;* Note, 68 COLUM. L. REV. 691, note 6 *supra.*

[81] ANASTASI, note 75 *supra,* at 60.

[82] CRONBACH, note 75 *supra,* at 306; Doppelt & Bennett, *Testing Job Applicants*

2. *That all or most psychological tests in common use are valid for whites but not valid or consistently less valid for blacks.*

Well-designed contemporary studies do not support the notion of differential validity for most commonly used employment or educational tests.[83] Sophisticated reanalyses of the data which led some earlier investigators to conclude that differential validity was a widespread phenomenon indicate that they were mistaken.[84] And recent reviews of the literature by respected authorities underline this conclusion.[85]

The methodological and statistical flaws which led some earlier investigators to reach erroneous conclusions are numerous, but the following are among the most common: (*a*) artifacts as a function of differences in the size of the black and white samples being compared; (*b*) artifacts that result from comparing samples from different institutions and confounding group factors with institutional ones; and (*c*) artifacts that stem from reliance on ratings as the criteria of test validity instead of using more objective criteria.

---

from Disadvantaged Groups, 57 Test Serv. Bull. (1967). See also Lerner, Therapy in the Ghetto: Political Impotence and Personal Disintegration 62 (1972): "Quite simply, if a valid test shows that poor people or black people do less well than rich people or white people, the correct interpretation is not that the tests must be biased and bad or that poor people and black people are no good: it is that poverty, prejudice, and racism are bad for people, and indeed, we have overwhelming evidence from multiple irrefutable sources that this is so. Ironically, many of the very people who speak out most eloquently against the evils of poverty, prejudice, and racism then turn around when considering victims of these forces and insist that they see no adverse effects, as if life were like a Hollywood movie in which an overwhelmingly outnumbered and outgunned hero is viciously attacked, yet emerges unscathed and even unmussed from the fray. Only in the movies."

[83] Campbell, Crooks, Mahoney, & Rock, An Investigation of Sources of Bias in the Prediction of Job Performance: A Six-Year Study (1973); Cleary, *Test Bias: Prediction of Grades of Negro and White Students in Integrated Colleges,* 5 J. Educ. Meas. 115 (1968); Kendrick & Thomas, *Transition from School to College,* 40 Rev. Educ. Res. 151 (1970); Maier & Fuchs, *Effectiveness of Selection and Classification Testing,* U.S. Army Research Institute for the Behavioral and Social Sciences, Research Report 1179, September 1973; Mitchell, *Predictive Validity of the Metropolitan Readiness Tests and the Murphy-Durrell Reading Readiness Analysis for White and Negro Pupils,* 27 Educ. & Psychol. Meas. 1047 (1967); Stanley & Porter, *Correlation of Scholastic Aptitude Test Scores with College Grades for Negroes versus Whites,* 4 J. Educ. Meas. 199 (1967).

[84] O'Connor, Wexley & Alexander, *Single-Group Validity: Fact or Fallacy?* 60 J. Appl. Psychol. 352 (1975); Schmidt, Berner, & Hunter, *Racial Differences in Validity of Employment Tests: Reality or Illusion?* 58 J. Appl. Psychol. 5 (1973).

[85] Anastasi, note 75 *supra,* at 194, 195; Bray & Moses, note 77 *supra.*

It is essential to grasp the fact about the first group of artifacts that the significance of validity coefficients varies with sample size. As a result, the same exact validity coefficient may be significant for a large sample but not for a small one. Because of this, it is easy—and meaningless—to "prove" that any test is valid for one group and not for another. All it takes is a large enough sample of one group and a small enough sample of another. The proper procedure for differential validity studies utilizing samples of different sizes is to evaluate the difference between the two validity coefficients, not to test separately for the significance of each.[86]

3. *That modern psychology has conclusively disproved the notion that there are such things as fairly general as opposed to very specific intellectual abilities and that tests of multiple specific abilities are always better predictors of vocational and academic performance than tests of general intelligence or aptitude.*

At the present time, there is no consensus in psychology on the nature and structure of intellectual ability. A minority of contemporary psychologists continue to adhere to the Spearman thesis that intellectual abilities are best conceptualized as reflections of a single, very broad factor sometimes called general intelligence. Another minority takes an opposite stance, arguing that intellectual abilities are best conceptualized as a multitude of very narrow and highly specific factors. The majority of contemporary psychologists adopt an in-between position, conceptualizing trait organization in terms of a number of moderately broad group factors, each of which may enter into different tests with different weights.[87]

A useful illustration of the sorts of evidence upon which the majority view is based is provided by some of the more sophisticated analyses of factors underlying scores on the Wechsler Adult Intelligence Scale. Initially developed in the 1930s as a test of general intelligence, the WAIS consists of eleven different subtests, originally conceived as a variety of ways of tapping general intelligence and/or the ability to utilize it effectively.[88] Factor analytic work in the '50s and '60s indicated that no single, general factor seemed to account for all or most of the total variance of the bat-

---

[86] APA Standards, note 77 *supra*.

[87] ANASTASI, note 75 *supra*, at 371, 373.

[88] WECHSLER, THE MEASUREMENT OF ADULT INTELLIGENCE (1939); WECHSLER, THE MEASUREMENT AND APPRAISAL OF ADULT INTELLIGENCE (4th ed. 1958).

tery.[89] However, a single, relatively broad general factor did seem to account for as much as 50 percent of it.[90] In addition, three major group factors were identified: a verbal comprehension factor, a perceptual organization factor, and a memory factor. It is, of course, possible to analyze these factors still further, *e.g.*, perceptual organization seems to represent a combination of spatial visualization and perceptual speed, while the memory factor seems to include immediate rote memory for new material, recall of previously learned material, and the ability to concentrate and to resist distraction. These components can, in turn, be broken down into a further set of constituent elements and so on and on. Disagreement arises about the utility of continuing the process of differentiation and about its relation to the organization and operation of intellectual abilities in living human subjects.

Multifactor batteries based on a more differentiated theory of intelligence than that underlying tests like the WAIS were developed in the last quarter-century to measure a large number of different types of intellectual abilities thought to be relevant to various sorts of educational and vocational performance.[91] Initially, the hope was that these multifactor batteries would prove markedly superior to the older, more general tests in terms of differential validity. Results thus far have been disappointing: multiple factor batteries simply have not made the hoped-for contribution to differential validity.[92] In the occupational arena, the problem may stem, at least in part, from the difficulty in obtaining satisfactory criteria of occupational success. In the educational arena, it seems increasingly likely that the problem inheres at least partly in some of the theories underlying the multifactor batteries: there is impressive evidence indicating that a single, relatively broad factor—verbal comprehension—makes a disproportionate contribution to achievement in all academic areas. Because most general intelligence tests are, in large

---

[89] See ANASTASI, note 75 *supra*, at 254; Cohen, *A Factor–Analytically Based Rationale for the Wechsler Adult Intelligence Scale*, 21 J. CONSULTING PSYCHOL. 451 (1957); Cohen, *The Factorial Structure of the WAIS between Early Adulthood and Old Age*, 21 J. *Consulting Psychol*. 283 (1957); Guertin *et al.*, *Research with the Wechsler Intelligence Scales for Adults: 1955–1960*, 59 PSYCHOL. BULL. 1 (1962); Guertin *et al.*, *Research with the Wechsler Intelligence Scales for Adults: 1960–1965*, 66 PSYCHOL. BULL. 385 (1966).

[90] See authorities cited at note 89 *supra*.   [92] *Id.* at 383.

[91] ANASTASI, note 75 *supra*, at 378.

part, measures of verbal comprehension, they function both as measures of previous educational achievement and as predictors of subsequent educational performance. Moreover, because material taught in the educational system is of primary importance in American culture generally, general intelligence tests are reasonably good predictors of performance in many occupations as well as in a wide variety of other activities.[93]

4. *General intelligence tests purport to be measures of hereditary intelligence unmodified by experience and impervious to change.*

This is a popular misconception. No group of contemporary psychologists—majority or minority—believes this and there is no reasonable basis, theoretical or empirical, for such a belief. Intelligent behavior, on tests as in any other sphere of human activity is, like all human behavior, a product of both heredity and experience and of the continuing interaction between the two. There are, at present, no pure measures of either and, absent a major scientific breakthrough, there is no likelihood of developing any in the foreseeable future. Such disagreement as exists among psychologists in this area pertains only to the relative contribution of each to the determination of scores obtained on certain tests by various population groups and not by any particular individual within such a group.

For reasons having little or nothing to do with the field of psychology, this particular misconception has proved itself to be as persistent as it is harmful. In despair of eradicating it by other means, some psychologists have suggested abandoning phrases like "intelligence test" or "intelligence quotient" altogether.

B. MISCONCEPTIONS ABOUT TEST CONSTRUCTION AND VALIDATION
   METHODS AND THE RELATIONSHIP BETWEEN THEM

5. *That there are two basic approaches to the scientific construction and validation of tests, an inferior approach which is purely theoretical and a superior approach which is purely empirical.*

Methods of test construction may be either theoretical or empirical. Methods of test validation are always empirical: there is no other scientifically acceptable way of determining whether a test measures what it is supposed to measure. The primary difference between validation methods is that some are both theoretical and empirical

---

[93] *Id.* at 350; CRONBACH, note 75 *supra*, at 290.

while others are purely empirical. This difference usually corresponds, at least initially, to differences in methods of test construction.

A test constructed on the basis of theory is one in which the test designer begins by developing a psychological construct, based on logic, observation, and, it is hoped, insight, which he hypothesizes to be relevant to whatever human activity or activities he is trying to study. He then designs or selects test items which reflect various aspects of the construct as he has defined it. At this point, his test has mere "face validity," which is not a form of validity at all but only a necessary prerequisite to the establishment of the validity of his test and of the hypothesis underlying it. To establish validity, he must then make a series of a priori hypotheses about the behavior of people who score high on his test as contrasted with that of people who score low on it, empirically checking the accuracy of these predictions against multiple, independent external measures of behavior. If all or most of his predictions are borne out and there are cogent, testable explanations for any instances in which predictions were not confirmed, test validity has been established. This particular sort of validity is called construct validity because, in addition to knowing what the test predicts, the test user can also explain why the test predicts whatever it does predict in terms of the underlying construct.

An alternative, atheoretical approach to test construction begins by focusing on the end result, a particular criterion that the test developer is trying to predict, and amassing a very large initial pool of potential test items, checking the correlation of each with the criterion. Items which do not show high correlations are eliminated. The resultant items may or may not suggest a coherent underlying psychological construct which allows the test user to understand, explain, and interpret his results, on a post hoc basis. If cross-validation utilizing a new sample indicates that the same items still successfully predict the criterion, test validity has been established. This particular sort of validity is called criterion validity.

6. *That one type of validity—criterion validity—is always superior to other types because it is simple, objective, problem-free, and noncontroversial.*

Criterion validity is, at best, as simple, objective, problem-free, and noncontroversial as the criterion itself. It cannot be more so, and may sometimes be less so. There are situations where the criterion is relatively easy to define and measure in quite satisfactory objective ways. Situations like that most often arise in a business context when what one is trying to predict is competence in performing a simple, repetitive task. In such cases, criterion validity is the obvious choice because it generally serves the employer's interest in the most efficient way, allowing him to select the best employees at the least cost. The fact that he may not understand why high-scoring applicants do better on the test and on the job than low-scoring ones is usually irrelevant for his immediate purposes. Being a businessman and not a scientist or a social worker, he is under no obligation to pursue knowledge for its own sake or to provide effective vocational counseling for failed applicants.

When, however, the criterion an employer is interested in predicting is competence in the performance of a complex, varied task, the entire validation enterprise turns on the adequacy with which the criterion—competence—has been defined and measured. Obtaining suitable criterion data in such situations is one of the most difficult problems that psychologists face.[94] The easiest, most common, and least satisfactory way of dealing with the problem is to rely exclusively on subjective supervisory ratings, comparing the scores of potential employees with those of incumbent employees who have received positive ratings from their supervisors.

It is obvious that such ratings can be and often are biased by a host of factors which are quite irrelevant to the actual merits of an employee's work performance. A test which claims legitimacy solely on the basis of its ability to correlate with a criterion can be no better than the criterion itself which, in many instances, means no good at all. Measured against such a criterion, a poor test may appear to be a good one and, conversely, a good test may appear to be a poor one. Moreover, a poor test which has a high correlation with a poor criterion may be more troublesome than the criterion itself because it may serve formally to institutionalize unfair selection methods, giving a gloss of pseudo-scientific respectability to egregious bias. An uncritical acceptance of criterion validity wherever results are statistically significant tends to foster such unfortunate outcomes. Statistical significance is necessary for scientific validation but it is not, in and of itself, sufficient. Statistics, and the theory of probability on which they are based, are powerful scien-

---

[94] CRONBACH, note 75 *supra*, at 127, 413.

tific tools, not a form of alchemy capable of turning leaden data into gold. Good researchers often express this idea more tersely in a revealing phrase: garbage in, garbage out.

7. *That construct validity is simply another type of validity and an inferior one at that because it is purely theoretical and not empirical and is therefore appropriate, as the EEOC Guidelines suggest, only "where criterion-related validity is not feasible."*[95]

Construct validity is not simply another type of validity: it is a comprehensive concept which includes the other basic types (content validity as well as criterion validity) and it is not merely theoretical but is both theoretical and empirical.[96] It differs from criterion validity not in obviating the need for empirical validation against an external criterion but in requiring multiple external criteria instead of permitting reliance on a single, unanalyzed criterion. The use of multiple empirical criteria systematically selected on the basis of a coherent set of theoretical assumptions lays the basis for an analysis of the meaning of various patterns of correlation between test scores and criteria, allowing one to understand why a particular test correlates or fails to correlate with any particular criterion, thus elucidating the nature of the criterion as well as the nature of the test.

As such, construct validation is a powerful means of advancing human knowledge. In fact, it is the very process by which all scientific theory is developed. In employment testing situations and other practical contexts, it provides a much-needed way of investigating the validity of criterion measures in general and of tests developed with reference to a single atheoretical criterion in particular. Results of such investigations can and often should lead to the modification or abandonment of criteria chosen to validate a test or used as a basis for other decisions in a host of contexts, including the employment context.

C. MISCONCEPTIONS ABOUT REASONABLE REQUIREMENTS FOR EMPLOYERS

8. *That employment tests cannot and should not be general but must be developed anew for each particular job.*

---

[95] *EEOC Guidelines*, note 80 *supra*, at § 1607.5 (a).

[96] ANASTASI, note 75 *supra*, at 161; CRONBACH, note 75 *supra*, at 142, 143.

There is no reasonable basis for such a blanket generalization. In each employment testing situation, management is confronted with a choice between using an old, established test and/or a combination of such tests or developing new tests specific to the positions they wish to fill. There are always advantages as well as disadvantages to either choice, and these vary from situation to situation. Intelligent choice results from a careful analysis of the factors that are operative and relevant in a particular situation, followed by a systematic weighing and balancing of the relative advantages and disadvantages of either choice in that situation.

The usual, accepted procedure is to start with a job analysis, identifying key elements necessary for the competent performance of a particular job and then to investigate the appropriateness of established tests for the measurement of those elements. When there is a reasonable correspondence between the two, established tests are likely to be effective and should usually be tried first[97] for two major reasons. It is cheaper to use an established test than to develop a new one. There is no guarantee that the new test will prove superior to already established ones, and no quick way of determining that. Development and validation of a new test and of the criteria against which it is measured take time as well as money, time to investigate whether the test actually predicts what it is supposed to predict and how well or poorly it does that for various population groups under various conditions. New tests that initially seem better than older, established ones often turn out to have unanticipated defects and disadvantages that counterbalance whatever advantages or seeming advantages they have. In this area as in so many others, there is no substitute for length and breadth of experience.

On the other hand, the fact that a particular test has been successfully used in a variety of other situations is never proof, in and of itself, that it will be effective in some new situation. And, when the new situation seems to have little in common with prior situations and to require skills and abilities that do not seem to be adequately measured by any existing test, it may actually prove more efficient in terms of ultimate cost-benefit ratios to start from scratch by developing a new test, tailored as precisely as possible to the particular requirements of the new situation, or at least to those requirements which it proves possible to measure.

---

[97] CRONBACH, note 75 *supra,* at 411.

9. *That it is realistic to require complete local validation in each new job setting in which a test is used.*

It is incontrovertible that this is the ideal procedure in all industrial contexts. It is equally obvious that full-scale, longitudinal validation is rarely a realistic possibility in any local industrial context.[98] The majority of American businesses simply do not have access to a large enough employee sample over a long enough period of time to conduct such a study. Even if this requirement were limited to apply only to very large industrial concerns, there are at least three major additional reasons why local validation studies, however competently carried out, are likely to yield uninterpretable results.

First, there may be an inadequate number of employees performing the same or closely similar jobs. Second, the fact that not all employees can be hired or followed up means that some pre-selection inevitably occurs, and this operates to limit group heterogeneity, restricting the range of scores and depressing the likelihood of achieving statistical significance. Third, there is the usually difficult and often insurmountable problem of obtaining local criterion data with sufficient reliability and validity.

On the basis of the foregoing, the following conclusions about reasonable standards of proof for the job-relatedness of employment tests seem warranted.

1. Criterion validity is generally preferable to other forms of validity only when the criterion itself is clearly valid or can easily be made so. This is usually the case when simple repetitive tasks are at issue. It is rarely the case when complex varied tasks are at issue. Therefore, it is usually fair to both employers and employees to require that criterion validity be established for tests used to select workers for simple repetitive jobs; it is unfair to both to make such validity an automatic requirement for tests used to select workers for complex varied jobs.

2. Construct validity is theoretically preferable to other forms of validity whenever the criterion itself is lacking in validity or possesses only questionable validity. This is usually the case when complex varied tasks are at issue. Hence, construct validity is theoretically preferable in these situations. Establishment of true construct validity for all the skills needed to perform any particular complex, varied job is rarely if ever a practical possibility. It is an ideal perpetually to be

---

[98] ANASTASI, note 75 *supra*, at 436, 437.

sought, not a workable standard which can be legally imposed. Reasonable substitutes include but are not limited to: (*a*) a test which measures at least one of the several skills which a reasonable job analysis shows to be required for adequate performance on that job, whether the skill in question correlates with supervisors' ratings of performance or not, or (*b*) a test which is at least partially content valid for the job itself, or (*c*) a test which predicts successful completion of a training program in an economically feasible amount of time, providing that the training program is reasonably related to the job itself, as demonstrated by analyses of the job and of the training program, respectively.

3. Regardless of the form of validity being utilized, statistically significant local results can be expected and required only when a particular employer has enough employees performing each separate job to provide an adequate mathematical data base for tests of significance. Thus, an employer with a thousand employees may not have an adequate data base to make such a requirement reasonably applicable to him, *e.g.*, if his workers are distributed into one hundred different jobs, whereas an employer with only one hundred employees may have an adequate data base if all are performing the same task.

When the local data base is inadequate, reasonable inferences by an employer about the relevance of a particular employment requirement—test or nontest—should be permitted as a legal substitute for empirical proof of scientific validity. In science, reasonable inferences are generally acceptable only as hypotheses; they are unacceptable when offered as a form of proof.[99] This idea is workable and useful in the realm of pure science in large part because decisions and conclusions in that realm can be postponed for as many years or centuries as may be required to establish or at least approximate a truly satisfactory empirical form of proof.

Meantime, however, the nonscientific work of the world must go on, on a day-to-day basis. Thus, employers, be they businessmen, scientists, or lawyers, cannot wait indefinitely for ideal empirical demonstrations of the validity of their hypotheses. Often, they must act within a relatively short period of time or not at all, deciding whatever questions arise as best they can on the basis of the best

---

[99] "Face validity" is the technical name for this scientifically unacceptable use of logical argument alone as a form of proof.

evidence that can be obtained in a practical amount of time and at a feasible cost. Judges are in a similar situation. They must decide all cases legitimately before them at or shortly after their presentation no matter how strongly they might prefer to postpone the entry of a final judgment until more and better empirical evidence is obtainable. In these circumstances, purely abstract or logical reasonableness has been found to be a workable standard. Throwing out all challenged selection methods, however reasonable, if they cannot immediately be demonstrated to be scientifically valid does not appear to be a better practical alternative. The adoption of such a stance by the courts would force very large numbers of employers to hire and promote on a first-in-time, first-in-priority basis, a random basis, or a quota basis.

IV. Job Selection and the Broader Social Context: Causes, Effects, Implications, and Interrelations

The necessity for an employer to select among job applicants occurs whenever applicants or potential applicants outnumber openings for any position or group of positions. This is a fact of economic life which no legal system can obviate. Options exist only with regard to the selection methods chosen or permitted, and these options, too, are quite limited. Basically, there are but two types of selection methods, each with three main subtypes: (1) Qualitative methods relying on (*a*) tests, (*b*) educational requirements, and/or (*c*) social characteristics, *e.g.*, prior experience and personal attractiveness; or (2) quantitative methods utilizing (*a*) quota impositions, (*b*) first-in-time, first-in-priority allocation, or (*c*) random selection.

The primary difference between qualitative and quantitative selection methods is that the former aim to foster and reward the development of excellence, while the latter do not. Of course, aiming for excellence is not the same thing as achieving it, but it increases the odds of doing so, with or without full scientific validation of each qualitative requirement used. In the aggregate, heightened probabilities for excellence are not a function of the validity of any particular selection device. Rather, they are a result of a total situation in which vast numbers of employers are free to experiment with an unlimited number of possible qualitative requirements, discarding those that seem unsatisfactory and replacing them with others that seem more promising, and so on and on, in a continuing, open-ended process.

The theory underlying this process should be familiar to lawyers in general and to constitutional scholars in particular because it is similar in essential respects to the rationale underlying the First Amendment: truth has the best chance to emerge and prevail if ideas are permitted the freest possible play consistent with the need for a degree of social order and security. Science itself operates similarly in all countries and ages in which it flourishes: no central authority has ultimate decision-making power over which lines of research are worth pursuing and which not. Science does differ in one major respect: the acceptance of technical standards of procedure for the empirical testing of hypotheses, irrespective of their specific content, and the insistence upon such empirical testing as the only acceptable form of proof by all who choose to call themselves scientists and who harbor realistic expectations of being accepted as such by the international scientific community.

Scientific standards of proof can be and have been usefully incorporated into the fabric of the law in numerous areas where their use has proved feasible and economical, *e.g.*, in the scientific identification of persons through fingerprints and X-rays. Matching persons with jobs is, however, a very different and very much more complex task than the mere identification of particular individuals as such. This would be so simply because no single person ever matches a job with the unique particularity with which each individual matches his or her own fingerprints.

The selection of candidates for jobs can never be an unequivocal process, and this would be true even if jobs had the same degree of core stability as do certain physical characteristics such as fingerprints. In fact, jobs have no comparable degree of stability. Particularly when complex tasks are at issue, the actual work performed tends to alter constantly over time as the conditions of each job and of the relevant universe impinging upon it change, develop and retrogress in response to both internal and external pressures, *e.g.*, market conditions, technological developments, governmental policies, and intellectual and social fashions.

This does not mean that it is not desirable to insist on scientific validation of employment tests which operate significantly to reduce the percentage of minority group employees where it is feasible to do so. It does mean that it is a bad idea to outlaw the use of all tests in situations where proper scientific validation is precluded by practical exigencies like those listed as a correction to "misconception 9."[100] It is a bad idea to adopt inflexible and impossible standards.

This first and most obvious danger inheres in the great discrepancy between standards for legal proof of the acceptability of test versus nontest qualitative requirements. Demonstration of the scientific validity of academic requirements for most professional jobs has never been required[101] and is not likely to be in the foreseeable future. Technical difficulties aside, it would require too massive an upheaval in the life of the nation and too extreme a disappointment of expectations built up over long periods of time by great numbers of students, teachers, and professionals in a multitude of fields, quite apart from any presumed effects on the level of competence of members of various professions.

Thus, setting impossible standards for the validation of test requirements in all situations,[102] and no standards at all for the validation of advanced degree educational requirements, results in the destruction of opportunities for objective merit selection and advancement for those with less formal education while preserving such opportunities intact for those with more formal education. One need not look far to see the intense resentment this generates among those with relatively little formal education who perform complex jobs and take pride in their ability to do so with skill by bringing relevant knowledge to bear on the problems which confront them. Policemen are one such group; firemen are another. Primary and

---

[100] See text *supra*, at notes 98–99.

[101] See Williamson v. Lee Optical Co., 348 U.S. 483 (1955); Graves v. Minnesota, 272 U.S. 425 (1926); Dent v. West Virginia, 129 U.S. 114 (1889); Lombardi v. Tauro, 470 F.2d 798 (1st Cir. 1972); England v. Louisiana Bd. of Medical Examiners, 246 F. Supp. 993 (E.D. La. 1965), *aff'd.*, 384 U.S. 885 (1966).

[102] Not quite all. In England v. Louisiana Bd. of Medical Examiners, 246 F. Supp. 993 (E.D. La. 1965), *aff'd*, 384 U.S. 885 (1966), Circuit Judge Skelly Wright, speaking for a three-judge district court, held that it was not a violation of the Equal Protection Clause to require chiropractors to comply with the Louisiana Medical Practice Act which prohibits any person from practicing medicine within the state unless he not only has an acceptable medical degree but also passes a medical examination given by the Board. The criterion validity of this examination was not discussed, nor was any other type of validity. *Compare* United States v. State of North Carolina, 400 F. Supp. 343 (E.D. N.C. 1975), where another three-judge court held that the North Carolina Board of Education had violated the Equal Protection Clause by requiring applicants for teachers certificates to achieve a minimum score of 950 on the National Teachers Examination, without first establishing criterion validity for that precise cut-off score.

secondary school teachers and administrators are also prominent on this list, along with many civil service functionaries, as witness the amount of litigation by members of these groups fighting for the retention of examination requirements they consider fair and relevant.[103]

To dismiss all of these protesting groups and individuals as mere bigots or unconscionable defenders of arbitrary personal advantage without even considering the reasonableness of their arguments in terms of the sorts of knowledge and skill required for job competence seems high-handed, to say the least, particularly when such dismissals come from professionals who have not even considered applying similar standards to the process by which they were selected for their own jobs. In psychometric terms, this is the equivalent of saying that face validity is always acceptable for the upper middle class and those above them in rank but never acceptable for the lower middle class and those below them in rank.

Comparative inconsistency and unfairness aside, the effects of such a stance are likely to be less than salutory for people without advanced degrees generally and for minority group members in that position particularly. In the first place, the fact that an employer of such people is precluded from selecting among them on the basis of an unvalidated test does not automatically force him to shift from qualitative selection methods to quantitative ones. Instead, the usual immediate result is for such an employer to shift from test and/or non-job-specific educational requirements to an assessment of social characteristics like vocational experience and personal attractiveness. The potential for discriminatory practices is not reduced by such a shift; it is heightened.

It is, of course, obvious that the potential for prejudicial decision-making is heightened when subjective evaluation of personal attractiveness becomes the sine qua non of employment selection. It is, perhaps, less obvious but equally true that such evaluations are likely to color judgments of all other social characteristics which are not objectively measurable,[104] e.g., what sort of prior vocational experi-

---

[103] See, e.g., amici curiae briefs in Carter v. Gallagher, 452 F.2d 315 (8th Cir. 1971); Chance v. Board of Examiners, 458 F.2d 1167 (2d Cir. 1972); Castro v. Beecher, 459 F.2d 725 (1st Cir. 1972); Vulcan Soc. of N.Y. City Fire Dept. v. Civil Serv. Comm'n, 490 F.2d 387 (2d Cir. 1973).

[104] Psychological researchers often refer to this phenomenon as a halo effect.

ence will qualify as relevant and what weight it should be given. Even when prior vocational experience alone is considered by decision-makers deliberately prevented from meeting potential applicants or otherwise learning about their race, sex, ethnic origins, or religious backgrounds,[105] it is rarely if ever a preferable selection device from the point of view of minority group job applicants. In a society where many vocational doors were long closed to such individuals purely on the basis of group membership, prior experience is unlikely to be evenly distributed.

The fact that test results may also differentiate between groups in ways that are not immediately enhancing for all minority group members should not blind us to a very fundamental difference here. Prior vocational experience is part of an individual's past history; current skills and abilities measured by tests are not. It is not possible for individuals, groups, or nations to change their respective pasts and not desirable for them to falsify such data. It is, however, both possible and desirable for all three to change their present and their future. Tests permit this; individuals can study and train for them now and groups and nations can do much to facilitate that process, regardless of past barriers, obstacles, and lacunae. Thus, the major difference between present test deficits and deficits in previous vocational experience is that the former can be remedied; the latter cannot.

It will be argued, however, that the educational deficiencies of many minority group members constitute too great an obstacle to overcome and too unfair a handicap to justify equal treatment on the basis of color-blind standards of objective merit for those society has made unequal. Such critics often seem to feel that the only fair procedure is to make the law into an instrument of coercion aimed at eliminating qualitative selection methods altogether and replacing them with purely quantitative ones for as wide a cross-section of jobs as society will tolerate. Only in this way, critics of this stripe insist, will it be possible to be fair to blacks and others who have been the victims of discrimination and to create true equality.

Whatever reservations one may have about the wisdom of such a point of view in terms of its consequences for American society

---

[105] Rating or scoring done without knowledge of extraneous factors which could affect judgment is called "blind."

as a whole and for its legal system, it seems, at first glance, to reflect a highly positive stance toward minority group members themselves, at least when seen in isolation from the rest of society. On closer analysis, however, there is reason to wonder even about that, and to fear that some of the assumptions about minority group members which underlie such a viewpoint may actually be quite inaccurate and unhelpful, even degrading.

Before examining and contesting the assumptions referred to above, it seems desirable to spell out those which premise this article. Taking black people as an example, the assumption here is that such employment-relevant skill deficits as have existed among them stemmed not only from inferior educational opportunity but also from a lack of motivation to develop skills in certain areas because of a perceived lack of opportunity to make use of those skills as a result of discriminatory employment practices. This assumption seems reasonable in light of the fact that in areas like sports and music where—in recent years at least—prejudice did not totally foreclose opportunity, very large numbers of black people have given unmistakable demonstrations of high levels of ability and strong motivation to develop it to the fullest through intense, self-imposed discipline, effort, and training. This being the case, it seems reasonable to assume that most black people would respond similarly to the removal of racial barriers to employment and advancement in the skilled trades and professions as well as in business, industry, science, and academia.

In fact, there seem to be only three major bases on which one might assume otherwise: (1) because one believes that black people are inherently inferior; (2) because one believes that black people have been and are being socialized into what is currently referred to as a nonverbal subculture; or (3) because one believes that it is impossible to equalize the schooling offered to black children and to extend the remedial educational opportunities available to black adults so as to give them a fair opportunity to learn the skills needed to compete successfully with whites for jobs.

Assumption 1 does not seem worth spending much time on. In scientific terms, the null hypothesis that there are no genetic differences in intelligence between races has never been convincingly disproved, despite sustained efforts to do so by a small minority of scientists who believed such differences existed and who worked diligently to demonstrate them, particularly in the early decades of this century.[106] The overwhelming majority of contemporary scientists feel that available data is inadequate to support any conclusions about innate group differences in intelligence between races.[107] Absent a major scientific breakthrough, more research is not likely to change this consensus in the foreseeable future because the fundamental methodological obstacles which rendered past studies inconclusive remain formidable. In what is likely to be a long meanwhile, it is important to remember that causality aside, the fact is that test score differences within groups greatly exceed any between-group differences which may happen to exist on any particular test at any particular time.

I have dealt with assumption 2 elsewhere. Accordingly, it seems most economical to simply reiterate some key passages here and allow those interested in pursuing the matter further to do so:[108]

> [I]n reality generally and in America particularly, there is no cultural or subcultural group that does not value human communication and there is no human group that does not rely heavily on verbal means of achieving such communication. The poor value verbal communication at least as much as the rich do and, in many instances, more. Afro-Americans, for instance, have an extraordinarily rich oral tradition, expressed through song, story, speech making, and just plain rapping. This tradition is as alive today as it has always been, and it lives among the Black poor as well as among the Black rich, as witness such orators as Martin Luther King, Jr., and Malcolm X, and their audiences, audiences which were dominated by those with blue

---

[106] Compare BRIGHAM, A STUDY OF AMERICAN INTELLIGENCE (1923), with Freeman, A Referendum of Psychologists, 107 CENTURY 237 (1923).

[107] See, e.g., LOEHLIN, LINDZEY, & SPUHLER, RACE DIFFERENCES IN INTELLIGENCE (1975), and reviews by Cronbach and by Crow, in 21 CONTEMP. PSYCHOL. 389–92 (1976); Society for the Psychological Study of Social Issues, Statement on Current IQ Controversy: Heredity versus Environment, 24 AM. PSYCHOL. 1039 (1969). See generally, ANASTASI, DIFFERENTIAL PSYCHOLOGY (3d ed. 1958).

[108] LERNER, note 82 supra, at 158. See also Lerner, Is Psychotherapy Relevant to the Needs of the Urban Poor? in EVANS & CLAIBORN, MENTAL HEALTH ISSUES AND THE URBAN POOR 49 (1974). From this vantage point, it is hardly surprising that studies comparing the performance of black people on verbal and nonverbal tests of intellectual functioning show no consistent trend toward inferior performance on the former. Indeed, to the extent that a differential exists at all, evidence thus far accumulated points generally in the opposite direction: black people as a group may tend to do somewhat better on verbal tests than on nonverbal ones. See, e.g., Bray & Moses, note 77 supra, at 551–52; Cleary, Humphreys, Kendrick & Wesman, note 76 supra, at 16.

collars and those with no collars at all. Most Blacks value
verbal skills and most have them. Those that do not are not
reflecting a cultural difference but a failure to be socialized
into their own culture.

Assumption 3—that it is impossible to equalize the schooling
offered to black children and to extend the remedial educational
opportunities available to black adults so as to give them a fair
opportunity to learn needed skills—is not so easily dismissed. Moreover, even when people assume that it is possible to do these things,
they often make the further assumption that it will take an unac-
ceptably long period of time, too long to make a school-focused
strategy an acceptable alternative to the immediacy of an approach
which simply abolishes qualitative employment requirements where-
ever possible.

The feasibility of rapid, large-scale school improvement is too
big a topic to be covered here in any depth. The following will
have to suffice: (1) an initial attempt to distinguish and separate
out those obstacles to school improvement which are extrinsic and
evitable as opposed to those that are intrinsic and inevitable; and
(2) a brief, initial listing of at least some of the reasons why a school
improvement approach is preferable to an approach which ignores
school quality or focuses upon it only as an excuse for downgrading
qualitative job requirements.

Regarding the first issue, an aggressive, single-minded focus on the
goal of school integration must head the list of extrinsic and evitable
obstacles to the improvement of school quality. Resources being
finite, it is an inescapable fact that money and effort made available
for massive busing and redistricting to achieve quantitative equality
is thereby made unavailable for the struggle to achieve qualitative
equality in education. This is not an argument for separate but equal
education in the old *Plessy v. Ferguson*[109] sense. Deliberate, governmentally imposed segregation through either the frank de jure or
the devious gerrymandered lines route was bad for people generally
and for their education particularly. Its abolition was a necessary
first step toward progress.

It does not follow, however, that deliberate, governmentally imposed integration is always good for people or likely to facilitate

---

[109] 163 U.S. 537 (1896).

their learning.[110] There is an enormous difference between removing arbitrary barriers and imposing blanket quotas. Quota enforcement seems reasonable and necessary when the distribution of schoolchildren of different races defies residential patterns. It is less reasonable and less necessary when it reflects residential patterns. And the more those residential patterns reflect free choices by black as well as white parents, the less reasonable and necessary it becomes. To the extent that residential patterns themselves reflect externally imposed constraints upon—rather than free choices by—black parents, it is the externally imposed constraints that are the evil to be abolished. The density of particular population groups in particular areas is simply not, in and of itself, an evil unless one is convinced that national homogeneity rather than freedom is the ideal.

To be sure, some blacks actively prefer integration per se; others have an intense investment in separatism. Both of these subgroups, however, represent only a fractional minority of the larger minority. Most blacks do not really care much about either of these causes. They have a profound and justified resentment of arbitrary barriers, but once these are removed, what they seek is quality, in education as in other areas. That, a least, is their first priority and the degree of proximity to whites or distance from them tends to be a very secondary concern, when it is a concern at all.[111]

Ironically, both black integrationists and black separatists have attracted strong support from groups of white professionals as well as strong opposition from other such groups. Alas, the ardent wishes of the great majority of black parents for an improvement in the quality of the education available to their children have not attracted any really comparable group of white supporters. White professionals who do champion this cause tend to be somewhat isolated from currently fashionable ideologies and to be quite vulner-

---

[110] Early hopes that integration alone would result in significant improvements in children's learning have proved naïve. See, e.g., COLEMAN, RECENT TRENDS IN SCHOOL INTEGRATION (1975); COLEMAN, KELLY & MOORE, TRENDS IN SCHOOL SEGREGATION 1968-73 (1975); MOSTELLER & MOYNIHAN, eds., ON EQUALITY OF EDUCATIONAL OPPORTUNITY (1972); ST. JOHN, SCHOOL DESEGREGATION: OUTCOMES FOR CHILDREN (1975); Coleman, Racial Segregation in the Schools: New Research with New Policy Implications, 57 PHI DELTA KAPPAN 75 (1975).

[111] See, e.g., MARX, PROTEST AND PREJUDICE 176 (1967); WATTS et al., THE MIDDLE-INCOME NEGRO FAMILY FACES URBAN RENEWAL (1964). See also Ralph Ellison, in Federal Role in Urban Affairs, Hearings before Subcommittee on Executive Reorganization, U.S. Senate, Committee on Government Operations, 89th Cong., 2d Sess., Part 5, 1155 (1966).

able to unfounded charges of racism by highly vocal demagogues of both races.

As a result of such factors, plus shortages of money and properly focused staff, there has been little if any improvement in the quality of education offered to poor children, black or white. Thus, most children from poor families attend poor quality schools, whether integrated or not, and emerge poorly equipped to compete in the job market. Teaching the young graduates of these schools to direct their hostility against white employers, schoolteachers, and standard setters generally instead of against the grossly inferior education which produced their vocational difficulties may create interesting political opportunities for a few but seems contrary to the best interests of the many.

In economic and psychological terms, the best interest of minority group members requires that they receive the best possible education. Real competence resulting from highly developed basic skills is a surer and less limited basis for vocational success as well as for individual and group pride and autonomy than reliance on temporary friends who insist that one's deficits don't matter, as long as one doesn't try to enter their protagonists' fields. This is especially true in light of the fact that the only purely quantitative selection method which assures blacks of adequate numbers of jobs—quota selection—is so fraught with insoluble problems and intolerable dangers in a society as heterogeneous as ours that its widespread use over any extended period of time must be ruled out as a realistic political possibility.

Caucasian members of the upper middle class may tend to identify themselves primarily as white majoritarians in a fairly undifferentiated sense. Members of the lower middle class and groups below them are much less likely to do so, unless they are also members of special organizations like the American Nazi Party or the Ku Klux Klan. Currently, few are, and those who are not tend to view themselves in highly differentiated terms, not as white people, but as Polish-Americans, Irish-Americans, Italian-Americans, Greek-Americans, Appalachian-Americans, and so forth. People who define themselves in these terms tend to see themselves, with some justification, as victims of bigotry, rather than as sources of it.

Governmental reforms aimed at improving conditions for some groups while ignoring the existence of the same conditions in other groups serve to intensify feelings of victimization and discrimination among people who define themselves in ethnic terms. Resultant frustration and resentment is magnified still further when these people feel that they are being forced to pay a higher proportional price for such selective reforms than that paid by more affluent whites. To characterize this resentment as a racist phenomenon is to risk the creation of a self-fulfilling prophecy. In addition, such a characterization or stigmatization ignores two hard facts: (1) Discrepant allocations of the burdens and dislocations occasioned by selective reform is a frequent reality. And (2) the discrepant burdens cannot be justified in terms of differential responsibility for the evils that the reformers are attempting to eliminate.[112] Working-class people in general and ethnically identified whites in particular bear a responsibility for those evils which is certainly no greater and may well be lesser than that shared by the more assimilated professional classes from which the liberal reformers usually come.

For all these reasons, and others as well, any blanket use of quotas for black people is likely to provoke increasingly vociferous demands for similar treatment for a multitude of other groups—demands which simply cannot be accommodated within the framework of American democracy and its legal system as we have known it. If and when the choice must be made, it is widespread quota imposition, not the overall American system, which is likely to be abandoned. Well-educated and highly competent black workers will not be affected; poorly educated ones are likely to be thrown back into the misery and want from which they emerged, more bitter and volatile than before.

Widespread quota hiring has other dangers. Employers who replace merit systems with quota systems are often forced to restructure old jobs to correspond to the new hiring standards. A common way of doing this is to break complex jobs down into their component parts in order to create a multiplicity of simple, repetitive tasks. Once this is done, broad individual competence becomes irrelevant: since all jobs are simple, all workers may be viewed as interchangeable parts in a larger system. Only the system itself remains

---

[112] The Burger Court's sensitivity to issues such as these may partially explain its recent decisions in Runyon v. McCrary, 96 S. Ct. 2586 (1976), and McDonald v. Santa Fe Trail Co., 96 S. Ct. 2574 (1976). See also the dissenting opinions by Chief Justice Burger and by Mr. Justice Powell in Franks v. Bowman Transportation Co., 424 U.S. 747 (1974), and especially at 788 n.7.

complex and only its top designers and managers need high levels of skill and intelligence.

This is, in fact, what happened to very large numbers of industrial jobs in the first half of this century, as the assembly line and the industrial union replaced the craft structure of industry and made the old craft unions obsolete in most areas.[113] Today, computer programming techniques provide a theoretical model for the extension of this process into vast new realms. The too-quick disparagement of unvalidated or incompletely validated merit selection methods as racist in impact may provide the ideological justification for just such an extension.

There are at least two major reasons to view such an extension with concern. In the first place, most complex jobs today are service jobs, not product manufacturing jobs, and there is reason to doubt the efficacy of the line-level simplification process in the service realm. Bureaucratization is, in many ways, the service industries' technical equivalent of the industrial assembly line but it has not resulted in comparable increases in efficiency. Instead, it seems to produce a sharp decline in the quality of service with no compensating advantages in cost-benefit ratios. Thus, employers and consumers stand to lose more than they gain from such a process.

The second major reason to view pressures in this direction with concern and caution rather than unmitigated enthusiasm has to do with the effect of the destruction of complex jobs on workers themselves. Simpler jobs do not produce simpler men; they produce frustrated and demoralized men who can no longer define themselves by their work or take pride in their vocational competence and uniqueness. This has already happened to large numbers of American workers and may help to explain the centrality of ethnic identity in the self-definitions of so many white Americans of modest means.

This is not to deny the fact that, to some extent, ethnic identity is simply a continuing phenomenon, long ignored by those outside the ethnic communities in question but nonetheless real for that.[114] The

---

[113] See, e.g., LYND & LYND, MIDDLETOWN 73–89 (1929); compare LYND & LYND, MIDDLETOWN IN TRANSITION 7–73 (1937). See also WEBB & WEBB, THE HISTORY OF TRADE UNIONISM (1950 ed.); THOMPSON, THE MAKING OF THE ENGLISH WORKING CLASS 234–68 (1963).

[114] See, e.g., GLAZER & MOYNIHAN, BEYOND THE MELTING POT (1963).

current centrality of ethnic identity, however, may also represent a reemergence or revivification of immigrant attitudes grown pale with the passage of time. Such reemergences may be a defensive response to the loss of opportunities for meaningful self-definition through work. If so, the cultural content of the new ethnicity may be very thin and, as a result, its potential for social divisiveness may outweigh its potential for enriching cultural diversity.

Pride in complex, work-related skills learned in well-functioning schools which give poor as well as rich children of all colors and backgrounds a real vocational chance and some real vocational choices seems a preferable alternative. Creation of such schools need not take forever, particularly if the American legal system plays a constructive role in the process.

HANS ZEISEL

THE DETERRENT EFFECT OF THE
DEATH PENALTY: FACTS v. FAITHS

I. The Problem

Once again in the 1975 Term, the Justices of the Supreme Court found themselves unable to express a unified position on the validity of the death penalty. The problem is a complex one because of murky precedents, disputed facts, and strong emotional commitments. It is proposed here to address just one of the issues raised in the cases, the question of the data supporting or controverting the deterrent effect of the death penalty.

In one of the opinions in *Gregg v. Georgia*[1]—there was no opinion for the Court—Mr. Justice Stewart, speaking for himself and Justices Powell and Stevens, stated: "Statistical attempts to evaluate the worth of the death penalty as a deterrent to crimes by potential offenders have occasioned a great deal of debate. The results simply have been inconclusive."[2] The Justice went on to cite with approval the position of Professor Charles L. Black, that no conclusive evidence would ever be available on the question of deterrence:[3]

Hans Zeisel is Professor Emeritus of Law and Sociology, The University of Chicago; Senior Consultant, American Bar Foundation.

[1] 96 S. Ct. 2909 (1976).

[2] *Id*. at 2930.

[3] *Id*. at 2931, quoting BLACK, CAPITAL PUNISHMENT: THE INEVITABILITY OF CAPRICE AND MISTAKE 25–26 (1974).

. . . after all possible inquiry, including the probing of all
possible methods of inquiry, we do not know, and for systematic and easily visible reasons cannot know, what the truth
about this "deterrent" effect may be. . . .
    . . . A "scientific"—that is to say, a soundly based—conclusion
is simply impossible, and no methodological path out of this
tangle suggests itself.

It is the purpose of this paper to show that both the Court's and
Professor Black's views are wrong; that the evidence we have is
quite sufficient if we ask the right question; and that the request
for more proof is but the expression of an unwillingness to abandon
an ancient prejudice.

II. The Structure of the Evidence

All studies that explore the possible deterrent effect of capital punishment are efforts to simulate the conditions of what is
conceded to be an impossible controlled experiment. In such an
experiment the population would be divided by some lottery process
(randomly) into two groups. The members of one group, if convicted of a capital crime, would receive the death penalty; the members of the other group, if convicted of a capital crime, would
receive a sentence of life in prison.

The random selection would assure all other conditions that could
possibly affect the capital crime rate remain the same—within the
calculable limits of the sampling error—in both groups, so that the
"death penalty–life sentence" difference remains the only relevant
difference between them.

Figure 1 shows the basic analytical structure of such an experiment.
This hypothetical graph, denoting the constellation that would confirm the existence of a deterrent effect, begins with two populations
of would-be murderers $(X + Y + Z)$, equal in every respect except
that the one lives under threat of the death penalty, the other does
not. (X) is the number of would-be murderers in both groups
deterred, even by the threat of prison; it can be read from the first
bar and projected to the second. At the bottom end of each bar (Z)
is the proportion of would-be murderers whom even the threat of
the death penalty would not deter. It can be read from the second
bar and projected to the first. The crucial test is whether a group
(Y) can be found which would be deterred by the death penalty but

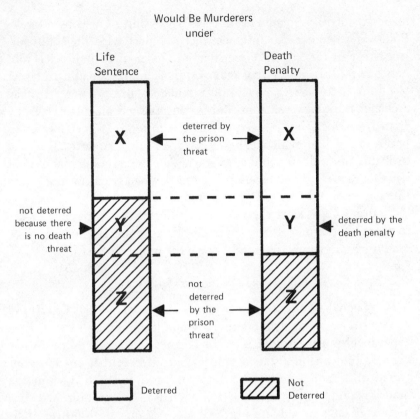

FIG. 1. Experimental paradigm showing a deterrent effect of the death penalty over the life sentence.

would not be deterred if there were only the life sentence. The statistical test that would establish the existence of group (Y) would reveal a significantly lower level of murders[4] under threat of the death penalty.

In principle, it should be possible to identify individual members in each of the three groups. As a practical matter one can identify only the murderers who have not been deterred.[5] Efforts have been

---

[4] The paradigm is limited to murder. See also, however, Bailey, *Rape and the Death Penalty: A Neglected Area of Deterrence Research*, in BEDAU & PIERCE, EDS. CAPITAL PUNISHMENT IN THE UNITED STATES 336 (1976).

[5] The task of tracing the effect of an experimental treatment through case histories of the persons who had been affected by it is less difficult if the treatment aims at a positive effect not a negative, deterrent one. See ZEISEL, SAY IT WITH FIGURES ch. 11 (1965 ed.).

made to identify members of the (Y) group. The Los Angeles
Police Department, for instance, filed a report with the California
legislature in 1960 to the effect that a number of apprehended robbers had told the police that while on their job they had used either
toy guns or empty guns or simply simulated guns "rather than take
a chance on killing someone and getting the gas chamber."⁶ Quite
apart from this being hearsay evidence reported by a very interested
party, this is poor evidence, if any, on the issue. The unresolved and
probably unresolvable difficulty is whether these robbers would not
have minded "killing someone," if the risk had been no more than
life in prison.

Figure 2 represents the paradigm diagram for proving the deterrent effect of increasing executions. Proof of deterrence would be
established if groups (Y_1) and (Y_2) were found to exist.

III. The Impossible Controlled Experiment

Such diagrammed evidence would be cogent if derived from a
controlled experiment. How morally and legally impossible such an
experiment is can easily be seen if its details are sketched out. In one
conceivable version a state would have to decree that citizens convicted of a capital crime and born on odd-numbered days of the
month would be subject to the death penalty; citizens born on even-
numbered days would face life in prison. A significantly lower number of capital crimes committed by persons born on uneven days
would confirm the deterrent effect. The date of birth here is a device
of randomly dividing the population into halves by a criterion that
we will assume cannot be manipulated.⁷

The equally impossible experiment that would test the effect of
differential frequencies of execution would require at least three
randomly selected groups. In the first group everybody convicted
of a capital crime would be executed. In the second, only every
other such convict (again selected by lot) would be executed. In
the third, nobody would be executed.

The data available to us for study of the deterrent effect of the
death penalty are all naturally grown; none derive from a controlled

---

⁶ Report of the California Senate on the Death Penalty 16–17 (1960).

⁷ Worried, expectant mothers, of course, could demand Caesarian delivery on an
even-numbered date. Such intervention, however, would affect the purity of the
experiment only if these mothers were also farsighted, *i.e.*, if their artificial birth-
dates would comprise a higher rate of future murderers than the normal deliveries.

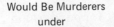

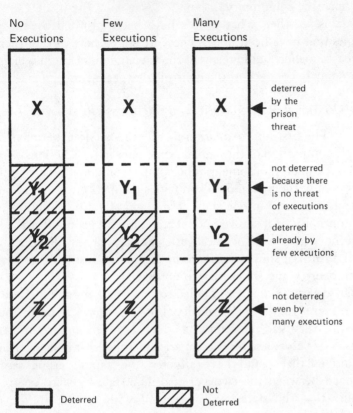

FIG. 2. Experimental paradigm showing a deterrent effect of increasing the rate of executions.

experiment. Yet they all are analyzed as if they had come from a controlled experiment. The structure of analysis is the same. What is missing is the prior randomization which insures comparability in all other respects. The analysis of naturally grown data must try to reproduce comparability by other means. Since none of these means is ever perfect, none of the studies based on naturally grown data ever completely simulates the impossible experiment.

It is this impossibility of the experiment and the unavoidable imperfection of nonexperimental data that account for despair of ever discovering "the truth about this 'deterrent' effect."[8] The despair is unwarranted. Even in the so-called natural sciences proofs that

---

[8] Note 3 *supra*.

are incomplete have nevertheless, for good reasons, been accepted by the scientific community.

Let us see then what proofs have been afforded by the many studies that have been done. They are stated here, not in their historical sequence, but in terms of the varying degree with which they approximate the ideal of the controlled experiment.

IV. Homicide Rates with and without the Death Penalty

The first approximation to the impossible experiment is the simple comparison of the capital crime rates in jurisdictions with and without capital punishment. The comparison could take two forms. Historically the first and most obvious comparison was made of the capital crime rate in one state before and after the abolition of the death penalty. If it showed no increase, it gave ground for the belief that the withdrawal of the death penalty had no ill effect.[9] The second form of simple comparison was between states that have the death penalty and states that do not have it.[10]

These early comparisons failed to show higher capital crime rates when there was no death penalty. But to take this as proof that the death penalty had no deterrent effect involved important assumptions. The before and after comparison implies that none of the other conditions that could have affected the capital crime rate had changed between the two periods. The state-by-state comparison implies that the states were identical with respect to the other conditions.

The first improvement on the simplistic structure of these comparisons was to put the before-and-after comparison side by side with developments in states which during that period had not changed their death penalty rule. Similarly, the comparison between

---

[9] The first comprehensive data on before-and-after comparison were presented by Thorsten Sellin to the Royal Commission on Capital Punishment. *The Deterrent Value of Capital Punishment*, REPORT OF THE ROYAL COMMISSION ON CAPITAL PUNISHMENT App. 6 (Cmd. 8932 1953). Sellin's memorandum is published in the MINUTES OF THE EVIDENCE, 647. *Cf.* also KOESTLER, REFLECTIONS ON HANGING App. (1956); UNITED NATIONS, CAPITAL PUNISHMENT, REPORT (1960); Samuelson, *Why Was Capital Punishment Restored in Delaware?* 60 J. CRIM. L.C. & P.S. 148 (1969).

[10] Sellin, *Homicides in Retentionist and Abolitionist States*, in SELLIN, ed., CAPITAL PUNISHMENT 135 (1967); Reckless, *The Use of the Death Penalty—a Factual Statement*, 15 CRIME & DELINQ. 43 (1969); ZIMRING & HAWKINS, DETERRENCE 265 (1973); Baldus & Cole, *A Comparison of the Work of Thorsten Sellin and Isaac Ehrlich on the Deterrent Effect of Capital Punishment*, 85 YALE L.J. 170, 171 (1976).

states was improved by limiting it to contiguous states, for which
the assumption of comparability seems more justified.

Table 1 provides an example of contiguous states comparison.[11]

Only in one of the five groups is the homicide crime rate in the
no-death-penalty state (Maine) higher than in the other two states.
In all others it is either the same or lower. This is neither evidence of
a deterrent effect of the death penalty nor clear evidence of its
absence. Even contiguous states are not strictly comparable. Over a
span of sixteen years, the period covered by this table, the conditions
favoring crime in those states may develop in different directions.

The state-by-state analysis becomes more convincing if averages
for a long time period are replaced by the annual figures from which
these averages were computed. In figure 3, the homicide rate in
Kansas is compared with that of its neighbor states, Missouri and
Colorado. Kansas was an abolitionist state until 1935.[12]

Figure 3 allows several observations. First, that annual rates exhibit
considerable random fluctuations. It suggests that changes from one

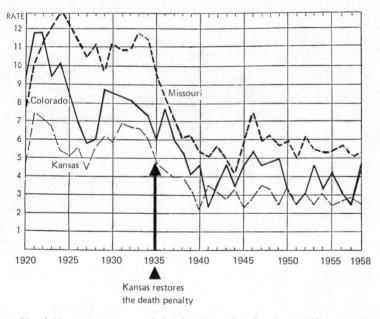

FIG. 3. Homicides per 100,000 population in Missouri, Colorado, and Kansas, 1920–58.

---

[11] ZIMRING & HAWKINS, note 10 *supra*, at 265.

[12] From SELLIN, note 10 *supra*, at 137.

TABLE 1

Homicide Death Rates in Contiguous States with[D] and without Capital Punishment, 1940-55
(Average annual rate per 100,000 population)

Midwest

Group 1		
	D	D
Michigan	Indiana	Ohio
3.5	3.5	3.5

Group 2		
	D	D
Minnesota	Wisconsin	Iowa
1.4	1.2	1.4

Group 3		
	D	D
N. Dakota	S. Dakota	Nebraska
1.0	1.5	1.8

New England

Group 4		
	D	D
Maine	New Hampshire	Vermont
1.5	0.9	1.0

Group 5		
	D	D
Rhode Island	Massachusetts	Connecticut
1.3	1.2	1.7

year to the next are unlikely to be significant. Figure 3 also shows that looking only at one state may lead to false conclusions. The Kansas homicide rate, except for the first two years, shows a sharp decline after 1935 and some early observers jumped to the conclusion that it was the restoration of the death penalty that did it. A glance at the homicide rates of Colorado and Missouri warns against this conclusion. The development of the Kansas rate does not noticeably differ from those of the two neighboring states, which had the death penalty throughout the entire span of years.

V. IMPROVING COMPARABILITY

Comparing the development of the capital crime rate in contiguous states with and without the death penalty has been challenged on the ground that contiguity is not a sufficiently solid guaranty of likeness. Three responses to this challenge have been forthcoming. One was to show that the contiguous states were in fact alike with respect to a great variety of factors that could, if they had differeed from state to state, independently affect the capital crime rate. Table 2 is an example of such efforts.[13]

TABLE 2

DEMOGRAPHIC PROFILE OF CONTIGUOUS STATES COMPARED IN GROUP 1 OF TABLE 1
(1960 data)

	Michigan	Indiana	Ohio
Status of death penalty	...	D	D
Homicide rate	4.3	4.3	3.2
Probability of apprehension	.75	.83	.85
Probability of conviction	.25	.55	.33
Labor force participation (%)	54.9	55.3	54.9
Unemployment rate (%)	6.9	4.2	5.5
Population aged 15–24 (%)	12.9	13.4	12.9
Real per capita income ($)	1,292	1,176	1,278
Nonwhite population (%)	10.4	6.2	9.8
Civilian population (000's)	7,811	4,653	9,690
Per capita government expenditures ($)*	363	289	338
Per capita police expenditures ($)*	11.3	7.6	9.0

* State and local.

---

[13] From Baldus & Cole, note 10 *supra*, at 178.

Michigan, the state without a death penalty, had no higher homicide rate than neighboring Indiana, even though it had a lower probability of apprehension and conviction, a higher unemployment rate, a larger proportion of blacks in the population, greater population density—all factors which should tend to increase the capital crime rate. On the other hand, it had a higher per capita police expenditure. Ohio had a lower homicide rate and a higher apprehension rate. On most of the remaining characteristics Ohio was in an intermediary position.

The second analytical device for improving comparability was to replace the comparison of entire states by comparing more homogeneous subsections of these states, such as communities of comparable size or counties of comparable income levels.[14] The third, most sophisticated response to the problem of comparability was to apply to it a tool called regression analysis. This is an instrument designed mainly to resolve problems such as this which call for separating the effect of one particular variable from the possible effect of a multitude of others.

Before discussing regression analysis in more detail, I turn to two additional efforts to sharpen the analytic approach aimed at detecting the existence of a deterrent effect for the death penalty.

VI. Sharpening the Measure of Capital Crime

If the death penalty deters murder, the rate of wilful homicides should show the effect. There are, however, grades of wilfulness and some types of homicide will have a higher likelihood of resulting in the death penalty. These types of homicide should provide a more sensitive index for detecting deterrent effect, if one exists, than the overall homicide rate.[15]

The difficulty of developing such an index, of course, is the lack of adequate data. With one exception, namely, the killing of a police officer, records are not generally separated according to the type of homicide committed. An effort has been made to obtain counts of

---

[14] Cf. e.g., Sutherland, *Murder and the Death Penalty*, 15 J. Crim. L.C. & P.S. 520 (1925); Campion, *Does the Death Penalty Protect the State Police?* in Bedau, ed., The Death Penalty in America 361 (1967); Vold, *Can the Death Penalty Prevent Crime?* 12 Prison J. 4 (1932).

[15] Zimring & Hawkins, *Deterrence and Marginal Groups*, J. Res. in Crime & Delinq. 100 (July 1968).

first degree murders from the country's prisons.[16] But these numbers are affected by regionally differing apprehension and conviction rates, and indirectly also by differential standards of plea bargaining and jury nullification. Suffice it to note that this effort too failed to detect a deterrent effect of the death penalty.

Killing a policeman is a genuine "high death penalty risk" category and it is well recorded and counted. Again it was Thorsten Sellin who investigated them; table 3 summarizes his findings.[17] Even this measure, rightly thought to be more sensitive than the general homicide rate, failed to reveal any difference between the threat of the death penalty and that of life imprisonment.

TABLE 3
RATE OF MUNICIPAL POLICE KILLINGS, 1920–54
(Per 10 years and 100,000 population)

No Capital Punishment		Capital Punishment	
Maine	.00	Vermont	.00
Rhode Island	.17	New Hampshire	.14
		Massachusetts	.22
		Connecticut	.14
Michigan*	.36	Ohio	.61
		Indiana	.64
		Illinois	.31
Minnesota	.42	Iowa	.56
Wisconsin	.53		
N. Dakota	.53	S. Dakota	.00
		Montana	1.58
		New York	.25
Detroit, Mich.	.85	Chicago, Ill.†	1.54

　° Without Detroit.
　† 1928–44.

VII. THE EFFECT OF EXECUTIONS

A sentence is likely to deter by the differential degree of fear it engenders in the would-be perpetrator. It has been argued, there-

---

[16] Bailey, *Murder and Capital Punishment: Some Further Evidence*, in BEDAU, note 4 *supra*, at 314.

[17] Sellin, *The Death Penalty and Police Safety*, in SELLIN, note 10 *supra*, at 138, 144, 145.

fore, that the dichotomy of jurisdictions with and without capital punishment is but a crude approximation to the reality of the threat. What matters was not the death penalty on the books but the reality of executions.

One response to this consideration was to transform the death penalty—life sentence dichotomy into the gradations provided by the number of executions carried out during any one year. I will return to this approach later. The other response was to try to find out whether publicized executions had a short-range depressing effect on the homicide rate.

Leonard Savitz recorded the homicide rates during the eight weeks before and after well-publicized executions in Philadelphia.[18] He found no depressing effect of these executions, although he used one of the potentially more sensitive measures of deterrence, the frequency of felony murders, rather than the overall homicide rate.[19]

A similar effort with California data showed an effect, albeit an ambiguous one. William Graves compared homicide rates during execution weeks with non-execution weeks.[20] He had the weeks begin on Tuesday in order to keep Fridays, the execution day in California, at the midpoint. The comparison (fig. 4a) suggested a depressing effect during the days preceding the execution and an increase in homicides on the days following it. Graves was puzzled; others considered the data as proof of a counter-deterrent effect. Conceivably the data could be rearranged, as in figure 4b, with the week beginning on Friday, the execution day. The results would then suggest a reduction of homicides during the first three days following executions compensated by an increase during the rest of the week. In any event, Graves's data show, at best, a delaying rather than a deterrent effect, and the failure of the more sensitive Philadelphia data to show any effect casts doubt on the strength of the California result.

---

[18] Savitz, A Study in Capital Punishment, 49 J. CRIM. L.C. & P.S. 338 (1958).

[19] A count of felony murders (for the non-lawyer: a homicide committed in the course of another felony such as robbery) can be made only with great difficulty and only in places, such as Philadelphia, where detailed police records are kept.

[20] Graves, The Deterrent Effect of Capital Punishment in California, in BEDAU, THE DEATH PENALTY IN AMERICA 322 (1967). (The rearrangement in figure 4b is not precise because the curves for Tuesdays through Thursdays will change under the redefinition.)

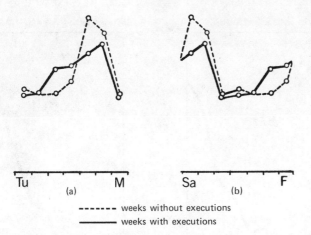

Tu   M   Sa   F
      (a)   (b)

------- weeks without executions
——— weeks with executions

Fig. 4. Homicides during weeks with and without executions.

VII. The Contribution of Isaac Ehrlich

Isaac Ehrlich was the first to introduce regression analysis to efforts designed to determine whether the death penalty had a deterrent effect beyond the threat of life imprisonment.[21] This was a new, powerful way of coping with the task of isolating the death penalty effect, if it should exist, uncontaminated by other influences on the capital crime rate. Ehrlich's paper was catapulted into the center of legal attention even before it was published, when the Solicitor General of the United States cited it with lavish praise in his Amicus Curiae Brief in *Fowler v. North Carolina*,[22] and delivered copies of the study to the Court. The Solicitor General called it "important empirical support for the a priori logical belief that use of the death penalty decreases the number of murders."[23]

In view of the evidence available up to that time, Ehrlich's claim was indeed formidable, both in substance and precision: "[A]n additional execution per year . . . may have resulted in . . . 7 or 8 fewer murders."[24] The basic data from which he derived this conclusion were the executions and the homicide rates as recorded in the

---

[21] Ehrlich, *The Deterrent Effect of Capital Punishment: A Question of Life and Death*, Working Paper No. 18, National Bureau of Economic Research (1973). The paper was subsequently published under the same title in an abbreviated form in 65 Am. Econ. Rev. 397 (1975).

[22] 96 S. Ct. 3212 (1976).   [23] Reply Brief, p. 36.

[24] Ehrlich, note 20, *supra*, 65 Am. Econ. Rev. at 414.

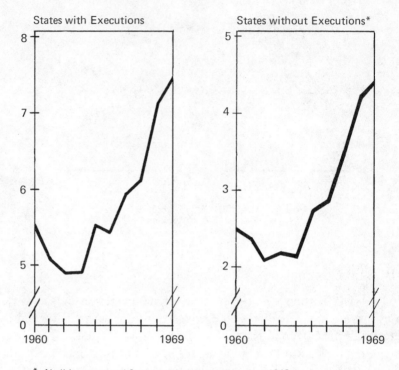

Fig. 5. United States homicide and execution rates, 1960–69.

United States during the years 1933 to 1969, the former generally
decreasing, the latter, especially during the sixties, sharply increasing.[25] Figure 5 presents the crucial divergence between 1960 and
1969. Ehrlich considered simultaneously other variables that could
affect the capital crime rate through calculations I shall discuss
presently.[26]

IX. Regression Analysis

Regression analysis proceeds essentially in the following manner. Suppose one knew for certain that, aside from the possible

---

[25] Data on murders from *The Deterrent Effect of Capital Punishment: A Question of Life and Death*, Sources and Data, May 1975, Memorandum by I. Ehrlich.
Data on executions from: National Prisoner Statistics, U.S. Bureau of Prisons.

[26] Ehrlich's analysis included the following variables: the arrest rate in murder
cases; the conviction rate of arrested murder suspects; the rate of labor force participation; the unemployment rate; the fraction of the population in the age group
14 to 24; and per capita income.

deterrent effect of executing murderers, there was but one other factor that influenced the capital crime rate: the proportion of men between the ages of 17 and 24 in the total population. The analysis would then begin by relating the capital crime rate in the various states to the proportion of young men in those states, as in figure 6.

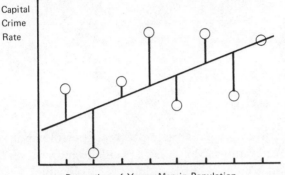

FIG. 6. Hypothetical relationship between the capital crime rate and the proportion of young men in the population.

The points in this graph may represent either different jurisdictions at one point of time, or different points of time in the same jurisdiction, or both. The straight line (the regression line) represents the best estimate of the relationship between the proportion of young men in the population and the capital crime rate. The vertical distance of each point from the regression line represents the residual part of the variations in the capital crime rate, the part that remains unexplained after the effect of the "proportion of young men" has been eliminated. One then proceeds to test whether these residuals are related to the frequency of executions, by plotting them against the number of executions in the respective states as in figure 7. If no relationship exists, a horizontal regression line will indicate that executions have no deterrent effect (a): No matter how executions vary, the capital crime rate remains the same. If a relationship exists (b), the downward slope of the regression line would indicate that as the frequency of executions increases, capital crime decreases. That graph, one will note in passing, is in appearance indistinguishable from the finding of a controlled experiment, if one could be made.

The complete apparatus of regression analysis is more compli-

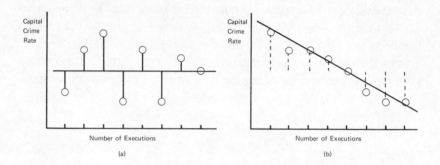

Fig. 7. Two hypothetical relationships between the frequency of executions and the residual capital crime rate.

cated, primarily by encompassing several control variables, not just one, as in our example. Many more problems must be resolved along the way. One requirement is to include all variables that affect the outcome. If one is omitted its effect could be erroneously attributed to one of the included variables. This danger of spurious correlation is particularly great if the analysis is concerned with so-called time series data, such as corresponding constellations of executions and capital crime over a series of consecutive years.

Another requirement is that the analysis account for feedback effects. Estimates of deterrent effects of punishment, for example, may be distorted if they fail to separate the simple statistical association between crime and punishment into its potential two components: the effect of punishment on crime, and the possible reverse effect of crime on punishment. For example, an increase in crime may overload the law enforcement system and thereby increase the defendant's chances of a lower sentence in the plea bargaining process.

All these and other technical refinements of the regression analysis have but one goal: to isolate, through a process of mathematical purification, the effect of any one variable upon the other, under conditions that exclude the interference from other variables. Regression analysis, thus, is but another effort to simulate with the help of nonexperimental data the experimental conditions outlined in figure 2 of this paper.[27] These examples suggest the sophistication

----

[27] A more elaborate effort by me to explain regression analysis to the non-statistician is in preparation and will be published in the *American Bar Foundation Research Journal*.

of this analytic instrument, but its sophistication is matched by a corresponding measure of delicacy. Applied to nonexperimental data, regression analysis is not a naturally robust instrument. Its results can be drastically affected by minor changes in the analytic pattern, for which the investigator has, as a rule, many options.

X. EHRLICH'S DETERRENCE CLAIM EVAPORATES

Ehrlich's study, because it ran counter to all the hitherto available evidence except that of Graves, and because it was introduced into a litigation of historic import, received extraordinary attention from the scholarly community.

First, Peter Passell and John Taylor attempted to replicate Ehrlich's finding and found it to hold up only under an unusually restrictive set of circumstances.[28] They found, for example, that the appearance of deterrence is produced only when the regression equation is in logarithmic form; in the more conventional linear regression framework, the deterrent effect disappeared.[29] They found also that no such effect emerged when data for the years after 1962 were omitted from the analysis and only the years 1933–61 were considered.[30]

An effort to duplicate Ehrlich's findings from Canadian experience also failed.[31] Kenneth Avio of the University of Victoria, after analyzing the thirty-five-year span, concluded that "the evidence would appear to indicate that Canadian offenders over the period 1926–60 did not behave in a manner consistent with an effective deterrent effect of capital punishment."[32]

During 1975, the *Yale Law Journal* published a series of articles reviewing the evidence on the deterrent effect of capital punishment. Included in this series was a second attempt to replicate Ehrlich's result by William Bowers and Glenn Pierce.[33] In replicating Ehrlich's work, they confirmed the Passell-Taylor finding that

---

[28] Passell & Taylor, *The Deterrent Effect of Capital Punishment: Another View*, March 1975 (unpublished Columbia University Discussion Paper 74-7509), reprinted in Reply Brief for Petitioner, *Fowler v. North Carolina*, App. E. at 4e–6e.

[29] *Id.* at 6–8.   [30] *Id.* at 5, 6.

[31] Kenneth L. Avio, *Capital Punishment in Canada: A Time-Series Analysis of the Deterrent Hypothesis* (mimeo, 1976).

[32] *Id.* at 22.

[33] Bowers & Pierce, *The Illusion of Deterrence in Isaac Ehrlich's Research on Capital Punishment*, 85 YALE L.J. 187 (1975).

Ehrlich's results were extremely sensitive to whether the logarithmic specification was used and whether the data for the latter part of the 1960s were included.[34] Bowers and Pierce also raised questions about Ehrlich's use of the FBI homicide data in preference to vital statistics data.[35]

Ehrlich defended his work in this series in the *Yale Law Journal* by addressing some of the criticisms raised against his study.[36] He refuted some, but not the crucial ones. In his article he referred to a second study he made of the problem, basing it this time on a comparison by states for the years 1940 and 1950. Ehrlich claimed that the new test bolstered the original claim. But he described these findings as "tentative and inconclusive."[37] In the meantime, Passell made a state-by-state comparison for 1950 and 1960 but did not find what Ehrlich allegedly had found. Passell concluded: "We know of no reasonable way of interpreting the cross-section [*i.e.*, state-by-state] data that would lend support to the deterrence hypothesis."[38]

A particularly extensive review of Ehrlich's time series analysis was made by a team led by Lawrence Klein, president of the American Economic Association.[39] The authors found serious methodological problems with Ehrlich's analysis. They raised questions about his failure to consider the feedback effect of crime on the economic variables in his model,[40] although he did consider other feedback effects in his analysis. They found some of Ehrlich's technical manipulations to be superfluous and tending to obscure the accuracy of his estimates.[41] They, too, raised questions about variables omitted from the analysis, and the effects of these omissions on the findings.[42]

Like Passell-Taylor and Bowers-Pierce, Klein and his collaborators replicated Ehrlich's results, using Ehrlich's own data, which by

---

[34] *Id.* at 197–205.   [35] *Id.* at 187–89.

[36] Ehrlich, *Deterrence: Evidence and Inference*, 85 YALE L.J. 209 (1975).

[37] *Id.* at 209.

[38] Passell, *The Deterrent Effect of the Death Penalty: A Statistical Test*, 28 STAN. L. REV. 61, 80 (1975).

[39] Klein, Forst & Filatov, *The Deterrent Effect of Capital Punishment: An Assessment of the Estimates*, Paper commissioned by the Panel on Research on Deterrence, National Academy of Sciences (June 1976).

[40] *Id.* at 18, 19–24.   [42] *Id.* at 14–17.

[41] *Id.* at 14.

that time he had made available.[43] As in previous replications, Ehrlich's results were found to be quite sensitive to the mathematical specification of the model and the inclusion of data at the recent end of the time series.

By this time, Ehrlich's model had been demonstrated to be peculiar enough. Klein went on to reveal further difficulties. One was that Ehrlich's deterrence finding disappeared after the introduction of a variable reflecting the factors that caused other crimes to increase during the latter part of the period of analysis.[44] The inclusion of such a variable would seem obligatory not only to substitute for the factors that had obviously been omitted but also to account for interactions between the crime rate and the demographic characteristics of the population.

Klein also found Ehrlich's results to be affected by an unusual construction of the execution rate variable, the central determinant of the analysis. Ehrlich constructed this variable by using three other variables that appear elsewhere in his regression model: the estimated homicide arrest rate, the estimated homicide conviction rate, and the estimated number of homicides. Klein showed that with this construction of the execution rate a very small error in the estimates of any of these three variables produced unusually strong spurious appearances of a deterrent effect.[45] He went on to show that the combined effect of such slight errors in all three variables was likely to be considerable, and that in view of all these considerations, Ehrlich's estimates of the deterrent effect were so weak that they "could be regarded as evidence . . . [of] a counterdeterrent effect of capital punishment."[46] In view of these serious problems with Ehrlich's analysis, Klein concluded: "[W]e see too many plausible explanations for his finding a deterrent effect other than the theory that capital punishment deters murder." And further: "Ehrlich's results cannot be used at this time to pass judgment on the use of the death penalty."[47]

The final blow came from a study by Brian Forst, one of Klein's collaborators on the earlier study. Since it had been firmly established that the Ehrlich phenomenon, if it existed, emerged from developments during the sixties, Forst concentrated on that

---

[43] *Id*. at 24, 25.

[44] *Id*. at 28–30.

[45] *Id*. at 17–19.

[46] *Id*. at 18.

[47] *Id*. at 33.

decade.[48] He found a rigorous way of investigating whether the ending of executions and the sharp increase in homicides during this period was causal or coincidental. The power of Forst's study derives from his having analyzed changes *both* over time and across jurisdictions. The aggregate United States time series data Ehrlich used were unable to capture important regional differences. Moreover, they did not vary as much as cross-state observations; hence they did not provide as rich an opportunity to infer the effect of changes in executions on homicides.

Forst's analysis is superior to Ehrlich's in four major respects: (1) It focuses exclusively on a period of substantial variation in the factors of central interest. (2) Its results are shown to be insensitive to alternative assumptions about the mathematical form of the relationship between homicides and executions. The results were also invariant to several alternative methods of constructing the execution rate, to alternative assumptions about the nature of the relationships between homicides, and other offenses, executions, and convictions and sentences, and to alternative technical assumptions. (3) By not requiring conversion of the data to logarithms, Forst's model does not require that false values be used when the true values of the execution are zero. (4) It incorporates more control variables.

Forst's study led to a conclusion that went beyond that of Klein: "The findings give no support to the hypothesis that capital punishment deters homicide."[49] "Our finding that capital punishment . . . does not deter homicide is remarkably robust with respect to a wide range of alternative constructions."[50]

XI. The Overlooked Natural Experiment

Forst saw that Ehrlich, by using aggregate data for the United States as a whole, was forced to disregard the differences between states that had capital punishment and executions, and states that had either abolished the death penalty or at least had ceased to carry it out. Ehrlich's model thus could not evaluate the natural experiment which legislative history had built into the data. If Ehrlich's thesis—that it was the reduction of executions during the

---

[48] Forst, *The Deterrent Effect of Capital Punishment: A Cross-State Analysis of the 1960s* (September 1976, mimeograph).

[49] *Id.* at 27.   [50] *Id.* at 29.

sixties that made the capital crime rate grow—were correct, then
no such growth should obtain in the states in which there could be
no reduction in executions because there had been none to begin
with. Yet as figure 8 shows, the growth of the capital crime rate
during the crucial sixties was as large in the states without executions
as in states with executions.

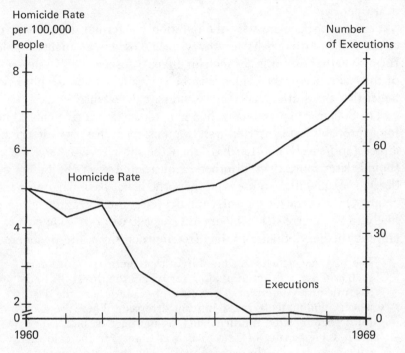

Fɪɢ. 8. United States homicide rate and number of executions, 1960–69.

XII. Evidence versus Ancient Sentiment

The evidence on whether the threat of the death penalty has
a deterrent effect beyond the threat of the life sentence, its normal
substitute, is overwhelmingly on one side. None of the efforts to
sharpen the measurement yardstick by replacing the overall homicide rate through more sensitive measures succeeded in discovering a
deterrent effect. Nor did any effort to sharpen the analytical instruments of analysis help. Even regression analysis, the most sophisticated of these instruments, after careful application by the scholarly
community failed to detect a deterrent effect.

This then is the proper summary of the evidence on the deterrent effect of the death penalty: If there is one, it can only be minute, since not one of the many research approaches—from the simplest to the most sophisticated—was able to find it.[51] The proper question, therefore, is whether an effect that is at best so small that nobody has been able to detect it, justifies the awesome moral costs of the death penalty.

I can only speculate why the question concerning the deterrent effect of the death penalty has always been posed in its unanswerable form: whether or not it has such an effect. I suspect that at the root of the resistance to the evidence is the very ancient and deeply held belief that the death penalty is the ultimate deterrent.

The Solicitor General has called it a "logical a priori" belief. The logic probably runs as follows: If punishment has any deterrent effect (and surely it often has) then the most severe punishment should deter more than all others. Confronted with the failure to detect such an effect, those who share the belief have narrowed the claim. Only certain types of capital crime, they say, not all, are likely to be deterred. The Court in *Gregg v. Georgia* gave two examples, the hired killer and the "free murder" by a life prisoner:[52]

> We may nevertheless assume safely that there are murderers, such as those who act in passion, for whom the threat of death has little or no deterrent effect. But for many others, the death penalty undoubtedly is a significant deterrent. There are carefully contemplated murders, such as murder for hire, where the possible penalty of death may well enter into the cold calculus that precedes the decision to act. And there are some categories of murder, such as murder by a life prisoner, where other sanctions may not be adequate.

If these are the best examples, the others must be poor indeed. The murderer for hire, knowing himself fairly safe from detection, is not likely to be concerned over the difference between death and prison

---

[51] The one exception pointing in the other direction, the dubious California finding that executions appear to postpone some homicides for a few days, is of small import. An effort to duplicate the finding in Philadelphia failed. See text *supra*, at notes 18 and 20.

[52] 96 S. Ct. at 2931. Further examples are afforded in a footnote: "Other types of calculated murders, apparently occurring with increasing frequency, include the use of bombs or other means of indiscriminate killings, the extortion murder of hostages or kidnap victims, and the execution-style killing of witnesses to a crime." *Id.* at n.33.

for life. The "cold calculus" that moves the hired killer must surely tell him how small the probability is that he will be caught.[53] A good part of his careful contemplation goes to avoiding traces.

The life prisoner who kills is even a more interesting example. At first glance, the argument seems so irrefutable, that this type of homicide is occasionally the last capital crime on the statute books before the death penalty is abolished. It is a prize example because on "logical a priori" grounds his is by definition the "free murder" under the law. Again, it is useful to look at the facts, which Sellin was the first to illuminate. He found that, in 1965, the year for which he collected the data, sixteen prison homicides had been committed by men convicted of murder. Since not all murderers in prison are there with a life sentence, the true number of these "free murders" is likely to be even smaller.[54] In fact, of course, the "free murder" is probably altogether a figment because most life prisoners have some hope of being released before the end of their natural life, a hope that would be destroyed by a second murder. A prison, moreover, has ways of its own of punishing such a double murderer.

It is only fair, however, to take these examples of the Court for what they are, efforts to bolster with reasons the unwillingness to abandon the ancient sentiment. In that sentiment, the belief in deterrence plays but a small part. It is the belief in retributive justice that makes the death penalty attractive, especially when clothed in a functional rationalization. The belief has ancient roots, even if the rationale is modern. The Court in *Gregg* approvingly cites *Furman v. Georgia*.[55]

> The instinct for retribution is part of the nature of man, and channeling that instinct in the administration of criminal justice serves an important purpose. . . . When people begin to believe that organized society is unwilling or unable to impose upon criminal offenders the punishment they "deserve," then there are sown the seeds of anarchy.

---

[53] An interview comes to mind with a former warden of the Cook County Jail who did not believe in the death penalty. The interviewer asked him, "You mean, you would even hesitate to execute a hired killer?" The warden's answer as I remember it was: "I shall cross that bridge when I come to it. In my many years here in the Cook County Jail, I have yet to meet the first hired killer. They are never caught, although Chicago would be a good place to catch them."

[54] Sellin, *Prison Homicides*, in SELLIN, note 10 *supra*, at 154, 157; see also Buffin, *Prison Killings and Death Penalty Legislation*, 53 PRISON J. (1974).

[55] 96 S. Ct. at 2930, quoting 408 U.S. 238, 308 (1972).

The depth of this feeling was revealed in a strange interchange during oral argument between Mr. Justice Powell and Professor Anthony Amsterdam, counsel for the petitioners:[56]

> *Mr. Justice Powell:*
>   Let me put a case to you. You've heard about Buchenwald, one of the camps in Germany in which thousands of Jewish citizens were exterminated. . . . If we had had jurisdiction over the commandant of Buchenwald, would you have thought capital punishment was an appropriate response to what that man or woman was responsible for?
> *Mr. Amsterdam:*
>   . . . We all have an instinctive reaction that says, "Kill him." . . . But I think the answer to the question that your Honor is raising, . . . [to] be consistent with the 8th Amendment to the Constitution . . . my answer would be, "No."

Mr. Justice Powell asked the same question again, this time about a man who might destroy New York City with a hydrogen bomb. Amsterdam's answer, of course, was again no.

Significantly, both examples went to the issue of retribution, not deterrence. It is hard to think of any crime that would be less deterred by the difference between the death penalty and life imprisonment, for instance, in Spandau prison. The sentiment in favor of the death penalty does not stem from the belief in its deterrence and perhaps we overestimate altogether the importance of that issue.

Nowhere was the worldwide decline of the death penalty significantly connected with arguments about its effectiveness or the lack thereof. In some countries abolition became simply the logical end-point of a gradual decline in executions, probably accompanied by a parallel change in moral sentiments.

In other countries, abolition was clearly an expression of moral sentiment. The first de jure abolition of executions in czarist Russia goes back to A.D. 1020. Capital punishment reappeared in the fourteenth century but was again abolished when Elizabeth ascended the throne in 1742. On both occasions, the issue was one of morality not expediency.[57] In Germany, the 1946 Constitution abolished the death

---

[56] The colloquy occurred during argument in *Woodson & Waxton v. North Carolina;* transcribed record No. 75–5491, at 20.

[57] "Do not kill anyone, either guilty or not . . . . Do not destroy a Christian soul, even in case death is well deserved." Testament of the Grand Prince of Kiev,

penalty as a deliberate act of repudiation of the Hitler era, when the death penalty, legally or illegally imposed, claimed millions of lives. In Great Britain, after a century of controversy, the abolitionists won when a man, protected by all the vaunted safeguards of British justice, was executed for a crime that he had not committed.

Ceylon abolished the death penalty when it acquired its independence, as an act of Buddhist faith. In Austria, the movement toward abolition reflected primarily moral sentiments. The parliament of the first Austrian republic unanimously abolished capital punishment as a renunciation of the monarchical past. In 1933, a semi-fascist chancellor restored the death penalty primarily as a political threat to the underground opposition. The second republic again abolished the death penalty, first in ordinary criminal cases and then also for cases triable under martial law, last used against the socialist political opposition in the civil war of 1934.

Abolition of the death penalty thus has reflected in the main a change in cultural sentiments, if not of the people, so at least of its legislators or its government. In the United States also capital punishment will end only when our cultural sentiments change. The people, a majority of whom now favor the death penalty, will be the last to change. The legislators will probably change before them; and our Supreme Court Justices conceivably may change even earlier.

Sentiment for the death penalty in the United States has grown during the last decade, stimulated by the unprecedented rise in violent crime during the second half of the sixties. In such times the demand for the death penalty grows because it is so easy to believe it will make law enforcement more effective. It is interesting to analyze the growth of this popular sentiment. In figure 9, four Gallup polls on the death penalty spanning sixteen years are analyzed. Sentiment for the death penalty did not rise until 1967, and then only among the white population. Black sentiment for the death penalty, always far below the corresponding figures for whites, remained unchanged. In the South, sentiment for the death penalty among whites and blacks has traditionally been below the average for the country. For the blacks, this is still true; their propor-

---

1125 A.D. Elizabeth purportedly promised God that if she were selected she would take no life. Adams, *Capital Punishment in Imperial and Soviet Criminal Law*, 18 AM. J. COMP. L. 575, 576 (1970).

tion favoring the death penalty has been declining, reaching in 1976 a new low of 24 percent. Among the whites, sentiment in the South has caught up with that of the country as a whole, at 70 percent.

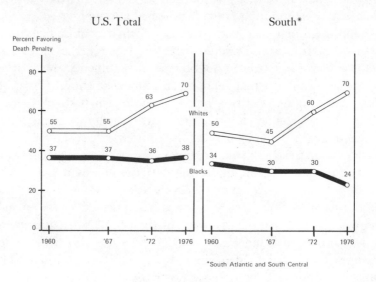

° South Atlantic and South Central.

FIG. 9. Proportion of whites and blacks favoring the death penalty, 1960–76 (Gallup Poll).

The petitioners in *Gregg* all came from the South. In the last analysis the Court held that it had no power to override legislation that was grounded in a belief that even some of the Justices must have shared.

Still, one must not give up hope. The realization that the deterrent effect, if it exists at all,[58] can be only minute, should force us to look

[58] Two of the best studies—those of Forst and Passell—showed even a counter-deterrent balance for the death penalty. In both studies it was statistically insignificant. The possibility of a counterdeterrent effect does not come as a total surprise. It has theoretical support of long standing. There is the suicide-through-murder theory advanced first by STAUB & ALEXANDER, THE CRIMINAL, THE JUDGE, AND THE PUBLIC—A PSYCHOLOGICAL ANALYSIS (1931); see also H. von Weber, *Selbst-mord als Mordmotiv*, MONATSSCHRIFT FÜR KRIMINALBIOLOGIE UND STRAFRECHTSRE-FORM 161 (1937). Then there is concern over the generally brutalizing effect of the death penalty which just adds one more killing in cold blood. Also, as long as some states still consider crimes other than murder (*e.g.*, rape) to be capital offenses, the old argument that killing the victim-witness may somehow "improve" the

once more at the balance sheet, and weigh against the, at best, minimal benefit, the awesome costs of the death penalty: the inhumanity of the act, the ever present danger of error, the ultimate impossibility to make a fair decision as to who is to die and who is to live.

For the committed who believe that there should be more search for the elusive deterrent effect, a new opportunity has arisen. By the grace of the Court we are in the midst of a new natural experiment. After a number of years during which, through *Furman*, the death penalty was held in abeyance throughout the land, some of our states will resume executions. There is thus another opportunity to see whether the capital crime rate in these states will decline compared to the states that still have no executions.

In the end one must remain skeptical as to the power of evidence to change ancient beliefs and sentiments. The greater hope lies in the expectation that with better times our sentiments will reach the "standards of decency that mark the progress of a maturing society."[59] Justices Brennan and Marshall thought—wrongly it appears—that we had already sufficiently matured.

The conclusion that the personal sentiments of the judges play a decisive role is strengthened by reading the decision of the Massachusetts Supreme Judicial Court in *Commonwealth v. O'Neal*,[60] which held a mandatory death sentence upon a conviction for rape-murder to be unconstitutional. That court had before it on the deterrence issue the very same evidence that was before the United States Supreme Court in *Gregg*. Yet the majority of the Massachusetts court accepted the evidence as proof of the inability of the death sentence to deter. The lack of proof of deterrent effect deprived the government of a "compelling state interest" to justify the death penalty.

Why did the Supreme Court and the Massachusetts court arrive at a different decision? The decisive factor was the simple fact that in the United States Supreme Court only two of the nine Justices felt that "the standard of decency" required abolition while on the Massachusetts court five out of seven felt that way.

---

criminal's situation is still valid. *Cf.* BEDAU, *supra* note 20, at 264 n.7. Consider also the case of Gary Gilmore, the Utah convict who succeeded in his objective to be the first person executed in the post-*Furman* period. See N.Y. Times, 18 Jan. 1977, p. 1.

[59] Chief Justice Warren, writing for the Court, in Trop v. Dulles, 356 U.S. 86, 101 (1958).

[60] 339 N.E.2d 676 (Mass. 1975).